The Human Basis
of
the Polity

Aldine Treatises
in Social Psychology
edited by M. Brewster Smith

The Human Basis
of
the Polity

A Psychological Study
of Political Men

JEANNE N. KNUTSON
The Wright Institute

Aldine · Atherton, Inc.
Chicago/New York

First published 1972 by
Aldine · Atherton, Inc.
529 South Wabash Avenue
Chicago, Illinois 60605

ISBN 0-202-24040-1
Library of Congress Catalog Number 70-159599

Printed in the United States of America

Preface

The field of political psychology, which for an unfortunate number of years was largely the idiosyncratic specialty of the few political scientists based at the University of Chicago who gave it birth, has suddenly developed into robust adolescence. For at least twenty years, political scientists wondered whether the child would ever mature, but the question today is rather the meaning his life will have within the family of subfields that compose the discipline of political science. Although some specialties—as occurs in every family—alternate between ignoring and expressing hostility toward their new sibling, most political viewpoints now show an appreciation of intrapsychic dynamics as well as institutional imperatives and sociological constructs.

While the decades of the fifties and the sixties have seen a phenomenal growth of psychically oriented political research, however, the problem of its overall relevance and meaning for political behavior and political philosophy has largely been neglected. Further, while there now exists a body of thoughtful psychobiographies and a multitude of personality related field research reports, this data has been collected and analyzed in terms of a variety of seemingly disparate perspectives. Thus the relationships between the dimensions of authoritarianism and anomie, alienation and dogmatism, efficacy and misanthropy, mental health and political participation have yet to be systematically explored. Hence—for a variety of cogent reasons—an attempt at synthesis has become necessary to help us see what we actually do know about the psychic dimensions of political man, as well as what relevance this knowledge has for our views of social goals, political institutions and the humanity which social and political systems are designed to serve—and, hopefully, to enhance. It is in terms of this need for integration and assessment (as well as reassessment) that this book was originally begun.

As work on this book progressed, however, it soon became apparent that what was required was not only a theoretical assessment of where political psychology has been and a speculative analysis of where future research efforts could be fruitfully directed, but it appeared additionally necessary to provide an empirical demonstration of what past theorizing has led us to expect. In the implementation of this goal, the National Institute of Mental Health, through a Research Fellowship Award (1-Fl-MH-37, 277-01 BEH-A), provided assistance, which I gratefully acknowledge.

The result of the foregoing thought process is found in the following pages. I hope that—in this era of the rapid proliferation of information and analysis—a theoretical summary of behavioral literature in terms of a holistic psychological perspective will be useful in assisting us to know which questions have been answered and which vital questions have not even been asked. The empirical demonstration is directed both to integrating previously separate research dimensions and to demonstrating the possibilities of employing a unified personality theory in survey research. Throughout, the reader will note many places in the discussion at which questions are raised in the process of synthesis that need a good deal more thought and attention than can be provided in an overview such as this. At various points it has been suggested that the personality theory upon which this book is based offers a valuable means of framing the hypotheses by which further research efforts may be directed.

In writing this book, I was made vividly aware of the fact that research is a social process—most enjoyably and productively so. The manuscript has benefited greatly, as have I, from the lengthy and thoughtful critiques of Professors James C. Davies, Joel Aronoff, Christian Bay, M. Brewster Smith, and M. George Zaninovich. My particular debt to Professor Davies and Professor Eric C. Bellquist is also avowed by the dedication of this book. I would also like to acknowledge the stimulation and personal encouragement provided by three individuals whose considerable knowledge of human behavior has been especially helpful to me: Professors R. Nevitt Sanford and Alexander L. George, and most particularly, the late Abraham Maslow, who truly actualized in his life the humanistic values to which his professional work was dedicated. Work on this book has benefited also from the knowledge of computer intricacies made available by Professor Michael Baer, as well as the encouragement of Professor Elizabeth Léone Simpson. Finally, I offer a word of public appreciation for the ever cheerful, heartening and gracious assistance of my husband, David.

Contents

With Gratitude and Esteem

this book is dedicated to

Eric C. Bellquist,
Professor of Political Science,
University of California, Berkeley

and

James C. Davies,
Professor of Political Science,
University of Oregon

for making personal the impersonal

A Modest Proposal

> The level of development of measurement models in
> the social sciences is a symptom of the status of the
> discipline as an empirical science, and the measure-
> ment studies done in this area in the last 14 years sug-
> gest, unfortunately, that we have neglected our profes-
> sional responsibility to measure concepts accurately
> and comprehensively. If we do not meet this responsi-
> bility with more vigor and rigor, we will continue,
> with the help of electronic computers, merely to ma-
> nipulate empirical cliches—at near the speed of light.
> (Struening and Richardson, 1965, p. 776)

The serious contemplation of avenues of political action and types
of political organization is an ancient and respected pursuit. From
widespread distress over America's involvement in Vietnam to
the equally heated—if more limited—debate over the possibility of
an era of unitary government that could supersede a dated nationalism, thinkers today are continuing a concern that stretches back
at least two thousand years. The discussion then as now centers
around the questions of what is the good in social life and how
man's behavior may be directed toward attaining it.

Political philosophy can thus be seen to deal with particular
time-bound causes and effects within a framework of more enduring questions. Further, underlying these perennial concerns, one
can detect a unitary preoccupation on the part of those varied and
numerous individuals who have made political philosophy their
task. The study of political philosophy can be seen as an attempt,
on the part of many diverse thinkers over a very long period of
time, to apply their particularistic view of human nature to the
study of political organization. For a view of human nature is assumed in any expression of conviction concerning the feasibility
and desirability of a particular ordering of political relations. Indeed, a view of man's nature inevitably delimits the "angle of vision" which Wolin (1960, chap. 1) describes so clearly as being
particular to each philosophy.

Some writers, in the tradition of Plato and Aristotle, have
opted for the view that man is a rational animal and is capable of
ordering his relationships with other men so as to achieve through
society (and only there) self-fulfillment and the "good life." Others,
Rousseau particularly, have considered man to be naturally good,
naturally fulfilled. In political society, man finds not the ultimate
in self-expression, but rather the corruption of his noble nature.

Still others, in the Hobbesian tradition, have pictured man as passionate, power-seeking, unsatisfiable and inherently at war with other men. It is only through the polity's strict control of his passions that man can find social peace and order. This social peace doesn't come from within; it is imposed by the great leviathan—the state.

Up to the present day, political philosophers have based their theories on views of human nature that were at times logically consistent, but certainly not empirically verified. (Until recently, the tools for such analysis were of course not available.) Furthermore, traditional political philosophy has made use of simplistic and uniform views of human nature. If, for example, the author felt (as Marx did) that human nature was perfectable to a point where the ordering of societal relationships would be a natural function of man's harmony with himself and the economic arrangements in his society, this view encompassed all men in society. Commenting on the "oversimplified, overoptimistic, rationalistic picture of man" presented by Marx, Eric Fromm notes:

> He did not recognize the irrational forces in man which make him afraid of freedom, and which produce his lust for power and his destructiveness. On the contrary, underlying his concept of man was the implicit assumption of man's natural goodness, which would assert itself as soon as the crippling economic shackles were released. . . . With their chains they have also to lose all those irrational needs and satisfactions which were originated while they were wearing the chains. (1955, p. 232)

Human nature has been seen, in other words, as monolithic—as possessing but one character type. Throughout political philosophy, social controls have been thought sufficient to eliminate deviant types. The only categorization offered has at times been between the rulers and the ruled (and here the differences are explained in terms of role expectations).

To an overwhelming extent, this situation unfortunately is still true today. Since the benchmark work of Sigmund Freud, however, political philosophers have been able to ask more penetrating questions about human nature. They have been made aware, through the accumulated clinical work of others, that human nature is not all of a piece; that there are various points along a continuum of mental health—mental illness, i.e., along the road to a maximalization of human potential. As Lucien Pye has noted: "In his insight into the full dimensions of man's inner nature, Freud made it embarrassingly clear that previous theories of political relationships were generally premised on impoverished and inadequate notions of human nature" (1961, p. 291). Further, cultural anthropologists have offered additional refinements of the patterns which human nature may display.

As a result of these insights, a few writers have attempted to get political philosophy out of the fact-free vacuum in which it had been contemplating human nature in relation to various types of social organization and confront it with the problems of social organization in the real world. (Machiavelli was the prototype of this species.)

The opening round in this confrontation between political philosophy and psychology is undoubtedly Graham Wallas' Human Nature in Politics. Wallas (1962) complained in 1908 that "The study of human nature by the psychologists has, it is true, advanced enormously since the discovery of human evolution, but it has advanced without affecting or being affected by the study of politics" (1962, p. 37). He went on, in a discussion of practical politics (interspersed with a multitude of examples drawn from his life experiences as a practicing politician) to explode the myth that political man is rational—that man's political actions are based on rational considerations. He concluded: "Political impulses are not mere intellectual inferences from calculations of means and ends; but tendencies prior to, though modified by, the thought and experiences of individual human beings" (p. 16). As A. L. Rowse says, in his introduction to Wallas' book, the keynote of the argument is "the leadership of the irrational by the rational" (p. 3).

Unfortunately for those concerned with the study of behavior, the dichotomy posed by Wallas sounds disturbingly simple today. As Heinz Hartmann has pointed out:

> What is called reasonable is actually frequently based in part on a set of implicit or explicit value judgments, the validity of which is taken for granted, and its meaning varies accordingly. If it is considered a legitimate aim of the individual to place certain personal interests above other considerations, an activity that serves this aim will no doubt be called reasonable; while looked at from the viewpoint of a different system of values, to sacrifice those interests will be considered the very essence of reasonable behavior. (1947, pp. 359-92)

While, as Hartmann goes on to say, rational behavior is generally correlated with adaptive behavior, there are some adaptive behaviors which are best performed if rational thinking and action "are temporarily kept in abeyance."

Thus, while pointing out the unreality on which many political assumptions had been based, Wallas confused the discussion of political behavior by offering an equally unjustifiable view of human nature, so simplistic as to be practically useless for present-day research work. One must only ask: "What is rational?" and "rational for whom?" to see that this view, although an undoubted improvement over past theorizing, is of little practical use.

Slowly, however, an increasing number of political scientists have begun to give recognition to the fact that politics and political behavior include a study of more than institutions and legal framework—important though these areas undoubtedly are.[1] In short, political scientists have begun to appreciate anew Plato's insight that prepolitical dispositions shape political institutions, and that "the stability of the constitution depends upon the moulding of the appropriate form of character (or personality)."[2]

The questioning of rationalistic assumptions of human nature had driven the beginning wedge. The next, and—from the fruitfulness of its consequences—far more important step in the dialogue between psychology and politics has been the work of Harold D. Lasswell.[3] In two widely known books (<u>Psychopathology and Politics</u>, 1960, and <u>Power and Personality</u>, 1948), in addition to numerous essays on the subject, Lasswell has popularized two major insights concerning the relationship between human nature and political behavior. One point involves a long-standing assumption which Lasswell has helped make more precise: the importance of experiences in formative years in shaping later political activity. Lasswell (1930, pp. 74-76) has discussed this in terms of a now well-known formula: $p]d]r = P$, which is conceptualized as "Private Motives/ Displaced on Public Objects/ Rationalized in Terms of Public Interest" being equated with "the political type" (1948, p. 38).

The second point which Lasswell has frequently made is that because politics can be conceptualized as a study of power relationships, the political personality can be considered as a particular type in which the need for power is the dominant value (1948, p. 17). Lasswell, commenting on this point in a later article, has said:

> The authoritarian type is the one most closely approximating the "perfect" politican in the sense of one whose primary goal value is power, whose preferred base value is also power (threat or use of extreme deprivations in any sphere), and whose basic expectations are that the most important human relations are matters of power. (1951)

As provocative as this second proposition is, to my knowledge it remains just that: an assumption undocumented by definitive empirical study. Furthermore, in another place, Lasswell himself has suggested (as Spitz [1958, p. 90] points out) that "all top leaders in democratic or totalitarian regimes . . . tend to be recruited from fundamental personality patterns that are <u>not</u> primarily ori-

---

1. For a useful discussion of this process of enlarging the scope of concern in the field of comparative politics, see Eckstein (1963).

2. To employ Lasswell's statement (1959) of this relationship.

3. Lasswell's impact on the study of political behavior is well illustrated in a series of essays in his honor. See Rogow (1969a).

ented toward power."[4] Finally, as Lasswell has recently discussed this "political personality" who "emphasizes the pursuit of power in preference to other values" as likely to be found in business as well as politics, one must question the justification for the label "political" being applied here at all[5] (1968, pp. 89-91).

The third round in the dialogue between psychology and politics came with the publication in 1950 of the massive psychoanalytic study of The Authoritarian Personality. The importance of this work for political scientists lies in the attempt, for the first time, to establish on a broad scale an empirical link between political ideology and personality. The particular focus of this study was anti-Semitism and generalized ethnocentrism. As the study progressed, however, an attempt was made to connect the basic personality type with other attitudes, including "political-economic conservatism." (As has been pointed out elsewhere,[6] this later connection is not theoretically justifiable on the basis of the assumptions made in this study.) The authors, through clinical evaluation, projective tests and attitude questionnaires established a strong correlation between a syndrome of intolerant attitudes and a type of personality concerned with power. The authoritarian personality is conceptualized as expressing deference to power figures, hostile and rejecting of outgroups (weak and low status groups and individuals) and given to stereotypy and over-generalization.

Since the publication of The Authoritarian Personality, a variety of different studies have been done using the F (for fascism) scale which had been developed to measure authoritarian character. Although the accuracy of this instrument has been questioned, both on technical grounds and as a measure of authoritarianism,[7] so many replications have established the connection between this authoritarian personality type and a variety of undemocratic characteristics that it has become an accepted basis for political understanding.

With the publication of The Authoritarian Personality came a

---

4. Browning and Jacob comment on this new emphasis by noting that Lasswell has recognized that "the power-hungry individual may be too compulsive and rigid to win power; he is more likely to be found at the fringes of the political system than at its center" (1964, p. 75).

5. This issue is discussed at greater length in chap. 2, below. Also see Lane (1959, pp. 124-28) and Milbrath (1965, pp. 81-89).

6. See Kecskemeti (1951); also the section on authoritarianism in chap. 3 of this book.

7. The most thoroughgoing critique is found in Christie and Jahoda, eds. (1954); also see Rokeach (1956); also the section on authoritarianism in chap. 3 of this book.

great many studies (see chap. 3, below) which analyzed the reliability and validity of the Berkeley research. Not only were the
methods of the original study carefully considered, but its theoretical assumptions were also subject to considerable scrutiny. One
point which became particularly apparent in this analysis is that
the authoritarian personality as delimited by the Berkeley study
was only one type of authoritarian, a type which rather imprecise-
ly could be typified as "right." A second point which was made in
the discussion following the Berkeley study of authoritarianism
was that a false dichotomy had been established: the absence of
agreement with a particular list of items measuring right authoritarianism did not qualify the balance of subjects to be labeled as
"democrats." In other words, it has been felt that the democratic
character type must be further refined by adherence to a positive
set of behavior-stimulating values. As Maslow comments:

> Unfortunately the great Berkeley study on authoritarianism
> defines the democrat in negative terms, that is, in terms of
> the number of authoritarian statements that he disagrees with.
> So far as their fascism scale is concerned, only two out of the
> thirty-eight items are characteristic of the democratic person
> in a positive sense, and even these are doubtful. In other words,
> there is no D for democracy scale. The democrat is defined as
> one who doesn't have fascistic symptoms. It tells what he is
> not; it doesn't tell what he is. This pressing task still remains
> to be done. (1957, p. 100)

Nevertheless, in spite of its detractors, The Authoritarian Personality remains one of the theoretical and empirical foundation
stones of behavioral research. Its importance, as its authors state,

> is the demonstration of close correspondence in the type of ap-
> proach and outlook a subject is likely to have in a great vari-
> ety of areas, ranging from the most intimate features of fam-
> ily and sex adjustment through relationships to other people in
> general, to religion and to social and political philosophy. Thus
> a basically hierarchical, authoritarian, exploitive parent-child
> relationship is apt to carry over into a power-oriented, ex-
> ploitively dependent attitude toward one's sex partner and one's
> God and may well culminate in a political philosophy and social
> outlook which has no room for anything but a desperate cling-
> ing to what appears to be strong and a disdainful rejection of
> whatever is relegated to the bottom. (Adorno, Frenkel-
> Brunswik, Levinson, and Sanford, 1950, p. 971)

A fourth major landmark in the dialogue between personality
and politics was the publication of Milton Rokeach's The Open and
Closed Mind (1960). Although this book has had, as yet, a much
more modest impact on the analysis of political behavior, its carefully described and clinically documented analysis of cognitive systems is potentially of great value in the study of politically relevant

behavior. Rokeach placed his subjects along a continuum of open-closed mindedness (or degree of dogmatism), which he showed to be a much more general measure of authoritarianism than the earlier F-scale. Subjects at the closed-minded end of the continuum were shown to be typified by a high state of anxiety (pp. 211, 367), a concern with the source rather than with the content of new information, and an inability to synthesize new information which is contradictory to their belief system. Further, the structure of various disparate belief systems was demonstrated to be similar, though the content differed (pp. 14-17).

Rokeach hypothesized that the most important factor in gaining knowledge of the nature of a belief system is understanding the content of what he calls the "central region" of the belief system. This region encompasses "primitive beliefs . . . about the physical and social world, the latter including the person's self-concept and his conception of others" (p. 40). In closing, he offers this provocative comment: "We suspect that if we knew more about the nature of such primitive beliefs, their organization, and how to modify them, we would know more about the conditions leading to the formation and modification of belief systems. This should have important implications for the psychology of politics, personality, mental health, psychotherapy, and education" (p. 409).

The potential value of Rokeach's contribution to the study of political behavior appears considerable. Not only is his conceptualization broader than that employed in the Berkeley study, it is also more directly relevant to a wide variety of political phenomena. (For example, the degree of individual dogmatism should be related to partisanship, proclivity to join extremist groups, decision-making and bargaining in periods of crisis and the fluidity of political opinions in time of stress.) Therefore, it is possible that Rokeach's work will have an impact as large as that stemming from the massive study of authoritarianism and thus it deserves an equal place in this discussion.

In the 1960s, the study of personality and its relevance to behavior has continued on three major fronts: psychology, sociology, and—running a poor third—political science. Other character traits and personality types have been uncovered and correlated with various attitudes and behaviors. Some of the most widely employed are anomia[8] (the personal dimension of anomie, as first conceptualized by Emile Durkheim), intolerance of ambiguity, political and personal efficacy, a sense of civic duty, and a feeling of generalized misanthropy (labeled "faith in people").

To this day, however, knowledge which has been slowly accumulated in the field of psychology through clinical observation, projective tests, psychoanalysis, et cetera—interesting though such

---

8. Leo Srole coined this term to distinguish the mental state from "anomie," the social state. (See the section on anomia in chap. 3 of this book.)

knowledge often is to political writers—has seen little application
(or the possibility thereof) in the study of political behavior. Equally important, the studies which have included an interest in personality have seldom attempted to show the relevance of their concern
to other approaches. David Easton, commenting recently on the
study of interest groups, emphasizes the current view:

> In effect, research students have been saying: Let us keep the
> motivations of the actors constant and thereby delete them
> from the situation. Whatever the feelings of the individuals
> within the group may be, if we are looking at the process from
> the point of view of any one group, then its decisions and ac-
> tions (policy) will be modified by the power of varying constel-
> lations of groups arrayed around it. (1964, p. 180)

Also unfortunately for the development of the field of political
psychology, the usefulness of these landmark conceptual schemes
has generally not been seen in the insights into motivation and personality which they offer to students of political behavior. What has
been too frequently seen is the facility with which it is possible to
apply carefully developed scales on easily available subjects, without benefit of theoretical sanctity. Thus, it is true, an increasing
number of studies dealing in general with political behavior are
published, but few writers have first scientifically delimited the
area of analysis before "charging off" to measure attitudes.

Further, the reader of research reports is not always sure—
because of the ambiguous titles of various scales which are not included for analysis in many reports—just exactly what is being
measured or how comparable—if at all—various findings are. Occasionally, for example, a critic will be forced to say, as was done
in the Christie and Jahoda book previously cited, that correlations
between two scales are apparently due to the inherent similarity
of the scale materials, leaving unanswered the problem of whether
the attitudes in question really do relate to each other in a meaningful way.[9] At times (as in the case of anomia, intolerance of ambiguity and authoritarianism, for example), several scales—each

---

9. Indeed, the reader at times is assailed with the most
amazing finds, due to labeling monstrosities. Thus, for example,
Eysenck in discussing the results of answers to the question "In
some countries medical certificates must be produced showing
that neither party to a marriage has V.D. Would you agree or disagree with this being made a requirement here?" notes that, as
the upper status group was more in agreement than the lower status group, there exists the contradiction of "the upper status group
behaving in a Radical direction [!] but the low status group behaving in a Conservative direction [!]" (1954, pp. 32-33). Findings
such as this—and McClosky's (1958) use of the label of "conservatism" which then correlates with mental illness—make the understanding of political behavior research difficult indeed.

purporting to measure the same trait—are in current use. The careful student may even find it impossible to see a copy of the scale that is used in reported research.[10]

Finally, because many political scientists are only lately developing an awareness of the value of a firm knowledge of statistics, the questioning in print of the research techniques in various studies has augmented their hesitancy to accept the conclusions of behavioral studies as important additions to our knowledge. A new breed of writers—the analysts' analyst—have frequently offered critical evaluations of the work of others in terms which are at times so technical that their meaning is not generally understood. In short, a new type of snobbery has sprung up, based on being "more statistically reliable than thou."[11]

Thus the majority of political scientists (concerned with International Politics, Political Parties or Public Administration, for example) are often as baffled today as earlier by the usefulness and applicability of psychology for the study of politics in their field of interest as each new monthly publication uncovers a new trait which correlates with yet another attitude—and they can but wonder what application the new study has to those findings reported earlier. Perhaps the acerbity of such comments as the following represents merely a "rational" response to the prevailing chaos: "We need no theory of human nature—it only confuses us [political scientists]. . . . To bring in psychological considerations . . . distracts us from our business, which is the study of what is said and done, not the study of motives for saying and doing" (Riker, 1965, p. 379).

In other words, in spite of the tremendous possibilities which have opened up for political scientists to truly understand—and predict—what is said and done in a variety of political subfields, the new tools remain largely unused. Although the value of understanding the effect of personality in political behavior has been amply demonstrated, political scientists, when attempting to measure behavior, generally continue to replicate studies of well-known effects of demographic variables because these are easily measurable and, in many ways, involve no intellectual risk-taking. Perhaps this attitude can be best typified by offering the comments

10. For example, the study of anomie by McClosky and Schaar (1965) employed a great number of specially constructed scales, only one of which—to my knowledge—has ever been made available. A similar complaint applies to McClosky's work on conservatism. (See Kendall, 1958, pp. 506-10.)

11. There is no intent here to suggest that incorrect use of statistical measures is ever defensible. The point is simply that, at times, argument over the applicability of a particular test has obscured consideration of the value of the research perspective and findings.

of one political scientist (anonymous), who was heard to remark:
"I'm not going to use psychological variables in any field study of
mine. The first time we ask a legislator whether he'd rather cro-
chet or play football, we'd be thrown out of his office. Besides, the
results are usually ambiguous and the terminology incomprehen-
sible to the audience I want to reach—usually involving something
about an 'unresolved oedipal conflict.'"

In a sense, this book is an attempt to answer just such reservations. It is an attempt to demonstrate the exciting possibilities
in field studies which do employ psychological variables (exclud-
ing physical ejection from the interviewee's presence). It specifically wishes to establish two points:

1) It is possible, in studying political behavior, to use personality and motivation theory without individually considering the specific, formative conditions of manifest behavior and attitudes. In an
academic division of labor, it is possible for political scientists to
apply—without consideration of idiographic causality—knowledge of
personality which has been clinically established and verified by
psychologists. Further, the use of personality variables is relevant to many specialties within the field of political science (as
well as sociology, anthropology and psychology).

2) This application may be done in the use of questionnaires
employed in a survey. While studies of individual personalities
are invaluable and basic to the understanding of political leadership and decision-making,[12] the questionnaire remains a necessary tool in the understanding of the behavior of man in the mass
—of political man in modern society.

In sum, it is my considered opinion (ignoring the biblical ad-
monition about judging not) that the underdeveloped field of political psychology has been typified by fragmented and haphazard applications, in many cases, of pseudopsychology to any seemingly
important behavior or, if carefully done, has seldom offered the
theoretical framework with which cross-cultural comparison is
possible.[13] Furthermore, and even more deleterious to the understanding of behavior, is the lack of any consideration which many
political scientists have given to the dimension of personality in
their study of behavior.[14] Instead, far too much emphasis has

12. For excellent examples, see Erikson (1958, 1969), George
and George (1956), Edinger (1965), Brodie (1966), and useful short-
er studies by Barber (1968a, 1968b).

13. See, for example, Dicks's (1950) most interesting work
with German prisoners (pp. 111-54). In their comprehensive survey of work on national character, Inkeles and Levinson illustrate
further how "the absence of standardization in analysis has led to
marked inconsistency in various studies and has thus made comparison difficult" (1969, pp. 412-13).

14. An excellent example of this is Wilson (1962). Wilson

been placed on isolated personality traits and discrete attitudes. But, as M. Brewster Smith has noted, an individual's separate attitudes—acquired in a variety of ways—are not likely to be of great value in either predicting or understanding his behavior (1968, pp. 15-28). What is needed is rather "a good map" to aid us in keeping "the whole Elephant in view."

Thus the thesis here is simply this: with the theoretical frameworks and empirical evidence at hand, the time has come for a synthesis of past research and the integrated analysis of personality and political behavior in terms that are both broader (to include all personality types rather than isolated, superficial traits or single personality syndromes) and deeper (to include a study of the causal conditions and need requirements of predispositions to various types of politically relevant behavior so that individual traits are seen as integrated manifestations of deep-seated motivational states). In other words, the time has come to turn the rather desultory dialogue between psychology and political science into a full scale debate. Instead of peeking, from time to time, into the Pandora's box provided by Freud, it is suggested that we courageously take the lid off! As a preliminary step, it is also necessary to bring together the disparate research interests currently employed and to attempt to assess what—at this point in time—is now known about the behavior of political man.[15]

In order to do this, one must have a theoretical framework within which to work—a framework which encompasses a wide range of human motivation and which clearly delimits basic types of personality. Such a framework is found in the work of Abraham Maslow. Its importance for the study of political behavior was pointed out initially by James C. Davies in his Human Nature in Politics. Several other students of politics have also recently noted the central theoretical relevance of Maslow's need hierarchy to the field of political psychology.[16] What is now required is an empirical demonstration of the value of Maslow's ideas in relation to political behavior, as well as a display of their relevance to other concepts popularly employed in behavioral research. This book is an attempt to satisfy this need.

The study of politics from the point of view of personality theory is indeed illuminating. The clues to the understanding of politi-

---

speaks at length about the amateur democrat but never tells the reader who (other than middle class members and, in New York clubs, predominantly Jews) the amateur democrat is, or what his motivations in joining are—that is, what satisfactions he seeks through political activity. These questions are left "to those with a taste for mass psychiatry" (p. 166).

15. An excellent step in this direction is found in Berelson and Steiner (1964).

16. For example, see Bay (1965, pp. 39-51); also Lane (1969) and Simpson (1971).

cally relevant behavior that may be gleaned from past studies are manifold. So much work has been done in so many diverse directions that it is like being confronted with a box full of the parts of a giant and complex jigsaw puzzle. This particular work is but an attempt to put enough of the pieces together that the dim outline of the picture may be visible. It will, I hope, raise more questions than it answers. If they are the right questions—if they lead to fruitful research—this attempt will have been justified.

Before turning to a consideration of the field of political psychology itself, however, discussions previously overheard among various sects within the academic community, as well as a study of the literature, strongly indicate the advisability of making ex-plicit what should be implicit in research on political behavior. Because, as Butler stated in another connection, "Criticism can . . . degenerate into a species of academic cannibalism . . ." (1958, p. 106) I hope that, by making my motives clear at the outset, the motives of the American variety of political man, as discussed in the following pages, can be examined in a dispassionate manner. Thus I offer a catechism for the use of psychological variables in the study of political behavior (where sociological variables have found such a comfortable home).

1. Psychological variables will be of greatest value as research tools when used to refine present knowledge gained from the application of general measures of social-economic status, role, political activity, et cetera—sociological variables which are now in popular use. (Both Silberstein and Seeman's [1959, pp. 258-64] highly informative analysis of the commonly accepted view that prejudice is correlated with mobility, in which they controlled for concern with status,[17] and McClosky and Schaar's [1965, pp. 14-40] work on anomie, in which anomie is studied as a psychological as well as a sociological dependent variable, exemplify the valuable results which are possible by incorporating psychological concepts into present research designs.) In other words, as Christie points out, "Any attempt to relate personality variables to political ideology without taking the social context into account is apt to be highly misleading as well as an oversimplification of some highly complex interrelationships" (1956, p. 428).

It is also important at this point to clarify the meaning which the construct "social class" has in the following discussion. The view here is that at best, social class membership is a compact label for a variety of basic, formative life experiences which predispose an individual to certain behaviors and attitudes— that is, which become internalized at various levels in his personality system. Insofar as the various indicators of an individual's social sta-

---

17. Also see the current works of Seeman (listed in the bibliography), which have continued to use this approach, as well as to attempt a synthesis of personality related learning theory and group oriented mass society theory.

tus are homogeneous and interlocking (for example, his past education, his present income and occupation), the likelihood is increased that his social class designation will be a fair approximation of the personality predispositions accompanying specific formative experiences. In other words, "Social class may be usefully
regarded as a statement of probability that an individual has had
or will have certain kinds of experience that shape his behavior
and orientations toward the society and toward new ideas, information, and concepts."[18]

2. It is recognized that, on the macro-level, the relationship
between personality and politically relevant behavior is likely to
be difficult to assess. It is not expected, for example, that it will
be possible to predict, by the use of personality variables, who
will join the Democratic party and who will become a Republican,[19]
or that personality (despite Lasswell's theories) will show who will
become a political leader and who will become a business official.
As Milbrath and Klein have pointed out in relation to their study of
Washington lobbyists

> . . . political participation seems to be a special case of a gen-
> eral social participation pattern. Personality factors requisite
> for general social participation are also requisite for political
> participation, but their presence does not necessarily produce
> political activity. We are not aware of any study which has iso-
> lated a personality trait which drives people specifically into
> politics; even the much discussed "drive for power" finds
> many alternative modes of expression.[20] (1962, p. 54)

It is also recognized that "the institutional imperative" has a great
deal to do with official behavior.

What personality should tell us, however, is the difference in
behavior and beliefs of political leaders stemming from their personality needs (as suggestively illustrated in the rough classification by Matthews [1960] of U. S. Senators); the type of Republican
or Democratic leader and platform that will be supported with vigor
or else ignored in a particular campaign and among a particular
group of voters; the probability that certain individuals will join intolerant groups (of Right and Left) and what their subsequent behavior will be; the political appeals and events which are most likely
to strike a responsive chord due to individual anxieties and individual needs. In other words, personality may not be of great predictive value in assessing who engages in many of the types of political

18. Hess and Torney (1967, p. 126). Also see Treiman's (1966,
pp. 651-64) discussion of the distinction between the "status-dis-
crepancy" effect and the "additive" effect of status.

19. Note, for example, the low correlations found by McClosky
(1965, pp. 44-45).

20. On this point, also see Prewitt (1965, pp. 96-111).

activities which are broadly popular (for example, being a Republican, voting). It will, however, tell us what <u>function</u> various types of activity (political office, marching in parades) serve in an individual's psychic economy, what appeals are likely to meaningfully engage certain individuals, what <u>kind of behavior</u> can be correlated with various personality types and, conversely, <u>who</u> is available for specific, limited kinds of political activities—particularly for activities the social importance of which outweighs their numerical representations. <u>The influence of personality bears a direct relationship to the specificity of the politically relevant behavior.</u>

No claim is being made for a one-to-one correlation between broadly measurable personality types and categories of political behavior—general or specific. The claim <u>is</u> made, however, that, by ruling out chance, strong relationships can be established which will increase our understanding and prediction of political behavior. In addition, an understanding of personality should make much seemingly contradictory behavior understandable. For

> even when there is little or no consistency at the level of behavior acts, there may be great stability or consistency in the hypothetical structures and processes that determine these surface acts. To borrow an attractive expression from Kurt Lewin, "the same heat that melts the butter hardens the egg." The same structure, when reflected in different circumstances, may have superficially different, even opposite, effects. This kind of consistency of determining structures and processes is of the utmost importance in personality theory. (Lazarus, 1963, p. 39)

It is suggested here that this same "consistency of determining structures" will also be of value in understanding political behavior.

3. Because adaptation and adjustment allow people to function much more "normally" than projective tests of their emotional needs would indicate, there is a very real value in studying motivation from the objective behavioral standpoint, rather than causally, from the subjective standpoint of inner dynamics and psychic tensions.

> The manner in which a person copes with his problems is the most revealing thing about him. . . . Insofar as one can single out a particular flaw in current views of ego defense it is that writers on the subject have failed to mention the tremendous importance of constructive strategies as a means of avoiding the vicissitudes that make crippling defenses necessary.[21] (Smith, Bruner, and White, 1956, pp. 282-83)

---

21. A useful discussion of ego psychology which elucidates this difference between defensive and coping behavior can be found in Kroeber (1963, pp. 178-98).

4. It is true that personality (considered as the totality of an individual's needs and his expression of them in behavior, values and attitudes) is not immutable; however, it shows great stability when studied over long periods of time, even during the formative years.[22] Thus adult subjects may be expected to fall into relatively stable personality types, concerning which future predictions can be made. Further, the study of any one individual personality will suggest what concrete types of personality changes will likely occur in response to specific types of life experiences. In other words, once personality is formed, its future development is shaped by its past organization and internalized experiences. Knowledge of the past will be predictive of the future: personality development is cumulative. (This point of view agrees with Smith's (1968, p. 277) statement that "personal and social development [is] inherently circular or spiral, rather than linear in terms of neatly isolable causes and effects" [1968, p. 277].)

5. While it is possible to study the functions which opinions, attitudes and behavior hold "in the economy of personality," without taking up the more complicated question of causation:

> . . . if, as current theories of learning and of personality development lead us to believe, people tend to learn those ways of thinking and behaving that, broadly speaking, work for them, the functional approach is not so remote from causal explanation after all. . . . The distinctions drawn by a functional analysis, in other words, are likely to be causally relevant.[23] (Smith, 1958, p. 7)

6. Finally, and perhaps most important, it must always be kept in mind that personality is but one of a triad of factors in consideration of which behavior must be studied. Equally important in determining behavior are cultural predispositions and the field stimulus.[24] Personality, it is readily acknowledged at the outset, is not the sole determinant of behavior. Thus Spitz is correct in stating that

> the difference between a "democratic" and an "authoritarian" personality is sometimes not in how he behaves but in how he is treated. In this respect Shaw's conversion of Eliza Doolittle from a flower-girl into a duchess attests to a greater

---

22. For example, see Frenkel-Brunswik (1942, pp. 121-265).

23. Also see Katz (1960, pp. 163-204).

24. One important consequence of this is the necessity of carrying out one's research design in a variety of field situations in order to test the reliability of correlations which have been established. See, for example, Davids and Eriksen's work on the questionable relationship between authoritarianism (as measured by the F-scale) and neuroticism (1957, pp. 155-59).

insight than that simplistic psychology which mechanistically
reduces adult conduct to its alleged infantile origins, or
equates it with a particular type of character structure. (1958,
p. 88)

While this is undoubtedly true, it is equally important to note that
the flower-girl never will be (as Shaw also so artfully demonstrated) the same kind of duchess which the born-and-bred upper class
variety could become. Personality alone is not synonymous with
behavior; yet neither is there a one-to-one relationship between
cultural or situational factors and man's actions. In short, while
the concern of this book is personality factors, a knowledge of
their influence will only be of value in the study of political behavior when they are considered in relation to cultural and situational
factors.[25] Thus the point of view here is decidedly a "field view"
of behavior.[26]

With confession of motives in the past, let us now turn to the
subject proper. In the first part of this book, Maslow's motivation
theory is presented in detail, as I interpret it. By drawing on various disciplines, Maslow's personality model is related to other
work in the field of behavior which is pertinent to an understanding of political behavior. Whenever possible, the specific relation
of the argument to the study of politics is brought out. The first
part, then, is seen as an attempt to integrate available research
reports involving a personality dimension with what is known or
theorized about politically relevant behavior—and to do this within the framework provided by Maslow.

A word here should be offered concerning the materials which
are presented in chapters 2 and 3. As has been discussed, work in
political psychology has just begun to provide a synthesis between
personality theory and political behavior. The political research
which deals with any psychologically meaningful variables is therefore quite fragmented. In going through the literature of psychology
and sociology, one finds a great amount of work which bears on our
interest here. Yet research in these disciplines is usually done
without consideration of political behavior. It is therefore often
necessary to present research findings as analogues of what would,
one hopes, result from a direct study of political behavior.

A good deal of the evidence which is presented in the first part
of this book is therefore politically relevant only by inference.

_____

25. As Sears notes: "To describe a person as having high
emotionality or low sensitivity or diffuse anxiety is systematically
acceptable only if other variables are added that will, together with
these internal personal properties, specify what kind of behavior
can be expected from him under some specific circumstances"
(1951a, p. 477).

26. For a detailed elucidation of this approach in a variety of
areas, see Yinger (1965).

Much of it is empirically verifiable—that is, based on "hard" data. Occasionally, however, work is presented which is theoretical, rather than empirical, or based on subjective analysis of a single case, rather than on objective appraisal. The rationale for including such material is the desire to demonstrate the congruence of one specific personality theory—Maslow's—with a wide range of past work and thinking in various behavioral disciplines. To put the matter in simple terms, it is often easy to dismiss one man's philosophy if it is believed to be idiosyncratic and isolated from the mainstream of professional interests. To show that a wide variety of separated workers have come to a similar—though less all-encompassing—view of human motivation is quite another story.

Then, in chapter 4, the discussion focuses on an original attempt to empirically verify the possibilities of using Maslow's theory of motivation to study political behavior. Too often, writers interested in developing the field of political psychology have limited their efforts to a discussion of the valuable possibilities of bringing personality into political research and to delimiting the areas of possible application. It is tantalizing indeed that, after all the years since Graham Wallas examined human nature in politics, so few political scientists have been willing to do more than to merely discuss the possibilities![27] Thus a concerted effort has been made here to illustrate the practical application of personality in political research as a necessary adjunct to the theoretical discussion.

Avoiding the Scylla of a sample size of four and the Charybdis of a study of that easily available research animal, the college student, an attempt was made to cast as wide a net as possible among various types in the working community. With the limited funds that were available, it was impossible to consider a probability sample of a significant area. Therefore, while diversity and size were achieved, representativeness was not. The value of the study which is central to this book therefore lies in the relationships which were uncovered as indicators of future research possibilities, rather than in any firmly established results.[28] It is realized of course that many valuable and legitimate subjects of study cannot be precisely quantified.[29] Yet a suggestive analysis of the relationships between mental health and politically relevant behavior will hopefully point to possibilities for fruitful theoretical and empirical work in the future.

27. Two recent articles by Greenstein (1967a, 1968) fall into this category. These exploratory arguments are expanded and reprinted in his recent book, Personality and Politics (1969).

28. These findings have, however, recently been replicated and their relevance expanded in a new study of political leaders. For a preliminary report of this study, see Knutson (1971).

29. A point which is made by Lynd (1958, p. 86).

Finally, the concluding chapter of this book focuses on the theoretical and empirical relevance of the foregoing material. The discussion will include a model for the use of personality variables in the study of political behavior based on previously outlined relationships. Further, in an effort to return to our point of departure, the concluding chapter also encompasses a discussion of the relevance to democratic theory and political philosophy of what is known today about personality and its effect on politically relevant behavior.

It is hoped that through this book the value (and practicality!) of using psychological variables in behavioral studies will be firmly established. This value is both predictive and intuitive—as an aid to understanding the phenomena with which we, as students of political behavior, are forcefully confronted: leaders and followers, radicals and reactionaries, activists and apathetics, democrats and authoritarians. But even more: the study of the selective process which prepares some men to be self-fulfilled and humanitarian leaders and others to be hostile, anxious and driven demagogues, which permits some people to react to the infinite and fluid field of political phenomena (marked by frequent crises) with open-mindedness and tolerance, while others are constrictive in their cognitive process and hostile in their attitudes toward others—such a study offers a fascinating mystery to the student of political behavior. This challenge perhaps has been best stated by George C. Homans, who said:

> There is only one paramount reason for studying anything but the multiplication table. Either you are so interested in a subject that you cannot let it alone, or you are not. In the end, it is a matter of intellectual passion. (1950, p. 2)

2

A Theory of Psychic Evolution

> The ultimate test of the validity of any construct and of
> the measures which enter into its definition is found in
> the utility of the construct in the process of reducing
> the matrix of events to some meaningful order. (Peak,
> 1953, p. 273)

Within the discipline of psychology—as within the discipline of political science—there is a variety of sects, each opting for its own
particularistic view of the phenomena with which it must deal. (As
Greenstein [1967] noted, this fragmented state of psychology is in
no small way responsible for the difficulties with which those interested in developing a field of political psychology must deal.)
Psychologists hold vastly different views of human personality;
consequently a wide variety of models[1] has evolved. The model
upon which this book is based belongs to a school of thought that
has been called the "growth actualization" school and whose most
well-known exponents are Carl Rogers and Abraham Maslow.[2]
    The growth actualization school becomes most distinct when
contrasted to the two more traditional conceptual approaches in
psychology. One of these approaches is of course the Freudian
psychoanalytic approach. Here human behavior is discussed in
terms of a philosophy of the residues of adjustments and compromises necessitated in the inevitable universal process of socialization and development. According to Maslow and others in the
growth actualization school, the basic defect in Freudian analysis
is its emphasis on pathology and its lack of explanation of the
forces and phenomena of mental health and human fulfillment. As
Bruno Bettelheim has stated, psychoanalytic theory "overstresses
the importance of the inner life to the neglect of the total man as
he deals with his human and social environment" (1960).
    "Growth" oriented psychologists point to empirical demonstra-
tions that man is driven by more than the desire to satisfy his sex,
hunger, sleep, and other psychological needs. In reference to the
traditional Freudian, Maslow commented

> Psychologists of this persuasion treat the human being as if
> he were an animal, which of course he is, but as if he were
> merely an animal, only an animal, so that the animal charac-

---

1. A useful summary is found in Hall and Lindzey (1957).

2. For a discussion of the contrast between this school and
traditional Freudian psychology, see Rogers (1961, pp. 90-92).

teristics which are unique to man are somehow not considered properly "scientific." . . . The assumption is that that which can be studied scientifically about the human being is what he has in common with lower animals. (1969)

Examples of efforts to widen the scope of traditional motivation theory beyond such narrow confines can be found in Harlow's work on the need for affection or "contact comfort,"[3] White's analysis of competence or "effectance" motivation[4] and Maslow's analysis of the need to know.[5]

In actuality, it does not do justice to the variety of approaches within the psychoanalytic tradition to dismiss all writers of this orientation as similarly negativistic. Perhaps the most well-known example of a creative extension of Freud's ideas is the work of Erik Erikson (Coles, 1970). Indeed, Erikson's discussion of man's life pattern in terms of stages from each of which is derived a tendency toward later mental health or illness is in many ways similar to the personality development explored by Maslow. Erikson states:

What the child acquires at a given stage is a certain ratio between the positive and the negative which, if the balance is toward the positive, will help him to meet later crises with a better chance for unimpaired total development. The idea that at any stage a goodness is achieved which is impervious to new conflicts within and changes without is a projection on child development of that success ideology which so dangerously pervades our private and public daydreams and can make us inept in the face of a heightened struggle for a meaningful existence in our time.[6] (1959, p. 61)

Certainly, Maslow would concur fully with the statement that "If we will only learn to let live, the plan for growth is all there" (p. 100).

A second, traditional, and to Maslow and his colleagues, equally crippling view of human personality is the behavioristic school which has discussed human behavior in terms of learned response patterns, specific stimuli and reinforcement through rewards (or extinction through lack of reward). Again, such "mechanistic" assumptions are attacked as providing an unsatisfactory basis of understanding for a great deal of human behavior. (As Maslow [1957a]

---

3. Harlow (1958, 1959) and Harlow and Harlow (1962).

4. White (1959); also White (1963).

5. Maslow (1963).

6. Yinger (1965), who develops this thesis in considerable detail, states "The character system being maintained is a moving equilibrium, constantly incorporating new experience which modifies the existing tendencies. It is an open system."

has remarked, he finds inadequate a philosophy of human behavior in which man is studied "as if he were no more than a complicated white rat." Further, increasing confirmation of the discontinuity between animal and human behavior (as well as of the specificity of any "laws" of learning) is coming from within the behavioral tradition itself (Breland and Breland, 1961; Seligman, 1970).

In juxtaposition to these two schools of thought, Maslow discusses a view of human motivation which he calls "the third force" or "humanistic" psychology.[7] The distinctiveness of humanistic psychology is seen as follows:

> Humanistic psychology parallels the Freudian model to the extent of seeing human needs as biological in origin. The major emphasis in Humanistic psychology rests on the assumption regarding "higher needs." They are seen as biologically based, part of the human essence or the species character. (Maslow, 1969)

The view of human personality that is offered by the growth-actualization school is dynamic, rather than static. It is based on the belief that man has certain inborn, basic needs which must be satisfied if the individual is to enjoy mental health and that, through the satisfaction of these basic needs, man grows to self-actualization. It is felt that throughout each culture and in the past as well as the present, the human personality has been shaped by these basic needs and the way in which they are satisfied or left unsatisfied. Finally, it is advanced that these needs are arranged in a hierarchy of importance so that after—and only after—the first and most basic need is largely satisfied does the next need become a motivating force.[8]

This emphasis on growth and fulfillment, rather than on the crippling compromises which social development often requires in turn for an individual's right to existence is not particular to the writings of Abraham Maslow. As Frieda Fromm-Reichmann points out:

> Goldstein's "self-actualization," Fromm's "productive character," Whitehorn's "mature personality" and the "self-affirmation" of the existentialists are formulations of the same concept. In the classical psychoanalytic literature insufficient attention has been given so far to the concept of self-realiza-

---

7. Two recent journals dedicated to this viewpoint are The Journal of Humanistic Psychology and The Journal of Transpersonal Psychology.

8. An epigenetic (to borrow Erikson's use of this term) psychological scheme has widespread appeal. Refer, for example, to Kohlberg's work on moral development (1966; 1968). Also relevant is Loevinger's developmental model (1966) and the work of Piaget (see Flavell [1963]).

tion as a great source, if not the greatest source, of human fulfillment. Freud has referred to it in his teachings on secondary narcissism and ego-ideal formation, but he has dealt more with the investigation of the origin of the phenomenon than with the elaboration on the psychological significance of the end-product, mature self-realization. (1960, p. 134)

Also relevant is the current analysis of psychic growth in terms of degrees of competence.[9]

In presenting Abraham Maslow's theory of this "hierarchy of needs," readers should be aware that the following discussion is based upon my own interpretation. An attempt is made here to discuss Maslow's theory in terms which will be understandable to those whose interests in the study of behavior lead them to a consideration of the importance of personality and motivation, not to those who are primarily interested in the psychological bases of personality formation. Professor Maslow set forth his own carefully described and clinically derived statements in a great variety of writings, the most important of which is his Motivation and Personality. Others, whose interests in the application of personality to behavior has led them to a consideration of Maslow's ideas, have offered their own versions elsewhere.[10] Therefore, while the following discussion is liberally salted with quotations from Maslow's writings, the serious student is directed to read further in the original discussion.

To begin with, Maslow offers a "holistic" view of personality. That is, he believes that one cannot meaningfully consider an individual attitude or piece of behavior aside from the total personality. Stated in another way, he suggests that each person is predominantly motivated by one or more psychic needs and that the importance of this need in the person's psychic economy colors or "flavors" all the attitudes and behavior in which a personality dimension is involved.[11] Thus each person has an integrated (though perhaps unarticulated) world view, based on his personal needs. Further, "Each act tends to be an expression of the whole integrated personality." However, because behavior also reflects the immediate situation and the particular culture, "a much higher correlation is found to obtain between character and impulse-to-behavior" (Maslow, 1943d, p. 549).

---

9. For a review and analysis of personality in terms of competence, see Smith (1968a).

10. See Appendix F for a summary of other work.

11. For example, Maslow exempts behavior which is reflexive - such as brushing a fly off one's nose; a momentary response to an immediate situation - such as jumping out of the way of an oncoming truck; or a culturally conditioned act - such as standing up when a lady enters the room (1943d, pp. 500-501).

Maslow thus discusses personality in terms of "syndromes" of motivation. By understanding the importance of a particular syndrome in a personality, one can hopefully understand and predict the person's behavior in specific situations which engage his psychic needs.

> In our definition of the syndrome, the main quality which characterizes the whole ("meaning," "flavor," or aim) can be seen in any of its parts if these parts are understood not reductively, but holistically. Of course this is a theoretical statement and we may expect to find operational difficulties with it. Most of the time we shall be able to discover the flavor or aim of the specific behavior only by understanding the whole of which it is a part. And yet there are enough exceptions to this rule to convince us that the aim or "flavor" inheres in the part as well as in the whole. (Maslow, 1943c, pp. 528-29)

Maslow's theory of motivation encompasses five basic need areas. These need groups or areas[12] are physiological, safety or security, affection and belongingness, esteem and self-actualization. The first four, as will be detailed below, differ in quality from the need for self-actualization because they are deficiency needs. That is to say, they are needs the gratification of which is the basic condition of mental health. The fifth need, the need for self-actualization, is the state of mental health or psychic fulfillment and results minimally from an individual's fulfillment of the other four basic needs. The furthermost reaches of psychic fulfillment are recognized to be but dimly understood.

At once, the reader will recognize that Maslow's need hierarchy encompasses far more than the powerful physiological drives of sex, hunger, thirst, et cetera. Maslow (1954) believes that knowledge of other needs is equally as important in an understanding of behavior because the frustration of these needs is equally devastating to personality development. At the outset, it can be seen that needs two through five will be much more important in research on western political behavior, while unresolved physiological needs offer a testable hypothesis for behavior differences among deprived groups within our own culture. In addition, this construct offers a culture-wide approach in nations (such as India, China, most of Latin America) where the majority of the citizens, it can be hypothesized, will exhibit unfulfilled physiological needs.

Maslow also advances the belief that the severe deprivation of

---

12. While both Maslow and this text usually refer to five "basic needs," it is important to realize that Maslow's need hierarchy is based in fact on five "need areas" (so that the physiological level, for example, refers to a variety of specific needs such as sex, sleep, thirst, hunger, etc.) and does not rest on a simplistic assumption that man's motivational patterns could be defined in terms of five single needs.

a need, particularly if it occurs in early years, will color or flavor the behavior of the individual throughout the remainder of his
life and will affect his ability to cope and manner of coping with
his life problems. In other words, without professional (psychiatric and/or social) intervention, a man who has suffered from a
lack of gratification of affection needs as a child will be forever
after bounded by operating in an environment which he perceives
to be unloving—which offers him no feeling of belonging.

> Once character structure has been formed it becomes rela-
> tively independent of its origins [sic] and it may thus come
> about that the insecure adult remains insecure even when of-
> fered safety, belongingness, and love, though the already se-
> cure person can retain his security in the midst of a threat-
> ening, isolating, and rejecting environment. (Maslow, 1952)

Thus, while personality is formed through the process of social
interaction, it soon attains a degree of autonomy which limits (but
does not deny) its further malleability.[13]
On the other hand, persons who have received full gratification of a basic need in their formative years will cease to be motivated by it. One can only speak of motivation in regard to unsatiated needs. In a future case of severe deprivation of this need,
the person will likely be able to tolerate its deprivation. Maslow
states:

> . . . it is precisely those individuals in whom a certain need
> has always been satisfied who are best equipped to tolerate
> deprivation of that need in the future and . . . furthermore,
> those who have been deprived in the past will react different-
> ly to current satisfactions than the one who has never been
> deprived. (1943)

The importance of this theory for students of behavior is obvious:
by understanding the syndrome which "flavors" the behavior and
attitudes of a given individual one can begin to understand the
meaning which his actions have for him and to predict what course
they may follow in a future situation. This may be possible even
though (if lacking psychiatric training) students of behavior may
not have the information or knowledge to adequately assess specific causes of the syndrome's existence. Thus the psychodynamics
and the psychogenesis of motivation become separable dimensions.

---

13. As Yinger states: "It is not simply that a child can discover himself only in the actions of others toward him, much as
he can see his face only in a mirror. More than that, the self is
formed out of the actions of others, which become part of the individual as a result of his having identified with these others and
responded to himself in their terms. Retrospectively, one can ask
'Who am I?' But in practice, the answer has come before the question" (1965, p. 149).

No attempt is made here to suggest that these five basic need groups encompass the totality of human motivation. Maslow himself would be the first to deny such a narrow view. Indeed his last work was concerned with the discussion of other needs which arise when the level of self-actualization is reached. (These needs [which he has variously called "B-values," or "meta-needs"] involve such dimensions as curiosity, the need to know and the need for beauty.)[14]

But while these five needs do not exclude other bases of motivation, they are—as the following evidence cumulatively indicates —fundamental motivational forces whose frustration causes debilitating and constricting personality dynamics. Further, as far as current knowledge indicates, these need areas are universal and vital motivational factors in all cultures. Finally, the search for their satisfaction is also, as is demonstrated below, of considerable value in the analysis and prediction of politically relevant behavior.

After the earlier, simplistic views of human nature which have been employed in political philosophy, Maslow's view of man—to use Henry Kariel's words—"as a structurally complex, open-ended system in an interminable process of transformation" (1968, p. 5) undoubtedly presents difficult research problems. This more complex model of man, however, will allow us to see more clearly what was earlier either dimly perceived or totally ignored in a simplified conceptualization of human behavior and needs.

Physiological Needs

Starvation can confine the freedom of expression more effectively than can political tyranny. (Bay, 1965, p. 15)

All this is far too difficult for me, I am only a small man.[15] (Dicks, 1950, p. 118)

The importance of the basic physiological needs is well-known through the work of Freud and his pupils and has also been demonstrated by animal psychologists in a variety of experiments. The need for sex, hunger, thirst, sleep, warmth, et cetera—all of the basic needs upon which physical health depends—are also impor-

---

14. Because the number of individuals who go beyond the minimum level of self-actualization is hypothesized to be numerically very small, for political research purposes it may not be necessary to sub-categorize the self-actualizers into distinct higher stages of mental health, although growth in self-actualization may be an important dimension to explore.

15. The statement summarizes the view of the German prisoners he studied who could be typified as "unpolitical men" and suggests the traditionalist's view of politics.

tant in psychological health. It has been shown over and over again, for example, that in situations characterized by severe deprivation of all needs (such as occurred in the Axis concentration camps in World War II), physiological needs become of prime importance.[16]

Two factors must be considered here. People who live at a starvation level are only peripherally concerned with the higher needs. The misunderstanding of this basic fact has again and again been the stumbling block of American foreign policy, as we have attempted without success to build democracy when the population is concerned with surviving physically.

The second point is that persons who have never had their physiological needs fulfilled will not be open to the concerns of those people who have—no matter what their current social status. To political scientists, physiological needs may most simply be thought of as needs for food, for shelter, for clothing. Maslow's point here is that a political leader—even though he may be President of his country and surrounded by all the creature comforts which civilization can offer—will nevertheless react in ways similar to those who are still daily experiencing the hunger and the cold—if he has been severely deprived in his formative years. To the leader, the hunger and cold are now psychic realities.

It would be a facile job to establish some cutoff point on a calorie chart as indicative of these needs, but, unfortunately for the researcher, each of Maslow's five needs is important in understanding an individual's motivation only when seen from within. In other words, I wish to emphasize the importance of a phenomenological viewpoint. To the middle class researcher, the peasant child with his half-empty stomach, who sleeps in a rude hut, may be a prime example of the need for physiological satisfaction. To the native, however—provided his simpler satisfactions have been adequate for his energy needs and regular in appearance, and provided he is not made personally aware of a higher standard which would make him feel relatively deprived—physiological needs may not be a source of motivation. His needs, in other words, may advance beyond a concern for physiological satisfaction.

There is an interesting similarity between this need and some traits associated with the Freudian oral character. Take, for example, the discussion by Dicks of Russian character, based on a study of twenty-nine male defectors. Remembering the severe physical hardships suffered by the peasantry in Russia who grew up during the establishment of Communism, and also keeping in mind that this oral character is found by Dicks to typify the peasants and not the elite that he studied, the following comments are of particular interest:

---

16. Maslow (1954, pp. 80-82). Also see Bettelheim (1960, p. 233), Nardini (1952), Davis (1948) and Davies (1963, pp. 11-15).

. . . there was a great deal of preoccupation with food and its acquisition, in men who had <u>for a long time</u> been well fed in western Germany. Anecdotes, war experiences, and attitudes to the various periods of Soviet history were evaluated in terms of the gratification or frustration of oral needs. Prodigious eating and the reminiscences of such feasts form high lights in their stories. The attitude to an officer or to the authorities as a whole was often determined primarily by their indulgence or withholding in matters of food, cigarettes, and vodka. This simple like or dislike was expressed in a way which showed that the informant was thinking only in terms of the direct relation of the authority to himself and his kind, and unable to think of the economic or logistic limitations imposed on the authority figure. It implied that authority either loved or did not love one. . . .

Indeed this passivity, "fatalism," and sense of mutability of life beyond one's control are themselves oral traits, linked to the helplessness of infancy at the hands of omnipotent parent figures. It would be interesting to discover to what extent the traits here described are characteristic of peasants generally, with their primary producer mentality and their dependence on fitful weather and markets, and to what degree they are specifically Russian. (1952, pp. 137-39).

This quotation is pertinent to our discussion in several respects. In the first place, Dicks found a preoccupation with food on the part of men "who had for a long time been well fed"—which suggests the correlation advanced by Maslow between early deprivation of a specific need and later attitudes and behavior. Second, Dicks found that this preoccupation colored the individual's relations with his human environment. Third, he describes more generalized traits as correlated with a concern with food: "passivity, 'fatalism,' and a sense of mutability of life beyond one's control." Finally, he offers the suggestion that these characteristics may typify others whose life subsistence pattern is uncertain.

In summary, it has been frequently demonstrated that when physiological needs are unsatisfied, this deprivation will color the attention, behavior and performance of a person. Even if later satisfied, long-standing deprivation of this need will leave its effects on the character of the individual. Persons with unfulfilled physiological needs are hypothesized here to be typified by the "traditional" (in Lerner's [1958] terms), the peasant who, having lived close to starvation all his life (and isolated from the main currents of his society) is fearful and conserving in all of his attitudes. It is assumed that <u>relatively</u> few Americans will fall into this category and that those who do will come primarily from a small number of specific socioeconomic groups (for example, migrant workers, southern farm workers, inhabitants of urgan ghettos).

But what of the typical American whose physiological needs
have been satisfied? In what terms do we then speak of motivation?
Maslow states:

> It is quite true that man lives by bread alone—when there is
> no bread. But what happens to man's desires when there is
> plenty of bread and when his belly is chronically filled?
>
> At once other (and higher) needs emerge and these, rather
> than physiological hungers, dominate the organism. And when
> these in turn are satisfied, again new (and still higher) needs
> emerge, and so on. This is what we mean by saying that the
> basic human needs are organized into a hierarchy of relative
> prepotency. (1954, p. 83)

The Need for Safety and Security

> Whatever words we use, there is character difference be-
> tween the man who feels safe and the one who lives his life
> out as if he were a spy in enemy territory. (Maslow, 1954,
> p. 114)

The five basic needs can be conceptualized as points along a
continuum, the ends of which would perhaps be indicated by "concern with self" and "concern with environment (and self in relation
to it)." The individual who is typified by unfulfilled physiological
needs exemplifies the concern with self in its most elemental form:
the need to survive physically. In all other relationships, his attitude is that of passivity. The person typified by the need for safety
and security has advanced one point along the continuum: he is
aware of the world around him and he is concerned with his relationship to it.

Full of anxiety over the chaos he perceives to be surrounding
him, this individual wishes to establish some form and order in his
world. Thus it is hypothesized that he will be intolerant of ambiguity
and highly dogmatic. His unfulfilled needs require him to arbitrarily
impose a pattern or design on the phenomena surrounding him. It is
also hypothesized that he will be hostile to that which he does not
understand—those people and ideas which are different from what
is known and therefore, safe. It is thought, however, that like the
person typified by unfulfilled physiological needs, he will be passive
in accepting roles which his environment makes available to him.
Though aware of his environment, he feels that it is unresponsive to
his needs. If he assumes any role, it will be that of a follower, rather than a leader—and this usually when crisis makes action necessary. It is also felt that a key to understanding him can be symbol-
ized by the word "control"—with little control over his own impulses, he worries about control over the unstructured events and
passionate people he perceives to comprise his environment.[17]

---

17. To this most important point of control, we will return at

Hadley Cantril's report on the famous Orson Welles Halloween broadcast illustrates the value of understanding and isolating security motivation (1940). While those who panicked tended to be lower class and poorly educated, Cantril found a personality variable was directly related to such behavior. Further, this variable was not limited to lower class or uneducated individuals.[18]

Cantril calls this factor "susceptibility-to-suggestion-when-facing-a-dangerous-situation." (It is important to note that this characteristic is not defined as a generalized suggestibility.) In other words, for certain persons, reports of impending doom act in the nature of a prophecy being fulfilled—a prophecy in which a great deal of affect is invested.[19]

Cantril describes this personality trait as follows:

> In the first place, . . . [it] implies a certain feeling of personal inadequacy. The individual is unable to rely on his own resources to see him through. He feels relatively helpless and believes his own best efforts at a better adjustment are insufficient. This means, furthermore, that the individual believes his life and his fate are very largely dependent on some forces outside himself—on chance, or economic conditions far beyond his control, or on the whim of some supernatural being. All this adds up to an intense feeling of emotional insecurity, one which is likely to be augmented as the situation surrounding the individual appears more and more threatening. (p. 138)

Persons who are insecure thus have special sensitivity to environmental cues that can be interpreted as threatening. While education helps to control the behavioral reaction to inner panic, it cannot overcome the individual's desire for a world of greater order, permanence and reward—for a world, in short, of greater safety and security.[20]

---

length in the section of this chapter entitled "Generalized Deprivation."

18. ". . . the differences between the vulnerability scores are much greater within each educational group than they are between the educational groups" (Cantril, 1940, p. 135). For two case study illustrations of the selective status effects of this variable, see pp. 172-79 of Cantril's study.

19. He found seven areas to be good predictors of this susceptibility: "Insecurity, phobias, amount of worry, lack of self-confidence, fatalism, religiosity, frequency of church attendance" (1940, pp. 131-34).

20. While Wolfenstein typifies Lenin as another example of one who is motivated by "an underlying receptivity to the danger signals of his environment," published accounts of Lenin's life do not appear to this author to place Lenin among those with an un-

Maslow sees the value placed on safety and security operative in the behavior of all people. In the child, it is

> his preference for some kind of undisrupted routine or rhythm
> . . . [his preference for] a safe, orderly, predictable, orga-
> nized world, which he can count on, and in which unexpected,
> unmanageable, or other dangerous things do not happen, and
> in which, in any case, he has all-powerful parents who protect
> and shield him from harm. (1954, pp. 86-87)

In the healthy adult, the value of safety is manifest in concern with insurance, a savings account and job tenure, "in the very common preference for familiar rather than unfamiliar things, or for the known rather than the unknown." In the insecure person—one whose need for safety has never been fulfilled—the value of safety takes on prime importance. The world is seen as "hostile, overwhelm-ing, and threatening. Such a person behaves as if a great catastro-phe were almost always impending, that is, he is usually respond-ing as if to an emergency" (pp. 87-88).

The causes of a need for security motivating adult behavior, while producing the same results, can be hypothesized as based on two disparate conditions. One type of an adult need for security is present in an individual's personality because the real world on which his primary home depended was unpredictable and chaotic. In this category would be the children of displaced persons and refugees, as well as the inhabitants of urban slums and ghettos. He reacts to a world which is perceived as a jungle because for most—if not all—of his life this has been an accurate and even nec-essary operational code. The other type of an adult need for secu-rity would be present in persons whose parents have been unable to provide an emotional atmosphere that is predictable and stable in their home lives as children.

Borel[21] has described such a home as follows:

> If the parents are themselves constantly anxiety-ridden by
> their own feelings of insecurity and unable to follow a constant
> predictable pattern of response, the child is faced with the im-
> possible situation of trying to find security in a desperate
> struggle where the rules are constantly changing. He repeat-
> edly tries to solve the dilemma by the alternative of indepen-
> dent action and is just as constantly thwarted until he finally
> gives up. He becomes conditioned to the attitude that what

healthy security fixation. It is more likely that Lenin was a men-tally healthy person whose revolutionary activities—and the politi-cal unpopularity of his family—led to a realistic appraisal of the world as hostile and threatening. (See Wolfenstein [1967]).

21. This article offers an interesting explanation of man's entire emotional range as well as his social history seen from the basis of a need for security.

little security is available lies in dependence on others and the anxiety-ridden struggle to constantly gain the approval and goodwill of others is the only way of life. He then spends his life acting out roles that he feels will gratify others while carrying a constant burden of anger and frustration. (1964, pp. 106-7)

On the basis of such a twofold classification of the development of an unfulfilled need for security, it is hypothesized that, taken as a whole, there would be a strong correlation between unfulfilled physiological and unfulfilled safety-security needs because the type one experience would tend to produce both. But the correlation, though strong, would be far from a perfect one-to-one relationship, because there is no necessary connection between the unfulfilled need for food, shelter, et cetera, and the type two childhood environment.

It is assumed, for the same reason, that there is a strong relationship between these first two needs and a low socioeconomic status. Again, however, the researcher cannot accurately classify a person on the basis of his life experience alone—it is necessary to ascertain what the subject's life experiences mean to him. Thus the same type of humble surroundings produced in Abraham Lincoln a basically fulfilled, "growth-oriented," political leader whose need for affection was used with great creativity[22] and in Joseph McCarthy, a politician who had—it must be assumed—severely unfulfilled and very basic needs.[23]

Of what value in the study of politically relevant behavior would it be to isolate in our research persons with an unfulfilled need for security? First of all, we have seen from Cantril's study that such motivation stimulates individual panic reaction in situations which are easily verifiable as nonthreatening. In situations more objectively frightening (for example, police reports of sniper activity during urban riots), these persons will be even more likely to be aroused to activity, rather than remain bystanders.

Second, Maslow tells us that the safety needs of such a person "often find specific expression in a search for a protector, or a stronger person on whom he may depend, perhaps a Fuehrer" (1954, p. 88). Sullivan, the anxiety-ridden, closed-minded Communist in Smith, Bruner and White's study of attitudes toward Russia, also falls into this category: "He was too insecure, his consciously formulated picture of himself and the world played too vital a role in his security system for him to tolerate discrepant features in his images of self and world" (1956, pp. 182-83). The need for

---

22. See Clark (1933). Clark's book is a particularly good blend of psychology and biography which does justice to both fields.

23. Anderson and May (1952); also see Rovere (1959), Davies (1966, pp. 85-87).

security also accounts for part of the motivation which Gerth found to impel individuals to join the Nazi party.[24]

In addition to being a candidate for <u>followership</u> in mass movements which offer strong leadership and a dogmatic world view, and in mobs reacting to danger cues, the person with an unresolved need for security appears to be <u>one type</u> of the prejudiced personality about which so much has been written in past years. As Helen Merrell Lynd states:

> Expectation and having expectation met are crucial in developing a sense of coherence in the world and in oneself.
>
> Sudden experience of a violation of expectation, of incongruity between expectation and outcome, results in a shattering of trust in oneself, even in one's own body and skill and identity, and in the trusted boundaries or framework of the society and the world one has known. As trust in oneself and in the outer world develop together, so doubt of oneself and of the world are also intermeshed. . . .
>
> Shattering of trust in the dependability of one's immediate world means loss of trust in other persons, who are the transmitters and interpreters of the world. (1958, pp. 45-47)

Allport, in <u>The Nature of Prejudice</u>, offers several pertinent comments. First of all, he notes that "In all cases of intense character-conditioned prejudice a common factor emerges which Newcomb[25] has called 'threat orientation.' Underlying insecurity seems to lie at the root of the personality" (1954, p. 373). Further, in citing a study of the causes of anti-Semitism,[26] Allport makes the following remarks.

> The findings of this research are important. It will be noted that the anti-Semite is not merely a bundle of negative attitudes. Rather he is trying to <u>do</u> something: namely, to find an island of institutional safety and security. The nation is the island he selects. It is a positive anchorage; it is his country right or wrong; it is higher than humanity; more desirable than a world state. It has the definiteness he needs. The research establishes the fact that the higher the degree of nationalism, the higher the anti-Semitism.
>
> Note the emphasis here is upon positive security.[27]
>
> (1954, p. 381)

---

24. Gerth (1940).

25. Reference is to T. M. Newcomb, <u>Social Psychology</u>, New York, Dryden Press, 1950, p. 588.

26. Reference is to Nancy C. Morse and F. H. Allport, "The Causation of Anti-Semitism: An Investigation of Seven Hypotheses," <u>Journal of Psychology</u>, 34 (1952), 197-233.

27. Gilbert also finds a connection between the search for se-

Finally, Allport mentions the well-documented correlation between higher education and increased tolerance.[28] He suggests that
"Perhaps it is because higher education lessens feelings of insecurity and anxiety" (p. 405). The relationship between education and
tolerance—which has often been established empirically—is an important area for future research. Too frequently it has been assumed that there is a simple causal relationship between increased
education and democratic attitudes. This is likely, however, to be a
two-way process, the second part of which has been left unconsid-
ered to date. That is, there may well be a high correlation between
unfulfilled basic needs and an inability to complete an education
commensurate with ability.[29] If it can be empirically demonstrated
that the educational process is unable to ego-involve students who
are psychically deprived, this would go a long way in explaining
why the educated (and those in leadership positions based on a completed education) are more tolerant. Education then becomes a selective process, where the likelihood of survival increases as a
person continues up the ladder of satisfaction of his basic needs.[30]

Those who do stay in school (because of social pressures, et
cetera) and who also have unresolved basic needs, would of course
evidence very different attitudes about the world than psychically
fulfilled individuals who are educated and in leadership positions.
Insofar as low socioeconomic status is correlated with psychic deprivation, this would help to explain the tantalizing variation that
Hyman noticed in his study of the socialization process: differences
by SES grow more profound with school level in spite of the fact
that low SES dropouts should make the school group more homogeneous (1959, pp. 63-65). This would suggest that attitude patterns
are determined early and are then intensified. To a person who is
psychically deprived, the educational experience (if he remains to
complete it) does not change his view of the world, but rather confirms his pessimism, anxiety and hostilities, through the process
of selective perception in the classroom as well as the social relationships which the school offers.[31]

---

curity and ardent nationalism, commenting as follows: "With the
expansion of the ethnic identification group from the primitive
tribe to the modern state, the socially identified security of the individual has been correspondingly extended. The aggressive nationalism that has characterized many dictatorships must be regarded as an enlarged manifestation of that continuing quest for security through group solidarity (1950, p. 8).

28. See, for example, Stouffer (1955).

29. Cervantes discusses the dropout girl's early marriage in
terms of a search for security (1965, p. 73).

30. This point is mentioned by Bettelheim and Janowitz (1964,
p. 18).

31. Some evidence for the hypothesis that the effect of educa-

Research on political socialization clearly shows that the lessons of citizenship in a participatory democracy are not learned in the classroom but that learning is rather largely shaped by predispositions brought into the classroom.[32] Lawrence S. Kubie sums it up by remarking that "there is an incessant interaction between universal but subtly masked neurotic mechanisms and the educational process, and . . . as a result of this interplay education is blocked and distorted. The relationship between the two is evidently so close, that both must be solved if either is to be solved."[33]

This discussion of prejudice should not be taken to mean that the need for security is identical with the need to be intolerant and to express hostility toward outgroups. The problem of prejudice will be brought up again in connection with other unfulfilled needs. Further, prejudice is of course a reflection of learned cultural values as well as individual personality needs. At this point, it is important only to note that one type of home from which the prejudiced individual comes is an insecure home. The literature on prejudice (and on the authoritarian personality) does not appear to describe a homogeneous population. Factor analysis done by others tends to confirm this.[34] An alternative explanation is the hypothesis that intolerance serves a different function and has a different meaning in personalities with different unfulfilled basic needs. To the student of political behavior, it is of value to recognize this difference.

The unfulfilled need for security—as a culture-wide concern—

---

tion on values is dependent upon the human input of an educational system is found in a study of Negro voter registration in the South. The authors found that "white education in southern counties is independently and negatively associated with Negro registration. Short of the highest levels, the more educated the whites the more actively and effectively they seem to enforce the traditional mores of the region against Negro participation in elections. The usual effect of an increase in average schooling for whites in the South as a whole appears to be to give the white people more of the skills that are needed to express effectively their anti-Negro sentiment. For example, the correlation between median school years completed by Whites and the presence or absence of a White Citizens Council or similar organization is +.32 . . ." (Matthews and Prothro, 1967, pp. 178-210).

32. See, for example, Hess and Torney (1967), Langton and Jennings (1968), Dawson and Prewitt (1969), Langton (1967, 1969), and Simpson (1971).

33. Quoted in the introduction to Jones (1960).

34. See, for example, reports in Eysenck (1954), O'Neil and Levinson (1953); also references below in chap. 3, section on authoritarianism.

has been discussed at length in the classic <u>Escape From Freedom</u>
by Erich Fromm. To Fromm, it is a pervading feeling of insecurity that has a historical explanation and serious political implications in this age of mass movements (1941, pp. 202-9). He lays
particular emphasis on the destructiveness which stems from isolation, powerlessness, anxiety and "the thwarting of life."

What are the political views of a person who is driven by a
need for security? As with others in the psychically deprived
group, they are likely to be undemocratic. Lane, in his intensive
study of a small group of working class men (1962), describes one
of them (Rapuano) in terms similar to those used to picture an individual with an unfulfilled need for security. In Lane's analysis,
such a person suffers from a loss of identity (which is also the
theme of Lynd's argument, discussed below). Lane's discussion
is useful in helping to theoretically delimit this type:

> I would argue that the most likely intellectual development for
> a man where nothing is anchored, nothing, including his con-
> cept of himself, is secure, is to put a high premium on stabil-
> ity, order, decisiveness, rationality. This is, I think, what has
> happened to Rapuano. Since confusion about himself, combined
> with ambivalence about political matters, and uncertainty
> about his occupational future are constantly framing questions
> in his own mind, and have made him chronically worried and
> badly ulcerous, he cannot bear more confusion and indecisive-
> ness in the world—such confusion as may appear in legislative
> processes. . . . Marginal man, a man without psychic country,
> he becomes, understandably, an undemocrat. (pp. 110-11)

To the political scientist, then, the need for safety has particular applicability to the study of politically relevant behavior.
Among this group of psychically deprived persons will be found
dogmatic, intolerant citizens, and followers in modern mass movements who seek to "escape from freedom" by accepting the identity
and particularistic world view which demagogues sell. They are
likely to support simplistic solutions to complex and threatening
problems such as riots ("shoot looters on sight") and police pro-
tection ("when guns are outlawed, only outlaws will have guns" or,
alternatively, "police are pigs") and to be intolerant of diversity
("America—Love it or Leave it").

The Need for Affection and Belongingness

> The theologian is right. Why not admit it? More than anything
> else, the world needs Love. These several hundred pages have
> shown that unless a human being is welcomed to this world
> with love, he might as well have been stillborn; that unless his
> widening horizon continues to assure him of this love, he will
> not grow; and unless the religious and political beliefs which
> secure this love are left unfouled, he will wander through life
> in a maze. (De Grazia, 1948, p. 187)

After the need for physiological satisfaction and the need for safety and security have been <u>largely</u> fulfilled, each person next becomes motivated by a need for love and affection, for warmth and a sense of mutuality in his relationships with his human environment. To return to our hypothesis that Maslow's hierarchy parallels a continuum running from "concern with self" to "concern with environment (and self in relation to it)" affection is envisioned here as the beginning point in psychic development of an active reaching out toward others. Persons with such a motivating need have moved one more point along the continuum of involvement with their environment. It is an anxious and uncertain reaching out, however, and perceived rejection is met with hostility (either suppressed or overt).

Thus, in our society of joiners, the person with an unfulfilled need for affection is envisioned as being particularly likely to be found among the membership of social groups. In ideology, it is assumed that these persons will be both susceptible to appeals of brotherhood and concern with others and undemocratic because of their mistrust of others to supply their needs. The importance of this need cannot be overemphasized. As Maslow states, "In our society the thwarting of these needs is the most commonly found core in cases of maladjustment and more severe psychopathology"[35] (1954, p. 89). To De Grazia, this need is the cause of simple anomie (pp. 72, 107).

From previous studies, it is expected that persons whose childhood homes lacked love and affection will be particularly likely to express hostility and prejudice toward others and toward themselves. As Berelson and Steiner (1964, p. 75) conclude, after an exhaustive study of behavioral literature: "In general, the unloved child tends to be an unloving adult, with a high degree of self-hatred (that is, unlovable)."

Evidence in this direction is offered by Bettelheim and Janowitz (1964) in their study of the relation between social mobility and prejudice among 150 veteran enlisted men. While they began by stating that there is no ideal type of prejudiced personality, they went on to note that in their study as well as in many others, "personal insecurity, subjective feelings of deprivation, anxiety, and hostility were found to be positively and meaningfully linked to prejudice" (pp. 68-69). In turning to a consideration of the early home life of the prejudiced subjects, the authors report: "A significant association was found between tolerance toward minority groups and the recollection of love and affection on the part of the parents, while intolerance toward minority groups was associated with the recall of lack of parental love and harsh discipline." The authors go on to say:

---

35. Lane refers to the prevalence of this need among two samples of college students (1969, pp. 100-101).

The most interesting aspect of the association between intolerance and recollections of parental strictness is that there
was virtually no difference (1 per cent) between stereotyped
and outspoken anti-Semites. Therefore, it may be assumed
that having had affectionate parents (or at least believing so)
is definitely related to tolerant attitudes, while the reverse,
though having some influence on intolerance, hardly influences the degree of tolerance. If this should be so . . . then
one might think that adverse childhood experiences, particularly lack of parental love, have much to do with the need to
discharge hostility in later life, but relatively little to do with
the intensity with which such hostility will be discharged. This
seems to corroborate the findings of other research workers
which indicate that ethnic intolerance is acquired relatively
late as compared with the development of a general need for
hostile discharge. (pp. 209-10)

Allport also mentions the effect of a home which lacks emotional warmth on the later development of hostility. In reviewing
a study of anti-Semitic patients who were undergoing psychoanalysis,[36] he mentions that "the rejection of the child by one or both
parents was the rule rather than the exception." Allport expands
on this point as follows:

> Without stretching the evidence too far, we may at least make
> a guess: children who are too harshly treated, severely pun-
> ished, or continually criticized are more likely to develop per-
> sonalities wherein group prejudice plays a prominent part.
> Conversely, children from more relaxed and secure homes,
> treated permissively and with affection, are more likely to
> develop tolerance. (1954, pp. 285-86)

In regard to early environment, it should also be noted that
the Berkeley study of authoritarianism discussed their highly intolerant subject's home life in somewhat similar terms. (However,
as each of Maslow's deprived groups may theoretically exhibit authoritarian tendencies, no one need group is identical with the authoritarian individual, as defined by the F-scale or by Rokeach.
Authoritarianism and intolerance will be found among all four deprived groups but, with differing intensity and serving far different purposes in the economy of the personality.) As discussed by
the Berkeley group,[37] the home life of their highly prejudiced subjects led to both outward glorification of and repressed hostility
toward parent figures. The fathers of these subjects were typified

---

36. Reference is to N. W. Ackerman and Marie Jahoda, Anti-
Semitism and Emotional Disorder, New York, Harper, 1950, p. 45.

37. Adorno, Frenkel-Brunswik, Levinson and Sanford (1950);
see especially chap. 10 by Frenkel-Brunswik, entitled "Parents
and Childhood as Seen through the Interviews."

as "distant and stern" with whom "the relationship seems to be barren of any affection." The image of the mother is summarized under the heading of "sacrifice, moralism, restrictiveness." Of great importance in character formation was the type of punishment used in these cold, authoritarian homes. It is described as "threatening, traumatic, overwhelming discipline . . . [which] forces the child into submission and surrender of his ego."[38]

Additional striking evidence for the existence of a need for affection and of the debilitating effects of its lack of fulfillment in early life can also be seen in the work of Harry Harlow and Rene Spitz. Harlow's (1958, 1959, 1962) work on monkeys shows an analogy that deprivation of mothering and "contact comfort" in young leads to a variety of neurotic symptoms, among which are the inability to give love and to join in meaningful relationships with others. Spitz's (1945, 1946) studies of children raised in an institutional setting where physical needs are well provided and emotional needs ignored illustrates both the emotional and the physical damage which lack of love can cause.

Various studies, then, have shown a relationship between a person's belief that he is lovable and his being able to be accepting of others. Thus the need for affection is important in considering the tolerance that must underlie a democratic, pluralistic society. This point was studied directly by Fey (1955) (using as subjects fifty-eight third year medical students). He reports that subjects with high self-acceptance scores tend also to accept others ($r = +.43$). Further, they tend to feel accepted by others ($r = +.71$), but are, in actuality, "neither more nor less accepted by others ($r = +.07$) than Ss with low self-acceptance scores." (Fey explains the later contradiction by stating that self-depreciating people are apparently well-liked because they are not seen as interpersonally threatening.) Fey found that there was not only a connection between acceptance of self and acceptance of others, but also between acceptance of others and feeling ($r = +.43$) and being ($r = +.20$) accepted by others. Thus individuals with a need for affection will likely have difficulty in accepting themselves and this difficulty will mar their interpersonal relations in many ways.[39]

A most interesting experimental study which bears on the relationship between acceptance of self and acceptance of others is reported by Jones (1960). He used as subjects a psychology class in a boarding school, with control groups both in the same boarding school and in another, more liberal, day school. His subjects, who were enrolled in a Self-knowledge Workshop, were tested be-

---

38. Also see Frenkel-Brunswik's comments in Christie and Jahoda (1954, pp. 236-37).

39. For further documentation on this point, see Sheerer (1949); also Stock (1949). For a study focusing on the relationship between self-acceptance and dogmatism scores, see Pannes (1963).

fore and after the session on various personality measures. Jones found that—in contrast to the two control groups—his subjects changed significantly in self-acceptance (the overt purpose of the class), but also—without purposeful and articulated class work— the subjects had simultaneously changed significantly in their acceptance of others (as measured by the Bogardus Scale). Surprisingly, however, their overt attitudes expressing hostility toward others (as measured by both the E- and F-scales) remained unchanged. Jones concludes that while increased self-acceptance had diminished the group's needs to project, it had not affected their antiintraception.

In a very thorough review, Goldfried (1963) summarizes the literature on this point. He links it to Adler's key concept that: "The stronger the feelings of personal inferiority, the greater the likelihood that a person will hold negative attitudes toward others." In spite of the difficulties in comparing the wide variety of research techniques which have been employed to study this problem, Goldfried found two hypotheses to be generally confirmed: "a) in general, there is a positive relationship between one's attitudes toward self and one's attitudes toward others, and b) individuals who are maladjusted tend to have more negative attitudes toward others."[40] Horney has summed up this psychological truth as follows: "The conviction of being unlovable is closely akin to the incapacity for love; it is, in fact, a conscious reflection of that incapacity" (1937, p. 113).

Lane, in his discussion of the origin of antidemocratic attitudes among the previously mentioned small group of workers he studied intensively, also helps us to further delimit the type of individual motivated by a need for affection.[41] He connects these attitudes with political alienation, a root of which he sees as a feeling of "homelessness."[42] He describes this feeling of homelessness as follows:

> It includes (1) the feeling that human companionship is too shallow and transient or, figuratively, the search for the human relations of the hearthside, (2) the lack of a sense that

---

40. Also see Berger (1952).

41. Other studies which aid in understanding the behavioral manifestations of this need are the case of Paul in Bettelheim (1955) and the motivations of many young survivors presented in Lifton (1967). (See especially page 259 for an archetypal analysis of individuals motivated by the need for affection.)

42. Lynd connects the feeling of homelessness with experiences of shame, stating: "Loss of trust, exposure, failure, the feeling of homelessness—these experiences of shame—become still more unbearable if they lead to the feeling that there is no home for anyone, anywhere" (1958, p. 56).

there is a certain place where I belong (and where others will recognize that I belong), and (3) the feeling that there is no special and defined job there waiting for me to do it, and hence the fear of loss of usefulness and function in society, (4) the sense of doubt about how to play the roles that as father, husband, worker, citizen, an adult must assume in society. (1962, pp. 179-81)

It is a feeling of lacking close rapport with others and lacking geographical roots. It is submitted here that in the person with an unfulfilled need for affection, this feeling of "homelessness" will be accompanied by a very active sense of a lack of being loved—or of being lovable.

Lane goes on to make a very useful differentiation. He notes that while both the authoritarian and the homeless tend to be "undemocrats," they are, at base, very different:

Where the authoritarian bases his human relations on calculations of strength and seeks subordination to the strong and domination over the weak, the homeless man seeks a penetrating intimacy in human relations, which he may not be able to find. Whereas the authoritarian conceives of his own group as the center of things, and others as "strangers" and outsiders, the homeless man constantly finds himself as the outsider, the stranger trying to enter or find a "we-group" to join. (1962, pp. 185-86)

Again, we may ask "Of what value to the study of politically relevant behavior is a knowledge of the need for affection as it operates in adult citizens?" As it affects democratic society, we have first of all seen that persons with an unfulfilled need for affection will tend, because of their anxieties and hostilities, to be authoritarian and undemocratic.[43] In interpersonal relations, these persons will tend to reject others. In social activity, it is likely that they will be members of a variety of groups, but that they will not be leaders of these groups. For example, Verba—while considering leadership as "a functional relationship within groups"—also notes research which "suggests that the ability of an individual to lead the group in its instrumental task requires a certain degree of immunity to hostile reactions. Insofar as the individual's personality needs are for group acceptance, he will tend to abandon the instrumental direction of the group" (1961).[44]

Because the need for affection, by its very nature, propels in-

---

43. Davies, for example, connects a "child's anxiety about his dependency on his parents" with the ability to develop a "warm and trusting attitude toward political authority" (1965, p. 15).

44. Maslow concurs, stating, ". . . I think most leaders have to be able to withstand hostility, that is, to be unpopular, without falling apart" (1965, p. 30).

dividuals to seek interpersonal relations, it is assumed here that it is important in understanding motivations to many types of political activity. While it places definite limitations on leadership capacities, it has been found to be an important factor in analyzing the motivations of political officials on several occasions. An example of this is found in Alexander and Juliette Georges' (1956) thoughtful study of Woodrow Wilson. Wilson is analyzed as being driven by needs for both affection and self-esteem. Some of their comments which are pertinent to our discussion here are:

> Wilson's own recollections of his youth furnish ample indication of his early fears that he was stupid, ugly, worthless and unlovable. . . . It is perhaps to this core feeling of inadequacy, of a fundamental worthlessness which must ever be disproved, that the unappeasable quality of his need for affection, power and achievement, and the compulsive quality of his striving for perfection, may be traced. (p. 8)

> Throughout his life, Wilson was greatly concerned with the problem of whether he was lovable and loved, and required an inordinate amount of explicit reassurance on this score. (p. 31)

In a concluding section, the Georges discuss this dual motivation (to which we will return in the next section). While Wilson was driven by a need for self-esteem, "power was not the only operative value in Wilson's political behavior. . . . His desire for power was mitigated by a simultaneous need for approval, respect and, especially, for feeling virtuous" (p. 320).

Maslow's need hierarchy offers one of its most rewarding uses in the analysis of leadership motivation. Its potential value can be illustrated by a few comments made here in connection with the study of Wilson. What does an unfulfilled need for affection tell us about the type of leadership and decision-making ability of an individual? He will be driven by "his need for a continuous flow of affection and approval" (p. 21), as the Georges show so clearly coloring Wilson's relationships with his wife, with Colonel House, with all of his associates. "To the man Wilson, identity of opinion and love were inseparably linked. He never learned that he and a friend could disagree and still retain a mutual affection" (p. 31). Further, as with other individuals who fall into Maslow's psychically deprived group, no accomplishment ever gave Wilson a sense of satisfaction. Wilson is quoted as saying "I am so constituted that, for some reason or other, I never have a sense of triumph. . . ." (p. 137).

It thus appears likely that the person with a great need to seek satisfaction and an inability to find it will provide a different quality of leadership from that of the self-actualizer to whom we will turn later. But even more important, the ability of such a psychically deprived individual to assess reality and to perceive new information will be severely restricted by his need to hear favorable information. (While Rokeach's closed-minded individual selectively perceives in order to accept only information congruent to his belief system, an individual in power who has a need for affection in addition forces his subordinates to selectively present information to him.)[45]

Another political leader motivated by a need for affection is included in Wolfenstein's (1969) discussion of revolutionaries. Leon Trotsky's need for the affection and approval of others can be analyzed as requiring him to place an undeserved amount of trust in those with whom he worked—a dangerous preoccupation for a revolutionary. Thus "betrayal and the unreliability of others' promises were to be [constant] elements of Trotsky's life" (p. 61). In addition to his unrealistic expectations of loyalty in others, Trotsky manifested a flamboyant need to gain attention and to remain center stage (p. 66)—again an unhealthy fixation, given the personalities with whom he had to deal!

Trotsky's need for affection undoubtedly also shaped his political beliefs and behavior. Wolfenstein quotes Trotsky as expressing an original dislike for Marxism (in favor of populism) because Marxism brings "dryness and hardness into all the relations of life" (p. 197). It is possible that this same need to bring warmth to politics led to Trotsky's concentration on a doctrine of "permanent revolution"—that is, to ever-continuing work of revolutionary brotherhood. Thus an unsatisfied personal need made it impossible for Trotsky to commit himself to ideals and causes as abstractions[46] (especially causes necessitating retreat and giving no opportunity for personal glory) and also—it may be argued—hastened his end, both politically and physically.

Another psychobiographic study which illumines the relationship between the need for affection and leadership capacities is Brodie's (1966) study of Thaddeus Stevens. While the author speaks of Stevens' flexibility, the overwhelming impression given is of his dogmatism and self-defeating inflexibility. Relevant for our interests here, this portrayal of Stevens also emphasizes his self-hatred (which, we have seen earlier is clinically related to hostility toward others); his drive for acceptance (and concurrent need for punishing those who do not accept)—a psychic need which was not manifest as a concurrent need for esteem by Stevens; his inability (like Wilson) to experience a sense of triumph and—most im-

---

45. Another leader apparently driven by a need for affection can be seen in the portrayal of Hermann Goering by Gilbert (1955, pp. 84-98). As with Wilson, the need for affection and the need for self-esteem both appear to be important in Goering's motivational framework.

46. Wolfenstein describes as Trotsky's "fatal flaw" his "indecisiveness about submitting or fighting" (p. 138).

portant—the psychogenesis of his political and personal attitudes in his physical "unlovableness" and (on many levels) his psychically debilitating abandonment by his father. A comparison of the personalities of Stevens and Lincoln—contemporaries who both evidenced needs for affection—would be of considerable value in elucidating the manner in which the intensity and psychogenesis of the need determines whether (as in Stevens' case) defensive ego behavior will predominate over coping strategies.[47] (The general employment of such defensive mechanisms implies a reduced sense of inner competence and the probability of behavior which is dysfunctional to the person's avowed goals.)

The need for affection also can be seen influencing the behavior of public officials in Barber's (1965) study of first term members of the Connecticut legislature. This need is exemplified by the type Barber calls the "Spectator"—a legislator classified by his high willingness to be returned to office and his low activity in office. He is "a person of modest achievement, limited skills, and restricted ambitions, political and otherwise. . . . If he is short on competence for political leadership, he is long on availability and . . . on caution, tact, and loyalty." Further ". . . his main pleasures in politics seem to come from being appreciated, approved, loved, and respected by others. And his complaints center around situations in which he is left out, rejected, or abused." His rewards are admission to a decision-making body, the prestige of its membership and approval expressed directly to him. He lacks self-confidence; he likes the respect he receives but doesn't feel that he deserves it. In short, the Spectator is concerned with adopting an approval-getting social exterior and clearly implies that "this protective exterior is necessary for approval, because the person behind the mask is unlovable" (pp. 25-43). In politics, then, he is a person who is acted upon rather than a "mover of men." His desire for approval colors his behavior in his legislative role.[48]

The public official who seeks approval to satisfy unfulfilled needs will not be numbered among the individualists, the nonconformists, the critics of a popular cause. If he becomes a leader, he is likely to be cast up into prominence by identifying particularly closely with broadly popular sentiment. In his desire for approval, he is likely to be prominent among those who bring their attitudes and opinions into conformity with those groups of which they are members. (There are indications in Newcomb's [1943] study

---

47. For a discussion of an ego model in these terms, see Kroeber (1963).

48. Barber (1968) also discusses Calvin Coolidge as an individual motivated by an unsatisfied affection need (a need which, developing gradually through loss of significant others, did not disallow the assumption of activist roles although it flavored behavior in them.

at Bennington college that this may be the factor behind at least
some of the girls' switches to the college liberalism. Indeed, a
great deal of the attitude change in Newcomb's book can be explained as a desire to conform so as to be pleasing to one's peer
group because one needs to be thought pleasing and acceptable.)

In political activity, such persons will also seek security in
personal relationships through the types of roles they assume.
For example, in a study of the motivations of fifty local elected
officials in Louisiana and twenty-three eastern businessmen-poli-
ticians, Browning and Jacob (1964) investigated the need for power
and the need for affiliation. (They distinguished the need for affiliation from a true desire for sociability or "liking to be with people," noting that the need for affiliation expresses a "concern with
warm, friendly, relationships" and may not be an "approach motive" but rather "a real barrier to dealing with people" because
of the anxieties which it raises.)

The results of this study by Browning and Jacob suggest that
a local politician type will probably vary, reflecting the types of
politics which exist: <u>factional, power politics will likely drive
away those with a need for affiliation</u>. It is likely that the need for
affection will propel individuals to seek secure positions, such as
are offered by civil service and, where factionalism is of minor
importance, in local government, rather than to engage in the
rough and tumble of "big time" politics except as a popular leader
of a well-established movement. (Leadership of mass movements
which emphasize brotherhood would, it is assumed, offer even
greater security than elective office.)[49] Such persons will also be
likely (as noted above) to seek to enhance their security by adopting approval-seeking behavior (that is, conformity to their reference group's values). That such affiliative needs may cause alli-
ance with other "social rejects" is well-illustrated in the life of
Thaddeus Stevens.

Lane, in a study of four students (out of 11 who displayed a
high need for affection in his original sample of twenty-four college students) offers some hints about the relationship between
this personality type and political ideology. He suggests that anxiety about one's personal acceptability may lead to an anxious type
of liberalism. He traces this "liberalism" to two causes:

1. insecure interpersonal relations encourage an emphasis
   on intellectual achievement (and to some extent vice versa),
   which, for these young men, in turn, led to a kind of problem-
   solving orientation where "reform" of some kind was cognitively and socially satisfying.

2. [a hostility to the] apparently integrated and secure repre-

---

49. In this connection, note Lasswell's (1960) discussion of
the agitator type who seems to be driven by needs both for affection and self-esteem.

sentatives of the dominant groups in their milieus. It is more specifically interpersonal than economic or political. (1965, p. 78).

In a similarly oriented study with a group of 538 subjects (mostly college students, with an admixture of various disparate adult groups), Nettler and Huffman (1957) come to conclusions which agree with Lane's findings. Using Maslow's Security-Insecurity Inventory and an originally devised Radical-Conservative Scale, the authors found that security was related to Conservatism.[50] However, the relationship between insecurity and radicalism was due to the insecurity of "the individuated, 'degrouped' radical . . . the group-protected radical, the ideologue of the left, scores as securely as his counterpart of the right." (However, they also found that the percentage of secure scores dropped from registered Republicans to Democrats to Socialists and Progressives.) These results are interesting in view of the thesis advanced later on that this measure of insecurity is particularly likely to register the needs for affection and esteem.[51]

The need for affection also appears to be important in an understanding of a major element in the process of political socialization: the school dropout (who constitutes one-fourth of all American children).[52] The major impression left by Cervantes' recent study, The Dropout (1965), is that the dropout is motivated by a need for affection ("I've never been able to find a good friend. . . . It's just that I felt left out.") plus a general lack of understanding and communication, and that this, in turn, stems from a disintegrate family (pp. 22-37). Cervantes found, for example, that the first noticeable characteristic for dropouts was fewer friends. One statement very powerfully sums up his data: "There is a positive correlation between number of friends and educational adequacy" (pp. 48-49; underline added). Cervantes pictures the dropout as motivated by a search for acceptance, both at home and at school,

---

50. This is the opposite of McClosky's (1958) findings.

51. Simmons (1965), however, discusses a study which does not support this conclusion. Using a sample of 400 students, he employed scales measuring five dimensions of liberalism (economic, religious, sexual, civil liberties and social problems), as well as Nettler's alienation scale and eight measures of disturbance (normlessness, powerlessness, social isolation, despair, misanthropy, life dissatisfaction, low self-esteem and attitude uncertainty). He concludes that not only is liberalism not undimensional (which has been variously noted elsewhere), but alienation is only related to religious liberalism—not to liberalism in general. Further, there was "little or no relationship between liberalism and personal disturbance."

52. Langton (1969, p. 56).

which leads him to spend an inordinate amount of time with a few peers. In analyzing the cause of this need for acceptance, he points to a recurrent theme in the literature of behavior: the faulty father-child relationship.[53] Lest these conclusions be brushed aside as simply a symptom of lower class devaluation of education, Cervantes notes that in a matched sample of dropouts and graduates, it <u>was not</u> objective conditions that made the difference (pp. 95-100). In his conclusions, Cervantes remarks that the dropouts' problem is made before they ever begin school—and must be cleared up before then.[54] Cervantes' work thus helps to substantiate the hypothesis that the educational process is <u>psychologically</u> selective.

Thus we can see that the need for affection is an important determinant of many types of politically relevant behavior. As it propels individuals into social relationships, it likely affects the composition of many politically important groups: it probably accounts for a major part of the membership of political clubs and interest groups and, to a lesser extent, the civil service and the legislatures. The need for affection appears to shape role behavior as well as role assumption. It is envisioned as being a handicap, but not an absolute bar, for those who seek leadership positions. Because one of the consequences of all four types of psychic deprivation is an inability to accurately assess reality, such leaders are not only likely to be ineffective in their interpersonal relationships but also unable to fulfill the need for making decisions in light of all relevant information. They will also be unlikely to be able to make a personal decision as to when to end their political careers—the maladaptiveness of their behavior will have made the decision for them. Finally, individuals with a need for affection will be likely to be intolerant and undemocratic in their views and found in large numbers among the explosive element of our urban centers: the school dropout.

The Need for Esteem

The person who is disappointed in himself, in his status in the eyes of the world, is also disappointed about the world that sees him this way. (Lane, 1962, pp. 106-7)

The need for esteem, lying as it does one point further along the continuum of involvement with one's environment, is of great potential importance in understanding political behavior. It is also, as described by Maslow, the most difficult to clearly conceptualize. It is conceived as both a spur to activity and, in other individuals, a barrier to participation. In other words, a need for esteem can

---

53. With this comes the oft-noted concurrent inability to accept authority.

54. A similar conclusion summarizes the analysis of the dropout presented by Silberman (1964, p. 277).

motivate some persons to seek recognition through assuming roles which have prestige. In others, the need for esteem can produce shyness and bashfulness and thus inhibit role-seeking. Political scientists have found the need for esteem to be a particularly important variable. As Barber notes, it has been useful both in voting studies where high self-esteem has been correlated with political activity and has also been assumed, especially by Lasswell, to be a spur to political role-seeking (and equated with the pursuit of power) as an individual with low self-esteem seeks compensation for this unfulfilled need (1965, pp. 217-25)

Harold Lasswell has undoubtedly been the leader in pointing to the importance of the need for esteem in the study of political activity, a need which he sees as motivating a pursuit of power "as a means of compensation against deprivation." (He further connects the pursuit of power with "the political personality.") In Lasswell's words, "Power is expected to overcome low estimates of the self, by changing either the traits of the self or the environment in which it functions" (1948, p. 39). Lasswell recognizes, however, that the need for power alone will not determine whether an individual will be active politically: not only must opportunities be present for displacement and rationalization of psychic need in terms of the public sphere, the necessary skills must also be acquired (p. 53).

This motivational assumption has been put more explicitly by Herbert Jacob (1962) in a model for the recruitment of elected officials. It assumes that there are three bars to political activity—"personality development, occupational choices, and political opportunities"—and that "negative performance on any of the three bars recruitment." Summarizing the personality factors which serve as propellants to political activity, Jacob theorizes that "the need for prestige, power, nurturance, exhibitionism and avoidance-of-friendship compose the most salient traits of the homo politicus."[55]

The pursuit of power as a compensatory personality goal is undoubtedly a significant motivational force in politics. I am suggesting here, however, that such a pursuit must be qualified and seen in perspective with other personality needs. The pursuit of power (like the pursuit of affection, security, et cetera) can stem from healthy as well as unhealthy personality drives. "To put it categorically, the normal striving for power is born of strength, the neurotic of weakness" (Horney, 1937, pp. 162-63). It is exceedingly dysfunctional for political scientists to consider neurotic all those who hold or seek power.

The neurotic pursuit of power, however, is an important variable to study in its own right—and this is due to two factors. Because persons with a need for esteem have moved a considerable

---

55. The relation of avoidance-of-friendship to political activism appears to be an unsubstantiated thesis.

way up the need hierarchy toward self-actualization, they are especially likely to be active in their social-political environment. Because of their specific personality needs and increased mental
health, they are the most likely of all deprived individuals to be
found in leadership positions and thus not only to be political actors,
but to play significant roles. Hence the behavior of these neurotic
individuals can have important and lasting political consequences. In
addition, the need to seek compensation for damaged self-esteem (to
which syndrome the neurotic pursuit of power belongs) shapes decision-making in unique and important ways. It is thus possible to outline a model for political behavior to which such individuals are likely to adhere.

In regard to the relationship between the need for self-esteem
and the pursuit of political office, Barber offers this further comment:

> Political candidacy is best seen not as a simple extension of
> citizen politics but as a shift into a different frame of reference,
> one involving a rearrangement of one's regular, normal com-
> mitments and, from a personal viewpoint, considerable uncer-
> tainty. Insofar as such a step depends on deeper motives, it is
> most likely to be taken by two kinds of people: those who have
> such high self-esteem that they can manage relatively easily
> the threats and strains and anxieties involved in this change;
> and those who have such low self-esteem that they are ready to
> do this extraordinary thing to raise it. (1965, pp. 223-24)

Thus Barber hypothesizes that among candidates for political office,
there is likely to be "more variation in self-esteem than will be
found among a matched group of non-candidates" (p. 225).

Thus it appears that the application to the study of political behavior of a carefully developed personality theory which encompasses the need for esteem will be of particular importance in helping
political scientists to structure the phenomena with which they must
deal regarding political activists. Such a personality theory will offer a way out of the tangled underbrush of competing hypotheses
previously sketched.

Maslow, in discussing this need, divides it into two parts: a need
to esteem oneself (to be a worthy individual) and a need to be esteemed by others (to be recognized as a worthy individual). He states:

> These [subsidiary sets] are, first, the desire for strength, for
> achievement, for adequacy, for mastery and competence, for
> confidence in the face of the world, and for independence and
> freedom. Second, we have what we may call the desire for rep-
> utation or prestige (defining it as respect or esteem from other
> people), status, dominance, recognition, attention, importance,
> or appreciation.[56] (1954, p. 90)

---

56. Also see the division of Maslow's need hierarchy offered
by McGregor (1961).

In attempting to conceptualize how the need for self-esteem can both force participation and cripple one's ability to do so, the need to experience esteem from others is conceptualized here as being temporally prior to the need to esteem oneself[57]—as being lower on Maslow's need hierarchy. Persons operating on this level (need for social-esteem) will be bashful, shy, retiring. Persons who feel themselves to be worthy in other's eyes but who experience no inner resonance of this worth would operate on a higher level of motivation and their behavior would be quite different: lacking a sense of inner worth, they would repeatedly seek confirmation of their value by fulfilling personal goals (and yet lack "a sense of triumph" when fulfillment occurs).[58] These persons, motivated by a need for self-esteem, are envisioned as particularly likely to be bitter toward those in power positions who have ability to grant them status, recognition and prestige (but can never do so to a degree which brings psychic satisfaction).[59]

Persons with a need for esteem thus can be considered to be motivated by either a need for social-esteem (psychically prior) or a need for self-esteem (esteem from others, a higher level of inner competence). Persons who share a general need for esteem will differ, therefore, in the vigor with which they seek prestige and recognition. While the distinction between self- and social-esteem is not made in the research presented in chapter 4 (or in most research reports which follow), it is a differentiation which would be of value to pursue.

A most useful study of the concept of esteem is presented by

---

57. This accords with generally accepted psychological theory. See, for example, Mead (1934).

58. Maslow further subdivides individuals with high self-esteem on the basis of the presence or lack of a concurrent need for security. (This is presumably based on individual performance on both his Security-Insecurity Inventory and his esteem test developed for college women [Social Personality Inventory for College Women] as well as on clinical observations.) Individuals with high self-esteem who are simultaneously high in security will operate in interpersonal relations "in a kind, cooperative, and friendly fashion." Individuals who are high in self-esteem and insecure are "interested not so much in helping weaker people as in dominating them and hurting them" (1954). See also Maslow (1942b). In my view, persons who are high in self-esteem and security are equivalent to Maslow's self-actualizers and will be discussed in the following section. Persons high in self-esteem and insecure (i.e., perceiving themselves low in the esteem of others) will be considered as operating at the top of the deprived category and actively engaged in status striving—i.e., as actively seeking confirmation of their worth.

59. See evidence on this point in Knutson (1967).

Coopersmith in The Antecedents of Self-Esteem. In addition to a
thorough theoretical discussion of this concept, Coopersmith (1967)
presents the results of a field study of elementary students which
employed an original Self-Esteem Inventory as well as a behavioral rating form which elicited the assessments of both teachers and
principal. In addition, the mothers also filled out a background
questionnaire and were interviewed. Coopersmith's results are
based on a sample of eighty-five subjects selected from 1748 public school children who were given his inventory. Individuals differing in self-esteem were also found to differ in other significant
dimensions:

> These differences in styles of responding to oneself, to other
> persons, and to impersonal objects reveal that persons with
> high, medium, and low self-esteem adapt to events in marked-
> ly different ways. They experience the same or similar events
> differently; they have different expectations of the future and
> markedly different affective reactions. . . . The behavioral
> differences are due to differences of anticipation, reaction,
> and willingness to trust and rely upon personal judgment as a
> basis for action. They are also attributable to the greater
> sense of exposure and self-consciousness experienced by the
> person low in self-esteem and which lead him to turn inward
> and dwell upon his difficulties. (pp. 46, 71)

As the test-retest reliability of the Self-Esteem Inventory
after three years is .70, Coopersmith hypothesizes "that at some
time preceding middle childhood the individual arrives at a general appraisal of his worth, which remains relatively stable and enduring over a period of several years (p. 5). However, it was found
in this study that subjective and behavioral measures of self-esteem
did not in every case coincide. Thus an individual could be high in
one dimension and low in the other. In underlining the "inner-direct-
edness" of mental health, popularity in school was found to be related
to behavioral, but not subjective estimates of worth (pp. 48-49). Pertinent to our discussion here is his additional finding that individuals
differing in self-esteem do not significantly differ in the number of
social groups to which they belong but that self-esteem is significantly related to more active group roles.[60] Also noteworthy is the
nonsignificant relationship which appeared between self-esteem and
socioeconomic status (p. 83). Finally, there was a close, negative
relationship between subjective self-esteem and anxiety, as measured by the children's form of the Taylor Manifest Anxiety Scale.
This negative relationship also occurred when self-esteem was
correlated with a variety of neurotic presenting characteristics. (It
is interesting to note that although Coopersmith assumes defensive-
ness and general lack of mental health for his two discrepant groups,

---

60. There are various indications here that part of these results may be also due to a need for affection.

those high in subjective esteem and low in teacher-principal behavioral ratings were the lowest of all groups here in anxiety
scores and in other ways appear as healthy as his high-high group.)

The relationship arising in this study between a child's self-
esteem and his home life forcefully points to the conclusion that
the low self-esteem group has quite accurately assessed and as-
similated the view of themselves which their parents hold. As
Coopersmith states:

> the mothers of children with low self-esteem are less affec-
> tionate and accepting and . . . their children perceive them in
> just this way. . . . The whole tenor of the results so far sup-
> ports the general hypothesis that parental rejection results in
> feelings of personal insignificance. (p. 174)

In this respect, esteem can be seen as a set of learned expectations that becomes, in later life, a self-fulfilling prophecy.

From a review of the literature, it is possible—by adding
Coopersmith's evidence—to derive a composite picture of the
shared characteristics of those with what Maslow calls the "esteem syndrome." First of all (as with others motivated by deficiency needs), it is envisioned that the anxieties of persons motivated by a need for esteem will preclude a tolerant acceptance of
others. A great deal of work regarding the relationship between
intolerance and the concern with status (considered here to be a
part of the esteem syndrome) has been done in the past few years,
under the direction of Melvin Seeman.[61] In a preliminary study
(with Fred B. Silberstein, 1959), the focus was on the commonly
found relationship between ethnocentricity and mobility—either upward (because of concurrent insecurities) or downward (because of
failure). The hypothesis being tested was that social movement will
be related to the insecurities that cause prejudice only if there is
a concurrent concern with status and, further, for those with a concern with status, "failure to move" itself can be of great importance in producing the hostilities of intolerance.[62] In a sample of
665 persons in Morgantown, West Virginia, the hypothesis was vividly confirmed. The authors concluded:

> In short, mobility alone does not predict prejudice; the status-
> seeking groups tend to be more prejudiced, regardless of mo-
> bility history; and the greatest prejudice is found among those
> who are status-minded and who have suffered status loss—the
> downwardly mobile M.O.'s [mobility-oriented]; but the down-

---

61. As mentioned earlier, Seeman's work illustrates the value of employing both sociological and psychological variables in
behavioral research.

62. For some samples of items used in these studies, see
the status-concern questions in Appendix A.

wardly mobile A.O.'s [those without concern for status] have
strikingly low prejudice scores. (Silberstein and Seeman, 1959,
pp. 260-61)

For the upwardly mobile, the same results occurred: mobility orientation, not movement alone, was related to prejudice (pp. 261-62).

Regarding the earlier correlations found between downward
mobility per se and prejudice, Seeman offers this comment:

> It may be that these positive results reflect harsher circum-
> stances of mobility—e.g., a decline that is rapid and highly
> visible (to self and others), and/or a decline that occurs in a
> social context that both heightens the insecurity involved and
> encourages its expression toward a minority target.[63]

In an earlier study, using as subjects fifty school administrators, Seeman (1958) also found that in certain major areas, mobility orientation correlated with leadership style.[64] This relationship
was important in view of the lack of predictive ability, in the study,
of intergenerational or individual career mobility.[65]

As has been stated earlier, each of the four deprived groups
is likely to be intolerant of others, though intolerance will play a
different function in the personality of each type. We have seen that
the individual with a need for affection comes from a home environment similar in many respects to that of the authoritarian described in the Berkeley studies. In the category of need for esteem,
we find another type of individual who exhibits some similarity to
the high F-scale scorers—most clearly because of a common concern with power and status.

For example, to discuss authoritarian character as portrayed
in an early article by Maslow (1943b), evidence concerning such
persons is summarized as follows: they possess a "strong drive
for power, status, external prestige." In placing people into in-
groups and outgroups, the authoritarians tend to grant superiority
by "external signs of strength, prestige or dominant status." Further, "The authoritarian can because of his nature practically never

---

63. Seeman, Rohan and Argeriou (1966). This study is a replication of the West Virginia research in Malmo, Sweden. In this
case, the correlations did not hold, suggesting that "Status-minded-
ness has a different meaning in Sweden than it does in America"
(p. 195).

64. Another study with a similar focus is reported by Robin
(1957). Also see Henry (1949).

65. In an experimental attempt to reduce anti-Semitism and
anti-Negro attitudes, Middleton reports that reduction of prejudice
was related to status concern (as measured by Kaufman's scale),
with those low in status concern more likely to reduce their prejudiced attitudes at a .01 level of significance. See Middleton (1960).

be ultimately satisfied. . . . The authoritarian must be perpetually and insatiably ambitious. This also means that he can never be happy except for a time." Frenkel-Brunswik (1952, 1948) has also variously noted that the prejudiced individual is success-oriented and concerned with status symbols. "He is indifferent toward the content of work and lays emphasis upon work mainly as a means to success and power" (1948, p. 300). Therefore, while persons motivated by a need for esteem are not isomorphic with the authoritarian personality, it is hypothesized here that they are likely to comprise a considerable segment of this well-studied personality group.

Kaufman (1957) reports an attempt to measure directly authoritarianism (using the F-scale and the A-S scale of the Berkeley study) as it is related to status concern. The latter was determined by an original scale which, Kaufman notes, "did not meet the 90 per cent reproducibility criterion for a Guttman scale," although it did appear "to have a reasonably consistent focus." (Impressionistically, his status concern scale appears to measure upper middle-class striving.) Using a sample of 213 non-Jewish college undergraduates, he reports correlations of .71 between the SC- and F-scales, .66 between the SC- and AS-scales and .53 between the F- and AS-scales. He also notes that, with status concern controlled, the correlation between the F- and AS-scales "drops to a nonsignificant .12." Kaufman suggests that "the F-scale measures in a diffuse way the sort of attitude measured more specifically by the SC-scale. Instead of a reflection of personality, the common element among these scales could very well be the function of an ideology of status achievement and maintenance" (p. 382). Thus it is a testable hypothesis that persons motivated by a need for esteem will be authoritarian and generally intolerant.

Finally, Rokeach (1956) offers the view that the individuals with a need for esteem may be highly susceptible toward dogmatism, as closed belief systems are a means of gaining a sense of power and security in comprehending one's world. Rokeach states:

> To varying degrees individuals and groups will become disposed to accept closed systems of thinking and believing in proportion to the extent to which they are made to feel alone or isolated in the world they live in, and thus fearfully anxious of what the future holds in store for them. Such a state of affairs leads to pervasive feelings of inadequacy and to self-hate. Attempts are made to overcome such feelings by becoming excessively concerned with a need for power and status. And along with such an over-concern are compensatory attitudes of egotism on the one hand and misanthropy on the other. These, in turn, lead to feelings of guilt and a generally disaffected outlook on life. (1956, pp. 5-6)

In addition to intolerance and mental rigidity, the need for esteem has been related to other politically relevant behavior. It is of considerable interest to discuss here the various findings regarding the influence of this personality type on degree of political activity. For example, this was the focus of attention in a random sample (n = 114 with 88 useable questionnaires) from 614 Washington lobbyists (Milbrath and Klein, 1962). Because the group were so similar in their vocation and their socioeconomic status, the authors attempted to differentiate them on the basis of personality factors. Using shortened subscales relating to sociability, dominance, self-control, social presence and self-acceptance from Gough's California Psychological Inventory, the authors isolated a "sociality-dominance-esteem syndrome" which was of important value in predicting whether or not individuals would run for elective office.[66] (In other words, this syndrome apparently led persons to seek the role of legislative decision maker over that of executive.) Further, the authors found that a short, five-item Esteem scale "worked remarkably well in discriminating between participants and nonparticipants in political activity."[67] This scale was strongly related to such political activities as campaigning, soliciting political funds, activity in nonpolitical groups and to scores on the dominance scale (.01 correlation with a onetailed test) and was also related to general party activity (.05 correlation with onetailed test).

A second field study, which also bears on the need for esteem, is reported by Robert Rosenzweig, who used as subjects sixteen candidates for public office in Massachusetts. In stating why they personally had run for public offices, nine subjects gave "issue-oriented responses" while the remainder "stressed the personal value of public office as a means of social or financial advancement or in terms of increased prestige" (1957, p. 166). When asked to generalize on why men go into politics, however, "the issue or social-service motive disappeared from the picture almost entirely and was replaced by a fairly clear picture of self-interest in which the most important elements were personal advancement and prestige." Rosenzweig feels that his data suggest that "the prestige-seeking individual will turn to politics if he sees a political career as being more prestigeful [sic] than his present activity and more prestigeful [sic] than possible alternatives." At this point, the reader can only wonder whether the interview technique forced the respondents to conform, in the first case, to the socially acceptable (to say nothing of politically acceptable) responses, or whether, in the second instance, political candidates—or politi-

---

66. This syndrome was not (as a similar study by Milbrath in North Carolina shows) important in determining who would hold appointive office.

67. In other words, individuals high on this scale like to be in public view. They have sufficient <u>social</u> esteem to seek <u>self</u>-esteem.

cal scientists—can accurately assess motivation on the basis of intuition and personal experience alone.

Another field study of political participation used a nonrepresentative sample of 138 voting age Arizonians, divided between political representatives and partisan activists vs. apoliticals, with both matched for socioeconomic status (Hennessy, 1959). In an attempt to determine why seventy-two were active in politics as opposed to sixty-six who weren't, Hennessy found that the politicals, by his measures, were significantly higher on a power scale and uniformly less willing to compromise than the nonpoliticals.

In contrast to Hennessy's findings are those of a study by Browning and Jacob (1964), previously mentioned under the need for affection. The seventy-three politicians and elected officials which comprised their sample were given tests of both the need for affiliation and the need for power. They found that "politicians we tested did not uniformly have any particular level of power motivation, and are not clearly different in power motivation from non-politicans of similar occupation and status."[68]

Donald Matthews, in his well-known U. S. Senators & Their World(1960), offers four possible motivations to political leadership, which are impressionistically based on his careful study of the U. S. Senate membership: (1) a desire for prestige and power, (2) "love of the game," (3) a clear-cut, personalized, view of the public interest and a strong emotional commitment to it, and (4) family influence (pp. 48-49).

Matthews typed his actual subjects on the basis of their social background and previous political experience into "Patrician Politicians," "Amateur Politicians," "Professional Politicians," and "Agitators." He found that these types correlated with several pertinent factors, such as choice of committee assignment and job security. While these categories aren't directly related to personality type or the need for esteem, of particular interest here is the Agitator group: lacking in professional accomplishment, prestige or prestigious social background, their background and behavior display characteristics similar to those of our psychically deprived groups in general.

Other studies also bear on the importance of esteem in the analysis of political activity. One of these is a study by Rosenberg (1962) using a random sample of high school juniors and seniors in New York State (n = 1,682, but not all subjects completed the questionnaire). This study suggests that low self-esteem is a barrier to political participation. Rosenberg found that students with low self-esteem were less likely to be interested in political matters, to follow news in the mass media or to show knowledge of

---

68. This study uses an outgrowth of the projective Thematic Apperception Test developed by Henry Murray and revised by David McClelland. Hennessy's "scales" are not tested scales, but simply groupings of similar items.

current political figures. Also (again on self-ratings), they are
less likely to participate in political discussions. By combining
the latter two items into an "index of intensity of political discussion," Rosenberg found that 53 per cent of those with highest self-
esteem were both frequent and active participants, as compared
to only 14 per cent of those with the lowest self-esteem; further,
those low in self-esteem said that they were rarely opinion leaders.

Rosenberg also employed an "index of interpersonal threat"[69]
which had a definite correlation with low self-esteem. He found
that individuals with low self-esteem did not participate in discussions, even though they were interested, and attributes this to the
fact that "they are inordinately afraid that they may elicit the
scorn, hostility, or ridicule of others" (p. 207). Rosenberg isolated two other factors which correlated with low self-esteem: lack
of confidence in the impact of their views on others and self-con-
sciousness. Finally, he found that people with low self-esteem are
also less interested in politics; they seem to turn their interest inward and were high on a day-dreaming scale. For example, low
self-esteem was correlated with the statement that "I often find
that I am distracted from public affairs by my personal problems"
(pp. 201-11).[70]

Thus, in past research, persons motivated by the need for esteem have been generally seen—compared with all other subjects—
to have a limited ability for sociopolitical participation. Further,
it appears that active participation—when related to esteem needs
—reflects a need for self-, not social-esteem. The contradictory
results which exist may be due to the lack of differentiation between
a need for self-esteem and a need for social-esteem, as well as to
the differing measures and subjects employed.

Robert Lane's detailed study of fifteen working-class subjects
contains a thoughtful analysis of the importance of understanding
an individual's self-esteem in assessing his politically relevant behavior—this time, his political ideology (1962). For example, in
discussing the causes of undemocratic views, Lane mentioned narcissism and, particularly, disappointed narcissism.

> The person who is disappointed in himself, in his status in the
> eyes of the world, is also disappointed about the world that
> sees him this way. If others do not appreciate him as he would
> like to be appreciated, they must be something less than men;
> Ferrera [one of the subjects] thinks of them as sheep, and if
> they are sheep, they are unlikely to be able to run a community
> council democratically, or to be worthy receptacles for decen-
> tralized power. In short, disappointment with the way others

---

69. See Appendix A.

70. It must be noted that there was no control for SES or intelligence.

see you leads easily to a disappointment with others in a more
general sense—in their judgment, their skill, their intelligence, their very worth in the eyes of God. (pp. 106-7)

In line with Lane's discussion of the behavioral predispositions of those with unsatisfied needs for social esteem is the hypothesized readiness of these individuals to join mass movements
which offer opportunities for revision of status criteria. In analyzing the membership of the Nazi party, for example, Gerth states:

The common element in the situation of all these different
strata was their despair and lack of social and economic security, the wide differential between self-esteem and actual
status, between ambition and accomplishment, between subjective claims for social status and the objective possibility
of attaining these goals through competitive orientation toward
"market chances," or opportunities for social ascent through
bureaucratic careers. (1940, p. 528)

Mass movements whose ideology states the necessity of over-
throwing the status quo should particularly appeal to those with a
concern for social esteem whose status is frozen in the present
social structure. As Lane notes (referring both to the Progressive
Movement under Theodore Roosevelt and also to the Nazi Party),
"the undervaluing by the community of an individual or a group
tends to lead such people into politics to redress their situation."

Not only may a discrepancy between the way a society esteems
a person and his own sense of worth lead to active political involvement, it is also true that a discrepancy between a person's
personal aspiration level and his achievement level has this
effect. It isn't the underprivileged who revolt, it is those whose
privileges, status, and opportunities do not correspond to their
expectations. (1959, p. 130).

In addition to a concern about the relationship between the need
for esteem and its influence on political participation and ideology,
political scientists have been particularly occupied with the effect
of an unfulfilled need for esteem on leadership behavior. This concern is evidenced in a group of intensive case studies of political
leaders (some of which have been referred to in the previous section). One of the studies which bears most clearly on the relationship between unfulfilled esteem needs and political behavior is the
previously mentioned study of Woodrow Wilson (George and George,
1956). (The authors explain Wilson's need for self-esteem as stemming from his relationship with his harsh Presbyterian father: ". . .
he [Woodrow Wilson] accepted his father's demands for perfection,
tried to emulate him, and interpreted his stinging criticisms as hu-
miliating evidence that, try as he might, he was inadequate." [p. 6])
The authors speak continually of Wilson's twin needs for affection
and power-achievement coloring his whole life and propelling him

to seek some sort of leadership role. Speaking of his early life, they say: "Exactly what it was he wanted to 'do' he seemed not to have decided. What attracted him, apparently, was the prospect of exercising leadership per se. He was then and, indeed, throughout his career, a leader in search of a cause" (p. 29).

The influence of Wilson's need for self-esteem is spelled out in more detail, as follows:

> It is our thesis that underlying Wilson's quest for political power and his manner of exercising it was the compelling need to counter the crushing feelings of inadequacy which had been branded into his spirit as a child. . . .

> His interest in power, in political leadership, was based, we submit, on the need to compensate for damaged self-esteem. The urgent inner need constantly to struggle against these mischievous self-depreciating legacies from his early years crippled his capacity to react objectively to matters at hand. . . .

> All through his career his most pressing commitment, not by choice but of inner necessity, was to prove to himself that he was, after all, an adequate and virtuous human being. He waged this private battle on fields furnished by his public life. He would become emotionally committed to certain measures the fate of which became in his eyes a test of his personal worth. With his self-esteem at stake, the struggle for the realization of such measures monopolized his energy and seemed to him of transcendent importance. . . .

> Where his personal involvement was smallest he could most skillfully respond to the demands of the situation. Where, however, he had harnessed an issue to the task of bolstering his self-esteem he involuntarily responded, in his reactions to what other people did, to his need for protecting his self-esteem. (pp. 114-16)

Finally, the Georges mention the loosely controlled aggressive impulses of Wilson, which haunted him all his life. Whenver he switched from being a power-seeker to being a power-holder, "he was no longer able to suppress his inner impulses toward aggressive leadership" (pp. 116, 160).

In much the same terms which Lasswell uses, the Georges discuss Wilson's political behavior as a search for power which "was for him a compensatory value, a means of restoring the self-esteem damaged in childhood." But they also note that Wilson couldn't seek naked power—always his leadership had to be committed to high moral causes. They explain this by stating that "His desire for power was mitigated by a simultaneous need for approval, respect and, especially, for feeling virtuous" (p. 320). Perhaps it would be more plausible to say that Wilson's need for self-esteem

was tempered, as it is with all men, by both the culture at large
and the specific familial values into which he was born—both of
which made it impossible for him to "seek naked domination over
others." In addition, it appears (as discussed above) that Wilson
was also motivated by a need for affection.

This biography of Wilson and his relationship with Colonel
House has been referred to at great length for several reasons.
First, it is one of the very few political biographies which is also
an attempt to include an integrated discussion of motivation and
personality and the result is quite illuminating. Second, it offers
for study a detailed picture of a political leader in our culture who
is motivated by a need for esteem (and, to a lesser extent, by a
need for affection). The field of political psychology will only advance by working back and forth between in-depth political biographies and broad field studies of larger samples. The Georges' book
is certainly a useful example of the former.[71]

Another political biography which offers the careful student
many insights concerning leadership motivation and its relation to
the need for esteem is Edinger's Kurt Schumacher (1965) based on
the German Social-Democratic leader. Loss of an arm in World
War I, when Schumacher was a youth, appears to have instilled in
a previously psychically fulfilled youth a need for self-esteem and
for safety, needs which shaped his subsequent political life. In
evaluating this political activity, Edinger offers various clues to
understanding the individual who is driven to seek political power.
Schumacher chose a political career "because it permitted him to
satisfy his private needs in a socially and ethically acceptable
manner" (p. 14). As a political leader, he was dogmatic and rigid
and—apparently to increase his self-esteem as well as to act out
his convictions—invited retribution by "militant anti-Nazi activities" (for which he spent ten years in a concentration camp). (Such
death-defying activity can also be seen as the mechanism of reaction formation, that is, an attempt to seek confirmation that—in
spite of inner anxiety—the world is safe and manageable.)

Edinger makes clear that throughout Schumacher's career,
politically useful and important people were ruthlessly pushed
aside "as soon as . . . [they] appeared a potential obstacle to his
drive for power" (p. 137). His hostile, aggressive manner was—if
anything—intensified after the war in his relationships with the occupation authorities and, as earlier, was "frustrating to his drive

---

71. Other useful examples of psychobiographies would be
Erikson (1958, 1969), Edinger (1965), Brodie (1966), and (except
for the section on Lenin) Wolfenstein (1967). For examples which
lack an integrated approach, see the controversial study of Wilson
by Freud and Bullitt (1967) (distinguished primarily for a personalized example of negativistic psycho-analysis) and Glad (1966) in
which the biography is unrelated to the brief personality analysis.
More useful is Glad (1968).

for power" and dysfunctional to his manifest goals. Thus his personality was characterized by rigidity and inflexibility and, in his inability to compromise even when it was to his political advantage to do so, was often compared to that of de Gaulle. (Of special interest in view of our discussion of self-actualization are Edinger's comments concerning Schumacher's lack of empathy (p. 188).

In summary, Edinger notes that his subject, from the time that he lost his arm,[72] was a deviant (in his political party and, even, in the concentration camp). Edinger sees much of his personal rigidity as reflecting "strenuous efforts on his part to maintain consistency in his personal beliefs—to the point of satisfying his inner needs at the expense of his political goals" (p. 275). In Edinger's analysis, ". . . Schumacher's behavior and attitude patterns point to character traits clinically identified with those of an obsessive-compulsive personality striving to adjust to the objective environment in a socially acceptable manner" (p. 275).

It is possible to analyze Schumacher's personality in terms of several different perspectives. Much of the discussion of Schumacher's personality centers around traits which have become well-known as indicators of authoritarian personality, for example, "refusal to compromise," the belief that "tolerance in politics was a sign of weakness" and "a very low degree of tolerance for disagreement with his views or actions"—in spite of "his professed belief in democratic practices" (pp. 279-80). In Rokeach's terms, Edinger also sees Schumacher as "a highly dogmatic personality with an extremely closed belief system."[73]

Erik Erikson has developed a concept which is also useful here, not only in evaluating Schumacher's behavior, but also in assessing other more common forms of deviant behavior. In discussing the "psychological need for a totality without further choice or alternation, even if it implies the abandonment of a much desired wholeness," Erikson states:

> When the human being, because of accidental or developmental shifts, loses an essential wholeness, he restructures himself and the world by taking recourse to what we may call totalism. It would be wise to abstain from considering this a merely regressive or infantile mechanism. It is an alternative, if more primitive, way of dealing with experience, and thus has, at least in transitory states, a certain adjustment and survival value. It belongs to normal psychology. (1954, p. 162)

---

72. This is seen as the prime determinant of his later life; its importance was heightened because it came during adolescence, at a time of identity crisis for young Schumacher.

73. Edinger includes a very interesting section on belief systems on pp. 282-94, much of which is based on the concepts of Milton Rokeach.

Erikson goes on to state that: "The necessity of finding, at least temporarily, a total stamp and standard at this time [adolescence] is so great that youth often prefers to find and to adopt a negative identity rather than none at all."[74]

Schumacher's personality can also be assessed in terms of the personality model developed by Maslow. It appears, from Edinger's discussion, that Schumacher was motivated both by a need for safety (and to impose order on the world) and by a need for self-esteem (to prove himself as a man, to win social recognition). It is likely that the need for safety was of greater importance (and theoretically, it is prepotent—that is, lower on the need hierarchy) for Schumacher never appeared consciously to doubt his own worth and rejected the status symbols of power which easily could have been his. This discussion suggests once again[75] that a search for identity (a concern of Schumacher which became primary with the loss of his arm) is closely tied with a need for safety—for form, order, structure in the world and in one's relationship to it.

Edinger, in conclusion, makes some comments (which also apply to other leaders discussed here) regarding the role which rigidity can play in political leadership:

> The actor who lacks cognitive sensitivity to political circumstances as they really are is likely to experience considerable personal frustration in his attempt to play leading political roles. The political system or subsystem demands that he adjust his goal-oriented behavior to the expectations of important counter-players, who can advance or frustrate his externalized personal drives. If he cannot make the requisite adjustments in his behavior, he is likely to encounter severe external sanctions, which, in turn, affect his outlook and subsequent conduct. (pp. 308-9).

In connection with this discussion of the relationship between the need for power and self-esteem and political leadership, one must also mention the recent contribution by Erwin Hargrove.[76]

---

74. Erikson states further: "Similarly, many young Americans from marginal and authoritarian backgrounds find temporary refuge in radical groups in which an otherwise unmanageable rebellion-and-diffusion receives the stamp of universal righteousness within a black-and-white ideology" (p. 169).

75. See, for example, the comments of Lane included in the section above on the need for safety.

76. Also see the relevant empirical studies of the relationship between authoritarianism and leadership done by Haythorn which are summarized in Kirscht and Dillehay (1967, pp. 116-17; also p. 125), and reported in Haythorn, Couch, Haefner, Langham and Carter (1956).

Hargrove (1966) discusses three "Presidents of Action" (Wilson and the two Roosevelts) and three "Presidents of Restraint" (Eisenhower, Taft and Hoover). This division is based upon the following assumption:

1. The presidents of action "were driven by the need for personal power and this was the initial reason for their choice of a political career. In each man the quality of the need to influence and direct others was different but this kind of drive is essential to great political skill" (p. 7).

2. The presidents of restraint, on the other hand, "were not driven by the need for personal power and therefore lacked the skills that follow from such a need" (p. 144).

Hargrove's discussion of Wilson, Hoover and Taft underlines the fact that—whatever his political philosophy—the successful politician must, first of all, be flexible (as Edinger outlined above). Hoover's portrait, for example, shows this clearly. He is pictured as being indecisive and hesitant in new situations and in those in which he was criticized. "He leaped from one fixed idea to another, some of which were contradictory, and held to each with great rigidity. . . . Hoover could not see facts that were not provided for in his conceptual framework" (pp. 112-13).[77] This inflexibility is suggested as the reason for his inability to offer federal relief action which "probably more than any other factor lost the 1932 election." (Hargrove [p. 113] quotes a study by Carl Degler[78] of this matter, in which Degler concludes that Hoover "was temperamentally incapable of doing what a politician has to do, that is, admit he could be wrong and compromise.")

While this book makes many tantalizing suggestions which would bear careful investigation in the light of personality theory, it also shows the inherent difficulties one faces when working without a theoretical framework based on an all-encompassing view of personality as well as when employing a simplistic view of the political personality. In Hargrove's discussion, the need for power (or its absence) is too facile an explanation for the personalities he discusses. No one can doubt that the three "Presidents of Restraint"—outside of their years in the White House—were very much concerned with the personal application of power in their particular spheres of competence. Their difference in political skill from the "Presidents of Action" is partly due to their differing concept of the Presidency (the values into which they were socialized); partly to their feeling of ease (and the concurrent enjoyment of) manipulating things rather than people; but perhaps even more—and especially in the case of Wilson—to various types of

---

77. For a useful discussion of Hoover's personality, see Barber (1968).

78. Reference is to Carl Degler, "The Ordeal of Herbert Hoover," Yale Review (June, 1963), 580.

psychic deprivation which disallowed objective consideration of the problems with which they were confronted.[79] (Most likely, Eisenhower should be excluded from this later category. It is probable that his concern with things and formal relationships rather than with the informal manipulation of men was the result, not of psychic deprivation, but of years of conditioning in a hierarchical and authoritarian military environment.)

In other words, on the basis of the discussion in this book, it appears a fascinating possibility that, at least in relation to our highest elective office, the question of who will be elected is largely decided in terms of competence in an important, public area plus the availability and propinquity to the selection process. However, the question of how well the individual will do in office (in terms here of the individual leader's ability to form a consensus, solve problems and carry out a program) will likely be determined not by the leader's drive for power (and hence, the acquisition of the necessary skills), but by his general psychic need fulfillment which allows him to both objectively assess the problems with which he is presented and (equally important) to partake in what could perhaps be referred to as an "enjoyment of the game." Certainly individuals who are anxious and insecure about the world's ability to grant them adequate security, or affection, or recognition, cannot—in the long run—be successful in the competitive and critical light of power politics.[80] Perhaps this enjoyment of the game is partly due to a sense of empathy, as displayed by the two Roosevelts (which is certainly a quality of self-actualization); perhaps it is partly what Hargrove calls "a sense of the artistry of power" (p. 133).

It might, in other words, be possible to place these six Presidents along a continuum of psychic competence, with Wilson at the low end, followed by Hoover and then Taft, then by Eisenhower and the two Roosevelts. (Certainly it is a misapplication [again] of conservatism to suggest that only liberals can be Presidents of Action. At least if "conservative" is considered to be synonymous, in this case, with "Republican," one could hardly imagine the dynamic and innovative Governor of New York, Nelson Rockefeller, as a "President of Restraint.")

---

79. As Wolfenstein notes, "there is a correlation between such things as intrapsychic flexibility and tactical flexibility in politics. The man who uses a rigid pattern of defense to control his own impulses, who cannot take advantage of the nonpathological possibilities for displacement and rationalization early in his life and in the private sphere generally, is not likely to operate effectively in political situations calling for subtlety and the ability to adjust to changing conditions" (1969).

80. All of these comments offer possibilities in analyzing the personalities of Lyndon B. Johnson and probably Richard M. Nixon.

In this connection, Maslow (1942) divides those political leaders high in self-esteem between those who are insecure and those who are secure. The individual who is high in security and self-esteem (that is, who is a self-actualizer) will not strive for leadership and power per se: "He will be interested in leadership only in fields in which he himself is interested and he will have such an interest for the sake of the task to be done, the advancement of the field in which he is interested, or for the good of society in general rather than for the sake of assuaging his internal frustrations and threats." The person who is high in self-esteem but is insecure (that is, who is conceptualized here as a person who lacks a sense of inner worth) will "continually strive for power, for status, for position, and most important, for leadership." Because we select our leaders from the ranks of those "who present themselves" for candidacy, "we may expect in the ranks of these self-appointed candidates for leadership, a much larger proportion of insecure ones rather than secure ones."

The two Roosevelts and John F. Kennedy, for example, because of the values and stimuli of their primary homes, likely considered politics as their field of interest. Hoover, Taft and Wilson, however, came to politics from other fields of competence not because politics was their field of interest, but because of the compensation which the role of President offered to their various unfulfilled needs.

At this point, it is possible to construct a model of leadership behavior for individuals whose personality is motivated by unfulfilled basic needs.[81] Various role requirements can thus be aligned with need requirements of individuals who are psychically deprived.

Information-seeking. Information will be gathered and assessed on the basis of its ability to allay anxiety and be supportive of personality needs. Information incongruent with personality needs will not be perceived or will be rejected as irrelevant.[82] Thus psychically deprived individuals will have great difficulty in accurately assessing the reality on which they must sit in judgment and which they must help to direct by their decisions.[83]

81. For a useful discussion of the general area of leadership and personality, see Tannenbaum and Massarik (1958).

82. Holsti (1962) discusses belief systems (the "direct link" to decision making) as composed of facts ("Images of what has been, is and will be") and values ("Images of what ought to be"). In actuality, fact and value become intertwined for psychically deprived individuals.

83. In an interesting observation on the homes of children with high self-esteem, Coopersmith (1967) notes that while these families had more rules than did the homes of children with low self-esteem, there was opportunity for discussion within the rules and—equally important—the rules were uniformly applied. He sees

Subleaders (assistants). Subleaders will be chosen who have
the empathic ability to understand and satisfy unfulfilled personality needs (for example, Colonel House). Subleaders who are not
chosen by the leader will find their access to him barred if they
are unable to meet this requirement. Thus, in their supportive
role, subleaders will further limit the leader's range of information by presenting only that information which the leader is psychically open to receive.

Characteristics of decision-making. Because of the cognitive
inflexibility and unmastered anxiety of persons with deficiency
needs, their leadership capacities will be especially inadequate in
situations marked by flux and uncertainty—that is, the norm in politics. Past decisions, involving as they must personal insecurities,
will be revised with great difficulty, if at all. In spite of available
evidence, action will be hesitant and delayed—out of rhythm with
the requirements of the period (for example, Stalin's inaction in
the face of incipient attack from Nazi Germany[84] and Lyndon Johnson's unwavering commitment to the Vietnam war). Most important,
their need requirements "aim primarily not at satisfaction but at
safety" (Horney in May, 1950, 1939).

Freedom in decision-making. Although conformity is not a
characteristic of all psychically deprived individuals,[85] a large
percentage of them are likely to be overconformists.[86] Thus the
independence which—like flexibility—allows successful leadership will be lacking. In an age of constantly reported public opin-

---

this as causally related to the better ability for reality testing
which typified his high self-esteem subjects. "Imposition of limits
is likely to give the child, on a rudimentary non-verbal and uncon-
scious level, the implicit belief that a definition of the social world
is possible and that the 'real' world does indeed impose restrictions and demand compliance with its norms. . . . In sum, imposition of limits serves to define the expectations of others, the
norms of the group, and the point at which deviation from them is
likely to evoke positive action; enforcement of limits gives the
child a sense that norms are real and significant, contributes to
self-definition, and increases the likelihood that the child will believe that a sense of reality is attainable" (p. 238).

84. For a detailed account, see Salisbury (1969).

85. In the Block's use of Lewinian concepts, psychically deprived persons can be either "over-controllers" or "under-controllers." (See Block [1950]; also Block [1951].) In addition, not
all conformity stems from unmet needs, as Di Palma and
McClosky (1970) have recently illustrated.

86. For example, compare the characteristics of the need-
oriented individuals discussed thus far with the personality tests
of the conformists studied by Crutchfield (1955).

ion polls, such lack of freedom can be particularly disastrous.
Perhaps the quality which is missing can best be seen in Coopersmith's description of his subjects.

> Favorable self-appraisals apparently have the effect of liber-
> ating the individual from the demands of social groups and
> from ordinary ways of responding to stimuli and life situations.
> By providing the assurance that one's judgment is worthy and
> one's abilities sufficient to the task, favorable self-attitudes
> lay the foundation for stable, anxiety-free performance. By
> generating the expectation that one's efforts will be followed
> by success and one's judgment borne out by subsequent events,
> high self-esteem enhances the likelihood of exploratory and
> independent activities. (1967, p. 63)

Efficacy of decisions. Because of these factors, the psychically deprived person enters political leadership roles with the
cards stacked against him. To borrow Kenneth Boulding's words,
"The elimination of error is accomplished mainly by feedback"
(1967). But for persons cognitively and perceptually walled in by
their anxieties, feedback is inefficient and incomplete. As was
noted in the case of Kurt Schumacher, their personal needs become
frustrating to a drive for power, and dysfunctional to the goals of
the leader and the group he leads. May has remarked that "Anxiety
restricts growth and awareness, shrinking the area of effective living . . ." (1950, p. 150). In politics, where crises come from every
quarter and every fresh problem must be met with a fresh solution,
a circumscribed life space is extremely hazardous.[87]

Because of their particular insecurities, persons with an unfulfilled need for esteem have been conceptualized as dogmatic, intolerant, concerned with status and susceptible to appeals of mass
movements which offer a new avenue to status and power. It is likely that this need will propel them to positions of leadership, but
that in these positions, their efforts will not meet with great success. Instead, their personality needs will prevent their functioning
with flexibility and ease and keep them from valuing information

---

87. This point is discussed more fully by Bensman and
Rosenberg (1960, pp. 194-95), under the heading of "Authoritarian
Misinformation": "The authoritarian administrator shies away
from independent criticism of his work. He demands subservience
of lower bureaucrats who feel that it is risky to provide him with
unpleasant information. Critical and independent views, like incon-
venient facts, are interpreted as personal criticism and as symptoms of disrespect or of impudence. This attitude conditions subordinates to feed him a steady diet of cheerful good news, automatic assent, and insincere agreement. The result is that he increasingly makes his decision in a vacuum." They note that such a process has had a particularly noticeable and deleterious effect in the
shaping of foreign policy.

per se. It has also been suggested that esteem needs will be found in all socioeconomic groups, because of the importance of subjective, as well as economic and social, deprivation—although the effect of social deprivation may show up in a weak, negative relationship between the need for esteem and SES.

There is a wealth of material which bears on this need and its relationship to political behavior. The material, it is true, is not of uniform scientific objectivity. Indeed, some is more speculative than scientific. Yet it all points to a widespread professional concern with the relationship between the need for esteem and political behavior—a concern that I am suggesting here—would benefit from being placed within a more general framework of personality needs. Further, whether scientific or impressionistic, the evidence points uniformly to particular characteristics which typify the man who seeks compensation for unfulfilled esteem needs—and for anxiety which can never really be assuaged.

The need for esteem has been particularly seen as propelling individuals to seek confirmation of their worth in interpersonal relationships (though not equally related to all types of activism). In its lowest form (on the need hierarchy), it is conceptualized as a need for the social validation of self worth and its characteristics are seen to be shyness, self-effacement and social unease. In its highest form, it is envisioned as a need for self-esteem, where confirmation is particularly to be sought in the winning of roles from which prestige, importance, power and a sense of mastery are derivable—and thus it is a variable of considerable political relevance. Both of these types will likely be insecure, anxious, and cognitively rigid because of their need for esteem, but the higher form will be more likely to be found in activists who assume social and political roles.

Finally, although the answer must lie in further research, it is strongly felt that persons who seek compensation because of unfulfilled esteem needs cannot be analyzed under a monistic drive for power. To state this differently, we are being cripplingly narrow to consider the pursuit of power as the primary compensation which an individual with damaged self-esteem is driven to seek. To be deliberately provocative, it is felt that to equate the need for esteem (taken in its broadest sense) with a need for power and to consider both the basic predispositions to political activity is based on several false premises.

In the first place, as Maslow points out, persons who are competent (which in some field of activity, is probably true of every political leader) but lacking in security of esteem (that is, in the security of a sense of inner worth), desire "reputation or prestige (defining it as respect or esteem from other people), status, dominance, recognition, attention, importance, or appreciation" (1954, p. 90). Based on a review of what is now known about political activists and on the need for self-esteem, two things seem apparent: (1) individuals with an unfulfilled need for esteem do seek the values listed above, but it is not necessary for a person to seek to achieve a <u>totality</u> of these values in order to reduce the anxieties which prompted the search; (2) the acquisition of power is connected directly to only <u>one</u> of these values—dominance—and further, many types of political activity may be high in status, attention, importance, et cetera, but have little undivided power which is associated with the role (nevertheless satisfying).[88] In fact, this is likely to be the case.[89] Therefore, from both standpoints, the fact that political activity is often not the best means of seek-power per se and because the acquisition of power may not be necessary to the individual needing esteem <u>if</u> some of the other values are amply acquired, I believe that the connection has been greatly over-stressed, to say the least, between damaged self-esteem and the pursuit of power—particularly in the area of political activity.

Second, in our culture the pursuit and acquisition of power is both officially circumscribed and also considered in pejorative terms by the average citizen.[90] This is clearly illustrated in the studies of various Presidents cited above, where the pursuit of power is <u>assumed</u> to be the motivating force but the existence of this motivation can only be seen—at best—indirectly, in connection with the pursuit of other values.

Third, it would be more realistic and add greatly to research clarity if political scientists thought in terms of the mere public

---

88. For a theoretical discussion of what specific conditions may engage power motivation in political leaders, see George (1968).

89. Many personnel managers, for example, may have—in their hiring and firing activities—more power satisfaction than a junior member of congress, whose office is similar to a broom closet and whose colleagues have given him the clear understanding that he must be satisfied for years with the worst committee assignment (that is, the least powerful and prestigious) and a passive legislative role. For members of the state legislature, this is even more likely to be an accurate description. This is not to say that politics doesn't offer roles of great personal power—but merely that many types of political activity (and particularly in party work) do not <u>primarily</u> offer the gratification of power. (The power which can be exercised in these roles is no greater than in many non-political roles with similar status.) And, because of the low opinion which many Americans hold of political activists, status and prestige are not ipso facto acquired in the assumption of a political role.

90. Lippitt and Sprecher (1960), for example, report a recent random survey in which more than half the adult population "believed politics to be dishonest or dirty." Also see various references in Matthews (1960).

attention, title, prestige and <u>propinquity</u> to power as desirable ends in themselves, rather than attempting (vainly) to reduce all politican activity to the base of power.

Indeed, it should be noted that there are a <u>variety</u> of relationships to power which leaders may assume. One relationship <u>is</u> undoubtedly compensatory, in which power is sought because of unsatisfied esteem needs. But a second—and equally important—relationship is instrumental, in which power is sought to further objective goals. Here men like John F. Kennedy and Franklin Roosevelt come to mind—men whose <u>cultural</u> values included a sense of public duty and a belief in their ability to influence public life in favorable ways. A third type of relationship occurs in cases in which the leader receives power while seeking other values and is uncomfortable in its use. Examples of this type of leader would be Calvin Coolidge and Leon Trotsky.

For many years, the political activist has, usually without explicit statement—been confused with the authoritarian personality, although research has made clear that such a personality does not function well in situations which are ambiguous, threatening and full of tension. It is strongly advanced here that this discrepancy should be clearly recognized and the previously held notion of <u>the</u> personality available for political activity, once and for all, laid to rest. For while the literature surveyed above suggests the likelihood that individuals motivated by a need for esteem will be politically active, nowhere is it indicated that these persons compose the universe of followers or leaders. In fact, the issue of their numerical importance has as yet to be assessed.

Generalized Psychic Deprivation

He who establishes his reputation externally as a means of asserting his inward worth develops a profound anxiety because the very center of his being is, as it were, outside himself. He tries to ingratiate himself everywhere and ends up belonging nowhere. At one and the same time he despises and depends upon those from whom he has bribed the gestures of approval and respect. (Carstensen, 1963, p. 15)

It is a miserable state of mind to have few things to desire and many things to fear. (Bacon, in Cantril, 1961, p. 7)

As we have seen, it is theoretically and empirically possible to separate persons who are "deficiency-oriented" on the basis of the most potent unresolved need (and occasionally <u>needs</u>) which motivate their behavior. Through this subcategorization, a much clearer picture can be achieved of the persons whose behavior political scientists must assess. For at least a decade, political scientists have been aware that psychically deprived individuals are dogmatic, authoritarian, insecure and anxious. But the above review of behavioral literature, by analyzing the various findings in terms of four potent human need areas, offers a much deeper understanding of such political men. For by considering a man's overriding psychic need (or needs), it is possible to assess more accurately the function which his beliefs and behavior, his attitudes and activity pattern, serve for him. Concurrently, it is possible to more accurately predict in what situations he will be predisposed to act and what directions his actions will take. Various specific behavioral models can be set up, analyzing, for example, the possibility of an individual with a need for security being aroused to followership in a revolutionary mass movement in such superficially similar but psychically and structurally disparate situations as the American depression, the aftermath of the Versailles Treaty in Weimar Germany and the period following the war and revolution which gave birth to newly Soviet Russia.

It is also of interest, however, to consider the shared characteristics of the persons in all four of the previously discussed deprived categories.[91] Such grouping will allow comparison with other studies of politically relevant behavior in which research categorization has been very broad. For a great deal of behavioral research continues to dichotomize subjects on an "either-or" basis in terms of one personality dimension. (It should also be noted that while the idea of hierarchy is an integral part of Maslow's personality model, it is only occasionally evidenced in the research relevant to Maslow's need groups, reported earlier.)

Genevieve Knupfer (1947), in her oft-quoted "Portrait of the Underdog" notes that "closely linked with economic underprivilege is psychological underprivilege: habits of submission, little access to sources of information, lack of verbal facility." (To this, we must add a view of the world as threatening and uncontrollable.) Because a plausible case could be made for linking at least three of these basic needs with the life situation of the low socioeconomic status individual (possibly excepting the need for esteem), low SES should show a statistical relationship to such characteristics as dogmatism and intolerance. However, it is hypothesized here that SES is an intervening variable and that each psychically deprived type, divided by each social level, should be statistically related to the attitudes and behavior discussed previously. (In computer terminology, the relationships should hold with SES controlled.)

---

91. At this point, it should be noted that lack of mental health here does not encompass psychosis because of its normal lack of political relevance. In other words, these psychically deprived or mentally ill people would probably not be seen in that light by laymen because they are able to function—albeit at a lower level—in economic, social and political roles. Thus the reader may find it useful to think of these personality types as being—in Smith's (1968) terms—more or less "competent," or, in Maslow's terms, more or less deficiency motivated.

Thus, students of behavior must have in mind the greater likelihood that psychic deprivation will be found among persons whose primary homes were economically underprivileged. Knowledge of statistics, however, necessitates the concurrent understanding that many of the psychically underprivileged group are expected to be found on the middle and upper SES levels. Further, the relationship between psychic deprivation and SES is hypothesized to be weaker for the affection and esteem needs than it will be for the physiological and safety needs.

What are the shared characteristics of the psychically underprivileged? A "sense of effectiveness in public affairs" has been found closely related to a sense of personal competence and a "satisfaction with [one's] present life condition" (unspecified). In this study by Douvan and Walker (1956) (based on a Survey Research Center probability sample of 316 members of the Detroit labor force who were employed or only temporarily unemployed), it is important to note that there was no significant relationship between demographic factors (such as education and occupation) and a sense of effectiveness.[92]

However, in spite of this lack of correlation, "the less effective groups . . . report feeling economically thwarted more often than the effective group." Also, "the low effectiveness group stresses personal factors when success is anticipated and environmental factors when they anticipate failure." These same individuals "consistently give more answers which reflect a picture of an oppressive, uncontrollable external reality." It is particularly interesting, in view of our previous stand that the successful Presidents were successful because of their ability to, and concurrent enjoyment of, manipulation of their world and the people around them, that the authors of this study found that "Those people who feel competent are more likely to reveal in their stories and answers an active interest in the environment, and anticipation of a pleasant, manageable world."

Douvan and Walker conclude that while some individuals, for reasons other than personality factors, may be "active and interested in the external world" while lacking this sense of effectiveness: "To make a strong commitment to events outside oneself would seem to require a view of the world as at least potentially manipulable and gratifying [emphasis added]".[93]

---

92. The authors suggest that this lack of correlation may be due to the narrowness of the sample and/or the fact that they had tapped a significant psychological dimension.

93. Douvan and Walker also found no relation between an individual's internal reality and his sense of competence. In the low competence group, "Reality is oppressive and uncontrollable, but not necessarily permeated by personal hostility that has been projected because it is unacceptable as part of the self."

　　　　　The Human Basis of the Polity

This Detroit study is important to our interests in political activists because it underlines the connection between an active desire to control one's environment and a degree of psychic competence—that is, the view of the world as pleasant, manipulable, and gratifying. It appears that the disbelief that the political world is amenable to individual efforts to control and possess gratification for such efforts is at the root of political inactivity, considered as a whole.[94]

A Survey Research Center 1958 nationwide sample confirms the results of this Detroit study.[95] The purpose of the SRC survey was to tap "basic evaluative orientations" toward the national government. Several factors were found to be related to positive feelings toward government. Positive evaluation was related weakly to education and also to living in an urban setting over 10,000. Relevant to our interests here, positive evaluation was clearly related to both political efficacy and a sense of personal competence, as the following tables show.

Table 2.1

RELATION OF ORIENTATION TO GOVERNMENT
TO SENSE OF POLITICAL EFFICACY

Attitude Toward Government	Sense of Political Efficacy				
	Low (N=140)	Low Medium (N=102)	Medium (N=371)	High Medium (N=241)	High (N=130)
Negative	29%	26%	16%	13%	7%
Intermediate	56	59	66	63	55
Positive	15	15	18	24	38
Totals	100%	100%	100%	100%	100%

Personality theorists have long noted a relationship between personal anxieties and generalized hostility.[96] From the SRC results, we can see that such generalized insecurity has a definite political dimension.

---

94. Because of the relationship of political efficacy to western industrialized democracies (see, for example, Almond and Verba [1965]), one can again point to the importance of psychic deprivation and its causes in comparative studies.

95. Stokes (1962).

96. Horney (1937) comments: "It makes a great difference whether the reaction of hostility and anxiety is restricted to the

Table 2.2

RELATION OF ORIENTATION TO GOVERNMENT
TO SENSE OF PERSONAL COMPETENCE

Attitude Toward Government	Sense of Personal Competence			
	Low (N=378)	Low Medium (N=233)	High Medium (N=352)	High (N=706)
Negative	24%	23%	13%	11%
Intermediate	61	64	64	64
Positive	15	13	23	25
Totals	100%	100%	100%	100%

Another study which reports similar results was based on a mailed-back questionnaire (with a 63 per cent return) given to a random sample (n = 1,230) of two Oregon cities who had been subjected previously to a personal interview (Agger, Goldstein and Pearl, 1961). Subjects were scored on the basis of three scales: personal cynicism (for example, "The biggest difference between most criminals and other people is that criminals are stupid enough to get caught"), political cynicism (for example, "Money is the most important factor influencing public politics"), and a well-known scale of political efficacy developed by Angus Campbell and used widely in national voting studies.[97]

Agger, Goldstein and Pearl found that while political cynicism was related to increasing age, low education and low income

> It is clear that even though people at each level of personal cynicism are consistently less politically cynical as their educational level increases, that is, that differences in educational level explain part of the relationship between personal

surroundings which forced the child into it, or whether it develops into an attitude of hostility and anxiety toward people in general. . . . [In unhealthy homes there is] an insidiously increasing, all-pervading feeling of being lonely and helpless in a hostile world. The acute individual reactions to individual provocations crystallize into a character attitude. . . . Because of the fundamental role this attitude plays in neuroses I have given it a special designation: the basic anxiety; it is inseparably interwoven with a basic hostility."

97. See Appendix A; also chap. 3 of this book for a further discussion of the use of this scale. This scale was employed in the SRC study discussed above.

and political cynicism, another major part of the relationship is independent of this variable.

The elderly were also found, as a group, to be _politically_ cynical because of a feeling of _personal_ cynicism, rather than because of increasing age alone. In regard to the measure of political efficacy, the authors again found that while it was strongly related to educational level as well as to political cynicism, "at every educational level the more potent are more trusting of politics and politicians than the less potent."[98] Hence again it is found that there is a strong relationship between a view of the world as hostile and unpleasant and a desire (in this case, the subjective feeling of capability) of taking part in and controlling external events.[99]

A fourth study which correlates personality characteristics with attitudes which are damaging to democratic political life is a study of 271 high school seniors by Harrison Gough (1951a, 1951b, 1951c and 1951d) concerning the relationship between intolerance (as measured by the Adorno E- and F-scales and the Levinson-Sanford anti-Semitism scale) and both psychological and sociological factors. In the four articles which discuss this study, a great many useful points are made regarding tolerance.[100] Of interest

---

98. That actual efficacy in demanding situations is related to past need fulfillment is suggested as the conclusion of a wide survey. "People who have had a stable past are more apt to manage during unexpected situations such as economic depression on [sic] unemployment than those who have experienced considerable prior deprivation. There is a difference in attitudes and coping abilities, dependent in part upon the early environment"; S. M. Miller, "The American Lower Classes: A Typological Approach," in Frank Riessman, et al., eds., Mental Health of the Poor, Glencoe, The Free Press, 1964, pp. 139-54; in (Beiser, 1965).

99. A later study by Litt (1963) suggests that political cynicism can be an acquired, community norm, as well as being based on personality need. In a random sample of voters from one middle class ward in the politically corrupt city of Boston, Litt found that while personal trust and political efficacy were related, they were not related, as in Agger's study, to political cynicism. When he took another sample in a suburb where there was "relatively effective and uncorrupted political rule" however, in addition to the correlations found with the Boston sample, Litt found that here political cynicism and efficacy were related. This study shows once again the importance of field in an understanding of personality factors.

100. One would question the relationship between lower intelligence and intolerance because of the difficulties which lower SES groups experience in test taking per se, in their lack of verbal skills and opportunities for enrichment. Greenstein (1965) for ex-

here is the correlation between intolerance and (a) low SES, (b) lack of sociability and participation in extracurricular activities, (c) "greater uneasiness and discomfort in social situations," (d) "greater tendency to complain of personal dissatisfactions, problems and annoyances" and "feelings of victimization and exploitation," and (e) four types of antidemocratic attitudes:

(1) "narrowness of outlook in regard to national and international affairs"
(2) "debunking attitude toward questions of political-social ideals and goals"
(3) "antagonism toward many outgroups, not just some particular outgroup"
(4) "emphasis on nationalism, chauvinism, and conservatism." (Gough, 1951d)[101]

Again there is a correlation found between lack of personal competence and both a lack of social competence and unhealthy political attitudes.[102]

The above findings suggest that psychic deprivation will have two politically important results: it will serve as a deterrent to the desire and ability to take part in political activity (from influencing friends to becoming President) and it will implant the all-pervasive view that the world is a hostile and threatening place where one's best defense is to attack—a place where people are means or instruments. (As Helen Merrell Lynd, 1958, p. 154) notes: "Certain possibilities in personal relations are already excluded, not only when the Others are regarded as a ridiculing and

---

ample, notes that the literature of educational psychology demonstrates that "in spite of heroic efforts to develop intelligence tests which are free of class bias, measures of basic ability also consistently differentiate between socioeconomic groups." Further: "If lower-status children are equipped with fewer intellectual skills, they also are equipped with a weaker desire to use such skills."

101. Hess and Torney (1967), in a study based on questionnaires given to 12,000 elementary school children, found that social and political participation were closely related to each other and to a feeling of political efficacy. Political efficacy, in turn, was related to high SES and (more closely) to high I.Q. It is most unfortunate that personality factors were not considered in this study.

102. Lester Milbrath (1965) offers further confirmation of the relationship between personality deprivation and politically relevant behavior, noting also that "absorption in personal problems" has been found to be a deterrent to activity (p. 70). (Milbrath also adds his voice to those pointing to the void in research relating mental needs to political behavior [p. 48].)

unfriendly audience, but when they are regarded as any kind of an audience.")

One of the most striking demonstrations of this lonely misanthropism is reported in a study by Sullivan and Adelson (1954). This study, based on a sample of 221 students in elementary psychology at a midwestern university, connects prejudice against specific groups with a generalized misanthropy, which—it will be developed later—is closely connected with a view of the world as hostile and threatening. The authors went through the original California pool of items for the E-scale and chose twenty-nine items that expressed intolerance against specific groups and then rewrote the items to indicate generalized prejudice. (For example, "People" replaces "Jews" in the item "Jews should be more concerned with their personal appearance and not be so dirty and smelly and unkempt.") The M (for misanthropy) scale and the E-scale (composed of items with different content) were correlated at the .001 level of confidence. To the authors, this indicates that while ethnic prejudice is related to misanthropy, the correlation isn't large enough to "demonstrate that prejudice is isomorphic with an underlying misanthropy or that the designation of particular minorities as objects of hate is adventitious, that is, free from social press."

What is most important in the results of this study is "the generality of reference of these attitudes. It appears, at least on the surface, that for many of the antidemocratic there may be no group other than the self." The authors, finally, suggest that in the E-scale there is (unfortunately for the interpretation of results) an implicit ingroup of "native, white, Christian Americans" which may not be the favored ingroup of the subject. They comment:

> The need for the separation of the tolerance and identification dimensions is suggested by Hartley's study[103] in which a completely fictitious group was presented for rejection or acceptance. That many persons manifested intolerance of this non-existent group reveals their prejudiced attitudes toward the strange and the alien. It does not, however, demonstrate contra-identification, for this term denotes, among other things, the association with the group in question of a set of attributes, learned either through experience or the propagation of stereotypes. (Sullivan and Adelson, 1954, p. 249)

A lack of political and personal efficacy or competence and a lack of tolerance for others are not the only dimensions along which, it is suggested, one may typify the deprived group. Another theme, which has again and again come to this author's attention while reading the reports of behavioral studies can be subsumed under the heading of control. The psychically deprived have little control over their drives and, at best, a tenuous control over their

---

103. Reference is to E. L. Hartley, Problems in Prejudice, New York, King's Crown Press, 1946.

behavior. The obverse of this is the fact that they have little control over their environment, in part because of their socioeconomic positions, but in larger measure because they perceive their environment as uncontrollable.[104]

This lack of control is intimately connected with the previously discussed feeling of uncontrollability of one's environment. As Erikson states: "The general state of trust . . . implies not only that one has learned to rely on the sameness and continuity of the outer providers but also that one may trust oneself and the capacity of one's own organs to cope with urges; that one is able to consider oneself trustworthy enough so that the providers will not need to be on guard or to leave" (1959, p. 61).

This theme of control is taken up in Lane's discussion of his small group of workers. He finds the key to the behavior of his "undemocrats" in their lack of ego strength and states:

> The core of the question of ego strength is control: control over impulse life, control over environmental demands. These four men do not know the meaning of control. Being unable to meet and control their private environments, they do not know in general how public events are controlled, ordered, or brought about . . . .
>
> There is a second sense in which personal experience colors an understanding of the world. If society is the man writ large, and if each individual understands mankind largely from his interpretation of himself, those low in ego strength will likely see society in the grip of irrepressible forces that are constantly challenging the rather ineffective regulators. We do not have to reach beyond the bounds of plausibility to conceive a person who experiences himself as barely able to contain the impulses that surge up within him finding the same situation in society. (1962, p. 125)

The importance of this concept is also seen in a study of social anxiety at the Tavistock Clinic, London, where an important subgroup factor within the general factor of social anxiety was found to be "fear of loss of control, especially bodily control." Because its subject doesn't seem to fit the other types of social anxieties which were isolated, the authors hypothesize that it is present "by virtue of a fear of loss of control of aggressive feelings" (Dixon, DeMonchaux and Sandler, 1957).

A most interesting contribution to the problem of control is a study by Siegel (1956) of the relationship between authoritarianism and hostility. Using as subjects sixty young male university

---

104. Individuals with problems of control can be classified as either over-controllers or under-controllers, depending upon their personality pattern of need gratification and tension release. For an explication of these concepts, refer to Block (1950).

students and sixty male veterans among those applying for treatment at the mental hygiene clinic of the Buffalo Veterans Administration Regional Office, the subjects' scores were established along three dimensions: authoritarianism (the F-scale), hostility as seen on a projective technique (the Elizur Rorschach Content Test on hostility which may indicate hostilities which the subjects are not willing to express), and a test of manifest hostility (which was developed for this study).

Results of this study showed a correlation that is statistically significant between high authoritarianism and manifest anxiety and a correlation between low authoritarianism and the projective test of hostility. The authors state that "contrary to expectations, the groups may not differ as greatly in amount of hostility they possess, but instead may differ in their readiness to express their hostility" [emphasis added]. While the results are tentative, it is plausible to assume that highly intolerant individuals will have less control over hostile impulses.[105]

Also in relation to our discussion of control, Gough (1951a), in his previously cited study of intolerance among high school seniors, found a lack of control among students who were high scorers on the E- and F-scales. He states that they "tend to be less discreet and prudent in self-description, are more prone to respond in unusual and uncontrolled ways, are less bland and accepting in their social outlook, are slightly more introverted" (pp. 241-42).

Additionally relevant here is Witkin's (1954, 1962) distinction between "field-dependent persons" and "independent or analytical perceptual performers" (a distinction noted by Rokeach in his discussion of the perceptual functioning of different belief systems). Witkin states:

> Field-dependent persons tend to be characterized by passivity in dealing with the environment; by unfamiliarity with and fear of their own impulses, together with poor control over them; by lack of self-esteem; and by the perception of a relatively primitive, undifferentiated body image. Independent or analytical perceptual performers, in contrast, tend to be characterized by activity and independence in relation to the environment; by closer communication with, and better control of, their own impulses, and by relatively high self-esteem and a more differentiated, mature body image.[106] (Witkin et al., 1954, p. 469)

---

105. For another study that deals with hostility and control, see John W. Thibault and Henry W. Riecken (1955).

106. Maslow has also suggested a connection between Witkin's field-dependent individuals, on the one hand, and poor mental health and lack of leadership skill, on the other hand (1965, p. 100).

The whole question of an individual's sense of control over his environment has been extensively studied in terms of Rotter's social learning theory (Rotter, 1966; Lefcourt, 1966) and tied, through a variety of research projects conducted by Melvin Seeman (1963, 1967, 1966), to the theory of mass society alienation. Briefly, Rotter has variously demonstrated that a person's belief in the locus of causality of behavioral reinforcements and the value which he places on those reinforcements is intimately related to his patterns of perception and learning. In sum, it appears from Rotter's evidence that

> the individual who has a strong belief that he can control his own destiny is likely to (a) be more alert to those aspects of the environment which provide useful information for his future behavior; (b) take steps to improve his environmental position; (c) place greater value on skill or achievement reinforcements and be generally more concerned with his ability, particularly his failures; and (d) be resistive to subtle attempts to influence him. (1966, p. 25)

The importance of Rotter's work for our purposes here lies in his demonstration that a person who feels that he cannot control his environment is likely to be disinterested in information relevant to problems of control and to make few attempts to do so. The obverse of this proposition has received little attention: that the person who has little feeling of competence in controlling his world feels a similar inefficacy in controlling his impulses (that is, in psychoanalytic terms, he has unresolved conflicts which are poorly defended). Rotter does note, however, studies of individuals who have given up or not taken up smoking which indicate that "this feeling that one can control the environment is also a feeling that one can control himself" (p. 21). Lefcourt (1966) also reports evidence which indicates that persons who "have a generalized expectancy that reinforcements are not under their control" tend to have high F-scale scores and (with the extreme "internal" controllers) to be relatively poorly adjusted (as measured by the Incomplete Sentences Blank).

M. Brewster Smith (in a recent paper which explores the relationship between personality and public opinion theory), ties the question of control to a research dimension to which we will turn in the next chapter—that of efficacy. Smith suggests that:

> how much self-determination a person exercises is bound up in a self-fulfilling prophecy: his feelings of efficacy, rooted in attitudes and concepts about the self, have much to do with what he will try and what he will accomplish. And these feelings of efficacy have their own social and personal determinants.[107]

---

107. Smith (1971).

I would suggest, in addition, that both externally and internally oriented feelings of inefficacy likely stem from a single type of early personal experience: the inability to at least minimally manipulate one's personal environment in ways that are consistently gratifying and the concurrent, considerable inner anxiety and hostility which such inefficacy generates.

How then can we relate the question of control to psychic deprivation as envisioned by Maslow? We have earlier hypothesized the existence of a continuum of concern with self—concern with environment (and self in relation to it) which parallels Maslow's need hierarchy. Concurrent with (and causally related to) this continuum can be envisioned a second continuum of control over self—perceived control over one's environment, that goes from high to low. As one moves higher and higher on the need hierarchy, in other words, he becomes better and better able to control his hostilities and anxieties: his emotions and his behavior. (In terms of an energy model, he has fewer unresolved inner anxieties which require defensive strategies.) With this control over self comes a concurrent growth of the view that one's environment is controllable and manipulable and a growing interest in (and knowledge of) control information. This continuum of control then helps to explain why, as a person moves up the need hierarchy, he becomes more and more socially and politically participant: as his inner need requirements and view of himself change, so does his view of the world.[108]

This discussion of control requires a point of clarification related to the study of political behavior. To political scientists, what is important is not that an individual has hostilities and insecurities (which, in any event, is a matter of degree), but rather that he is able to control them and to be objective about them, so that they do not hinder his successful functioning and assessment of reality.[109] In a like manner, Bettelheim and Maslow (as mentioned previously)

---

108. The dimension of control is apparently of considerable importance in understanding the motivations of George Wallace. For example, his biographer (Frady, 1968) notes that, in spite of their political sympathies toward him, Wallace "had a genuine aversion to the Klan. He just, in some vague way, didn't trust them. Anything that's basically uncontrollable makes him feel a little uneasy; he'd just rather stay away from it, whether it's for him or against him." (Wallace, as portrayed here, is a useful example of the relationship between psychic deprivation and political behavior. His view of life [see p. 14 of Frady's book] is typical of someone with very basic unfulfilled needs.)

109. In fact, as will be detailed below, findings suggest the ability of self-actualizing individuals to be objective about their problems and thus to discuss them more freely than deficiency-oriented persons—so that the former may appear on surface to have more problems.

have both commented at length on the negativism of psychoanalytic theory, with its lack of "attention to the positive powers of life and to how much they predominate over the crippling influence of neuroses."

In their study of the importance of Russia to their subjects, Smith, Bruner and White (1956, pp. 281-83) come to this same conclusion: "The pattern of a man's expressed opinions and values tells one much, often more when it comes to prediction than his responses to projective masochism and self-destructiveness." In other words, "The manner in which a person copes with his problems is the most revealing thing about him." Relating his comments to the life of Mahatma Gandhi, Erik Erikson concurs, noting:

> We must try to reflect on the relation of such a youth to his father, because the Mahatma places service to the father and the crushing guilt of failing in such service in the center of his adolescent turbulence. Some historians and political scientists seem to find it easy to interpret this account in psychoanalytic terms; I do not. For the question is not how a particular version of the Oedipal Complex "causes" a man to be both great and neurotic in a particular way, but rather how such a young person, upon perceiving that he may, indeed, have the originality and the gifts necessary to make some infantile fantasies come true in actuality, manages the complexes which constrict other men. This one cannot learn from Freud because he primarily described the conscience which inactivates ordinary people, and neglected to ask aloud (except, maybe in a cryptic identification with Moses) what permits great men to step out of line.[110] (1969, p. 113)

In any study of behavior which is concerned with motivation, therefore, one must be aware of the relationships to actual behavior. Here, these relationships are often only suggestions, but—for political psychology to make an important contribution—they will have to be definitively established. For a field view of personality[111] offers a more comprehensive and illuminating model than a view concerned only with inner dynamics.

There is, then, an important relationship between psychic deprivation and politically relevant behavior. These individuals, taken as a group, will comprise the "undemocrats" of whom Lane writes. It is hypothesized that they will be generally politically in-

---

110. In a moment of considerable insight, Erikson adds: "This, then, is the difference between a case history and a life-history: patients, great or small, are increasingly debilitated by their inner conflicts, but in historial actuality inner conflict only adds an indispensable momentum to all superhuman effort" (p. 363).

111. See Yinger (1965) for a detailed discussion of "personality as behavior."

active, until reaching the level of needs for affection and esteem, when their needs will propel them to seek satisfaction through social activity. Passive or active, however, they will be untrusting and intolerant of a world which they believe is hostile and rejecting of them.

Perhaps nothing shows more strongly the need to truly understand and predict the behavior and attitudes of this group than the voting analysis which Walter B. Simon (1959) has done of the years in Austria and Germany immediately preceding Hitler's rise to political power. Simon's analysis shows that the Nazi vote was not an ideological vote, but a protest against the status quo and came from those who were politically apathetic and uncommitted; that is, those who had not voted before or who had voted for minority parties. (In Austria the pattern was somewhat different, but the general interpretation is the same.)

In the May, 1928 election in Germany, the Nazis got slightly less than 3 percent of the total. In September, 1930, they received 17 percent of the total. In July, 1932, the figure had jumped to 37 percent. The gain of nearly 13 million votes from May, 1928 to July, 1932 "did not come even in part from the major party vote [emphasis added]." The major party vote actually increased during this period and the Socialist loss "was more than balanced by a Communist gain." The Nazi vote came from losses of minor parties and increased voting participation from 70 percent in 1928 to 88.5 percent in 1933. "At this election [1933] Germany's minor parties virtually disappeared, but the major parties held their own remarkably well, with the Catholic vote remaining nearly one million above what it had been in May, 1928 and the combined Socialist and Communist vote falling less than 0.4 millions short of its 1928 level."[112]

Thompson and Horton, in summarizing an analysis of these Nazi elections, state:

> The suggestion is that political inefficacy may result in political alienation which involves not only apathy or indifference as a response to awareness of powerlessness, but also diffuse displeasure at being powerless and mistrust of those who do

---

112. The relevance of this to American elections can be seen in the fact that in each U. S. election between 1940 and 1960, approximately 15-20 per cent were new voters—persons who has just come of age, but mainly persons who had not voted in the last election. Key (1966) comments: "Though we commonly ascribe great significance to the switchers, they are in many elections outnumbered by the 'new voters.' In some elections, indeed, the 'new voters' contribute significantly to the outcome, if they do not determine it. . . . The significance of the group is suggested by the fact that in 1950 on the order of eight or nine million persons voted who had not voted in 1956" (pp. 21-22).

wield power. Given the opportunity for expression, political alienation would be expected to be translated into either an undirected vote of resentment or an organized vote of opposition. (1960)

This hostility toward political authority emphasizes the importance of considering politically <u>relevant</u> behavior to be equally <u>inactivity</u>, as well as the well-categorized types of political activity. It also again points to the importance of psychic deprivation.

This relationship between apathy and alienation is also evident in some additional findings of the SRC national survey discussed above. The subjects were asked to place themselves on a continuum of political commitment ranging from strong Democratic through independents to strong Republican. For most Americans, such self-placement was easy to do. A small group, however, saw no relationship between themselves and any type of commitment to the American party system. Between partisans and independents, on the one hand, and these "apoliticals" on the other hand, the difference in attitudes toward government is striking, as the following table (Stokes, 1962, p. 69) illustrates.

Table 2.3

RELATION OF EXTENT OF PARTY IDENTIFICATION
TO ORIENTATION TO GOVERNMENT

Attitude Toward Government	Extent of Party Commitment		
	Apoliticals (N=52)	Independents (N=349)	Party Identifiers (N=1373)
Negative	42%	16%	15%
Intermediate	48	66	62
Positive	10	18	23
Totals	100%	100%	100%

A study by Hastings (1956, 1954) of voters in a Massachusetts community also focuses on the politically apathetic. He found a direct relationship between increase in voting and (1) social involvement in general, (2) having information and opinions on political issues, (3) concern with broad political issues and foreign policy (rather than issues such as taxation and the cost of living that more directly affect voters' lives), and (4) identification with the wealthy or above average socioeconomic strata (rather than with the below average and poor). These results held when age, income, education, sex, and religion were controlled.

Angus Campbell (1964) has noted that an estimated 10-15 per-

cent of voting age adults will "rarely, if ever, go to the polls"—
even if laws regarding restrictions based on residence, literacy,
etc., were changed. More important here, Campbell points out
that while education is always correlated (and assumed to have a
causal relationship) with voting, over the last thirty years there
has been little change in the percentage of the eligible who vote,
in spite of the great increase in general level of education. Nor
has increased awareness of political activities through television
(now in nine out of ten households) stimulated voting activity.[113]

Horton and Thompson (1962) report another field study which
focuses on the dimension of political negativism. Their subjects
were some 400 voters in two New York communities who were interviewed soon after they had defeated some school bond propos-
als. A strong relationship was found between low SES and rejection of the bond issue. From the characteristic attitudes of these
"rejectors" a dimension of psychic deprivation can also be seen:

> Alienation and low socioeconomic positions were found to be
> related both to each other and to a cluster of attitudes, a
> world view, which seemed to underlie the particular political
> response of the underdog. Certain recurring themes in this
> world view and, consequently, in the political style of the pow-
> erless were: the feeling that the world is a threatening place
> inhabited by the powerful and the powerless; suspicion of out-
> siders and of people in general; pessimism about the future;
> despair; and the tendency to debunk education and other val-
> ues necessary for success in a competitive society. (Horton
> and Thompson, 1962)

Horton and Thompson conclude that "voting down local issues may
be in part a type of mass protest, a convergency of the individual
assessments and actions of the powerless who have turned politics
into a 'phobic' sector by projecting into available political symbols
the fears and suspicions growing out of the alienated conditions of
their existence."[114]

Political interest, then, can be seen as part of a more general
social involvement, both—it can be hypothesized—stemming from
feelings of competence and positive effect toward one's world.
Hannah Arendt puts this issue in historical perspective:

> The success of totalitarian movements among the masses
> meant the end of two illusions of democratically ruled coun-
> tries in general and of European nation-states and their party

---

113. Dwight G. Dean (1965), writing in 1965, notes that in the
last seven Presidential elections only between 50-60 per cent of
the eligible voters did in fact vote.

114. For a more detailed analysis of this study, see John E.
Horton, "The Angry Voter, A Study in Political Alienation," unpublished Ph.D. dissertation, Cornell University, 1960.

system in particular. The first was that the people in its majority had taken an active part in government and that each individual was in sympathy with one's own or somebody else's
party. On the contrary, the movements showed that the politically neutral and indifferent masses could easily be the majority in a democratically ruled country, that therefore a democracy could function according to rules which are actively recognized by only a minority. The second democratic illusion ex-
ploded by the totalitarian movements was that these politically
indifferent masses did not matter, that they were truly neutral
and constituted no more than the inarticulate backward setting
for the political life of the nation. Now they made apparent what
no other organ of public opinion had ever been able to show,
namely, that democratic government had rested as much on the
silent approbation and tolerance of the indifferent and inarticulate sections of the people as on the articulate and visible institutions and organizations of the country. (1951, pp. 305-6)

The danger to an open society which is posed by such psychically deprived individuals is due to their predispositions to hostility, violence and rejection of the status quo in an effort to restruc-
ture the world closer to their needs. As Kornhauser states:

Apathy born of alienation from community may persist under
more or less stable conditions. However, the underlying disaffection of which apathy may be an expression readily leads
to activism in times of crisis, as when people who have previously rejected politics turn out in large numbers to support
demagogic attacks on the existing political system. (1959, p.
61)

Although in most national elections, such persons do not have an
opportunity to "vote their prejudices" (which Thompson and Horton see as being more likely to occur in local elections where one
may vote against an issue), the danger is nevertheless present and
real, in a land in which—on the average—40 percent of eligible
voters do not use this right. To this danger, we will return in our
final chapter.

In conclusion, Maslow's comments concerning psychic deprivation well underscore the political relevance of unfulfilled basic
needs.

The needs for safety, belongingness, love relations and for
respect can be satisfied only by other people, i.e only from
outside the person. This means considerable dependence on
the environment. A person in this dependent position cannot
really be said to be governing himself, or in control of his
own fate. . . .
    Because of this, the deficiency-motivated man must be
more afraid of the environment, since there is always the

possibility that it may fail or disappoint him. We now know
that this kind of anxious dependence breeds hostility as well.
. . .

This dependence colors and limits interpersonal relations.
To see people primarily as need-gratifiers or as sources of
supply is an abstractive act. They are seen not as wholes, as
complicated, unique individuals, but rather from the point of
view of usefulness. What in them is not related to the perceiv-
er's needs is either overlooked altogether, or else bores, ir-
ritates, or threatens. This parallels our relations with cows,
horses, and sheep, as well as with waiters, taxicab drivers,
porters, policemen or others whom we use. (1962, pp. 31-33)

Persons who are, in Maslow's terms, "deficiency-motivated"
have specific needs which shape their attitudes and behavior in differing ways. But psychic deprivation, whatever its motivational
components, can be hypothesized to be the foundation of a more
general philosophy of deprivation. This philosophy views human
beings as both weak and untrustworthy, human needs as insatiable
and our human environment as insecure, hostile and unmanageable.
Such a philosophy necessitates a mental posture of defense, generally equates inaction with security and makes action—when un-
dertaken—fearful and extreme because it is a response to a threat
which is both fearsome and desperate. Thus both the apathy of this
group and the psychic conditions which will require their response
must be included in any model of behavior in a participant democracy.

The Need for Self-Actualization

Even if all these needs are satisfied, we may still often (if not
always) expect that a new discontent and restlessness will soon
develop, unless the individual is doing what he is fitted for. A
musician must make music, an artist must paint, a poet must
write, if he is to be ultimately at peace with himself. What a
man can be, he must be. This need we may call self-actualization. (Maslow, 1954, p. 91)

The need for self-actualization, which represents the general
state of mental health, is not a need in the sense in which the four
earlier levels have been discussed. The needs for physiological,
safety, affection and esteem satisfaction are deficiency-related because they are seen as "external qualities that the organism lacks
and therefore needs." Self-actualization, however, is not "extrinsic to the organism . . ."; it is the process of the unfolding of the
human personality to its fullest extent—because its needs have been
met (1954, p. 183). In other words, only on this level of motivation
do we speak of the stage of human fulfillment commonly termed
mental health.

The beginning of self-actualization can be thought of as a benchmark or plateau in an individual's growth toward mental health and individual fulfillment. At its incipience (which is all that can be of practical concern for political scientists) it represents the fulfillment of our basic needs: physiological, security, affection and esteem. Cognitively and perceptually, it means that the individual's personality system tends to be open, rather than constricted, that his ability to assess reality is good and that his anxieties are controllable so that his personality needs do not hinder his successful social functioning.

But the boundaries of self-actualization, unlike those of the four lower needs, are not as clearly delimited in psychological theory. For the upper reaches of self-actualization—presumably attained by only a few—are but partially understood today and measures for their assessment are generally lacking. All that can be said with confidence is that growth in self-actualization leads to increased creativity, increased awareness of self and others, increased universality in thought and values, and increased curiosity. For persons who live in this higher realm of "peak experiences," Maslow has coined the phrase "transcenders."[115]

In accordance with his belief that in research, far too much attention has been placed on the causes and results of the lack of mental health, Maslow has studied and discussed at great length the phenomenon of self-actualization. He has been especially concerned with the weakness of what he calls man's "instincts" for growth, which can so easily be repressed "by one's culture, by learning, by defensive processes" (Maslow, 1964).

It is obvious, as a beginning to our discussion, that the self-actualizer will exhibit in greater or lesser degree the opposite of those characteristics which typify the psychically deprived group. That is, the mentally healthy individual is conceptualized as being relatively tolerant and secure; low in anxiety and hostility (and able to control the unhealthy impulses that do exist), that is, those that require defensive rather than coping behavior; undogmatic; and socially and politically concerned[116]—that is, concerned with his environment and with his relation to it.

But even this does not do justice to Maslow's (1954) concep-

---

115. Maslow (1964a); also Maslow (1969b). For the true self-actualizer, Maslow sees at least four conditions as necessary for growth: "not only that he be (1) sufficiently free of illness, (2) that he be sufficiently gratified in his basic needs, and (3) that he be positively using his capacities, but also (4) that he be motivated by some values which he strives for or gropes for and to which he is loyal" (Maslow (1967).

116. He is not necessarily an extreme activist; in fact he is likely to be highly selective of those activities which merit his time and energy.

tualization of the self-actualizer: being "growth-motivated" instead of "deficiency-motivated," there is a whole different quality
to his being. Through Maslow's detailed clinical studies, the following picture of the self-actualizer emerges. He is able to assess the world in a more realistic manner because he does not
consider the phenomena with which he must deal as inherently
threatening or hostile. In general, he will "judge people correctly
and efficiently." His personality needs, in other words, do not get
in the way of his observations.

Most important for our later discussion of Rokeach's work is
Maslow's hypothesis that "this superiority in the perception of reality eventuates in a superior ability to reason, to perceive the
truth, to come to conclusions, to be logical and to be cognitively
efficient, in general" (1954, p. 205). This is connected with Maslow's belief that "fear of knowledge of oneself is very often isomorphic with, and parallel with, fear of the outside world" (1962b,
p. 57). Thus, it is hypothesized here that anxiety and insecurity
are statistically related to the maintenance of closed belief systems.

To this we must also add Allport's comment that "perhaps
the most momentous discovery of psychological research in the
field of prejudice" is the discovery that there is a difference between the cognitive processes of prejudiced and tolerant people
(1954, pp. 170-71). In other words, as Maslow has noted, cognition
and perception in the self-actualizing person are relatively unmo-
tivated; the opposite is the characteristic of the unfulfilled person
(1954, p. 295). We can hypothesize, then, that there is a difference
between the cognitive processes of persons who, in Maslow's
terms, are self-actualizing and those who have unsatisfied basic
needs.[117]

Healthy individuals not only relate more realistically to their
environment, they also can more realistically assess their own
personalities. While they are accepting of themselves, they are
both aware of and concerned about their shortcomings and those
of their culture. "The general formula seems to be that healthy
people will feel bad about discrepancies between what is and what
might very well be or ought to be" (1954, p. 208).

Not only is the self-actualizer actively involved in his environment and able to manipulate it, but to an important psychological
degree—he is independent of it. In other words, the self-actualizers
spontaneously relate to their world (to use Erich Fromm's [1955]
terminology for this phenomenon); further, they "are not dependent
for their main satisfactions on the real world, or other people or
culture or means to ends or, in general, on extrinsic satisfactions"

---

117. Not only is the self-actualizer relatively undogmatic and
tolerant of ambiguity, he is accepting of and comfortable with the
unknown and often is "even more attracted by it than by the known"
(1954, pp. 205, 259).

(Maslow, 1954, pp. 213-14). This is most relevant to the concern
today over modern man's desire to "escape from freedom" through
overconformity and "other-direction." In opposition to this perceived trend, self-actualizers maintain an inner feeling of detachment from the culture—selectively accepting what seems right to
them.[118] They have less "national character" and are more "international people." This is certainly very different from the passive
yielding to cultural influences displayed, for instance, by the ethnocentric subjects of the many studies of authoritarian personality.
In fact, Maslow suggests that his need hierarchy may correspond
to another continuum—one "that ranges from relative acceptance
of the culture to relative detachment from it" (1954, pp. 226-27).[119]

Thus self-actualizers are likely to stand aloof from popular
movements to which there is a great pressure to conform but which
are not based on humanistic values. On the other hand, they are
likely to hold deeply to many values on which our democracy depends—in spite of counter-pressures. All of Maslow's self-actualizers (who were subjected to clinical study) were "democratic people in the deepest possible sense." They evidenced a great affection for and identification with other people—though occasionally
annoyed and angered by their shortcomings. This basic tolerance
is seen as motivating self-actualizers to avoid extremist politics,
because of the dogmatic, intolerant attitude of such groups. Their
proclivity to cultural detachment also means, however, that they
would not avoid the role of protector when they felt society to be
transgressing on their personal (and universalistic) values.

Self-actualization is not restricted to intellectual or aesthetic
fulfillment. The man with his prize rose garden, the woman who
fulfills herself through motherhood and creativity in domestic
skills, the fisherman, the teacher, the builder—in countless roles
and types of activity, creativity is possible. "Capacities clamor to

---

118. Cantril (1963) suggests that this may be an important
factor in progressivism—in a desire to experiment with the status
quo. He notes that not all people equate self-regard with social recognition. For some liberals, dissatisfied with life around them,
"social recognition and social status are not synonymous with self-
regard" (pp. 44-45).

119. Nettler (1957) reports developing an alienation scale
which differs from those commonly used in that it measures a
trait that is not isomorphic with mental illness. (For example, it
correlates + .309 with Srole's anomie scale, + .25 with Rosenberg's misanthropy scale and does not relate to the social dis-
tance-prejudice scale used.) The alienated were (at a .02 level of
significance) less prejudiced than the unalienated, however. Nettler suggests that alienation (as he measured it) can lead to creativity and altruism (e.g., Schweitzer) as well as to antisocial and
unstable behavior.

be used, and cease their clamor only when they are used sufficiently. That is to say, capacities are needs, and therefore are
intrinsic values as well" (Maslow, 1962b, p. 144). Therefore, self-
actualization should not be conceptualized as limited to any one
social or economic group. (The previous correlation between deficiency causation and low SES, however, should be kept in mind.)

The self-actualizer—considered in his full range—is thus not
only the epitome of mental health (that is, of human competence),
he is also conceptualized as being isomorphic with the democratic
personality—the opposite of the authoritarian. In his relations with
others the self-actualizer respects people as distinct and different
from each other, as ends in themselves (while the authoritarian
dichotomizes people on the basis of superiority-inferiority and
sees them as means to ends). The self-actualizer values strength
(the "capacity to solve problems external to the subject's psyche")
and competence, while the authoritarian values power. Finally, the
self-actualizer "will tend to recognize many scales of values and
is much more ready to consider scales of values which are different from his own. Furthermore these scales of value tend to be
specific and functional." (As noted by his willingness to become a
social activist when his humanistic values are threatened, this
does not mean that the self-actualizer is ambivalent in value-ori-
entation.) The authoritarian, on the other hand, uses only one scale
of values (the symbols of power and status) and will "defer to these
superior people [possessing these values] no matter what the field
may be, no matter what the question at issue, simply because they
rank high on the dominating scale of value" (Maslow, 1943b).

The democratic character structure of the self-actualizer,
once developed, is likely to be autonomous of an individual's current life situation (as is also true of the other needs, as we have
seen). To explain this phenomenon, Maslow has developed the hypothesis of "frustration-tolerance through early gratification."

> People who have been satisfied in their basic needs through-
> out their lives, particularly in their earlier years, seem to
> develop exceptional power to withstand present or future
> thwarting of these needs simply because they have strong,
> healthy character structure as a result of basic satisfaction.
> (1954, pp. 99-100)

Maslow goes on to suggest that "the most important gratifications
come in the first two years of life. That is to say, people who have
been made secure and strong in the earliest years, tend to remain
secure and strong thereafter in the face of whatever threatens."
This discussion is important to political scientists, not only in
suggesting again the stability of basic character, but also in pointing to the supreme value to society of efforts to make a child's
first years "secure and strong."

The point has also been variously made that mentally healthy
people possess more of what Allport (1954) calls "social sensitiv-

ity" and are "more accurate in their judgments of personality."
This is to say, self-actualizing people are characterized by empathy. The fact that Allport finds empathic ability to be "a prominent feature in personalities possessing ethnic tolerance" (that is,
persons who are likely to be found self-actualizing on other measures as well) is of great interest because of the fascinating basis
of understanding which it offers in studying individuals in transitional situations who can make the leap to a new identity through
use of this characteristic. Suggesting this hypothesis is Daniel
Lerner's well-known field study (1958) in which empathy is seen
as the key to personal adjustment in the fluid world of Middle Eastern society. It is the psychological factor which separates rural
illiterates lacking in media exposure from their peers, which gives
them opinions and the desire to become a member of a modern,
participant society.[120]

This is a small but important clue that Maslow is correct in
stating that psychic health, like physical health, is a unity which
knows no cultural or national boundaries. It may well be that individuals who have reached the level of self-actualization are more
"fit to survive" in the deepest sense (that is, to adjust, to be flexible, to feel out the most basic requirements of a situation), in
spite of the vicissitudes of life (and pressures to conform) which
may send them into isolation—or to the concentration camp. Because of this ability to be aware of the personality needs of others
and of himself, as well as the capacity to assess reality accurately and to be open-minded (that is, cognitively flexible, not value-
less), the self-actualizer is likely to be successful in leadership
roles. For creativity is "possible only to an individual who can afford to risk the unknown, to engage in the 'freely searching, scan-
ning, shaking-together process, which we call free association.'"[121]

Harold Lasswell (1951) has come to conclusions similar to
Maslow's about the components of democratic character. The most
outstanding characteristic of this personality he hypothesizes to be
the maintenance of an open ego—by which he means a warm and inclusive attitude toward others. The other characteristics which

---

120. See particularly chap. 2 of Lerner's book. While Lerner
notes that modern society encourages the development of empathy
as a skill (through mass media, literacy and voting, as well as
physical mobility), he makes clear that this is a personality characteristic which stimulates one Traditional to become "the cash
customer, the radio listener, the voter" (that is, Transitional),
while other Traditionals continue to conform to custom because of
their "constrictive" personalities—personalities which serve them
well in Traditional society. This personality distinction is not
made by Pye (1961)—unfortunately, because it forms a basis of his
theoretical argument.

121. Lawrence Kubie, quoted by Glad (1968).

Lasswell correlates with democratic character are a multivalue
rather than a single value philosophy (with little value attached to
the exercise of power per se), "deep confidence in the benevolent
potentialities of man" and freedom from anxiety.

Lasswell, in Power and Personality (1948), also discusses the
importance to the formation of democratic character of the lack of
social anxieties (conceptualized as "acute concern for the deference responses of others, and includes the incorporation and application to the self of deprivational appraisals"). For "democratic
character develops only in those who esteem themselves enough to
esteem others (to use a phrase of Harry Stack Sullivan's)." Lasswell also recognizes the continued importance to an individual's
life style of once achieving a healthy personality—in spite of the
deprivations to which he may be subjected in later life.

> Such a basic character formation operates selectively as an
> enduring predisposition in subsequent life situations. It makes
> it possible for the person to supply himself with indulgence in
> circumstances in which a favorable ratio of indulgence is not
> accorded to prodemocratic conduct by the environment. . . .
> Democratic characters have a durable positive image of the
> potentialities of human nature. (pp. 161-63)

How does a personality develop to the level of self-actualization? What factors of the primary home stimulate this "growth
motivation"? In addition to fulfilling the child's need for physiological satisfaction, for security, love and esteem, the optimal
situation (in home or school or anywhere) for allowing the democratic personality to develop "is a combination of emotional ma-
turity, of self-confident strength that permits both respect and
healthy control and discipline, of warm or cool affection, and of
training in democratic techniques and philosophy" (Maslow, 1957b,
pp. 105-8). Thus the development of democratic character, according to Maslow, depends not only on the quality of interpersonal relationships, but also on socialization into democratic values. Basic need gratification alone is not sufficient. "Responsibility for
oneself and for others, especially in the democratic use of power
over other people, demands education and knowledge, as autocrat-
ic submission or laissez-faire nonchalance do not."[122] Because
of this, one must again point to the social tragedy of the hypothe-

---

122. Lasswell concurs regarding this need for education and
notes that: "People need to be equipped with knowledge of how democratic doctrines can be justified. They cannot be expected to remain loyal to democratic ideals through all the disappointments
and disillusionments of life without a deep and enduring factual
knowledge of the potentialities of human beings for congenial and
productive human relations. As a means of maintaining a clear and
realistic appraisal of human nature, there must be deeply based
recognition . . . [that] the laborious work of modern science has

sized psychological selectivity of the educational process.

In an interesting discussion which emphasizes the twin factors of psychic fulfillment and the process of socialization in forming democratic character, Money-Kyrle relates characteristics that proved discriminating in studying German prisoners of war. Most important in separating authoritarian from democratic personality type was the existence of what Money-Kyrle calls a "humanistic conscience." In some individuals, however, such a value orientation was clearly external to their personality needs. These persons—as was true of other authoritarians—were "obsessively loyal to whatever authority they served."

> If it was a Catholic or Lutheran code of Christian ethics the resultant type of conscience might resemble the humanistic, but sometimes only in external form. Its deeper motives might be profoundly different. In some cases one had the impression that they were humanist in behavior only, and not in feeling, because they feared their God but did not greatly love their fellow men. Even this external resemblance to a humanistic conscience was absent when the authority to be obeyed was secular. (1951, p. 12)

Thus—as behavior is the outcome of cultural and personality factors interacting in a particular situation—it is possible to build a model of behavioral predispositions, as shown on page 94. In actuality, a field view of behavior would require a more complex model which allowed for disparity as well as similarity between the supportive influences of the larger culture and value learning in the primary group. Thus a self-actualizing person could receive humanistic value training from his family while still being a part of a larger authoritarian culture (a process which is likely producing unrest in Czechoslovakia today).

Types II and III (Table 2.4) are alienated individuals. (This points to a major thesis to be detailed subsequently: alienation as a construct is not equivalent to any one state of psychic competence. Thus, for example, alienation is only mistakenly considered as inherently symptomatic of the powerlessness which Rotter [1966] is studying.) The personalized world view of Type II and III persons is not supported by the culture in which they live. At times, when called upon to act, these persons will experience cultural demands as extreme forms of tension. As this tension increases, so will the chances that they will engage in culturally and politically devi-

---

provided a non-sentimental foundation for the intuitive confidence with which the poets and prophets of human brotherhood have regarded mankind. Buttressing the aspirations of these sensitive spirits stands the modern arsenal of facts about the benevolent potentialities of human nature, and a secure knowledge of the methods by which distorted personality growth can be prevented or cured" (Lasswell quoted in Bruce L. Smith [1969, p. 96]).

Table 2.4

	Authoritarian Culture	Humanistic Culture
Psychically deprived individuals	I. Gestapo members Ku Klux Klan Arab terrorists	II. Politically quiescent except in crisis situations. With needs for affection or esteem, may be active in extremist movements.
Self-actualizing individuals	III. Apolitical—creative in vocational roles. Rebellious when required to act as Type I or to deny their creativity.	IV. Active in politics when their particular values are engaged (for example, Vietnam war protest, defense of threatened value of patriotism).

ant behavior. This is true of the Type II individual who is asked to stand by while leftists mock his flag, his protectors, his way of life and his sense of order. It is equally true of the Soviet soldier ordered to put down an uprising in Hungary or Czechoslovakia or the Soviet citizen expected to be supportive (on many levels) of such actions in a civilian role. (In addition, for the Type III individual, creatively using one's talents may become a political and very rebellious act—as numerous Soviet cases have shown.) For the stability of a political system, it is thus necessary for there to exist tension-releasing mechanisms for such potentially deviant types—mechanisms which do not simultaneously endanger the political order in other ways.[123]

The recognition of the interplay between culture and personality is helpful in analyzing work on value and attitude change. Milton Rokeach (1968), for example, has recently been concerned with value change by making a subject aware of discrepancies between his professed beliefs and his value ordering. In an attempt

123. Examples of such mechanisms would be official days honoring veterans in the United States, as well as official addresses to the American Legion Convention and the existence of a President whose way of life and philosophy can be identified with by "personality conservatives." In the Soviet Union, such mechanisms might include officially permitted periods of self-criticism in literature, as well as the official concern for peace and friendship with all peoples.

to reduce dissonance in line with personality needs, it is possible
that self-actualizing people, socialized into the culture of the
American South for example, could be made to adopt more humanistic values because these values reflect their underlying optimistic, tension-free view of the world. For psychically deprived persons whose basic values do not support their verbal agreement
with democratic procedures, it is unlikely that an attitudinal or behavioral change in an experimental situation will be reflected in
changes in beliefs and behavior because such change would be in
the direction of increased dissonance. Further, in attempting to
change beliefs one must not overlook a most basic belief—whether
or not it is threatening to brave social norms.

The study of the behavioral predispositions of democratic
character is closely related to the issues with which political science must deal. Several students of behavior have particularly
been concerned with this type of personality. For example, in the
studies of tolerance (such as Samuel Stouffer's ground-breaking
Communism, Conformity, and Civil Liberties), it has been repeatedly found that tolerance correlates with optimism, leadership
roles and education. I would suggest that self-actualization is the
most common (and causal) factor behind all three of these relationships.[124] Indeed, it is probable that increasing concern with one's
environment and the ability to accept leadership positions are likely, as is continuation of one's education, to be correlated with satisfaction of basic psychic needs. Such psychic satisfaction, and
concurrent feelings of personal competence, are likely to result
in a view of the world as pleasant, gratifying and non threatening—
that is, in an optimistic frame of reference and in a willingness to
be participant in such an environment.

A study by Martin and Westie (1959) of "The Tolerant Personality" sheds further light on the self-actualizer. The study used a
probability sample of the blocks of Indianapolis which contained no
Negro residents. The subjects were scored on a scale measuring
attitudes toward Negroes, with choice options ranging from anti to
pro and tolerance being defined as those scores clustered around
zero (and prejudice being defined as those scores which were anti-
Negro). Prejudice correlated (at the .001 level of significance) with
the following scales: nationalism, intolerance of ambiguity, super-
stition, threat-orientation,[125] high F-scale scores, approval of

---

124. Regarding the relationship between tolerance and optimism, Stouffer (1955) mentions psychological theory to the effect
that "the individual who is very troubled, for whatever reason,
needs to blame someone aside from himself for his troubles."

125. Threat-Competition Orientation was measured by an 8-
item scale (see Appendix A) which was designed to measure "an
attitude of suspicion, distrust, and competitiveness; a misanthropic, 'jungle' outlook."

authoritarian child-rearing measures and religiosity ("the tolerant person tends to reject the fundamentalistic, doctrinaire, and
conservative outlook in favor of a more humanistic orientation."
There was no significant relationship between tolerance or prejudice and any type of church activity). The tolerants were also less
distrustful of politicians and more interested in politics.[126]

While this study largely defines the tolerant personality by
showing the characteristics he does not possess, we can nevertheless form the following picture, which is similar to that of the
self-actualizer. The tolerant personality is likely to be politically
conscious, concerned with a frame of reference broader than a
jingoistic nationalism, not disturbed by uncertainty or lack of concreteness (which typifies so much of politics), generally tolerant
toward others and humanistic in values. In a later article, Martin
(1961) is more explicit about the tolerant personality. Here his
discussion of the characteristics of the tolerant personality makes
it even more apparent that the key to his tolerance scores is what
is here called self-actualization.

There are other aspects of the healthy personality that are of
political importance as well. We have discussed previously the
findings of Milbrath and Klein that a "sociality-dominance-esteem
syndrome" worked very well in discriminating between individuals
who seek elective and those who seek appointive office (being positively correlated with elective office). In an earlier study, Milbrath (1960) sampled 100 contributors to both parties in North
Carolina (randomly drawn from official lists). To these subjects,
a 36-item personality test was administered; only a four item "sociability scale," taken from Gough's California Psychological Inventory, proved discriminatory. Sociability was positively related
to both socioeconomic status and to political participation. Status
factors, when controlled, accounted for "a considerable portion but
not the entirety of this relationship." This factor positively correlated with all types of political participation studied except holding
public office and making a political contribution. This study, although not correlated with all types of political activity, is suggestive again of the importance of ease in interpersonal relationships
(probably based on lack of anxiety and hostility) in allowing indi-

---

126. The significant statistics are:

	Means for Tolerant	Means for Prejudiced	CR
Nationalism	+1.02	+9.06	7.30
Intolerance of Ambiguity	-7.41	+3.79	10.77
Superstition	-7.85	- .19	8.81
Threat Orientation	-4.68	+1.86	5.95
F-Scale	-4.39	+5.07	8.01
Child Rearing Attitudes	- .93	+11.39	46.40
Religiosity	+5.46	+11.35	3.10

viduals to take an active part in their environment. Such social
ease can be related to characteristics (especially empathy) which
are part of the self-actualization syndrome.

One of the most provocative (though tentative) confirmations
of Maslow's views about self-actualization and its relationship to
politics comes from a study by Mussen and Wyszynski (1952). The
purpose of this study was an attempt to confirm the suggestions
which have been put forth in this regard by Riesman and Glazer.[127]
The sample for this study was composed of 156 University of Wis-
consin undergraduates.

The sample was given projective questions used by Levinson
in the California study of authoritarianism; the results are so pertinent to our interests here that they are discussed at length.[128]
The politically active (with low correlations at significant levels
varying from .05 to .10) showed a greater awareness of self
(based on their greater number of statements that were interpreted as "disappointment in self"). In answer to the question "What
might drive a person nuts?" the politically active group gave "a
significantly greater number of answers in the inability to adjust
to situations and/or face reality category." In short, the politically active were more able to assess and analyze their own personalities in a realistic fashion—one quality which has been connected
with self-actualization.

The politically apathetic, on the other hand, showed more "undifferentiated worry and indecision" which, the authors felt, "may
have their roots in vague, but deep, feelings of insecurity in the
face of what appears to be a generally threatening environment."
Further, the apathetic were very concerned with "social blunders"
(for example, convention), but not with the feelings of others. To
the authors, "The insecure, dependent individual needs sets of rules
to help him cope with the environment which seems generally
threatening. Because he does not accept his real feelings, he lacks
spontaneity in social situations, and established rules provide the
major basis for maintaining interpersonal relationships; hence he
is distressed (embarrassed) when he violates these rules."[129]

---

127. Reference is to D. Riesman and N. Glazer, "Criteria for
Political Apathy," in Studies in Leadership, ed. by A. W. Gouldner,
New York, Harper, 1950.

128. The subjects were also given the A-S, E-, F- and PEC
(Political-Economic Conservatism) scales from the Berkeley
study. These scales did not differentiate between the two groups.
To the authors of the study, this suggests once again that there
are other than personality reasons for prejudice.

129. Lynd also makes this point: "Codes or conventions, says
Conrad, provide ways of assorting, assimilating, and bearing experience. . . . Except for the person sufficiently deep-rooted in his
identity to be freely exploring, whatever cannot be codified, classi-

In answer to the question "What experiences would be most awe-inspiring?" the politically active showed a greater sensitivity and concern for self-expression, as well as their "ability to accept and enjoy intense emotional experiences."[130] In answer to the question "What would you try to instill in your child?" while the apathetics emphasized the importance of obedience, manners, formalized religion and morals and "success" orientation (for example, conventionalism), the politically active gave answers which the authors summarized as showing the activists' "fundamentally social orientation and social consciousness, his awareness of the importance of his own and others' emotions, and his relative freedom from conventional thinking."

As the hypothesis has been presented earlier that Maslow's need hierarchy correlates with a continuum, the low end of which could be epitomized by "concern with self" and the high end by "concern with environment (and self in relation to it)" the conclusions of this study demand lengthy quotation. Mussen and Wyszynski find two separate life patterns in the responses of their two groups:

> The apathetic's characteristics—inability to recognize personal responsibility or to examine—or even accept—his own emotions and feelings; vague, incomprehensible feelings of worry, insecurity, and threat; complete, unchallenging acceptance of constituted authority (social codes, parents, religion) and conventional values—form a self-consistent pattern which, in a clinical situation, would be labeled <u>passivity</u>. The deep and pervasive nature of this passivity is demonstrated further by the relative absence of responses emphasizing self-expression, ego-strivings and satisfactions or warm interpersonal relationships.
>
> From this point of view, political apathy itself may be regarded as one aspect of the individual's fundamentally passive orientation. (1952).

On the contrary, the active group shows

> an emphasis on strivings for ego-satisfactions, independence, maturity, and personal happiness. Instead of vague, unmanageable feelings of threat which form part of the passive pattern, active attempts to achieve self-understanding . . . are characteristic of the politically interested group.
>
> The sensitivity to others' feelings, emotions, and conflicts which is revealed by the politically active may also be interpreted as part of a generally active orientation, since it may

---

fied, labeled is potentially threatening, and can lead to a sense of being lost, unconnected" (1958), p. 65).

130. This agrees with Maslow's (1969b) conceptualization of the "transcenders."

represent an outgoing response: an attempt to understand, and empathize with, others. The final aspect of this coherent pattern, the active group's great social consciousness and emphasis on social contribution and love giving, involves a positive, active relationship with society generally. (p. 78)

The authors conclude that "Political activity may be regarded as one aspect of the politically interested subject's outgoing social responses and social consciousness [emphasis added]." Social consciousness alone, however, is not enough: to be politically active, one must be free from the anxieties which cripple one's ability to act.

This study of the personality correlates of political participation, though not a stated attempt to confirm Maslow's thesis, offers strong support for the personality theory which is advanced here. Individuals who participate in their environment in social and political ways differ in important aspects from those persons who are apathetic about their environment. In view of the widely held assumption in political science that political activity most likely reflects the pursuit of power as compensation for damaged self-esteem, it is extremely important that Mussen and Wyszynski found, on the contrary, that among the politically active, there was a strong tendency toward mentally healthy attitudes and beliefs. Finally, we must underline again that it is these same attitudes and beliefs which are the basis of democratic society.

But the subjects of this study were students, and many were below voting age: can these relationships be found in the "real world" of politics? In view of the wealth of knowledge available through psychological studies, it is amazing to report (as discussed in chap. 1) that very little has been done empirically in studying the type of personality which is active in political life. Perhaps the most direct evidence comes from an oft-quoted study by John B. McConaughy (1950), done more than twenty years ago! This study tested eighteen South Carolina legislators, state senators and representatives. The subjects were given a group of standardized personality tests, including the Bernreuter Personality Inventory, the Guilford-Martin Inventory of Factors G-A-M-I-N, the Edwards Unlabeled Fascists Attitude Test and the Lentz C-R Opinionaire.

The legislators' scores on these tests gave the following results: compared to the general population, they were less neurotic, greatly less introverted, showed much less nervous tenseness and irritability, were less inclined to fascist attitudes AND were in the top 36.22 percent on conservatism (this score declined quickly "when legislators are from counties with high retail sales, which is an index of prosperity"). On the other hand, the legislators, again compared to the general population, were more self-sufficient, and showed more general pressure for overt activity. They were ascendent in social situations (as opposed to submissive), masculine in attitudes and interests (as opposed to femininity), and much more self-confident (lacking in inferiority feelings) than the average. On this point, the author remarks: "Only 23.17 percent of the total adult male population ranks higher in lack of inferiority feelings than the average South Carolina political leader tested." Thus, in this study, as in Mussen and Wysznski's study, <u>mentally healthy characteristics are correlated with political activity.</u>[131] This underlines the wisdom of an early question by Maslow: "Why is there so much neglect of the fact that leadership in democracies is very often sought for the opportunity of service rather than to have power over other people?" (1954, p. 374)

In our discussion of self-actualizers, it is useful to return once again to Hargrove's (1966) study of six Presidents. (Because of the paucity of careful, analytic studies of political leaders, much of the evidence given here must unfortunately be impressionistic.) What is attempted here is to suggest a type which seems to fit Maslow's theory as a basis for making this theory operant in behavioral research. Hargrove's study is of value to us in highlighting the functioning of six well-known leaders and in showing the influence of their personalities on leadership style.

As presented by Hargrove, Franklin Roosevelt compares well with our view on a self-actualizer. The author notes that FDR evidenced psychological strength, and appeared free from anxieties. FDR's cognitive and emotional functioning also conforms to that of self-actualizing persons. "He was open-ended in his reaching out for attention and support and his genuine liking for people. He was open-ended mentally and ideologically, and in both his mental habits and ideals he sought to create ties of affection and support with people" (pp. 58-59). Perhaps even his attempt to pack the Supreme Court, which Hargrove attributes to overconfidence, can be seen as the characteristic of self-actualizers which Maslow describes as spontaneous, that is, marked "by lack of artificiality or straining for effect. . . . [The self-actualizer] practically never allows convention to hamper him or inhibit him from doing anything that he considers very important or basic" (1954, pp. 208-9).

Since self-actualizers will be found holding various types of political opinions (impressionistically, at least, no one party has a monopoly on self-actualization . . . or psychic deprivation), it must be remembered that political checks and balances are important even under conditions of healthy leaders and healthy followers.

---

131. For two pictures of self-actualizers, see Smith, Bruner and White (1956). One of these men (Chatwell) admires others because of their proficiency and competency. "His perception of the world followed in general the demands of his major expressed strivings rather than of unresolved inner tensions" (p. 111). For Osgood, "friendships always involve mutual esteem" (p. 236). Because this study focuses on the functions served by opinions held and the basis of their flexibility or inflexibility, it offers a great deal of useful background for the student of behavior.

If a person is self-actualized, it <u>does not</u> mean that he should be given political <u>carte blanche</u>, or that his political tactics will be valued by a majority of voters—even by a majority of the self-actualizers![132] It <u>does</u> mean, however, that his leadership will allow more problems to be solved (because of lack of rigidity, greater ability to assess reality, greater understanding of the motivations and needs of self and others, et cetera) and more people to be included in the decision-making process—that is, to be more democratic in arriving at decisions. This much we can say, based on the personality studies of political leaders which are now available: there is a vast difference in style and quality of leadership between a competent individual who is free from anxieties so as to be flexible in meeting the problems with which he must deal and realistic in assessing them and—on the other hand—the person whose unfulfilled psychic needs keep him rigid, inflexible and unable to function well in situations marked by stress and ambiguity.[133]

It is suggested here that this conclusion rests on substantially the same foundation as the conclusions which were reached by the late V. O. Key, Jr., in his landmark study of public opinion in America (1964). In assessing "particular distributions, movements, and qualities of mass opinion," Key repeatedly was forced to consider "that thin stratum of persons referred to variously as the political elite, the political activists, the leadership echelons, or the influentials." In spite of the contradictory and often intolerant views which compose mainstreams of American public opinion, Key noted that the opinions which serve as a basis for official decision-making are largely democratic and capable of forming a consensus. The answer to this apparent inconsistency was found in the motives and values of political activists. Key advanced the proposition that "these political actors constitute in effect a subculture with its own peculiar set of norms of behaviour, motives, and approved standards." Most important for our discussion is the fact that, among the leadership, Key found a broad agreement around modal beliefs, the prime one of which is "a regard for public opinion, a belief that in some way or another it should prevail."

---

132. For example, a very interesting study of an open-minded and healthy personality active politically is found in the life of Malcolm X. Far from being a rank-and-file extremist, Malcolm X's cognitive framework was, throughout his career, open to assimilate new ideas and new information. (His life is also a useful example of the prohibition against assuming psychic deprivation because of objective life experiences.)

133. For additionally supportive research on self-actualization, including an original measure of this dimension, see Shostrom (1964). Another use of Shostrom's Self-Actualization Inventory is reported by Murray (1968).

Key saw the causes of this restraint in "exploitation of public opinion" in the fact that political leaders come from competing centers of social and economic power and in "the indoctrination of those admitted [to leadership roles] in the special mores and customs of the activist elements of the polity." To these reasons, we must advance a third: in our culture at least, on the basis of present evidence it can be hypothesized that <u>individuals who achieve leadership roles tend to have self-actualizing personalities</u>.[134] This means both that they will not desire power per se and that they will share the important democratic belief concerning the value and the capabilities of the persons whom they lead. While, as leaders, they will be concerned with competent problem-solving (and their own views of successful solutions), they will also be respectful of the views of others.

The study of the phenomenon of self-actualization appears to be of great potential importance in understanding and predicting politically relevant behavior.[135] It is hypothesized that these persons—while not comprising all political activists—will be a statistically important segment of the influential—elite—leadership stratum. Their flexibility and competence as well as their ability to realistically assess the situations with which they must deal in the light of new information will make them valuable leaders. Finally, it is hypothesized that in our democratic society this group has an important social contribution to make. Relatively tolerant and open-minded in personal relations and in cognitive functioning, more able to resist the pressures of mindless conformity, these individuals are the bedrock of a participant democracy. Our concern should be in furthering the conditions which foster this type of character growth.

The Need Hierarchy as a Whole

". . . everyone is as God made him, and often a good deal worse."—Sancho Panza

---

134. On the basis of available studies of political activists as well as clinical research on levels of competence, I would suggest the possibility that national leaders (Congress, party officials, etc.) might be composed 60 per cent of individuals who are minimally self-actualized, 30 per cent of individuals needing self-esteem or affection, and 10 per cent of individuals operating on the lower levels of the need hierarchy. These figures would probably be revised downward as you descend the level of importance of political activity.

135. Certainly the empirical evidence is adequate to refute the assertion that "mental health is a moral concept, not an empirical one." For an exposition of this unfounded assertion, see John H. Schaar (1961), especially pp. 56-69.

As I have stated elsewhere (Knutson, 1967) Maslow's hierarchy can be seen as analogous to plant life: as with each human personality, each bud is formed with the possibilities of development
into a perfect, whole flower, but first it must successfully bypass
the vicissitudes of life which may blight its development. If the
bud is attacked by insects, disease, et cetera, it may continue to
unfold somewhat, but it will never become the perfect flower which
it inherently could have been: it will always (even after professional intervention) bear evidence of its earlier deprivation. Finally,
just as only the bud which has successfully reached the stage of
full development is considered to be whole and wholesome, so the
human personality which, having its earlier needs met is able to
develop to its fullest potentialities, is spoken of as having fully attained the level of mental health.

As we have previously noted, Maslow has called his theory of
human motivation a "holistic" analytic theory. By this, he means
that he is concerned with studying the whole individual, in seeing
individual traits, attitudes, and behaviors in relation to the functioning of total personality and in viewing specific needs as bearing a definite (knowable) relationship to other needs. What has been
suggested thus far is that it is possible for political scientists also
to deal with the total personality as a meaningful way of integrating
the disparate findings which past research has gathered and in
pointing the way to the type of questions whose answers we should
seek in the future. It is possible, in other words, for the political
scientist to work with various "syndromes" of personality. While
the purpose of each and every action can only finally (if then) be
known by in-depth personality analysis, the categorization of political man on the basis of broad general (and interlocking) types
would be a great advance over the haphazard analysis which has
been done in the past, especially as the "flavor" of specific personality needs is likely to cling to a wide variety of politically important attitudes and behaviors.

It is because we are dealing with motivational syndromes that
a common theme has run through our discussion. This theme concerns the resonance of a person's Weltanschauung with his specific personality needs. As Fichte has remarked:

> The kind of philosophy a man chooses depends upon the kind of
> man he is. For a philosophic system is no piece of dead furni-
> ture one can acquire and discard at will. It is animated with
> the spirit of the man who possesses it. (quoted in Cohen, 1960,
> p. 542)

Though perhaps unarticulated and fragmented in many cases, each
person nevertheless possesses a coherent philosophy which covers
such vital issues as the nature of man, of human relationships and
of his environment. His political philosophy is but an extension of
this personal philosophy, expressed through the political concepts
which are offered in his particular political culture. His political

behavior is shaped by his political philosophy, as well as the opportunities which exist for him to actualize his personal philosophy and the cultural and situational bars which obstruct its actualization.

It is not claimed that every person is motivated by just one need and that he progresses lockstep from one need to the next. Rather it is assumed that as a lower need area is largely satisfied, it recedes in importance and another need area becomes dominant in motivation. It is also assumed that the vast majority of persons can be classified on the basis of their predominant motivating level, although it is also realized that in some cases, individuals may move up the need hierarchy without having fully satisfied a lower need (so that, in effect, they are motivated by more than one need).

It has also been mentioned that personality is but one of a triad of variables which hold the key to understanding and predicting behavior. In addition to the great task of learning more about the effect of personality on politically relevant behavior, it is also necessary to simultaneously concern ourselves with the effect of a wide variety of specific field situations and (the third variable) with the influence of cultural values. For while Maslow has hypothesized that psychic health is universal, he has also underlined the importance of education and socialization in shaping individual behavior and attitudes. To this we must add the problem of assessing the support or dissonance which exists between cultural values on the one hand, and individual personality needs on the other, as well as the opportunities which the social structure provides for acting out.[136]

Thus, in this present work, the reader must keep in mind the culture-bound nature of the relationships which are suggested.[137] At the same time, with the growing importance of comparative studies, it is useful to be aware that Maslow's need hierarchy offers a useful basis for cross-cultural comparison. Maslow suggests, in this connection, that while the means of personality gratification may vary individually and culturally, the ends will be stable (1954, pp. 65-71). Indeed, "Our classification of basic needs is in part an attempt to account for this unity behind the apparent diversity from culture to culture" (p. 102).[138]

---

136. As Greenstein (1967, p. 50) points out, in studying the relationship between personality in the aggregate and politics, it is not simply a matter of numerical strength. For example, the balance of authoritarianism in the population as well as the positions held by this personality type are, in many cases, more important than absolute strength.

137. For example, Bettelheim and Janowitz (1964, p. 53) state that prejudice can weaken or strengthen an ego—depending on social norms.

138. Maslow also points to the importance of culture, not

Perhaps the greatest obstacle to the development of political psychology has been the lack of a conceptual framework within which to order the disparate findings reported with growing frequency—the lack of a common frame of reference among those working in the field. I have attempted to show that Maslow's theory of motivation and personality provides such a sorely needed theoretical framework.

By considering the various disparate findings in behavioral research in the light of Maslow's personality model (with its inherent hierarchical viewpoint), it has hopefully been illustrated that we can better understand their significance. Where these findings are similar to the need hierarchy conceptualized by Maslow, they have been presented under the various need levels in order to show the rich possibilities which such an application affords. (Of course, arrangement of the material presented above must be regarded as tentative and impressionistic—lest a charge of "egregious serendipity" be leveled!) Further, not all political studies can be so classified, even on an impressionistic basis. On the positive side, however, it must be stated that no behavioral studies have been uncovered, the results of which contradict any of Maslow's theses on the motivation levels of the human personality. On the contrary, an effort has been made to show that often (with much less clarity) the studies have arrived at similar conclusions.

From our overview of past behavioral research (and anticipating the material to follow), it is suggested that Maslow's theory performs well the three functions of theory as discussed below:

> First, and perhaps most basic, it makes possible the ordering of data. . . . It gives order and meaning to a mass of phenomena which without it would remain disconnected and unintelligible. . . . The ordering of data can help the observer to distinguish uniformities and uniqueness.
>
> Second, theory requires that the criteria of selection of problems for intensive analysis be made explicit. . . . Theory can serve to make more fully explicit the implicit assumptions underlying a research design and thus bring out dimensions and implications that might otherwise be overlooked.
>
> Third, theory can be an instrument for understanding not only uniformities and regularities but contingencies and irrationalities as well.[139]

---

only as a shaper of personality and behavior, but—for the self-actualizer—it is also a "reservoir-of-gratifications." He quotes, in this connection, A. Meiklejohn's question: "Is culture a set of problems or a set of opportunities?" (1954, p. 376).

139. Quoted from Kenneth Thompson, in McClelland (1960, p. 303). It is also suggested that Maslow's theory of motivation conforms to the model of personality theory put forward by Sears (1951, p. 477). "In any case, it is clear that an effective approach

By providing such a consistent theoretical framework within which to work, the application of Maslow's personality theory would be of decided benefit to the developing field of political psychology.

With this background in mind, let us turn to an examination of other approaches to the study of politically relevant behavior in a further attempt to explicate the relevance of Maslow's theory of personality and motivation to concerns of the political scientist.

---

to the problems of the development of personality and of the influence of personality on the behavior of groups requires a theory that has the following properties: its basic reference events must be actions: it must combine congruently both dyadic and monadic events; it must account for both on-going action and learning; it must provide a description of personality couched in terms of potentiality for action; and it must provide principles of personality development in terms of changes in potentiality for action."

3

Toward Greater Integration

While the tenor of our introductory discussion was critical of the state of political psychology, our theoretical analysis would be incomplete without a presentation of a more positive side. For the concrete knowledge which we have about the functioning of personality is available because of accumulative, painstaking research by others who have approached the study of man's behavior (political and otherwise) by employing a variety of conceptual schemes. While some of the research work presented here has explicitly been unrelated to the concerns of political scientists, on a basic level it will be shown that all of these studies contribute parts to our growing portrait of political men.

The research discussed in this chapter is the result of work in three disciplines: sociology, psychology and political science. Some of it comes under the joint heading of "social psychology," and is applied to a concrete social problem. Other work reported here, or elsewhere in this book, is the result of pure research on a highly theoretical level in one of the three disciplines. All of it helps form a picture of man's personality in which mental health —a state of low and well-managed anxiety which allows a creative interest in one's environment—is seen as the natural end process of development to adulthood, and the presence of tensions, anxieties, hostilities are seen as evidences of a defective, less competent, unfulfilled personality which has been warped in the process of growth. Of particular interest is the variety of research concerns which have built a complementary picture of personality— complementary to Maslow's theory of personality needs.

Perhaps one can more clearly envision the personality orientation employed here by again noting what it is not. Helen Merrell Lynd, in her book On Shame and the Search for Identity, includes an interesting discussion of Freudian psychology as "a theory of compensation"—a theory of what a person must do to live in society by overcoming his "primary antisocial and undesirable tendencies." In other words, the emphasis is on adjustment (Lynd, 1958, pp. 87-98). The examples Lynd gives show how at variance this traditional approach is to that offered by Maslow. She notes that such theories (and those of Parsons and Lasswell) "appear to concentrate on the tendency of both individual and social organism to maintain equilibrium at the expense of directing attention to the tendency to change and grow." Field theory (holism) is concerned, on the other hand, with "the recognition of the importance of dynamic factors" and the attempt to discover "significant wholes" (instead of "the identification of isolable, unambiguous items of behavior that can be reduced to nothing—but statements devoid of surplus meaning" [p. 126]).[1]

This emphasis on dynamic factors which lead to personality growth is the frame of reference in which the following research is presented. Various perspectives are discussed here in an attempt to show that, instead of providing yet another conceptual scheme by which to analyze behavior, Maslow's need hierarchy makes possible the use of a more economical research model because of its theoretical relevance to the major approaches now employed in behavioral research.

Dogmatism: Milton Rokeach

A major research interest which offers a great wealth of ideas to the political scientist is the long-standing concern of Milton Rokeach with belief systems. On the basis of a large variety of experiments and related research, reported over a period of years, Rokeach has developed a picture of man's cognitive and perceptual functioning that is widely used (though not always explicitly acknowledged) in explaining the causes of political behavior.

Rokeach (1960) has demonstrated that each person has a belief system and a disbelief system. Further, belief systems can be placed along a continuum of open-closed mindedness, based upon the degree of dogmatism with which they are structured. This differentiation is possible because of a variety of characteristics of an individual's cognitive and perceptual functioning which Rokeach has delineated. These characteristics have been correlated with both behavior (for example, difficulty in problem-solving) and attitudes (for example, tolerance vs. intolerance). Rokeach has made, however, a clear distinction between the content of belief systems and their structure, finding, for example, that a person can hold dogmatically to democratic beliefs[2] as well as to intolerant beliefs. Thus he offers dogmatism as a concept of much wider applicability than F-scale authoritarianism, because it will differentiate many types of authoritarianism while the F-scale has been frequently

---

1. Lynd's differentiation of personalities on the basis of whether they live on the "guilt-axis" or the "shame-axis" is similar to Maslow's view of people, with individuals operating on the "shame-axis" being self-actualizers, while those operating on the "guilt-axis" being psychically deprived.

2. For example, Kurt Schumacher is presented by Edinger in this light. Also see Rokeach (1960, pp. 4-5 and 14-17). Rokeach states, in other words, that while dogmatism "is assumed to involve both authoritarianism and intolerance, [it] need not necessarily take the form of fascist authoritarianism or ethnic intolerance" (p. 202).

criticized for measuring only right authoritarianism (Rokeach, 1956; Shils in Christie and Jahoda, 1954).

Rokeach has divided each person's belief system into three parts: central, intermediate and peripheral (pp. 39-42). The center or core of a person's belief system contains his beliefs about himself and others and about the world around him. Centrality of belief may be defined "not only in terms of cognitive connectedness but also in terms of the extent to which a given belief serves to enhance or deflate the ego" (1968, p. 48). These central beliefs are referred to as pre-ideological or primitive beliefs, which are defined as "any belief that virtually everyone is believed to have also." It is on this level that much of the preceding chapter has focused. For example, a person's belief that the world is hostile, threatening and insecure would be a primitive belief. It is inseparably connected with the personality needs of the individual: it is unquestioned; usually it is formed prior to the person's ability to verbalize it (1964, pp. 191-92).[3]

The intermediate region covers those beliefs a person holds about which authorities have a positive and which have a negative valence. These beliefs, like those in the central region, are absolute, but they can be differentiated from primitive beliefs "because the person who believes them knows that there are others who do not." It is because of these positive and negative authorities that people are able to classify what they hear as "true" or "false"— as "good" or "bad." As our previous discussion suggests, it appears that for some highly dogmatic individuals (for example, Kurt Schumacher—after becoming a political figure or Woodrow Wilson —after his father's death), there is no positive authority but themselves. To borrow Ibsen's phrase, they are truly "a majority of one."

At the outer level of a person's belief system lies the peripheral region wherein are found all the person's attitudes and opinions that are derived from his positive and negative authorities "regardless of whether such beliefs are perceived consciously as being thus derived by the person himself (1960, p. 47).

While each person has a belief system which is divided into these three regions, the nature of his central beliefs differentiates his belief system, not only because of the content of these central beliefs, but also because of the manner in which these beliefs

---

3. In Beliefs, Attitudes and Values (1968), Rokeach adds a new distinction: Primitive beliefs are divided between those for which there is a general social consensus and a second type which "is also learned by direct encounter with the object of belief, but its maintenance does not seem to depend on its being shared with others. . . . Examples of such beliefs are those held on pure faith —phobias, delusions, hallucinations, and various ego-enhancing and ego-deflating beliefs arising from learned experience . . ." (pp. 8-9).

structure the person's views about the nature of authority. (As Rokeach points out, what distinguishes an authoritarian from a non-authoritarian is not "because the first relies on authority and the second does not. Rather, they have different ideas about the nature of authority, different theories about the way to employ authority as a 'cognitive liaison system' mediating between the person and the world this person is trying to understand (1960, pp. 43-44).

A person who feels threatened by his environment, who feels insecure and uncertain in his life situation, will hold dogmatically to his beliefs about authority. To use Rokeach's terminology, his belief system will be closed—the function of preserving himself from threat will be uppermost in importance. (Rokeach states that all belief-disbelief systems have two conflicting, but simultaneous functions: "the need for a cognitive framework to know and to understand and the need to ward off threatening aspects of reality. To the extent that the cognitive need to know is predominant and the need to ward off absent, open systems should result (1960, p. 67).

The closed-minded person will be unable to assimilate new information which is incongruent with his previously held beliefs (which have been accepted because they have come from positive authorities).[4] As a result, incongruent new information will either (1) be perceptually distorted in such a way that it can be accepted (because it is now congruent to his other beliefs), (2) rejected out-of-hand, (3) accepted (because it stems from a positive authority) but not integrated with previously held beliefs, or (4) if it comes from a positive authority and requires a belief change which he cannot or will not make, "he will alter his beliefs about the positive authority itself; he will become more negative or more disaffected with the authority and, in the extreme, he will even formulate new beliefs about new authorities to rely on" (1964, p. 194). Thus persons who are dogmatic (as the Berkeley study of authoritarianism showed so well) will tenaciously hold opinions which are inherently contradictory.[5]

---

4. Rokeach differentiates between rigidity ("resistance to change of single tasks or beliefs") and dogmatism ("the resistance to change of a total system of beliefs") (1960, p. 23; also 1954, p. 196).

5. This discussion again underlines the fact that in attempts to experimentally change attitudes or values, it is necessary to consider each individual's cognitive framework as an independent variable. For a study which confirms that open- and closed-minded individuals differ "in their ability to differentiate between and evaluate independently messages and their sources in a communication context" see Powell (1962).

Rokeach, in view of our previous discussion, makes another important distinction between the open and the closed mind:

> We here consider the assumption that the closed mind, through fear of the new, is a passive mind. It achieves its systematic character "for free," through the external authority's efforts rather than its own. When left to its own devices, like a fish out of water, it cannot integrate new beliefs into a new system because it cannot remember them. The reason it cannot remember them is because there is a dynamic unwillingness to "play along," to "entertain" strange belief systems. (1960, p. 23)

Rokeach also differentiates individuals with open vs. closed minds on the basis of their anxiety of which a "central feature . . . is a dread of the future, . . . for the future is the most ambiguous and unknowable medium in man's cognitive world" (p. 367). Rokeach has stated, in another place, that, because dogmatism is based on "a disaffected conception of the present," it is postulated to be related to "the belief that a drastic revision of the present is necessary. . . . The greater the dogmatism the greater the condonement of force (1954, p. 200). Whether or not fear of an "ambiguous and unknowable" future will be found in the same dogmatic individuals who seek "a drastic revision of the present" should be carefully studied. From our previous discussion, it would appear that persons operating at the base of the need hierarchy would fear the future but hold tenaciously to what they now have except in periods of crisis while persons operating at the higher levels (3, 4 and 5) would be more willing from their various perspectives to seek change in the status quo.

On the basis of Rokeach's evidence, the following hypothesis is offered: dogmatic individuals will make ineffective political leaders because their personal needs (that is, their central or primitive beliefs) do not allow them flexibility in assimilating new information or an "openness" in their perception of reality. They do not function effectively in changing, challenging or ambiguous situations.[6] (It is likely that, over the long run, this would be true in all cultures.) While it is undoubtedly correct (as Edinger [1965, pp. 312-13] points out in his conclusion), that dogmatic, authoritarian individuals can serve useful political ends at times, because

---

6. Rokeach (1960, p. 211) has found that in new and different situations, persons with closed minds, because of their anxieties, simply cannot function effectively. Further, this inability to function is due to their perception of the world as threatening, rather than to their intellectual ability. In a replication of Rokeach's work (in a study which analyzed all of the range of scores, not just the extremes), Samuel Fillenbaum and Arnold Jackman report that "dogmatism and performance in a task requiring the subject to synthesize and organize a new set of beliefs that differ from the stan-

political conditions are inherently in a state of flux it is hypothesized here that, <u>sooner or later, a dogmatic individual will be self-defeating as a political leader (for example, his actions will be dysfunctional in terms of his political goals</u>).

In going through the writings of Rokeach, I have continually been made aware that—though their interests and approaches differ—Rokeach and Maslow are, in actuality, talking about the same personality phenomena. The person who maintains a closed belief system is a psychically unfulfilled or debilitated person—moreover, he is unfulfilled (that is, psychically deprived) in ways which have been specifically described by Maslow. Conversely, the person who holds an open belief system is described as bearing characteristics which mark him as a self-actualizer ("the alternative to accepting and rejecting others on grounds of belief congruence is to accept others without evaluating them at all" [Rokeach, 1960, p. 63]). Whether these two theories are describing identical or only roughly similar personalities must, of course, be determined empirically.

As mentioned in chapter 1, Rokeach has stated, "We suspect that if we knew more about the nature of such primitive beliefs, their organization, and how to modify them, we would know more about the conditions leading to the formation and modification of belief systems. This should have important implications for the psychology of politics, personality, mental health, psychotherapy, and education."[7] He has also tentatively advanced the view that "a full description of a person's belief-disbelief system is also a full description of his personality" (1956, p. 38). I would suggest that while Rokeach has been concerned with the nature and organization of belief systems, Maslow (though not explicitly) has been concerned with "the formation and modification of belief systems." If the very substantial contribution of both these scientists can be meaningfully fused, students of behavior will have taken a long step toward understanding human behavior. Specifically, it is hypothesized here that <u>Rokeach's continuum of open-closed mindedness closely corresponds to Maslow's need hierarchy</u>. Open-mindedness (with its accompanying characteristics) is seen as part of the syndrome of self-actualization.

On the basis of this theory of cognition, Rokeach has devel-

---

dard operation procedures of every day life holds not only for extreme scores on dogmatism, but also over the range of scores, the more close-minded the person the more trouble he has on such a test" (1961, p. 214).

7. It is relevant to note that "the origins and sources of control orientations and the operations for altering such orientations" are seen as the major unexplored dimension in Rotter's work on the sense of control over behavioral reinforcements (Lefcourt, 1966, p. 218).

oped a "Dogmatism Scale" which is "designed to measure individual differences in the extent to which belief systems are open or
closed." It has been widely used in behavioral research (some of
the results of which use are presented in this book). In the original research presented in chapter 4, Form D was used (with permission from Dr. Rokeach) to test the hypothesis on open-closed
mindedness.[8]

Although, by this point in the discussion, the reader is undoubtedly aware of the political relevance of the types of cognitive
functioning described by Rokeach, such useful clues to understanding the behavior of political man are provided thereby that it is
well to include here other remarks made by Rokeach. In this world
of mass movements and "true believers," it behooves political scientists to become knowledgeable about the belief system of their
subjects. The following comments by Rokeach are suggestive of
their application to political research.

1. Dogmatic individuals are susceptible to appeals from authorities that to them are positive, appeals that they may act on
without analysis. "A party-line thinker [a close-minded person] is
a person who not only resists change but can also change only too
easily. What he does depends on what his authorities do, and his
changes and refusals to change conform with authority" (1960, p.
225).

2. Open-minded subjects take considerably and significantly
longer in problem solving when they are given the clues "on a silver platter" (all at once) than under a "working-through condition"
because, it is assumed, "the open-minded subjects are not using
all this 'extra' time to synthesize, but to analyze, because they reject 'silver platter' handouts" (p. 240). Open-minded individuals
are likely, in other words, to analyze new information no matter
how the ideas are presented.

3. On the contrary, with the "silver platter condition," the
results for dogmatic individuals are quite different: ". . . problem-
solving proceeds more smoothly in closed persons when new beliefs are presented all at once than when presented gradually" (pp.
287-88). While closed-minded individuals are more resistant to
new ideas—by presenting completed sets of ideas (an ideology) as
a whole, resistance is lowered as the ideas can now be accepted
without being analyzed (providing the authority from which they
come is positive).[9]

4. Rokeach further suggests that "those with relatively closed
belief systems will by virtue of relatively greater isolation within

---

8. Troldahl and Powell (1965) report a sub-scale of 20 of
these items which has suitable reliability for field research work.

9. For additional research on learning differences between
open- and closed-minded subjects, see Restle, Andrews and Rokeach (1964).

their belief systems, be unable to see logical contradictions between beliefs" (p. 245). Equally important: "In the language of politics, isolation within a belief system may be thought of as the
structural basis for party-line thinking, and also of the inability
to defect from an inherently contradictory system" (p. 288). Thus
persons with closed belief systems, because of the isolation between their beliefs, may sustain contradictory ideas, become
"trapped within impossible systems without knowing it" and struggle for unobtainable solutions (p. 254).

The effect of closed-mindedness probably has important consequences for various types of political activity. For example, research into voting patterns has shown that the more strongly partisan the person, the more likely he is to insulate himself from
contrary points of view. . . . In short, the most partisan people
protect themselves from the disturbing experience presented by
opposition arguments by paying little attention to them" (Lazarsfeld, Berelson, Gaudet, 1944, pp. 89-90). It is possible that strong
partisanship (when accompanied by an inability to see any light on
the other side) may be an indication of closed-mindedness. Thus
an understanding of a person's cognitive framework, as well as of
the social pressure which he experiences to conform to his primary group's voting pattern and his family's political tradition,
may help to predict his voting choices.

Some very interesting research has been done, based on
Rokeach's theory of dogmatism. One of the questions which has
been extensively studied is the connection between the authoritarian individual and the dogmatic individual. Rokeach's own research
has indicated that dogmatism and conservatism are correlated in a
small, but consistently positive degree (1956, p. 29). However,
Rokeach has also shown that the F-scale becomes more ineffective
in its discriminatory powers the more the person who is authoritarian moves away from right authoritarianism.

Edwin Barker (1963) reports two studies which focus on this
problem. (One used 160 graduate students in the New York area in
1957; the other used forty-five student activists and a control
group of sixty-one at Ohio State University in 1963.) In both studies, he found that the F-scale was significantly related to only
right authoritarianism. However, an interesting difference appeared in Barker's second study (which was far less homogeneous
regarding amount of organizational activity and strength of political opinions). He found that:

> when one is dealing with subjects who range only from mildly
> conservative to mildly liberal, one will find no apparent rela-
> tion between authoritarianism and conservatism. However,
> when the range is extended—when one has some committed
> conservatives and leftists in the sample, the differences in
> general authoritarianism begin to show. . . . General authori-
> tarianism is more associated with rightist ideology than with

leftist ideology, although not as significantly as is "pre-fascist tendency" (F-scale). (Barker, 1963, p. 70)

By lumping together all the extremists in the Ohio study, Barker found that there was such a thing as "generalized extremism"— these individuals did not differ significantly (by ideological group) on any scale given to them. While Rightists and Leftists, in other words, differed from each other in the political opinions which they held, the extremists in both groups (compared to the rest of their ideology group) were higher on the F-scale, and in dogmatism, and in desire to censor radio and television participation by prominent persons and organizations connected with their opposing ideology group.

However, Barker also came up with a very interesting and most unusual finding which suggests that (at least his) Rightists may be much more psychically deprived (operating on lower need levels) than his Leftists: (1) Compared with dogmatic Leftists, dogmatic Rightists were higher on the F-scale (which can be explained away if it is considered, as it often is, a measure of political ideology as well as of personal intolerance), and (2) while the dogmatic Leftists wished to censor Rights' freedom of speech, dogmatic Rightists expressed a desire to censor both Leftist and Rightist organizations and individuals, "thus receiving a higher total censorship score" (pp. 71-72). (Again, the operation of the "self as the in-group" is a useful hypothesis.)

Rokeach has suggested that extremists can be found in any ideological position. The possibility exists, however, that because conservatism is often (but not always) operationalized as a rigid, uncritical adherence to the status quo, measures of conservative dogmatism would differentiate those who operate at the lowest two levels of the need hierarchy (need for physiological satisfactions and for security), while dogmatic extremists who wish to overthrow the status quo would represent (because of their central beliefs or personality needs) those persons who actively seek and cannot find affection and esteem in their present environment. This would help to explain the relationship which has variously been found between the particular rightist conservatism discussed above and various indicators of neuroticism. In sum, it is the thesis here that such an ipso facto relationship is spurious because it is not a conserving view of the world that is necessarily correlated with psychic deprivation, but a rigidly and anxiously held conservatism which stems from fear of social chaos.[10]

---

10. Thus, within the field of political science, there are numerous exponents of the view that mental health is likely to be related to positions on the left of the political spectrum, such as Merelman (1969), who says: "Left movements, in their call for innovation and their emphasis upon the secular over the sacred and equity over expiation, appeal to high levels of moral and cognitive

Dogmatic persons not only tend to be extreme in ideology (and perhaps skewed toward the conservative end), they have also been shown to tend to conform without question to the opinions of authorities that, for them, are positive. Just as the authoritarian person grants positive authority to individuals who have the outward symbols of status and power, there is some suggestion that dogmatic persons (undifferentiated, however, as to type) evidence a similar phenomenon. For example, Vidulich and Kaimon (1961) report a study of 307 undergraduates who were given Rokeach's Dogmatism scale. The top thirty and bottom thirty students were then selected for an experiment with the autokinetic phenomenon of apparent light movement.[11] Half of each group was placed with a "high status" stooge and the other half placed with a "low status" stooge. A correlation was found between high scores on the Dogmatism Scale and agreement with the high status stooge. An analysis of the findings showed that both the source's status and the subject's dogmatism are "highly significant sources of variation when considered alone . . . but that the interaction of these two variables again produces the greatest effect. . . ." The results were unrelated to intelligence.

It is also suggested that subjects differing in degree of dogmatism and authoritarianism will differ in the number and width of categories which they use for classification, if and only if, however, the stimulus is highly relevant to this personality dimension.[12] One study focuses on the classificatory behavior of twelve high and twelve low students (in dogmatism and authoritarianism), chosen from 410 tested. While the low students used significantly more categories in differentiating between undesirable social acts (the high relevancy area), there was no difference in their judgment of occupations (the low relevance area). According to the authors,

---

development. Movements of the right stress the need to respect authority, tradition, and punitive law. In so doing, they appeal to the earliest inculcated and most 'natural' forms of thought. Therefore, more people are capable of reaction than reform." So far as can be determined, such views are—at present anyway—based on what definitions are employed and the wishful thinking of the writer. Frenkel-Brunswik (1948) attacks this same problem in misapplying "liberalism." She notes that while "liberalism" is a political creed, humanitarianism is a much broader category and (hopefully) includes tolerant individuals besides those who are political liberals.

11. For an explanation of this phenomenon, see Verba (1961, pp. 77-78); also Jahoda and Cook (1954, pp. 211-30).

12. For additional research on this problem, see Coffman (1967). Theoretically, this question bears some interesting similarities to the value which Rotter's subjects place on control relevant information. See Rotter (1966).

this finding indicates "that the tendency of authoritarian and dog-matic individuals to render black-white judgments does not per-vade their usage of conceptual categories in all judgmental tasks" (White, Alter and Rardin, 1965).

A great deal of research, both by Rokeach and others, has em-ployed his concepts and research instruments. The preceding is but a suggestive outline of these findings. Yet it allows us to draw some general conclusions about the applicability of Rokeach's the-ories to the purposes of political science and their relation to per-sonality theory as developed by Maslow.

Theoretically, dogmatism is associated with what Maslow de-scribed as basic need deprivation. But more—it is likely that there is a causal relationship between these two factors. For persons motivated by unsatisfied basic needs appear to adhere to a partic-ular philosophy of deprivation. In Rokeach's terms, we would say that such deprived individuals exhibit an interlocking group of cen-tral ideas about themselves, others and the world. These ideas stem from a basic feeling of anxiety; they are pervaded by a sense of threat; they result in a dogmatic cognitive system.

It is possible to conceive of a direct, inverse relationship be-tween dogmatism and self-actualization, with dogmatism scores falling as individuals ascend the need hierarchy. But it is also pos-sible that all deprived persons will be highly dogmatic (although dogmatism serves a differing psychic function for each group) be-cause of the great difference between deprivation and growth mo-tivation as well as the general posture of defense that typifies psy-chically debilitated individuals. (We must also remember Ro-keach's comment that persons lacking in self-esteem are likely to be extremely dogmatic.) Therefore it was hypothesized that, in the field study presented in chapter 4, there would be found a direct relationship between general psychic deprivation and dogmatism and an inverse relationship between dogmatism and self-actualiza-tion. No hypothesis is offered regarding varying strength of dog-matism among various deprived groups.

In assessing the political importance of Rokeach's work, one must keep in mind the previous discussion of mental rigidity, in-flexibility and general dogmatism which several case studies (for example, of Hoover, Wilson, Schumacher) have shown to be the mark of an ineffective and dysfunctional leader (in relation to the person's avowed political goals). One must also remember the partisanship with which a dogmatic citizen is likely to hold his opinions, as well as the (hypothesized) inherent but unperceived contradictory nature of those opinions. Finally, students of politi-cal behavior should note the prime importance of a positive au-thority—an authority which speaks to personality needs, and not to the logic of the situation, in determining how a dogmatic person will assess the new information that the world in which he lives and breathes and has his being constantly presents him—and on which he must find a basis for opinions and action.

Authoritarianism: T. W. Adorno, Else Frenkel-
Brunswik, D. J. Levinson and R. N. Sanford

In a classic form of understatement, one must begin this section with the well-worn remark that "the scope of the present study
does not permit an exhaustive review of the material." The Berkeley
study of authoritarian personality has had such far-reaching influence on the knowledge which nonpsychologists have about personality that it is easily possible to count in the hundreds the discussions
and applications of the Berkeley group's findings. This proliferation
has been compounded by the easily available F-scale which—because of its effortless application—has been included in research
instruments measuring a mind-boggling variety of supposed traits,
attitudes and behavior.[13]

Out of this chaos must come order. To begin in the Paleolithic
age of behaviorial research, when to the average political scientist
"scale" referred to piscatory matter, density or music, a few influential writers (for example, Fromm, Maslow and Lasswell) began to warn about the dangers to democratic society of an authoritarian personality type: overconforming, conventional, sadomas-
ochistic in interpersonal relationships, concerned with power and
status and with his relationship to their perceived loci, he was presented as democracy's antichrist. With the events in Nazi Germany
which frightened tolerant men everywhere, a more concerted effort
was made to understand the phenomenon that is authoritarianism.

In 1944, the American Jewish Committee provided support for
a series of studies concerning prejudice.[14] The work entitled The
Authoritarian Personality was undoubtedly the most seminal and
provocative of these studies. Through continuously refined research instruments measuring both prejudice toward specific minorities and generalized ethnocentrism, the Berkeley group developed the now famous F- (for fascism) scale which—without being
explicitly connected with prejudice, or specifically directed toward
any minority group—was remarkably effective in discriminating
between tolerant individuals and those who were, in fact, ethnocentric and anti-Semitic. Further research was also done, both through
personal interviews and various projective tests, to demonstrate
that the findings of the F-scale were valid—that it was able to measure a specific personality type, with which a specific syndrome of

---

13. For a more inclusive current summary of work applying
the F-scale, see Kirscht and Dillehay (1967).

14. The results of these studies are: The Authoritarian Personality, Dynamics of Prejudice (Bettelheim and Janowitz, reis-
sued as Social Change and Prejudice, 1964); Anti-Semitism and
Emotional Disorder (Ackerman and Jahoda), Rehearsal for De-
struction (Massing) and Prophets of Deceit (Lowenthal and Guter-
man).

attitudes, as well as a specific type of primary home relationship, could be correlated.[15] Perhaps no one study has done so much to delimit the characteristics of a type of neuroticism (or, in our terms, a syndrome related to deficiency needs).

Paul Kecskemeti sums up the impact of this massive study as follows:

> The main lesson derived may perhaps be stated as follows: ethnic prejudice in general, and anti-Semitic prejudice in particular, is a symptom of deep, unresolved conflicts within the personality of the prejudiced subject. It is not a kind of hostility which might be explained "rationally" in terms of, say, economic competition or fear of deprivation as based upon experience. It is a hatred that is self-hatred as much as hatred of the other; the prejudiced subject seeks to annihilate the object which is in a way a hated and feared part of the subject himself. (1951)

Perhaps even more important for our interest here, the Berkeley study clearly demonstrated "that the views people hold on various subjects are not combined at random but form 'clusters,' so that a person who on one topic has an opinion belonging to one of those clusters is likely to have opinions belonging to the same cluster concerning many other topics" (Kecskemeti, 1951, p. 287).

The publication of The Authoritarian Personality set off a wave of discussion, replication and reanalysis. Foremost among this was the collection of critiques edited by Richard Christie and Marie Jahoda, entitled Studies in the Scope and Method of "The Authoritarian Personality." Besides the criticisms embodied in this work, additional studies discussed the "response-set" factor[16] which had been found to influence the results of the F-scale answers. (As the items were all stated so that agreement was scored as authoritarianism, a person who tended toward agreement—for example, one whose verbal ability was poor—would likely be found in the authoritarian group, whether or not such placement reflected authoritarianism as defined in the study.[17]

---

15. The generality of this personality type is underlined by two studies employing Jewish subjects: See Adelson (1953); also Himelhoch (1950).

16. The seminal discussion of response sets is found in Cronbach (Winter, 1946).

17. See, for example, Chapman and Campbell (1957); Christie, Havel and Seidenberg (1958) (who report, after a survey of response set studies: "Roughly an eighth of the variance in response to the F-scale would then be attributable to response set" in college samples, and perhaps the figure would be even less for more sophisticated groups); Weatherley (1964); Berkowitz and Wolkon

The path toward the improvement and analysis of research techniques did not stop here. It has also been suggested, for example, that individuals who are "Yea-sayers" in pencil and paper tests differ in personality characteristics from those who are "Nay-sayers" (Milbrath, 1962; Couch and Keniston, 1960; and Rorer, 1965). With these criticisms in mind (which have also been shown to apply to Rokeach's Dogmatism Scale [Lichtenstein, Quinn and Hover, 1961]), new F-scales were constructed which reversed items to account for this factor. But the debate went on—not only questioning what these new versions in fact measure, but also pointing out further difficulties. For example, it has now been hypothesized (Brim and Hoff, 1957; Berg, 1955) that extreme scorers (whether pro or con) will differ in personality characteristics from individuals who mark a more central choice in a Likert-type scale! Where will it end?

The discussion around the report of the Berkeley group has not only concerned how adequate its techniques are (of which the above is but a small sample of the charges leveled) but has also questioned just what is being measured. (Sarnoff and Katz [1954], for example, suggest that the F-scale may not be purely a personality measure "since the authoritarian values it measures may well reflect the individual's values rather than other basic personality characteristics."[18]) Further, some of the basic assumptions of its authors have been questioned. For example (as we noted above), Rokeach and others have shown that the F-scale primarily measures "right" authoritarianism (because of the content of its items), and does not discriminate equally intolerant, dogmatic individuals who hold beliefs which could be termed "left" or "center" (Kecskemeti, 1951). Dogmatism is now seen as referring to the structure of a belief system, the individual's central ideas about the world and the attitude that he has toward authority—not to any particular type of intolerance which is dogmatically espoused.

(1964); and the most interesting analysis by Rorer (1964), an analysis which is criticized by Bentler, Jackson and Messick (1965).

18. The best rejoinder to this criticism is provided by the wealth of other types of personality measures which the Berkeley group found to be correlated with the F-scale scores. However, no suggestion was made that authoritarianism is the only cause of ethnocentrism or that prejudice cannot be culturally conditioned. See, for example, the data on southern social leaders in Prothro (1952); also Christie and Garcia (1951) (in which the authors found —comparing a Berkeley and southern college sample—that "residence with such a social climate [permissive to discrimination] was conducive to greater acceptance of items relating to both prejudice toward minority groups and an authoritarian view of society" [emphasis added]).

It has also been mentioned that the assumption that <u>low</u> F-scale scorers are ipso facto democrats has been (for the above and other reasons) severely questioned. A particularly pointed critique of this allegation is included in the thoughtful analysis by Paul Kecskemeti, who notes that the Berkeley authors, by adopting, unexamined, all of the liberal-socialistic "myths" and further, by assuming that those persons scoring low in ethnic prejudice are by definition a "pro-democratic social force" lead to the conclusion that "the degree of biased naivety shown in this volume is seldom equaled" (Kecskemeti, 1951, pp. 290-92).

Finally, it has been demonstrated that while a strong general factor runs through the F-scale items, clustering suggests that several different dimensions are being tapped.[19] The preceding chapter of this book suggests some of these dimensions.

In spite of the wide variety of criticisms of the Berkeley study,[20] however, a great deal of its message stands intact. After the numerous replications which have been made (some of which will be discussed below) there is no question that this study represents a great advance in our knowledge of personality and its social importance. Though the response set factor has inflated results, it alone does not account for them.[21] The same can be said of cultural factors.[22] Though persons low in F-scale scores are not synonymous with democratic personalities, persons who receive high scores have been shown to be, in a very profound sense, undemocratic. Finally, although authoritarian personalities may be adequate for certain situations and innocuous in others, "the various forms of rigidity and of avoidance of ambiguity, directed as they are toward a simplified mastery of the environment, turn out [as we have seen in the case of several political leaders] to be maladaptive in the end . . . [because] stereotypical categorizations

---

19. See, for example, the analysis reported by Eysenck (1954, p. 152); a more detailed analysis in O'Neil and Levinson (1953); and an interesting discussion of the multidimensionality of authoritarianism in Weitman (1962).

20. For a good general critique of the Berkeley study, see Luchins (1950).

21. Rorer (1965) is particularly pointed in attacking "the illusion that acquiescence is widespread and of great importance, especially in the California F scale." (An informative, thorough discussion of acquiescence can be found in Bentler, Jackson and Messick [1965].)

22. This whole area represents an excellent example of the need to employ a field view of personality. See Prothro (1952), Pettigrew (1958), Smith and Prothro (1957), and Prothro and Melikian (1953).

can never do justice to all the possible aspects of reality"
(Frenkel-Brunswik, 1954, p. 187).[23]

Indeed, authoritarian character is an implicit danger to our
society. True, it has been stated that an authoritarian individual
can act democratically in times of a permissive, open, anxiety-
free situation (Spitz, 1958). Further Shils criticizes the Berkeley
study for its lack of "realization of the extent and importance for
the proper functioning of any kind of society . . . [played by] adap-
tiveness to institutional roles." Specifically,

> Persons of quite different dispositions, as long as they have
> some reasonable measure of responsiveness to the expecta-
> tions of others will behave in a more or less uniform manner
> when expectations are relatively uniform.[24] (Shils in Christie
> and Jahoda, 1954, p. 43)

However, in times of stress (which is, to some extent, the norm
of politics, if not for modern society), it is also realized that the
authoritarian personality's anxieties will lead him to project his
hostilities in situations involving choice (for example, political activities) in ways which are harmful to the maintenance of an open
society and of equalitarian interpersonal relationships. Thus, although it has been suggested in all seriousness that no personality
type could rate the plethora of pejorative adjectives used to describe the authoritarian personality ("some of my best friends are
authoritarians") and that researchers have let their personal values and political concerns dim their perspectives,[25] it is also
widely agreed that authoritarianism in individuals is a serious
though often dormant danger to our society.

---

23. For a report of experimental research which found a difference in leadership characteristics of individuals high and low
in F-Scale scores, see Haythorn, Couch, Haefner, Langham and
Carter (1956).

24. Shils further states that "Even authoritarian personalities are especially useful in some roles in democratic societies
and in many other roles where they are not indispensable, they
are at least harmless" (p. 49). (This depends upon the type of role
—e.g., economic, military, political. Regarding the latter, this
would be highly debatable!)

25. Another example of this is found in an article by Masling
(1954), who goes on to attack a straw man—that is, the belief that
authoritarians are neurotic—by showing that authoritarianism, in
four studies, was not significantly related to social functioning (remaining out of mental clinics, becoming leaders, et cetera). However, the general thesis in research on authoritarianism has not
been that it is debilitating—that persons so "afflicted" are so out
of step in our society as to be hospitalized or denied leadership
positions—indeed, usually the reverse has been feared!

In addition to their lack of ability to function adequately in times of stress, one must also keep in mind their basic antihumanitarian bias. As Frenkel-Brunswik notes, "Sympathy for the weak cannot develop where there is ingrained fear of weakness and where the weak furnishes the only practical target of aggression" (1954, p. 195). As Christie (1954, p. 166) summarizes previous studies of prejudiced personalities, "These are uncomfortable people in an unpleasant and unpredictable world"—surely not an adequate foundation for a stable, open society grounded in humanistic values.

Let us turn now to research that has employed the F-scale to see what possible relationships it may have to the motivation and personality theory which is the focus of this book, as well as to politically relevant behavior.

Several studies have been concerned with the relationship between authoritarianism and both anxiety and intolerance of ambiguity. An unpublished dissertation study by Siegel (1954) reports work in this area. Using as subjects a random sample of one hundred Stanford freshman women, Siegel differentiated them (on the basis of their scores on the Berkeley E- [ethnocentrism] and F-scales) for expressed authoritarianism. He then found significant relationships between their authoritarianism scores and their scores on the Taylor Manifest Anxiety Scale, their tendency to stereotype, their concern with status (based on whether the subject's first choice for the next year's housing was the prestigious "row" houses or not) and "affect-identification" toward national and ethnic groups (based on percentage of a list of national and ethnic groups which the subject indicated that she either liked or disliked). Siegel found, however, that there was a significant relationship between authoritarianism and an originally devised "Tolerance-Intolerance of Cognitive Ambiguity Test" only by applying an uncommonly used test of significance. Finally, he noted that a group of low E-F scorers who performed similarly to high E-F scorers on other tests were also authoritarian (in Rokeach's terms, one would say that they each displayed different types of dogmatism), though "prejudice-resistant." (Siegel noted that the high scorers' performances were much more predictable than the low scorers'.)

Davids (1955) reports another study which used measures similar to those employed by Siegel.[26] Using as a sample twenty male undergraduates at Harvard who volunteered for psychological testing and were demographically diversified, Davids em-

---

26. Davids (1963) further pursues the analysis of this variable. (This study suffers from a fundamental difficulty—that is, confusing tolerance of ambiguity with the denial that ambiguity exists by subjects who are psychically unable to creatively order and meet with enjoyment the challenge which ambiguity can pose.)

ployed the F-scale, the Taylor Manifest Anxiety Scale and tested
(by noting reactions to visual and auditory stimuli which were ambiguous) the subjects' intolerance of ambiguity. As in the study by
Siegel, Davids found a significant relationship between authoritarianism and manifest anxiety and no significant relationship between
authoritarianism and intolerance of ambiguity (though the relationships were in the predicted direction).[27] (Davids also reports a
significant inverse relationship between authoritarianism and intelligence. However, as this was based solely on lower grades, it
can only be taken to show a lack of ability to function well in educational situations—leaving the question of intelligence unmea-
sured.)

As hypothesized in chapter 2 of this book, intolerance of ambiguity, seen as an attempt to impose order on an insecure world,
should be strongly related only to the lower levels of the need hierarchy. It is therefore possible that it would only be shown in authoritarian persons functioning on this level which, for reasons
previously discussed, would probably include relatively few college
students.[28]

Closely associated with intolerance of ambiguity is generalized mental rigidity. Various research projects have focused on
the unclear relationship between authoritarianism and the factor
of rigidity. Neuringer attempted to measure this relationship as
it was affected by anxiety, hypothesizing that in previous experiments, in which the anxiety had been experimentally induced, the
stress was insufficient to affect the relationship. He used a control
group of mentally healthy individuals and, as subjects, two groups
of individuals typified by noticeable, behavior-affecting anxiety:
(1) a group, each of whom had made a serious attempt at suicide
and (2) a group, each of whom were suffering from debilitating psychosomatic ailments. He found that authoritarianism (as measured
by the F-scale) and rigidity were related and that the relationship
was enhanced when anxiety was present. Neuringer (1964) suggests
that when an authoritarian person becomes anxious, his defense
mechanism is heightened rigidity under stress.

Research by Meresko, Rubin and Shontz (1954) also suggests
that the authoritarian person, like our psychically deprived group,

---

27. The lack of relationship to intolerance of ambiguity, Davids notes, also occurred in a study reported by C. W. Eriksen and
D. Eisenstein, "Personality Rigidity and the Rorschach," Journal
of Personality, 21 (1953), 386-91, which raises the question as to
whether authoritarians are indeed intolerant of ambiguity.

28. For a study which also bears on the authoritarian's need
for structuring his world—in this case, his need to change his perceptions of a leader to conform to election results, see Paul (1956).
Regarding the perceptions of authoritarian vs. nonauthoritarian individuals, see Scodel and Mussen (1953); also Kanwar (1958).

lives in a world perceived as hostile and threatening, upon which
he must impose artificial, rigid order. Employing a scale measuring rigidity of attitudes regarding personal habits as well as the
F-scale to a randomly selected group of college students in beginning psychology, the authors found a relationship which was significant beyond the .01 level. The authors describe their scale as directly and/or indirectly implying "threatening consequences for
not following a rigid pattern in one's personal habits."[29] They further state that individuals whose behavior is based on a rigid pattern, appear to fear the use of spontaneity, flexibility and their
own judgment in coping with daily living.

That authoritarian individuals may be intolerant of ambiguity
as well as of others has several politically important ramifica-
tions. Intolerance of ambiguity motivates the search for decisions
which are sweeping, obvious, forceful and decisive—but above all,
for decisions! In politics, where inaction may be as potent a weap-
on as action, such persons press for actions which disallow finesse
or manuever—that call for the troops to be called home NOW—or
the enemy to be atomically destroyed NOW. Any consequences are
easier to face than the lack of decision from which consequences
can flow. Mental rigidity, of course, further narrows the scope of
solutions to be considered and evidence to be assessed.

A good deal of research has also gone into the relationship
between F-scale authoritarianism and socioeconomic status. For
example, a study by MacKinnon and Centers (1956-57), based on a
quota sample of 460 residents in Los Angeles County (taken from
four census tracts chosen to vary demographically) found a correlation between authoritarianism and increases in age in manual
workers. While this correlation generally held in nonmanual workers, there was a drop in the twenty and thirty year age brackets.
The authors question whether this drop is due to "life-situational
factors" or reflects "differences between individuals resulting
from their having been born in different periods of a changing culture." (To illustrate the latter hypothesis, the authors suggest the
possibility of greater hardship during the Great Depression and
the two World Wars for manual workers. They also suggest that
"the older generation may have matured in a stricter moral climate and received less education than the younger generation.")
Not only was occupation correlated with authoritarianism, but education was also found to be a factor, with authoritarians the predominant group in the nonhigh school graduates and the reverse
true among the college graduates.

The results from two national samples (n = 1,227), given a
shortened form of the F-scale developed by F. Sanford,[30] showed

---

29. See the discussion in chap. 2 concerning the Threat-Orientation and Interpersonal Threat Scales used in the study reported in chap. 4.

30. Dropped from Sanford's scale was the item "Obedience

similar relationships. High authoritarianism (scored by agreement with at least four of six items) was correlated with age, lack of education and lower socioeconomic status. One-fourth of the sample fell into this category. The authors report: "For the middle class, fuller education brings about a significant drop in the level of authoritarianism while for the lower class more education appears to have no significant effect on authoritarian tendencies" (Janowitz and Marvick, 1963). Authoritarianism was also related to isolationist attitudes, lack of political efficacy, and nonvoting in the 1948 election, but not to party preference. This study is suggestive again of the possibility that authoritarian tendencies can be positively influenced by education, providing they are peripheral (based on social values) to central personality needs. It is possible that the lack of influence of education in the lower socioeconomic group may be partly due to the greater severity of deprivation (another cause could be the physical, mental and social deficiencies which lower SES children bring to the classroom).

The relationship between authoritarianism and socioeconomic status remains ambiguous. Lipsitz (1965), for example, in a secondary analysis of three opinion surveys done in the early 1950s, finds that the relationship between authoritarianism and lower SES is not as clear-cut as once thought. He found that by controlling for SES, in many of the relationships the lower class group was no longer most authoritarian. In focusing on the subjects with a high school education or less, Lipsitz notes that while some of the comparisons are nonsignificant, "many indicate lower authoritarianism within the working class. Clearly, the lower authoritarianism of the middle class samples is due primarily to the greater frequency of post-high school education in the middle class."

There is, however, another and equally plausible explanation for this finding and for the fact that middle class subjects of high school education or less are more authoritarian than lower class subjects. It is possible that the reason that a lower SES person does not continue his education beyond high school is more likely to be economic and/or social. However, the inability of the middle class person to continue his education—in spite of economic and social pressures to do so—may indicate a greater likelihood that psychic factors are again acting selectively to determine that education is of little benefit (in this respect) to the psychically deprived, and that it is "growth-motivated" persons who are more likely to continue their education.[31] Thus, while an inverse rela-

---

and respect for authority are the most important virtues children should learn" because over 86 percent showed some agreement.

31. Farris (1956) has found (in a random sample in Tuscaloosa, Alabama of 454 people) that with political confidence held constant, the relationships between authoritarianism and intolerance wash out except for the confident subjects. Noting that Srole (see Anomia, below) found that intolerance and authoritarianism

tionship between SES and authoritarianism has appeared in numerous studies, deviant case analysis here would illumine our knowledge regarding the operation of motivational patterns and how they interact with social conditions. Certainly, there is no simple relationship between one's place in the social structure (present or past) and authoritarianism.

Another area which has been subject to study has been that of social participation and authoritarianism, concerning which the findings are also unclear. Harned (1961) reports a study based on a 1953-54 random sample of forty-one ward committee chairmen in New Haven, Connecticut and, as a control, twenty-seven men and women inactive in politics (paired for SES). The subjects were given three projective questions from the Adorno study in order to assess authoritarianism. Although F-scale scores were unrelated to either party activity or memberships in social organizations, authoritarian committeemen tended to place more emphasis on the importance of party organization per se, while committee chairmen with lower authoritarian ratings were found to be more likely to consider themselves active participants in more associations.[32] Finally, high authoritarian ratings were associated with low scores on an "ideological partisanship scale," suggesting that the purpose served by party work was not that of furthering ideological beliefs. Thus authoritarianism, in this study, was found to be neither a barrier nor a stimulus to participation, although the meaning of participation appears to differ between the authoritarian and the nonauthoritarian. (According to the model used in this book, whether or not authoritarianism is found to be a barrier to participation would be dependent upon which psychically deprived —and authoritarian—group was being measured. It is not authoritarianism per se which is related to participation, but rather the specific unfulfilled need which gives rise to authoritarian tendencies.)

Another study concerning the relationship between authoritarianism and participation is a secondary analysis by Lane of a national sample taken by the Survey Research Center as a 1952 post-election study which incorporated a 10 item F-scale (from which Lane drew up a four item Guttman scale). Lane (1955) noted that, with education controlled, there was no difference in voting and only slight difference in political activity between authoritari-

---

were only related in his upper status group, Farris suggests that people may need some confidence in and attachment to the political system before authoritarian tendencies can be observed. He also notes that such a relationship would be consistent with Maslow's theory of motivation—a point which is not clear to me.

32. Harned mentions that Sanford (1950) reports that while they tend to join organizations, authoritarians aren't likely to actively participate.

ans and "equalitarians." In the lower class only (determined by educational level), did the authoritarians express less political efficacy. No difference was found in expression of a sense of political duty, a point to which we will return. One most interesting difference (in contrast to the findings of Harned)[33] is the fact that authoritarianism was correlated with group participation, as can be seen from the table below.

Table 3.1

AUTHORITARIANISM AND NUMBER OF FORMAL GROUP MEMBERSHIPS

	Authoritarianism	
	Equalitarian	Authoritarian
Non-high school graduates	(N=60)	(N=172)
0-2 group memberships	72%	62%
3 or more group memberships	28	38
	100%	100%
High school or college graduates	(N=68)	(N=97)
0-2 group memberships	68%	51%
3 or more group memberships	32	49
	100%	100%
$x^2 = 6.58 > .05$		

In explaining this relationship, Lane hypothesizes that the authoritarian seeks membership because of some personal or material advantage. (Lane notes that Sanford found that the authoritarian—in comparison with the equalitarian—"is reluctant to join the less prestigeful groups but eager to 'head up' some community committee work.") In party preference, Lane notes a strong relationship at each educational level between authoritarianism and Republicanism. But while the authoritarian 1948 nonvoters who voted in the 1952 election went almost solidly for Eisenhower, most of them still did not vote, while of the equalitarian 1948 nonvoters, who divided their votes between the two parties, exactly half were induced to vote in 1952.

In analyzing the same data, however, but using three divisions and a different measure of authoritarianism, William Kornhauser (1959, p. 72) found an inverse relationship between authoritarian-

---

33. Harned's group was probably more homogeneous demographically and of higher status.

ism and (1) number of memberships, and (2) number of active memberships. Thus the relationships here are ambiguous, to say the least!

In opposition to Lane's findings relating authoritarianism to participation is the result noted by Milbrath and Klein (1962) in their previously discussed study of Washington lobbyists. Using the Christie version of the F-scale with half of the items reversed to account for response set, the authors report that authoritarianism appears to be a barrier to partisan political activity. "The barrier is no absolute, a few high scorers are active, but the tendency for high scorers to shun political activity is clear." Milbrath and Klein propose, as Sanford didn't control for SES or environment, that this is "the first clear-cut finding that a high score on F reflects a barrier to political participation." (The correlation between the Esteem Scale and the F-scale, for example, was -.13.) As this study concerns only the most active individuals (within a narrow demographic range)—persons who play prominent political roles—it is possible that the influence of authoritarianism may be more clearly a barrier here while not serving as an impediment to less conspicuous and perhaps less successful forms of activity.

While the relationship between authoritarian personality predisposition and sociopolitical participation remains unclear, it seems likely that this relationship will vary, given the type of activity and the type of authoritarian being studied. Indeed, according to Maslow's personality model, such varying results are to be expected. For—as a variety of studies have shown—authoritarianism is not unidimensional. It can be hypothesized that authoritarian individuals operating on lower need levels will be nonparticipant, while those motivated by unfulfilled needs for affection or esteem will join or lead—using available organizations or seeking those to whose membership prestige is attached—depending upon their individual personality needs.

The relationships with SES and social participation do not exhaust the research interests of those who have employed the F-scale. Another politically relevant dimension, which has been frequently studied, is that of political partisanship. Lane, as discussed above, found that authoritarianism correlated with Republican voting—when studying the 1952 election. A most interesting report of studies regarding this factor has been written by Leventhal, Jacobs and Kudirka (1964), testing the hypothesis that there will be a clear relationship between authoritarianism and political choice only when liberal vs. conservative ideology is clearly at issue in a campaign. First, the authors tested sixty-six undergraduates at Yale two weeks before the Kennedy-Nixon election. Here they found a significant relationship between F-scale results and preference both for Nixon and also for the Republican party.

Second, during the 1962 Congressional Elections, 189 randomly picked students from four Yale dormitories filled out question-

naires. They found, as did the Berkeley study, that there was a
strong relationship between high F-scale scores and high scores
on the Berkeley PEC ("political-economic conservatism") scale.
They also found, in three situations of hypothetical candidate
choice: (1) When the choice was between a conservative Republican and a Liberal Democrat, authoritarianism was significantly
related to the choice of a conservative Republican; (2) when the
choice was between a conservative Democrat and a Liberal Republican, however, authoritarianism was significantly related to
the choice of the conservative Democrat, (3) when both candidates
were "middle of the road" in philosophy, there was no relationship
between authoritarianism and candidate choice.

The authors conclude: "Evidence in support of the hypothesis
that high F subjects are oriented toward a 'community-wide' party
norm is quite unsatisfactory."[34] Clearly, the authoritarians pre-
ferred conservative values (as offered in this study), not the Republican party.[35] Also important, since the low F-scale scorers
were equally consistent in liberal choices, the results cannot simply be explained by the view that high F-scale scorers are other-
directed and tend to conform to the dominant values at Yale. Not
only does this study show again that personality and political choice
must be discussed in terms of the total field situation, it also emphasizes once more that both for growth- and deficiency-oriented
personalities, political ideology is an expression of an all-inclu-
sive Weltanschauung.

The supposed relationship between political conservatism and
various indices of neuroticism demands some clarification here.
Past confusion has stemmed, I would suggest, from a confusion of
the "radical rightist" with the true conservative—that is, one who
seeks to conserve and preserve, not to punitively reject or de-
stroy. Hofstadter (1965) has made a similar distinction, calling
the former "pseudo-conservatives" because of their proclivities
to attack, rather than defend, traditional values and institutions.
As Hofstadter states, exponents of rightist views, "although they
believe themselves to be conservatives and usually employ the
rhetoric of conservatism, show signs of a serious and restless dissatisfaction with American life, traditions, and institutions" (p. 43).
Bunzel amplifies this point in stating, "If the Burkean or moderate
conservative seeks to remind us of the continuity and universality
of certain traditional values, the radical rightist, in fusing his own

---

34. These results are reminiscent of the ease with which individuals in the authoritarian south switched to the Republican
party once a candidate was offered (that is, Goldwater) who ap-
pealed to their sensibilities.

35. An actual situation which illustrates this point is the rejection of Thomas Kuchel, California's liberal Republican Senior
Senator, by many of his party's regulars.

values the fundamentalist religion and morality, makes absolute judgments about them and demands their total acceptance" (1967, p. 83).

Herbert McClosky (1958), in his controversial study of the personality dimensions of conservatism, found a clear relationship between traditional conservatism and various measures of psychic deprivation.[36] As his conservatism scale has never been made available, one's judgment must be impressionistic, but it appears that what he was measuring was the rightists' belief in the fallibility of human nature and the untrustworthiness of human relationships—not the belief in the value of things established and the necessity of their but slow modification.[37] Two field studies help to amplify this distinction.

One study is based on a random sample of male Conservative party members in the state of New York and a control group of forty-eight Republicans.[38] By employing the Rosenberg misanthropy scale[39] and the authoritarian-equalitarian scale developed by SRC, Schoenberger (1968) found that his group of conservatives were less authoritarian, more supportive of civil liberties and "When asked if they could think of any organization hurting the conservative cause (only 7 of 45 thought any was helping), 71 percent named the John Birch Society. . . ." The issues that concerned these conservatives were social and economic, rather than more philosophic issues relating to the characteristics of human nature and human relationships.[40]

Schoenberger makes the following distinctions:

> Despite some elements of overlap, it may be in order to hypothesize that two major strains of right-wing attitudes and behavior are distinguishable on the basis of (1) political grounds—one concerned primarily with questions of economic and social policy, the other with a powerful and conspiratorial domestic Communist threat; (2) social differences—one a segment of the young, educated, technologically competent and economically successful middle to upper-middle class, the other older, less competent and less 'successful'

---

36. For a critical review, see Kendall (1958).

37. For further discussion of the use of McClosky's conservatism scale, see Kirscht and Dillehay (1967, p. 60).

38. All but one of the conservatives was a former Republican. (Schoenberger's article is based on his unpublished Ph.D. dissertation, University of Rochester, 1966.)

39. See Appendix A.

40. As distinguished from McClosky's sample and the conservatives in the Berkeley study of authoritarianism, this group had relatively high SES.

on these dimensions; and (3) psychological differences—one
reasonably well adjusted to their environment and able to
cope with, though dissenting from, the major political tendencies of their time, the other hostile toward many of the social
forces of the era and less able to keep their social-psychological balance when confronting them. (1968)

He concludes that while "The former group of inactive, ineffica-
cious, alienated and largely ill-educated individuals may be psychologically conservative . . . no evidence has been offered to demonstrate a consistent relationship to any broad variant of political
conservatism."[41]

A second study which attempts to measure conservative attitudes selected four aspects of conservatism for study: economic,
fear of communism, against "socialist and atheist" opinions (that
is, the dimension of tolerance), and isolation.[42] The data was acquired by drawing names randomly from registration lists in census tracts which varied in SES in two California counties. Important for our discussion here, no general conservatism factor was
found. However, as discovered many times before, "people who
feel involved in politics tend to have more consistent conservative
or liberal attitudes than others."

It appears likely that the definition of "conservatism" that is
employed in research will determine the mental health ratings of
individuals who fall into the category of "conservatives." Because,
as was discussed in chapter 2, the personal philosophy of psychically deprived persons encompasses a pessimistic belief regarding human nature and human relationships, when a conservative
response is couched in these terms it will likely be agreed to by
persons who exhibit unsatisfied basic needs. On specific issues,
ranging from the danger of Communism to Federal aid to Education, however, there is no psychological imperative that places
persons on one side or the other—if the issue is not stated in a
threatening manner which coincides with the "philosophy of depri-

---

41. He further remarks that while it is likely that many radical rightists are recruited from McClosky's extreme conservatives, "McClosky himself found that the correlations '. . . between
classical conservatism . . . and . . . party affiliation, attitude on
economic issues and liberal-conservative self-designation . . .
tend to be fairly low.'"

42. Anderson, Zelditch, Jr., Takagi, and Whiteside (1965).
The authors explicitly exempt from their study McClosky's dimension of "human nature conservatism"—that is, "assumptions about
the essential and inherent frailty of human nature" as they believe
that this dimension can refer also to liberals. They regret, however, not having included a fifth dimension—"aggressiveness in
foreign affairs."

<u>vation</u>." As Bunzel has noted, it is this "threat-orientation" which divides rightists from conservatives:

> the right-wing extremist has a longing for safety, definiteness, and authority. His 'island of safety' mentality, which fears the future and the unknown, seeks protection from the menace that seems to be present on all sides. His is basically a threat-orientation to life, which when translated into political terms leads him to object to democracy because it fails to maintain the strict order and dominance of authority he feels is necessary for the operation and survival of society. (1967, p. 84)

Levinson reports another study which concerns the relationship between authoritarianism and politically relevant behavior. Using as subjects two classes in education and one in social relations at Harvard in 1951, Levinson employed an "International-Nationalism Scale" which he had developed. Hypothesizing that nationalism is a part of general in-group thinking, he found that the IN Scale correlated .77 with the 16-item E-scale. (A 12 item F-scale correlated .60 with the IN Scale.) Levinson noted:

> Although nationalists glorify America as a symbol, they are inclined to regard most of the American population as an alien out-group. They are activated, it would seem, less by love of Americans and their heritage than by a sense of hostility and anxiety regarding other nations and "outsiders" generally. Internationalists, being under less compulsion either to glorify their own nation or to condemn others, show a more genuine attachment to their cultural traditions. (1957)

Levinson concluded, on the basis of this research and other work done with a "traditional family ideology scale" and a "religious conventionalism scale," that while one individual will "hold a nationalistic outlook" because of his anxieties to which it is "deeply gratifying,"

> Another individual holds a roughly similar outlook on the basis of a more superficial acceptance of what is "given" in his social environment; in this case, personality factors may play a relatively incidental role in the formation and maintenance of ideology.

He ends with a useful discussion of the relationship between personality and political ideology, subsumed under three factors:
(1) "receptivity" of the individual to only a limited selection of possible ideologies, (2) "immanence" of an individual's personality needs in his ideology, and (3) "relative consistency" of an individual's ideology, "not necessarily in a logical sense but in the sense that similar values, conflicts, and the like will be reflected throughout."

Also politically relevant is the research done by Canning and Baker (1959) which involved three autokinetic tests and differentiation based on a scale of religious authoritarianism,[43] in which authoritarian individuals were found to be highly susceptible to group pressures.[44] While all types experienced a change of judgment due to group pressure (the nonauthoritarian individuals changed more than double their mean scores—11.2 inches vs. 5.5 inches), "the mean scores of the authoritarian on the group test were more than five times greater than scores on the individual test (21.4 and 4.2 inches). . . ." This finding is consistent with our view of psychically deprived persons being "other-directed" due to their reliance on satisfactions emanating from other persons to alleviate their anxieties.[45] It is also related to Rokeach's finding that dogmatic individuals will make abrupt and radical changes in belief—if this change involves conformance with positive authority and does not violate their central beliefs (or, one may add, their psychic needs).

Finally, the authoritarian person has been found to be generally superstitious and to express belief in powerful and unseen forces which control his world. Such belief is seen as "a substitute for an underdeveloped self-reliance; and it is apparently this same feeling of helplessness, together with underlying destructive impulses, which leads the ethnocentric subject to agree more often than others with questionnaire statements which describe or predict doom and catastrophe, the spread of contagious diseases, and so forth" (Frenkel-Brunswik, 1952).[46] Thus authoritarian persons are predisposed to agree with the existence of a secret conspiracy, whether it be McCarthy's "treason in high places," the ideology expressed in The Protocols of the Elders of Zion or the "Establishment" ("power elite," "military-industrial complex") purposefully waging wars for profit and power while disallowing the necessity of alleviating pressing social ills.[47]

---

43. Reference is to a scale developed by Mark K. Allen and reported in "Personality and Cultural Factors Related to Religious Authoritarianism," unpublished Ph.D. dissertation, Stanford University, 1955.

44. Another study focusing on conformity and its relationship to authoritarianism is discussed in Crutchfield (1955).

45. In a study of a youth camp for minimum offenders, it was shown that the more authoritarian individuals (as measured by a form of the F-scale) were more cooperative and had more favorable opinions of the camp. It was noted, however, that the inmate subculture might not hold in a strict authoritarian maximum security prison, where cooperation is anathema (See Grusky, 1962).

46. Also see the discussion of tolerance and optimism in the section on self-actualization in chap. 2.

47. As Hofstadter (1965) notes, "The distinguishing thing about the paranoid style is not that its exponents see conspiracies

This discussion, fragmentary though it is, is suggestive of the breadth of uses of the Berkeley group's work in the study of political behavior. Perhaps because the F-scale measures only one type of dogmatism, perhaps because various measures for this authoritarianism have been employed, perhaps because these "right" authoritarians may be further differentiated on the basis of the individual's particular psychic deprivations—these reasons may explain the conflicts in results, where these exist.

It appears that authoritarians (as a general group) are likely to participate in sociopolitical activities only under certain conditions and that further, the quality and meaning of their participation will differ from that of nonauthoritarians. As is probably true with all men, authoritarians also appear to "vote their prejudices" (and thus likely to be somewhat flexible in party alignment over time)—although there is some indication that they also probably both use their votes to express rejection and hostility to the <u>status quo</u> and to abstain from voting. Furthermore, their personal behavior, their outlook on life and their political beliefs appear to be flavored by their perception of the world as threatening, and by their generalized intolerance. The conclusion which comes forcibly to our attention is that the F-scale, in spite of known faults, is a powerful measure of personality that, in many vital dimensions, is able to differentiate subjects in a way that is meaningful and <u>psychologically consistent</u>.

Fred Greenstein (who offers an incisive description of the authoritarian personality in German folklore as "the bicyclist's personality. . . . Above they bow, below they kick") presents a good summary of this personality type. His listing of the traits which have been attributed to <u>the</u> authoritarian personality again points to the fact that authoritarianism is not psychologically unidimensional. Greenstein speaks of

> the tendency of such individuals to <u>think</u> in power terms, to be acutely sensitive to questions of who dominates whom. [need for self-esteem] Only at a slightly further remove from politics is the pervasive rigidity in the authoritarian's manner of confronting the world. He is, in Else Frenkel-Brunswik's phrase, "intolerant of ambiguity." He likes order and is made uncomfortable by disorder; where the phenomena he is exposed to are complex and subtle, he imposes his own tight

or plots here and there in history, but that they regard a 'vast' or 'gigantic' conspiracy as <u>the motive force</u> in historical events. History <u>is</u> a conspiracy, set in motion by demonic forces of almost transcendent power, and what is felt to be needed to defeat it is not the usual methods of political give-and-take, but an all-out crusade. The paranoid spokesman sees the fate of this conspiracy in apocalyptic terms—he traffics in the birth and death of whole worlds, whole political orders, whole systems of human values."

categories upon them, ignoring their nuances. His thinking therefore makes more than the usual use of stereotypes. [need for safety and perhaps physiological satisfaction?] Another of the traits composing the character type is "conventionalism." The authoritarian . . . is described as being particularly sensitive to "external agencies" and, especially, to the prevailing standards of his own social group [need for affection, for self-esteem?] (1965)

Based on the discussion in the last chapter, it is hypothesized that the personality dimension of authoritarianism will be isomorphic with that of psychic deprivation (needs one through four), although it is also recognized that some intolerance is culturally conditioned and the F-scale alone may not be able to make this distinction. In testing this hypothesis in the research presented in chapter 4, fifteen items were employed.[48] These items were taken —in spirit and mostly in wording—from various items of the original F-scale. (A few of the items were made more current and specific—that is, into more intolerant statements.) No prediction is made as to the specific relationship between F-scale scores in general and these four groups. It is felt, however, that by studying F-scale scores in relation to the type of basic need motivating such persons, many ambiguous research reports (for example, regarding their SES and their degree of participation) will become clearer.

Manifest Anxiety: Janet Taylor

Anxiety . . . is a diffuse, irrational fear, not directed at an appropriate target and not controlled by self-insight. Like a grease spot, it has spread throughout the life and stains the individual's social relationships. (Allport, 1954, p. 346)

The role played by anxiety in the personalities of the psychically deprived has been frequently noted here. It is mentioned in chapter 2 as shaping the attitudes and behavior of various types of persons motivated by unfulfilled basic needs. Rokeach has stated that "dogmatism and anxiety are clearly shown to emerge together as part of a single psychological factor (1960, p. 349).[49] Not only has anxiety been discussed as generally associated with intolerance and authoritarianism; one type of anxiety—manifest anxiety—has also been shown, on at least two occasions (discussed above), to correlate with high F-scale scores.

---

48. See Appendix A.

49. Fillenbaum and Jackman (1961) also have found a relationship significant beyond the .01 level between dogmatism and anxiety. (However, they found no relation between generalized anxiety and performance on the Denny Doodlebug problem.)

Anxiety level is a particularly useful variable to assess in studying behavior. For anxiety presses for relief and this pressure can be seen as a potent factor in political behavior on the macrolevel, as well as within such more limited situations as the decision-making process. As Neumann has stated: "The external dangers which threaten a man meet the inner anxiety and are thus frequently experienced as even more dangerous than they really are" (1960, p. 273). At the same time, these same external dangers intensify the inner anxiety.[50] Thus extreme actions become "rational" responses to situational factors, because the latter are seen as extremely threatening.

In theory, anxiety has traditionally been particularly associated with middle-class persons because of the supposedly greater frustrations to which they are subjected during the childhood developmental period. It has thus often been assumed that in lower class children, raised in a more permissive environment, less anxiety will develop than in middle-class children. However, current research is suggesting that the particular deprivational experiences which are commonly associated with lower class membership, in addition to the frustration of being judged (and required to outwardly accept) middle class standards, lead to an inverse relationship between anxiety and SES (Sewell and Haller, 1959). Such a relationship, in terms of the model employed throughout this book, would suggest that lower class persons are relatively more psychically deprived.

Various measures of anxiety exist, which have been employed in questionnaire research. Rokeach used an index developed by Welsh, composed of four subscales from the Minnesota Multiphasic Personality Inventory (Hypochondriasis, Depression, Hysteria and Psychasthenia [Welsh, 1952]). In doing the research that culminated in his Political Ideology, Robert Lane employed a 24 item anxiety scale developed by S. B. Sarason and I. Janis and revised for that particular occasion by David Sears. This scale (made available by Dr. Lane), includes measures of both social and neurotic anxiety. As mentioned earlier, a 26-item social anxiety scale has also been developed by the Tavistock Clinic in London (Dixon, de Monchaux and Sandler, 1957), tested on 250 patients there and then factor analyzed. (The four factors which were isolated are social timidity, fear of loss of control, a fear of self-display and a fear of revealing inferiority.)

Perhaps the most widely applied scale in behavioral research is the Manifest Anxiety Scale developed by Janet Taylor. This scale consists of items which were taken from the Minnesota Multi-

---

50. Neumann goes on to state: "The painful tension which is evoked by the combination of inner anxiety and external danger can express itself in either of two forms: in depressive or in persecutory anxiety. The differentiation is important because it helps us to evaluate the political function of anxiety more correctly."

phasic Personality Inventory and then judged by clinicians as expressive of manifest anxiety. The scale was developed "as a device for selecting subjects for experiments in human motivation." The items in the original scale have been subjected to several revisions in efforts to shorten their number and simplify their wording.

There have been some criticisms that the Manifest Anxiety Scale is negatively correlated with intelligence. However, after a careful analysis of these studies by others, in addition to performing a replication of their own, Mayzner, Sersen and Tresselt (1955) came to the conclusion that if a negative correlation is found between intelligence and manifest anxiety, it is because of the degree of threat present in the testing situation; thus, in attempting to measure for anxiety, the degree of threat must be carefully controlled. (A careful review of the literature brought Sarason [1960] to a similar conclusion.)

Sarason, after a detailed review of the literature relating to studies of anxiety, offers some general conclusions. In general, the difference between high and low scorers is the fact that ". . . high anxious Ss have been found to be more self-deprecatory, more self-preoccupied, and generally less content with themselves than Ss lower in the distribution of anxiety scores. . . ." These differences are most likely to be seen in the subject's ability to cope with various situations; thus, differences in behavior and attitude may only appear in stress situations. In other words, subjects can be differentiated "in the response tendencies activated by personally threatening conditions. Whereas low scoring Ss may react to such conditions with increased effort and attention to the task at hand, high scoring Ss respond to threat with self-oriented, personalized responses." In conditions requiring an automatic response, those high in anxiety do better; in more complex situations, the situation is reversed.

We have noted in the preceding section that in studies by Siegel (1954) and Davids (1955c), a significant relationship was found between F-scale scores and scores on the Taylor Manifest Anxiety Scale.[51] Sarason comments:

> If scales of anxiety, or at least the Manifest Anxiety Scale, are measuring a variable related to obsessive-compulsive tendencies, then the positive correlations reported by some investigators between the Manifest Anxiety Scale and measures of authoritarianism perhaps might be explained in terms of the dogmatism and rigidity often observed in neurotic obsessive-compulsive personalities. (1960)

---

51. Davids also notes that the Taylor scale has been shown to be "highly related to several other measures of personality, such as the psychasthenia scale from the MMPI, The Winne Scale of Neuroticism, and the Psychosomatic Inventory" (1955c, p. 417).

It is possible that both the Manifest Anxiety Scale and the F-scale are measuring the way in which psychically deprived individuals cope with deep-seated personality needs—that is, both by a rigid, power-oriented structuring of the world into in-groups and out-groups and by symptoms of manifest anxiety (excessive worrying plus somatic strain).

In our previous discussion of political activity, a constant theme has been the crippling effects of anxiety. It has been suggested that each of the psychically deprived groups will, for different reasons, have anxieties which will interfere with the way in which they handle the problems which the world presents to them —that will color their interpersonal relations. Erik Erikson states as his first clinical postulate:

> That there is no anxiety without somatic tension seems immediately obvious; but we must also learn that there is no individual anxiety which does not reflect a latent concern common to the immediate and extended group. An individual feels isolated and barred from the sources of collective strength when he (even though only secretly) takes on a role considered especially evil, be it that of a drunkard or a killer, a sissy or a sucker, or whatever colloquial designation of inferiority may be used in his group. (1963, p. 35)

While Lasswell (1959) postulates the nonexistence of "anxiety-free personalities" in modern society, it has been frequently demonstrated that individuals do differ in the amount of their latent and their manifest anxiety. Because anxiety has been shown to be crippling in many ways, it is important to include this variable in our study of the political dimensions of personality. Because our concern is to relate our results to the main trends in behavioral research, the means of testing this hypothesis were the frequently used 28-item Taylor Manifest Anxiety Scale. Explicitly, the hypothesis to be tested is that there will be a direct and significant relationship between anxiety and psychic deprivation, as discussed by Maslow, and an inverse relationship between anxiety and self-actualization. Because anxiety is theoretically associated with each type of unfulfilled basic need, no prediction is made about the specific relationship between anxiety and need levels one through four.

Intolerance of Ambiguity: Else Frenkel-Brunswik and Stanley Budner

Like anxiety, intolerance of ambiguity is another thread which has run through all facets of our previous discussion of psychic deprivation. It is hypothesized to be a manifestation of some types of anxiety; it is seen in the dogmatic person's need to impose a rigid cognitive structure on his world; it has frequently been mentioned as a correlate of authoritarianism.

In addition, I would suggest that intolerance of ambiguity is

likely to be the most expressive or symptomatic form of the need
for safety or security. Intolerance of ambiguity is described as
"the tendency to perceive (that is, interpret) ambiguous situations
as sources of threat"; thus, a desire to structure one's world will
influence most areas of a deprived person's life. Tolerance of ambiguity, on the other hand, is "the tendency to perceive ambiguous
situations as desirable" (Budner, 1962)—as challenging, as stimulating, as interesting, as opportunities. It has been frequently noted
by Maslow to be a corollary of self-actualization. Indeed, Maslow
has stated categorically that creativeness is correlated with the
ability to withstand lack of structure, lack of future, lack of predictability, lack of control, tolerance of ambiguity, and planless-
ness (1965, pp. 184-88).

In discussing ambiguity, Budner states:

> An ambiguous situation may be defined as one which cannot be
> adequately structured or categorized by the individual because
> of the lack of sufficient cues. It is possible to identify three
> such situations: a completely new situation in which there are
> no familiar cues; a complex situation in which there are a
> great number of cues to be taken into account; and a contra-
> dictory situation in which different elements or cues suggest
> different structures—in short, situations characterized by
> novelty, complexity, or insolubility. (1962, p. 30)

From this description, we can see that intolerance of ambiguity is
an important variable to include within our study because of the
similarities between an ambiguous situation and the essence of politics.[52]

In a most interesting project conducted by Brim and Hoff
(1957), it was shown that the intolerance of ambiguity or "the desire to structure the universe" is a consistent personality trait.
The authors felt that this trait is also expressed by a response set
of giving extreme answers. They report two studies designed to
test this hypothesis. In one study, different groups of college students were given a "desire for certainty test," which asked them
to rate thirty-two statements according to the probability that many
or few would agree (for example, "The chances that an American
citizen will believe in God are about ____ in 100"). The students
were also asked to mark, from one to five, how sure they were of
their answers. (In this part of the study, scores were obtained by
multiplying the percentage given in each answer by its associated

52. Budner makes the following distinction between rigidity
and intolerance of ambiguity: "Briefly, intolerance of ambiguity
may be conceived of as a content characteristic of the individual,
as a tendency to evaluate particular phenomena in a particular
way; rigidity, as a formal characteristic of the individual, as a
tendency to manifest certain modes of response irrespective of
the phenomena being dealt with" (pp. 30-31). I would consider both
to be "formal" characteristics.

[one to five] certainty value.) In addition, extreme response set measures were taken both on single items and also by extreme position answers on various scales for four different groups. A consistent relationship (at a significance level of .01) was found between extreme response position and the subjects' scores on the certainty test for three of the groups. A relationship (significant between the .10 and .05 levels) was found between extreme scorers (high and low) on the F-scale and the desire for certainty was obtained for the fourth group. In the second experiment, the desire for certainty was measured after a lot, a little and no induced stress. It was found that the desire for certainty was increased by stress. Thus the trends for both groups of studies suggest that the desire for certainty is a consistent personality trait.

In regard to intolerance of ambiguity, it is of interest to note the suggestive relationships found by Davies in his study of the role of charisma in the 1952 election. Of a sample (n = 1799) taken by the Survey Research Center, only thirty-two cases were found "in which three judges agreed unanimously that charisma was predominant in the candidate perception." These thirty-two showed an "intolerance of ambiguity of action" in their concern that action (particularly strong action) be taken in Korea. They also showed "intolerance for ambiguity of perception," as they were highly likely to see parties and candidates in black and white terms. Finally, they were significantly more likely to report that it made a difference who won—but this was not reflected in a significant increase in their voting rate (Davies, 1954).

Although intolerance of ambiguity appears to be a stable personality characteristic, its relationship to other personality measures is not presently clear. For example, in our discussion of authoritarianism (above), it was noted that on two occasions no significant relationship was found between intolerance of ambiguity and F-scale scores. Siegel (1954) employed an original test which asked the subjects to match pictures of people with statements. The score of the individual was the number of statements he attributed to persons in the pictures. Only by using a contingency coefficient was a significant (p = .001) relationship to the E- and F-scales found. (This means of testing significance was used because "the data did not meet the prerequisite assumptions for the more conventional measures of association.") Again, Davids (1955c) also found an insignificant relationship between F-scale scores and a visual and auditory intolerance of ambiguity test.

An interesting experiment suggests, however, that intolerance of ambiguity is related to authoritarianism and that factors in the preceding experiments may have been the reason why lack of significant results were obtained. Seeing the "need to structure" and the "tendency toward closure" as "a coping reaction to the tensions underlying intolerance of ambiguity," Jeanne and Jack Block (1951) reasoned that "the rapidity with which an ambiguous situation is structured represents an operational manifestation of 'intolerance

of ambiguity.'" To test this hypothesis, they employed Sherif's experiment with a point of light, utilizing the autokinetic phenomenon
of apparent light point movement in a darkened room. The subjects
(sixty-five males enrolled in an elementary psychology course)
were asked in 100 trials (in forty-five minutes) to push a button
the moment they saw the light move (which shut the light off) and
then to note the length of movement. The subjects were also rated
on ethnocentrism, based on their scores on the Berkeley E-scale.

Independent raters then assessed the subjects' records and
tried to establish the trial at which each subject had established a
norm or frame of reference. It was noted that many subjects never
established such a norm for the degree of light movement; finally,
the subjects were simply divided on the basis of whether or not
they were able, in an ambiguous situation, to establish a frame of
reference. A significant relationship (at the .02 level) was found
between the establishment of a norm and authoritarianism.

The authors theorized, in making this experiment, that both
intolerance of ambiguity and ethnocentrism are "subordinate manifestations" of a more central personality dimension which writers
have labeled "ego-control." In line with the literature on ego-control, the Blocks classified their subjects as over-, appropriate-
and under-controllers. Over-controllers "bind their tensions ex-
cessively. Their various needs tend toward indirect means of expression." Under-controllers "do not bind their tensions sufficiently." Their various needs tend toward relatively direct and un-
modulated expression. Appropriate-controllers, on the other hand,
evidence a healthy control of their tensions and the means of their
expression. The subjects in this experiment had previously been
placed in one of these groups on the basis of their ego-control. It
was found that over-controllers were highest in E-scale scores,
followed (surprisingly) by appropriate- and then under-controllers.
(These relationships were significant at between a .05 and a .01
level.) For norm establishment, again over-controllers were most
likely to have established a frame of reference, followed by appropriate-controllers, while the under-controllers were least likely
to have established a norm (at similar significance levels).[53]

Because of these suggestive relationships between intolerance
of ambiguity and various indicators of psychic deprivation, it is
theoretically important to include this variable in the research design of the present study. After a survey of the literature, it was

---

53. Note the discussion in chap. 2 (section on generalized
deprivation) regarding control. From the comments made there it
would appear that the results would most likely show over-controllers and under-controllers as ethnocentric and intolerant of
ambiguity, with appropriate-controllers likely to be low in both
dimensions. It is possible that the under-controllers are lowest
on the E-scale because of an inability which showed up in the autokinetic experiment—the inability to set a norm.

felt that a scale devised by Budner offered a useful instrument for this purpose. The scale is composed of sixteen items, each of which taps at least one of the three ambiguous situations described by Budner, plus at least one of the four indicators of perceived threat which he theorized to be response modes to ambiguity.[54] The scale is composed of an equal number of positively and negatively worded items. Through testing on seventeen groups (mostly students), it was determined that the scale is relatively free of "both acquiescent and social desirability response tendencies."

Budner has found a consistently positive relationship between the intolerance of ambiguity scale which he devised and the F-scale (the version developed by Christie in 1958).[55] While the relationship between authoritarianism and intolerance of ambiguity was significant and consistent, analysis also showed that "these are two complex, overlapping constructs rather than different manifestations of the same one."[56]

Thus, in the following research, Budner's scale is included. Specifically, it is hypothesized that while intolerance of ambiguity will be generally associated with authoritarian tendencies and related to psychic deprivation, the desire to structure a threatening world will show a particularly strong relationship to the need for safety and security.

The Security-Insecurity Inventory: Abraham Maslow

Running through our discussion of all types of psychic deprivation is the theme of insecurity in a threatening world—a world which lacks the means of gratification or safety. In addition, we have been particularly concerned with Maslow's hierarchy of basic needs, which posits the existence of a need for security and safety which is second in importance only to man's physiological needs.

In 1952, Maslow published a standardized Security-Insecurity Inventory, which has a respected place in psychological testing. Its purpose is to provide a general measure of insecurity ("<u>Only</u>

---

54. Budner lists four types of response: "Phenomenological [having to do with 'individual perceptions and feelings'], denial (repression and denial), phenomenological submission (anxiety and discomfort), operative denial (destructive or reconstructive behavior) or operative submission (avoidance behavior). . . ."

55. Also, as expected, he found a negative relationship usually held between the intolerance of ambiguity scale and Christie's Mach Scale.

56. In the field study presented in chap. 4, there is a Spearman correlation of .38 between these two factors (significant at > .001).

those symptoms of insecurity which are characteristic of most or
all insecure people"), for available tests only registered particular types of insecurity (Maslow, Hirsh, Stein and Honigmann, 1945).
Maslow has listed fourteen factors which make up the syndrome of
insecurity, with the first three considered prior or causal and the
other eleven effects or consequent factors "even though they have
equal priority and 'causal' efficacy in the cross-sectional, contemporaneous, dynamic analysis of the personality." The three
prior factors are listed as:

Insecurity	Security
1. Feeling of rejection or being unloved, of being treated coldly and without affection, or of being hated, of being despised.	1. Feeling of being liked or loved, of being accepted, of being looked upon with warmth.
2. Feelings of isolation, ostracism, aloneness, or being out of it; feelings of "uniqueness."	2. Feelings of belonging, of being at home in the world, of having a place in the group.
3. Constant feelings of threat and danger; anxiety.	3. Feelings of safety; rare feelings of threat and danger, unanxious.

As is immediately apparent from these factors, the Security-
Insecurity Inventory is concerned with more than just a need for
security and safety; it is equally concerned with a need for belonging, for being loved—by definition, with Maslow's needs two and
three. The first aspect above also is concerned with acceptance,
and hence, it appears to relate to the dimension of esteem, although Maslow (1942c) has stated that questions that correlated
with self-esteem were removed from the test. Impressionistically,
then, it seems that the Security-Insecurity Inventory is a measure
of generalized psychic deprivation—specifically, of the needs for
safety, affection and self-esteem. In other words, what Maslow described as a "security syndrome" in 1952, he refined in later years
into separate need levels.

The construction of this inventory is discussed in detail in the
manual which accompanies it, as well as elsewhere. The total inventory includes seventy-five items. However, these seventy-five
items are divided into three groups of twenty-five each "thus making three equivalent and interchangeable forms of the test." Each
subtest is designed to measure the same factors as the total inventory. While, as with most tests, the reliability is higher when it is
given in its entirety, Maslow reports that each of the subtests "correlates with the total score over .90 and each may, therefore, be
considered to be a valid test of security."

Maslow notes that the validity of this Inventory is subject to the same limitations as other pencil and paper tests. However, scores on this test have been shown to be such useful guides to personality needs that Maslow reports, in connection with college students: "We have found it valid to treat any individual scoring low in S-I as if he were asking for psychotherapy, no matter what overt statement he may make."

In the research reported in chapter 4, the first twenty-five questions of Maslow's Security-Insecurity Inventory were employed to measure generalized security-insecurity.[57] It is hypothesized that high scores will be associated with each of the four levels of psychic deprivation. No prediction is made as to the specific relationships to each of the four need levels.

Anomia: Leo Srole

In recent years, a good deal of behavioral research has included an interest in anomie—a state of normlessness in society, characterized variously by the breakdown of social cohesion, the use of unapproved means to attain socially desirable goals or the meaninglessness of social regulations governing behavior, conflict between belief systems or the disintegration of belief systems. Traditionally, writers have been concerned with anomie as an objective, sociological reality—and have dealt with questions involving its socially structured causes, the relative amount of anomie present in a given society at a particular time, social groups in which it is likely to be found, and its relation to sociological problems such as various forms of deviancy. In doing so, they follow the approach first defined by Durkheim. However, because of the difficulty of measuring anomie directly, sociologists have been forced to employ measures of individual behavior, though such acts as anomic suicide and withdrawal from social pursuits because of perceived meaninglessness may occur in a non-anomic society and, on the other hand, an anomic society may contain many persons who do not display anomic patterns of behavior.[58]

Much current research, in addition—recognizing the differential existence of anomie in any given social group—has studied anomie from the viewpoint of the individual: as a subjective, psychological condition marked by disaffection of the individual from his social environment. To indicate the difference in emphasis, if not in kind, Leo Srole has referred to this later phenomenon as "anomia" to distinguish it from the social state of "anomie." This later condition is also sometimes referred to as "alienation," a psychological and social state which, it is maintained by some

---

57. Permission for the use of this Inventory was granted by Dr. John D. Black of the Consulting Psychologists Press, Inc.

58. For an excellent discussion of the whole area of anomie, see Yinger (1964).

writers, represents a separate dimension from either "anomia" or "anomie." (Although many writers use anomia and alienation interchangeably, a separate section is included at the end of this discussion of anomia in order to explore the distinction between the two concepts. However, it is felt in the deepest sense that anomia is alienation—though the opposite is not always true.)

According to Robert K. Merton (1949, 1964), the sociological concept of anomie clearly refers to objective conditions: "Anomie refers to a property of a social system, not to the state of mind of this or that individual within the system. It refers to a breakdown of social standards governing behavior and so also signifies little social cohesion" (1964, p. 226). Anomie, it is hypothesized by Merton, comes about in the United States because upward mobility is considered an almost absolute value, but—because of differential access to the opportunity structure—"appreciable numbers of people become estranged from a society that promises them in principle what they are denied in reality. And this withdrawal of allegiance from one or another part of prevailing social standards is what we mean, in the end, by anomie" (p. 218).[59]

To de Grazia and Merton, such anomie as this stems not from a lack of rules, but rather, from conflict between the directives of two belief systems. De Grazia notes that one belief system—which represents the religio-political dimension—is based on familial inclusiveness, equality and solidarity. The other type of belief system is economic, representative of modern capitalism. With its stress on competition, its directives conflict with those of the co-operative religio-political value system. This—in de Grazia's terminology—is "simple anomie" and its symptom is "the need for belongingness" or affection which modern life does not satisfy (de Grazia, 1948, pp. 72, 107). Acute anomie is then defined as the disintegration of the community of beliefs, due to the inability or indifference of the rulers. Its typical symptom is "anxiety accompanied by the image of a menacing world."[60] In other words, anomie arises not simply because some people have no access to opportunities for social mobility (this probably has always been so), but because of (1) the conflict in value systems and/or (2) the perceived indifference of the rulers.

Anomie—the condition of denying legitimacy to and failure to be guided by official standards, rules and mores—may affect, ac-

---

59. As Seeman's work shows (see chap. 2, section on esteem), blocked mobility among those concerned with status is most likely to cause individuals to feel alienated from their fellowman.

60. His discussion, in Gaetano Mosca's terms, of the difficulties which arise when the ruler and the ruled belong to two different environments offers some fascinating parallels to modern American ghetto problems. (See p. 74; also the section on Political Estrangement, beginning on p. 115.)

cording to Merton (1964), either psychically competent or psychically deprived people. Further, while anomie is dysfunctional for a particular society, the questioning of the legitimacy of social rules may also be a means to progress.[61]

> In the history of every society, one supposes, some of its culture heroes eventually come to be regarded as heroic in part because they are held to have had the courage and the vision to challenge the beliefs and routines of their society. The rebel, revolutionary, nonconformist, heretic or renegade of an earlier day is often the culture hero of today. Moreover, the accumulation of dysfunctions in a social system is often the prelude to concerted social change that may bring the system closer to the values that enjoy the respect of members of the society. (Merton in Clinard, 1964, p. 20)

In other words, anomie does not necessarily have moral or psychic connotations.

What Merton is really talking about is a theory of social deviance largely unrelated to the dimension of mental health, a theory which could, perhaps, be most easily explained in Marxian terms: when the legal and cultural norms (superstructure) no longer reflect the social groups' desires (base), when behavioral expectations are not clear, it is a condition of anomie. Perhaps social control (the use of the authority and power adhering to the superstructure) will bring the society back into line with the superstructure; or, perhaps questioning and deviant individuals will act as the antithesis through which a new synthesis is possible. Certainly, it is often an accurate description of social conditions to explain the disjunction between official norms and actual behavior in such a way; it is also possible to empirically test such a proposition. That is, it is possible to measure whether official norms of behavior (as taught in schools and churches, as pronounced by government officials, etc.) are (a) agreed with verbally and (b) conformed to behaviorally. Whether or not they are believed in does not alone, however, constitute an objective, social condition—though such beliefs have considerable social relevance. Neither the existence of anomia nor faulty socialization (as tested by learned norms) can be equated with anomie—a disintegration of the social structure.

In view of the great importance in behavioral literature of the concept of anomie-anomia as a means of assessing the possibilities of both social integration and political stability, it behooves us to question what light personality measures can throw on the subject as well as what inferences can reasonably be made from anomia to anomie or vice versa. If, for example, there is a conflict

---

61. Yinger (1964) also points out the necessity of distinguishing between "anomic value disagreements"—that is, those that "disrupt the workings of the society" and "pluralistic value disagreements."

between the economic and community belief systems, is this conflict differentially perceived? According to Merton, the answer is
affirmative—those groups whose upward striving is unsuccessful
will be those whose social bonds will weaken. Merton also mentions that personality factors are likely to enter in. Is it possible
that those who feel the competitive nature of the economy destroy-
ing the cooperative social framework will be those, <u>throughout the</u>
<u>social structure</u>, whose personality needs lead them to perceive
the world as hostile and unmanageable, persons who—in Maslow's
view—are psychically deprived? Further, will some individuals
feel powerless and normless although they are, in fact, socially
powerful members of the norm-setting and norm-enforcing establishment?

　　To ask another question: even if the disjunction or disintegration of values (as occurred in Weimar, Germany) is equally perceived, will not personality shape individual response? De Grazia
(1948), for example, discusses several factors which determine
what an individual's adjustment to anomie will be. A major factor
is the "incidence of anomie, simple or acute, in the community."
"Once the perception that many others are in the same miserable
state occurs, a greater inclination appears toward attempting adjustments in concert" (pp. 131-32). But does not the desire to attempt "adjustments" also depend upon the individual's view of
whether or not the sociopolitical world <u>is adjustable</u>—that is, responsive to individual or group action? Further, if action is keyed
to <u>the perception</u> of widespread, deteriorating socioeconomic conditions, does not personality—as well as objective conditions—determine the manner in which conditions are perceived? To be specific, given a broad similarity of cultural values and deteriorating
social, economic and political conditions from which few if any
were immune, what caused some non-Jewish individuals in Weiman,
Germany to be responsive to Hitler's appeal early, some late, and
some not at all? When one is concerned with <u>behavior or percep-</u>
<u>tion</u>, personality predispositions are again variables which must be
considered.

　　Finally, it appears essential to attempt to separate persons
who deny legitimacy to and fail to be guided by official standards,
rules and mores from persons who feel strong ties to the dominant
belief system—a system which is viable for them—and who <u>never-</u>
<u>theless</u> feel personal despair about their own life chances. In other
words, it appears possible to separate individual-to-society alienation (as discussed above) from alienation of an individual-to-him-
self. It is possible that a person can perceive his social world as
meaningful and purposeful in general—but feel that his own life
lacks meaning. In sum, <u>it is necessary to distinguish anomia from</u>
<u>anomie and to consider separately the sociopolitical importance of</u>
<u>each</u>.

　　It is possible, at least theoretically, that persons who despair
about the responsiveness, manipulability and orderliness of their

world would nevertheless agree on sociocultural values and give them at least passive support until a weakened social structure gave these persons an opportunity to act out their hostilities and anxieties. A study of delinquency illustrates how this might occur. Two areas within the city of Cambridge, Massachusetts were chosen for study. Both were similar in SES, but differed sharply in their delinquency rate. The authors (Maccoby, Johnson and Church, 1958) found, as expected, that the social structure was comparatively weak in the area of high delinquency and the residents were less homogeneous socially. Yet—nullifying one of the research hypotheses—the authors also found that when the residents of both areas were questioned about seven different kinds of deviant activity, their ratings bore a striking similarity in what they considered to be serious acts—as to what, in other words, social values were for them.[62]

Hypothetically, it is possible that the distribution of personality types (the number of psychically deprived) and the degree of socialization in the two areas generally approximated each other. Where the social structure was weakly knit, however, those persons with aggressions, anxieties, and a view of the world as hostile and threatening had the social opportunity to act out their aggressions, and a high rate of deviancy resulted. Thus psychic predispositions would be as relevant in predicting behavior as the strength of social ties and the precipitating field situation and become a necessary part of an interactional model—a thesis to which we will return. Hence a preoccupation with norm agreement as indicative of social stability is by itself likely to be of little predictive value.

Because of the proclivity of sociologists to consider anomic persons as indicative of the state of a society, one additional point can be made. In a thoughtful analysis of the concepts of anomie and alienation, John Horton states:

> Of course, neither Marx nor Durkheim would have tested their cases by measuring attitudes. One can be falsely conscious (not conscious of de facto alienation). There are also Freudians, religionists, and hip existentialists who see egoism and anarchy as the human condition (accepting of anomie).[63] (1964, p. 293)

---

62. Similarly, in a survey of high school students in areas which differed greatly in SES, Sherif and Sherif (1964, pp. 200-201) found no difference in the expressed value of education and "high school students in different neighborhoods did not differ markedly in knowledge of the limits of acceptable behavior and the points at which deviation is subject to sanctions by adult authorities."

63. For example, in relation to our previous discussion of the likelihood that psychically deprived individuals would be susceptible to extremist mass movements, it is of interest to note the con-

One must be aware that in measuring feelings, one is measuring predispositions—not actual behavior—and predispositions of various social groups are probably not equally likely to affect social conditions. As McClosky and Schaar state:

> the leap from the subjective feelings expressed by individuals to statements about objective social conditions is a perilous one. What people believe about a society may or may not be an accurate reflection of its nature: perceptions and feelings are never a literal copy of what is "out there" but are always powerfully shaped by the needs, motives, attitudes, and abilities of the observer. Hence, we can never confidently assume that because some people feel anomic the society is anomic. (1965, pp. 18-19)

This most definitely does not mean that the existence of anomic individuals is not of actual and potential sociopolitical import. It does mean, however, that it is very possible to have a sick society and healthy individuals who are disaffected (a point frequently made by Fromm and Maslow). It is also possible, however, to have a generally healthy society and psychically deprived persons who despair whether life has any meaning—in spite of objective opportunities to satiate objective needs.

Whether or not our social structure is characterized by anomie is—for all its political relevance—beyond the scope of this book. Whether its members can be characterized as exhibiting anomia and the meaning this has for our political and social structure, however, bears directly on our concerns here. The measurement and isolation of anomia offers a fruitful avenue for those concerned with the propensity for social (and hence, political) change and stability, given specific social conditions. Here we are concerned, not only with what people do today but with what they may do tomorrow—and thus place major emphasis on the interpretations which they put on the world around them. Especially because the political condition in a democracy is more fluid than the social structure (as individuals are frequently given opportunities to vote sweeping changes in the light of specific issues), anomia is an important variable for research in political psychology. (As has been previously stated, however, role expectations and position in the social structure may keep an individual's behavior from reflecting the anomia which he feels.)

The impetus for the current research interest on anomia in the study of behavior has been due to the work of Leo Srole. Srole's work is based on an initial 1950 study (401 randomly picked

nection which de Grazia sees between acute anomia and the rise and maintenance of Nazi power: "The most persuasive argument that could be made to keep them [the German people] in line took the form of a question: 'Would you rather go back to the chaotic days?' The terrible end was chosen instead" (1948, p. 182).

transit riders in Springfield, Massachusetts) and a replication included in the New York City Midtown study in 1952. Srole's thesis is that people can be fitted along a "eunomia-anomia" continuum based on MacIver's definition of anomie as "the breakdown of the individual's sense of attachment to society."[64] Specifically, Srole is concerned with testing the hypothesis that anomia—a personal state of "social malintegration"—is positively related to prejudice.

Srole has suggested five dimensions to anomia.

1. the individual's sense that community leaders are detached from and indifferent to his needs, reflecting severance of the interdependent bond within the social system between leaders and those they should represent and serve.

2. the individual's perception of the social order as essentially fickle and unpredictable, i.e., orderless, inducing the sense that under such conditions he can accomplish little toward realizing future life goals.

3. the individual's view, beyond abdication of future life goals, that he and people like him are retrogressing from the goals they have already reached.

4. the deflection or loss of internalized social norms and values, reflected in extreme form in the individual's sense of the meaninglessness of life itself.

5. the individual's perception that his framework of immediate personal relationships, the very rock of his social existence, was no longer predictive or supportive. . . .[65] (1956, pp. 712-13)

It is apparent from a reading of these items that what Srole is measuring (with the possible exception of the first dimension) is not directly related to social structure, but rather is expressive of a personalized view of the world—a view which very closely approximates that of our psychically deprived group.

Five items, each based on one of the above factors, were

---

64. Reference is to R. M. MacIver, The Ramparts We Guard (New York: The MacMillan Company, 1950), pp. 84-92.

65. In his study of the survivors of the Hiroshima A-bomb, Lifton (1967, pp. 503-5) discusses a syndrome found also in concentration camp survivors, which is reminiscent of anomic individuals. This syndrome includes both psychic and somatic symptoms (particularly associated with neurasthenia). Lifton sums up the syndrome as "a pervasive tendency toward sluggish despair— a more or less permanent form of psychic numbing which includes diminished vitality, chronic depression, and constricted life space, and which covers over the rage and mistrust that are just beneath the surface."

drawn up to test Srole's hypothesis. Analysis showed that these items were unidimensional and, in the New York City study, that they satisfied the requirements of a Guttman-type scale.[66]

In the Springfield study, Srole found a correlation of + .45 between his anomia scale and a shortened 5-item F-scale. Based on analysis of his data, Srole came to two conclusions: (1) Using education to indicate status, Srole found that social status was only slightly related to prejudice toward minority groups, a little more to authoritarian tendencies and "to a moderate degree," social status was related to anomia;[67] (2) anomia was related to prejudice "independently of the personality trends measured by the authoritarianism scale." However, F-scale scores are not closely related to prejudice "independently of the anomia factor."

> With the F factor partialled out, the correlation between A [anomia] and M [prejudice] remains more or less intact in all three strata. On the other hand, with A controlled, the correlation between F and M in the Low stratum is nearly extinguished; in the Middle and High strata the correlation is considerably reduced, but F retains value as a secondary factor contributing independently to M.

Had Srole isolated a powerful new variable with which to measure predispositions to prejudice? Was, in other words, anomia primarily responsible for the low status authoritarian's rejection of outgroups and secondarily responsible for the ethnic hostilities of the middle and high status authoritarian?

Roberts and Rokeach (1956) attempted to replicate Srole's study, using a probability sample (n = 86) of Lansing, Michigan. In addition to employing the Srole Anomie Scale, the 5-item F-scale and the 10-item Ethnocentrism scale, age, education and income were recorded. Agreeing with Srole's results, they found that authoritarianism and anomie were "about equally related to ethnocentrism." Contrary to Srole's findings, however, Roberts and Rokeach found that when anomie was held constant, the correlation between authoritarianism and ethnocentrism dropped only from .64 to .53, while—with authoritarianism held constant—the correlation between anomie and ethnocentrism dropped from .55 to .37 at the .01 level of significance. Further, while Srole found that anomia was related to status, Roberts and Rokeach—by using income and holding education constant—found that anomia correlated only

---

66. Srole's scale can be found in Appendix A, below.

67. Srole's findings to date indicate that anomia is connected to mental health, however, only if the disturbance is severe. See McClosky and Schaar (1965, p. 18); also see Srole's "Interdisciplinary Conceptualization and Research in Social Psychiatry," unpublished paper read before the American Sociological Society, Detroit, 1956.

- .22 with income. With income held constant, the correlation between anomia and prejudice dropped only from .55 to .51.[68]

Roberts and Rokeach thus came to two conclusions, based on their replication of Srole's study. First, status "whether measured by income or education or both" has no direct relationship to anomie, authoritarianism or prejudice. Second, while anomia is an important new variable in the study of prejudice, it is not as important as authoritarianism. "In particular, our findings do not support Srole's conclusion that the correlation between authoritarianism and ethnocentrism is spurious, being accounted for by the high relationship between authoritarianism and anomie, which, in turn, is significantly and independently related to prejudice."

In an analysis of both of these studies, McDill (1960) carried out a second replication of Srole's original work in Nashville in 1957, using a sample of 266 white, non-Jews, randomly drawn from three census tracts, each of which represented a different social stratum. McDill employed the Srole Anomia Scale, the 5-item F-scale and 7 of the 10 items of the E-scale. As in the Rokeach and Roberts study, controlling for status had no considerable effect on the correlations.[69]

McDill attained a similar correlation between anomia and prejudice and also between authoritarianism and prejudice. In controlling first anomia and then authoritarianism, McDill found—contrary to both earlier studies—that both correlations dropped by the same amount. He concludes that "there is a common dimension underlying these three attitude areas which accounts for the almost identical correlations among them."

In order to study this further, McDill carried out a factor analysis. He found a strong general factor with all anomia and authoritarian items and six of seven prejudice items having their highest loadings on this factor. The factor is called a "negative Weltanschauung" and is explained as a view "of being mastered by threatening forces beyond one's personal control" (which fits closely with de Grazia's theory of acute anomie and with our earlier discussion—in Maslow's terminology—of psychic deprivation). McDill comments that the high loadings on the F-scale items suggest the way in which this threat is met—that is, by a rigid structuring of the world power dimensions of ingroups and outgroups.

---

68. Milbrath (1965), after a survey of the literature, had surmised that anomie appears to be highly correlated with lack of education.

69. The results of these studies are a direct refutation to the acerbic comments of Gordon Rose that—not only is Srole's scale merely an artifact of class differences, but that "It is difficult to believe that five agree-disagree statements are likely to describe anything but the vaguest of feelings." (This in 1966!) See Gordon Rose (1966).

"Finally, the high negative loading of education on this factor indicates a definite relationship between the sociocultural environment to which one has been exposed and one's general social perspective." In essence then, both replications raise doubts "about the validity of Srole's conclusion that although both the authoritarianism and anomie scales are unidimensional, they nevertheless measure two discrete latent continua."[70]

Still, however, the relationships between anomia, authoritarianism and prejudice are not clear. In a study based on a random sample (a mailed questionnaire plus an interview follow-up of nonrespondents) of a Teamster's Union in Minneapolis, Rose (1966) found results similar to those of Srole's original study. In fact, he found a correlation between prejudice and anomia that was <u>higher</u> than that between prejudice and each one of the nine subscales of authoritarianism taken from the Berkeley study (a total of forty-six authoritarian items).

In a second study, Rose selected a random sample (n = 251) of two lower class communities in Rome, Italy. (No measure of prejudice was included.) On Srole's anomia scale, Rose found that the Italians were highly anomic. In discussing the finding that Italians are more likely to feel there is no use writing public officials, Rose states:

> if this is true, then Italy is factually a more anomic society than the American one, as the citizen's relationships to public officials is an important part of the social situation which defines anomie. In other words, since anomie refers to a social situation, questionnaire items which refer to important and relevant aspects of that social situation are likely to be adequate measures of anomie.

Here we can see other pitfalls of making socially relevant inferences from the existence of highly anomic individuals—this case of circular reasoning illustrating the impossibility of employing anomia in assessing social integration without the definition of an absolute set of social values from which people may fall.[71] If there is no such universal standard, then what is anomic in one society—whether it be writing to public officials or seeking suc-

---

70. Rhodes (1961), after using the anomia and F-scales in a sample of 1,027 high school seniors, found "a definite but imperfect relationship" between these two scales (with SES, Protestant fundamentalism and the subject's organizational participation controlled). He concludes that the relationship between the two scales "is not due to a low general correlation among all items of both scales; rather it is due to high correlations among specific items which are similar in wording or to F-scale items which measure submissiveness."

71. A point which has been made by Horton (1964).

cess and upward mobility—will not be a sign of defection from social health in a society which does not emphasize these particular
cultural values.

An attempt to summarize anomia findings was made by Meier
and Bell (1959). In pointing out that anomia scores are highest in
groups isolated from the mainstream of social life, they suggest
that the "degree of anomia is dependent . . . on the importance to
the individual of the life goal being blocked, the degree to which
its achievement is blocked, and the availability of substitute
goals."[72] In substantiating Merton's hypothesis that limited access to the opportunity structure would be reflected in normlessness, they found that greater anomia scores were consistently related to lower status groups, whether measured by SES, age, religion, subjective class identification, lack of occupational mobility
or social isolation.[73] Based on these factors, Meier and Bell constructed an "Index of Life Chances." They found that the percentage of anomia decreased (as measured by Srole's scale) with each
level of increase of access to life goals. (While they note that
these low status factors could be the results, instead of the causes
of anomia, they feel that this is unlikely.)

In a study with a different emphasis—one which, in general,
agrees with the thesis being developed here—McClosky and Schaar
(1965a) suggest that the psychological dimension has not received
adequate study in research on anomia. Even in Srole's work, SES
is considered to be the major factor related to anomia. They suggest that the question concerning current studies should not be
whether or not society is anomic, but rather what groups are so
cut off from "patterns of communication and interaction that [their
position] reduces [s] opportunities to see and understand how so-

---

72. In a study based on the 1958 annual SRC Detroit Area
Study (n = 627) which employed the Srole scale, Olsen (1965) found
that particularly among the working class, Negroes were much
more anomic. Anomia was strongly related to occupation, education and income, but the relationship was due almost entirely to
occupation. Differing from other studies, Olsen also found a strong
relationship between anomia and political preference, with the
highly anomic being 23 percent Republican, 25 percent Independent,
21 percent Democrat and 53 percent no preference (which held with
occupation and race controlled).

73. Their data was based on four San Francisco census tracts,
selected to vary in SES, but to contain few non-whites or foreign
born. From these four tracts, a probability sample of men over
twenty-one was taken, with a total of 701 interviews. For a discussion of additional data on the relationship between social participation and anomia taken from this study, see Bell (1957). Another
field study focusing on the relationship between participation and
anomia is reported by Mizruchi (1960).

ciety works, and what its goals and values are."[74] They criticize,
in other words, current research for treating the problem of anomie sociologically, rather than psychologically. However, in their
discussion of the fact that past research efforts have found the
high anomia scores to be among the isolated, low status individuals—positions in the social structure that limit "patterns of communication"—it would seem that McClosky and Schaar are still advancing a sociological explanation—here to mask a discussion of
intra-psychic dynamics. (It is possible, according to the argument
of McClosky and Schaar, that if these people were to move to social positions where they would have "little difficulty in finding order and meaning in society," that their anomia scores would drop
—possible, that is, if the difficulty is an objective pattern of faulty
communication.)

McClosky and Schaar (1965a), in other words, suggest that
anomic feelings are learned through faulty socialization and posit
(at least) three factors that are involved in this process: (1) "Cognitive factors that influence one's ability to learn and understand"
(including both poor cognitive and intellectual equipment),
(2) "Emotional factors that tend to lower one's ability to perceive
reality correctly" and (3) "Substantive beliefs and attitudes that
interfere with successful communication and interaction." They
employ their own "anomy scale" in preference to the commonly
used Srole scale. This original scale appears to measure a sense
of bewilderment and longing for "the good old days."[75] Using a
cross section of Minnesota (n = 1082) as well as a national sample
(n = 1484) to which mail-back questionnaires were given, the authors employed a wide variety of scales for which—most unfortunately—the construction procedures, but not the scale items, are
available.

McClosky and Schaar found an inverse relation between their
anomy scale and cognitive functioning. With the possible exception
of a "Mysticism" scale, cognitive behavior here appears likely to
be a function of socioeconomic status. That is, it is measured by
year of school completed, and scales to test information and response set. In regard to the emotional factors influencing learning, a significant relationship was found between anomy and original scales measuring inflexibility, rigidity "in the employment of

---

74. While it has been found that social participation is inversely related to anomia (see Bell, 1957, and Mizruchi, 1960), no causal
relationship can be based on these findings. It is possible, for example, that anomia is responsible for an individual's social isolation because a person expressing such despair about his life situation may be unwilling or unable to engage in meaningful social relations.

75. They also prefer the spelling "anomy" for reasons discussed in their article.

defense mechanisms," obsessiveness, anxiety, disorganization, bewilderment, low ego strength, hostility, paranoia, intolerance of human frailty and contempt for weakness—that is, a world view which de Grazia's concepts and McDill's factor analysis would lead one to connect with anomia.

In regard to substantive beliefs, the authors found a relationship between anomia and totalitarianism, fascist tendencies (an original scale), left and right wing attitudes, lack of tolerance, of faith in people, Calvinism (that is, judgmental, Protestant ethic), elitism, inequalitarianism and ethnocentrism. Although independent assessment cannot be made of the scale items, it would appear that these social and political views fall along the same dimension as the emotional factors which were also correlated with anomia.

The authors found also that by controlling for seven sociological variables (education, age, size of community, occupational status, race, sex and region), "high anomics continue to differ from low anomics on the same psychological variables we have been analyzing. Furthermore, the differences remain in every instance large enough to leave no doubt that personality factors determine Anomy independently of social influence." In sum, McClosky and Schaar "regard anomy as a byproduct of the socialization process—as a sign of the failure of socialization and of the means by which socialization is achieved, namely, communication, interaction and learning. . . ."

> Contrary to Srole's claim that anomy reflects mental disturbance only when the latter is "severe," and that social dysfunction is the independent variable producing anomy both with and without psychopathology, we found that personality factors are correlated with anomy at all levels of mental disturbance, and that they function in all educational categories and in all sectors of society. (p. 39)

The discussion by McClosky and Schaar is a most worthwhile addition to the conceptualization of anomia, though the descriptive terms are sometimes unfortunate. Their results are important in showing that anomia is indeed a personality variable—that is, it is a result of poor psychic competence. But to conclude that such emotional and sociopolitical attitudes which the authors found to be correlated with anomia stem from faulty socialization is to use the terms "socialization" and "learning" in ways that do not reflect the conclusions to which McClosky and Schaar come.

For socialization refers to the manner in which (primarily) infants learn "to adjust to the group by acquiring social behavior of which the group approves."[76] McClosky and Schaar, however,

---

76. A Dictionary of the Social Sciences, ed. by Gould and Kolb (1969, pp. 672-73).

are not dealing with social behavior—indeed, they are not dealing with behavior at all. Their concern is rather with the results of faulty psychological growth—results which, it is maintained here, though often accompanied by a certain position in the social structure, do not uniformly affect individuals in any one social position and are found in all status groups (as they note). Further, these psychic beliefs are—in Rokeach's terms—central beliefs about the world. They are not learned as we learn, for example, that democracy is the best form of government in every situation or that the world is round (beliefs which may change over time). They are unconsciously developed as the individual develops basic physical skills (breathing, sucking, crawling)—and are just as inseparable parts of him. Thus, while the contribution of McClosky and Schaar to widening our understanding of the psychological dimensions of anomia is substantial, their conclusion, by discussing anomic development as the result of faulty socialization, has obscured the unique personality aspects of the study, so that these have, unfortunately, been generally overlooked.

Gwynn Nettler (1965), in a critique of the work of McClosky and Schaar, makes two points. First, he notes that while the hypothesis is that anomic feelings stem from inadequate socialization "reflected by an inaccurate view of reality," McClosky and Schaar "offer no data to support their own conception of American modal values . . . nor do they test the relative acuity of the anomic eye." It would seem that while it is incumbent upon those who are interested in anomie as a social condition to discuss what the ideal state is assumed to be, in considering anomia (or anomy) as a psychological variable it is very clear what the ideal state should be: mental health with its attendant capacities for growth-oriented functioning.

The second point which Nettler makes deserves quoting as it illustrates the inherent difficulties in considering anomic attitudes as stemming from faulty "patterns of communication and interaction that reduce opportunities to see and understand how society works, and what its goals and values are."

> I should like to propose an alternative view of the interesting reports by McClosky and Schaar, Srole, and others who have written about "anomic" persons. These people are simply down-and-out, run over by life, "invisible," joyless, miserable, quietly desperate—Mama Oswald. Nothing need be said about a discrepancy between their status and their aspirations. Aspiration has long since died, if it ever lived.
>
> Srole's anomia and the present Anomy scales are measures of despair. To say of these desperate ones that they are in their depths because they don't see things accurately smacks of Dr. Pangloss. And it remains an assumption to be tested.

That anomia is a measure of despair has been mentioned by

others (and is acknowledged by McClosky and Schaar [1965b]).[77] There is probably no question that the adjectives which Nettler uses could be applied to such anomic individuals. The point is, however, that as scientists interested in predicting and explaining (and perhaps—improving) the world around us, what does matter is both why certain persons (and not others with the same disadvantaged position from which to view the world) exhibit such despair (and some exhibit it who are not at all objectively disadvantaged), and, second, what direction their anomia is likely to give to their behavior—what effect it will have on our social and political systems. The problem of a faulty view of reality is not simply the problem that anomic views may not accurately reflect social reality, but that these views have an autonomy of their own—once formed, they will likely be maintained regardless of the individual's life situation.

McClosky and Schaar suggest that Srole has been unfortunately narrow in considering anomia as a sociological problem (though causally related to personality factors). They suggest that anomia can be considered a problem of differential learning of social reality—based on one's position in the social system. (They do not suggest that such learning is uniform in any one social group.) Here we are attempting to refine the analytical model further, and posit the thesis that certain persons in each social strata are psychically deprived (the antecedent variable) and thus have an unhealthy (anomic) view of the world (the dependent variable). While this psychic deprivation is likely to be closely related to a marginal or low-status position in the social system and thus give the appearance that social position is the causative agent, anomic persons may also be found in fortunate positions in the social system —both originally and subsequently to the formation of their view that the world, for them, is meaningless and lacking in security.

Anomia is of interest to us here (as measured by Srole) because it does appear to be a good measure of generalized despair and thus is related to psychic deprivation.[78] Further, it has been

---

77. Meier and Bell (1959), for example, writing six years previous to Nettler, mention that Srole's scale appears to measure a "generalized despair"—"that is, utter hopelessness and discouragement. A person agreeing strongly with each of these questions is beyond simple apathy; his is a condition of sadness and distress in which he is unable to exercise any confidence or trust that his desires or wishes may be realized, and in the extreme may reach the point described by MacIver as 'unquiet introspection and self-torture.' . . . It is despair, however, which is in part turned toward one's fellows and the social order with the particular implication that no one is bound by any effective norms of responsibility toward others."

78. A poignant, personalized expression of the growth and in-

shown elsewhere that anomia is connected with nonparticipation in political life,[79] as well as to general social isolation. Indeed, as has been detailed above, the existence of anomic individuals is likely to be a better indication than verbal agreement with modal values of the stability of the social and political systems in times of crises. Thus, in the research discussed in chapter 4, Srole's 5-item scale has been employed[80] (with item 3 reversed, as has been suggested by Tumin and Collins [1959]), with the hypothesis that anomia is directly related to psychic deprivation. To be even more specific, it is advanced here that anomia is a result of unsatisfied basic needs.

It was also felt that Srole's scale should be included in the research instrument used in chapter 4 because, in addition to attempting to demonstrate the possibilities of utilizing Maslow's ideas to discriminate meaningfully between subjects, an attempt is being made to show the wide applicability of Maslow's need hierarchy to other methods of studying behavior. It is hoped that thus a variety of approaches can be linked to common concerns and a common measure of discrimination, enabling economy in research design within a single theoretical framework.

Alienation

As has been noted above, the distinction between anomia and alienation is usually unclear in research reports. Where a distinction is made, anomia usually refers to disorganization: to feelings of ineffectiveness or "inability to control one's destiny" (McDill and Ridley, 1962) and to feelings of lacking direction and values in one's life. Alienation, on the other hand, suggests "A more active

---

trapsychic meaning of anomia can be found in the late Richard Wright's description of what happened to him upon moving to the alienating society of Chicago and finding all meaningful social opportunities barred to him: "Slowly I began to forge in the depths of my mind a mechanism than [sic] repressed all the dreams and desires that the Chicago streets, the newspapers, the movies were evoking in me. I was going through a second childhood; a new sense of the limit of the possible was being born in me. What could I dream of that had the barest possibility of coming true? I could think of nothing. And, slowly, it was upon exactly that nothingness that my mind began to dwell, that constant sense of wanting without having, of being hated without reasons. A dim notion of what life meant to a Negro in America was coming to consciousness in me, not in terms of external events, lynchings, Jim Crowism and the endless brutalities, but in terms of crossed-up feeling, of emotional tension" (Quoted in Silberman, 1964, pp. 48-49).

79. Milbrath, 1965, pp. 78-79.

80. See Appendix A.

rejection of politics than the passive withdrawal or detachment of anomie" (Milbrath, 1965).

Perhaps a useful distinction can be made by conceptualizing anomia as a diffuse feeling of separation from formal, institutionalized society and from the informal society of their social milieu by persons who cannot discern a social interest, apart from their individual interests. Alienation, on the other hand, is exemplified by a more active and specific feeling of separation from the society of other men by persons who discern a generalized social interest, but reject it. As Nettler (1957) states, "an 'alienated person' is one who has been estranged from, made unfriendly toward, his society and the culture it carries." Thus while anomic individuals are alienated, all alienated individuals are not anomic.

In actuality, in measuring anomia you are thus, in a profound way, measuring one form of alienation. For a person who is alienated from other people will likely be simultaneously alienated from the society and polity which these others compose.[81] Active rejection, however, is more likely to be based not on this type of alienation per se, but rather on opportunities for its expression. We have previously noted William Kornhauser's incisive statement that:

> Apathy born of alienation from community may persist under more or less stable conditions. However, the underlying disaffection of which apathy may be an expression readily leads to activism in times of crisis, as when people who have previously rejected politics turn out in large numbers to support demagogic attacks on the existing political system. Because apathetic people may not manifest their discontent directly, we must measure their availability in terms of their lack of proximate attachments. (1959, p. 61)

Thus it is of interest here to note the specific consequences for political behavior which alienation, when expressed, may take, as well as the psychic components of alienation which exist independent of objective social-political conditions.

Melvin Seeman (1959) has been a pioneer in the study of alienation and some of its relationships to behavior. In an essay entitled "On the Meaning of Alienation," Seeman conceptualizes alienation in terms of five dimensions:

1. Powerlessness—"the expectancy or probability held by the individual that his own behavior cannot determine the occurrence of the outcomes, or reinforcements, he seeks."

2. Meaninglessness—when "the individual is unclear as to what he ought to believe—when the individual's minimal stan-

---

81. This is of course borne out by the social and political non-participation scores of anomic individuals noted above.

dards for clarity in decision-making are not met." This dimension is characterized by a "low expectancy that satisfactory predictions about future outcomes of behavior can be made."

3. Normlessness—which is the dimension Seeman sees defined by Durkheim, is a situation in which "there is a high expectancy that socially unapproved behaviors are required to achieve given goals."

4. Isolation—"the alienated in the isolation sense are those who, like the intellectual, assign low reward value to goals or beliefs that are typically highly valued in the given society."

5. Self-estrangement—related to Erich Fromm's view of man as "insecure, given to appearances, conformist." This dimension can be seen in "the degree of dependence of the given behavior upon anticipated future rewards, that is, upon rewards that lie outside the activity itself [rather than enjoyment of activity for itself]."

In regard to these five dimensions, Horton notes that the dimensions of self-estrangement and powerlessness probably come closest to Marx's view of alienation, while normlessness and meaninglessness are probably close to Durkheim's view of anomie, and isolation could fall in either category (Horton, 1964, p. 293). In other words, there is an obvious (and acknowledged) overlapping between the dimensions of anomie-anomia (both Durkheim's and Srole's varieties) and alienation (as alienation is defined by Seeman).

Further, using Seeman's five dimensions, there is no basis for a relationship between alienation and psychic deprivation, as categorized by Maslow (while such a relationship does appear to exist between anomia and psychic deprivation). Indeed, as was pointed out above, self-actualizers are seen by Maslow as being independent from their cultural milieu. Nettler (1957) has shown (by the use of an original alienation scale, as previously discussed) how alienation can typify creativity and altruism as well as deviant behavior.[82] Impressionistically, it appears likely that an individual alienated in Seeman's sense will be so because of intrapsychic needs or objective, social conditions, while persons characterized by anomia will be alienated because of unfulfilled basic needs.[83]

---

82. Nettler's measure appears to have high loadings on the fourth and fifth dimensions delimited by Seeman.

83. For example, Seeman (1966) has found a relationship between powerlessness and lack of organizational activity that is erased when formal membership becomes active in a work organization. (Results held with education, income, occupational status, prestige, age and mobility controlled.) Of course, it could also be

Lewis Feuer (1962) implicitly recognizes such a distinction in his discussion of alienation. He notes that Seeman acknowledges an inability to distinguish alienation from a rejective and critical view of one's society because this is "the essential intent behind the idea of alienation, and a multitude of alienated persons would be dissatisfied equally with conditions of power-possession, meaningfulness, norm-orientedness, involvement, and self-acknowledgment" (pp. 128-29). While Seeman defines meaninglessness in terms of a low ability to predict outcomes of behavior, Feuer points out that social determinism is indeed a widespread cause of alienation today! Thus Feuer discusses alienation in terms of six modes "in which, from the sociological standpoint, alienation is said to characterize the experience of modern people." These modes are the alienation of class society, of competitive society, of industrial society, of mass society, of race and of generations.[84] Thus alienation, as it has been historically conceived, is based—like the Durkheim-Merton theory of anomie—on a reaction to a measurable social condition.[85]

The complex relationship between alienation and both objective and personality causes can be seen in a study by Clark (1959) —a study which illustrates the necessity of including the variable anomia in an analysis of social alienation. Defining alienation as "the degree to which man feels powerless to achieve the role he has determined to be rightfully his in specific situations," Clark studied the membership of an agricultural cooperative as an example of a social system in action. Using a random sample of 361 of the 3,000 members, he asked questions designed to measure their relationship to the coop, their satisfaction and participation in it and knowledge of its activities. He found that alienation was negatively related to participation (-.37), to knowledge (-.30) and particularly, to satisfaction (-.62). But an individual's feelings of alienation were not simply related to organization-as-entity, for alienation was also negatively related to the number of others members known (-.17) and to the number of memberships which the person held in other organizations (-.21). Thus Clark's hypoth-

---

argued that it was the mentally healthy individuals who were officers, and thus did not feel powerless.

84. Schaff (1967), in his discussion of alienation, makes a distinction between alienation (which is a possible but not necessary part of the human condition) and "auto-alienation in which alienation is not based upon subjective appraisal but on the objective situation.

85. However, as Manheim (1965) correctly notes, such a reaction may vary from fatalism to "an attempt to explore and manage an emerging new condition," again removing alienation from the realm of psychic deprivation.

esis was confirmed: the more powerless an individual feels, the more generally physically and mentally estranged he will be from various aspects of social interaction. But, as the cooperative was assumedly impartial in its treatment of its members, we must still consider the personality dimension (which Clark did not do) in order to clearly understand this phenomena. (In addition, we note that alienation was not related to age, size of dairy herd or years of membership in the coop.)

In an unpublished dissertation using a random sample of voters in four wards in Columbus, Ohio (1,108 questionnaires delivered, 38.8 percent returned), Dean (1960, 1961, 1965) also studied the effects of alienation (conceptualized in terms of powerlessness, normlessness and social isolation) and types of apathy (interest, influence and behavior), analyzing their relation to voting behavior. He found no relationship between these measures of alienation and voting apathy and nonsignificant relationships between alienation and other types of apathy.

In a study based on a stratified probability sample in three small Iowa towns, Erbe (1964) employed Dean's measure of alienation, plus measures of socioeconomic status and involvement in organizations in a study of political participation. He found that:

> Alienation is of some importance as a predictor at the zero order, but higher order partialling raised grave doubt as to whether alienation affects political participation independently of socioeconomic status and organizational involvement.

In other words, analysis "suggests that alienation, as well as political participation, is an effect of socioeconomic status and organization involvement. . . ." In conclusion, Erbe states "The high correlations of measures of alienation and anomia with socioeconomic status indicate the desirability of scales that are not such direct expressions of class culture."[86]

Templeton (1966) also notes that similar results are produced by employing either Srole's anomia scale or various measures of alienation. In a random sample (240 interviews in Berkeley in the fall of 1960), he found that social status was negatively related to alienation and that alienation was not related to party preference or voting intentions in either 1956 or the coming 1960 election. While alienation was not related to participation per se, however,

---

86. In a random sample of Columbus, Ohio (using a mailed questionnaire with a 57 percent return), Neal and Seeman (1964) found anomia scores were not closely related to scale scores on powerlessness or normlessness. Neal and Rettig (1963), who report the same study, state "In both the manual and the non-manual categories, powerlessness, normlessness, and Srole's anomie scale emerged as a separate and unrelated dimension." (Impressionistically, a good part of the difficulty here lies in the inadequacy of Dean's measures.)

it was related to lack of strength of party attachment and withdrawal from politics in knowledge and interest. He found that both in acceptance of Negro efforts at improvement and of the local community power structure, the alienated were much lower in acceptance.
The rejection of three local ballot issues was also related to alienation, most strongly white collor workers.

Templeton concludes with the important observation that the
stability of our political system may well be due to the lack of opportunity for the expression of alienation (though the presence of
extremist groups show its existence). The alienated thus withdraw
from the political process or vacillate between parties as there is
seldom an opportunity for a protest vote. The greatest opportunity
for the alienated to vote their protests is found, Templeton feels,
in local politics, when local ballot issues call for acceptance or
rejection.[87]

McDill and Ridley (in a 1959 probability sample of 268 suburb-
an residents of Davidson County, Tennessee) studied the effects of
anomia and alienation on the defeat of a proposed consolidated met-
ropolitan government (1962). They suggest—congruent with the distinction presented above—that while anomia is "a belief in the inability to control one's destiny," political alienation involves a distrust of leaders and a generalized resentment that will be expressed
in voting. They found the effects of education, anomia and political
alienation (in an originally devised scale for that area) on both voting behavior and on attitude toward the issue to be additive, with
anomia and alienation contributory factors to the relationship between education and the election. As Campbell (1962) notes, in relation to the on-going studies of alienation at the University of
Michigan (with alienation defined as hostility, suspicion and cynicism in regard to politics): "It would appear that some part of political apathy is more than simply passivity. With some individuals
an active rejection of political matters is involved."

A recent study by Finifter (1970) sheds some additional light

---

87. This theme is also discussed in Thompson and Horton
(1960). However, as considered here, alienation can also lead to
social action (for example, Stokley Carmichael) as it is unrelated
to mental health—that is, it is not necessarily related to psychic
deprivation which hinders participation. It is anomia, rather,
which is related to both despair and (usually) to apathy. Also see
the study of political alienation by Horton (1960). Like the other
studies discussed here, Horton also considers both political protest and political apathy as differential responses to political alienation. Unfortunately for his model of behavior, Horton considers
"psychological alienation" as "a function of actual powerlessness
as judged by the observer" (p. 48). Unfortunately, because the statistically inverse relationship between alienation and SES indicates
that though these factors are usually related, they are far from
existing in a simple cause-and-effect relation to each other.

on the construct of alienation. The author measured two aspects
of alienation, powerlessness and normlessness, using a refined
sub-sample of a nation-wide probability sample drawn in 1960 for
the Almond-Verba study (1963). It was found that political participation was the variable most highly correlated (r = -.64 with powerlessness and that education was the most important social predictor
(r = -.44) of this variable. In regard to normlessness, however, the
most highly correlated variable was faith-in-people (r = -.37) and,
secondly, race (r = .22). (Faith-in-people also correlated -.37 with
powerlessness, indicating that it was an equally powerful predictor
of both types of alienation.) The data of Finifter's study suggest
that different persons—socially and psychically different—fall into
two rather separate (r = .26) dimensions of alienation. Tying them
together, however, is a shared misanthropy.

A final group of studies which bear on the subject of alienation is the earlier mentioned research on powerlessness conducted by Seeman (1966, 1963, 1967, 1964) and his associates. In these
studies (measuring powerlessness by Rotter's Internality-Externality Scale), it has been found that on a psychological level an individual is likely to perceive and retain control relevant information if he feels that he can utilize such information. Concurrently,
on a sociological level, it has been shown that a sense of power or
intrapsychic competence is positively related to membership, active membership and officership of an organization. Although some
suggestive data has been offered, it remains to meaningfully integrate these two levels before any statements of causality are made.
From the viewpoint of our previous discussion, it is the more
competent person who would seek to participate in his environment. It is equally important to note, however, that experience
which increases a person's opportunities to understand and manipulate his world (for example, education, or group activities) appears to be related to heightened feelings of efficacy, and hence,
to psychic growth.

In an attempt to delineate, as Srole has done in his work on
anomia, a psychological dimension of a social state (that is, persons who are in fact alienated but due to psychic rather than situational causes), I would delimit the psychological dimension of
alienation as feelings of incompetence, of misanthropy and cynicism,[88] as well as of anomia. All of these indicate lack of positive effect for and estrangement from human relationships (and
hence, from one's political system). In relation to its psychic dimension, Davids (1955) remarks that alienation "may be defined
briefly as a syndrome composed of the following interrelated personality dispositions: egocentricity, distrust, pessimism, anxiety,
and resentment. Previous research has shown that people who are

88. In chap. 2 (see section on Generalized Psychic Deprivation), the possible relation of cynicism—both personal and political—to psychic deprivation has previously been explored.

high on any one of these dispositions tend to be high on all of
them."

A good measure of part of the personality dimension of alienation is thus likely to be Rosenberg's "Faith in People" Scale,
which was developed in a 1952 study of students at Cornell and has
been used widely since then.[89] Rosenberg found that this scale correlated with a political cynicism scale, a scale showing willingness
to restrict freedom of speech, as well as the view that political deviants should be suppressed, and other attitudes that are reminiscent of generalized intolerance similar to the questions included in
the F-scale. Thus, in the study reported in chapter 4, the Faith-in-
People scale was employed (in addition to Srole's anomia scale and
the political efficacy scale) to tap some of the personality predispositions of political alienation. It is hypothesized here that misanthropy will be directly related to psychic deprivation. Because
each of the four deprived groups have psychic reasons to distrust
others, it is predicted that the strength of this relationship will
not diminish until the level of self-actualization is reached.

In summary, it appears that the subject of alienation can be
tackled from its sociological or its psychological dimension. The
sociopolitical dimension of alienation, so clearly discussed by
Marx, is based on objective conditions that isolate men from each
other and from their sociopolitical systems and impart to them
feelings of powerlessness, normlessness and isolation, such as
Seeman has delimited. The psychological dimension, it is hypothesized here, is based on unfulfilled personality needs that also isolate people from each other (and cause person-to-person rejection) but which objective conditions will not ameliorate—although
this distinction is seldom made.

Thompson and Horton state:

> As we see it, political alienation is a peculiarly sociological
> concept [similar to Merton's view of anomie]. Although prob-
> ably related to the "quasi-paranoia" of misanthropy, it is not
> a personality variable in the usual sense . . . political aliena-
> tion is most accurately understood as an emergent response
> to social structure in action, a reaction to perceived relative
> inability to influence or to control one's social destiny. (1960)

They note that while alienation as a sociological factor is related
to community power distribution, it is also related to a generalized lack of faith in people. They suggest that political alienation
and personality factors, while both important, will exercise an independent influence—far from a one-to-one correlation.

I have suggested here that misanthropy, as well as anomia
and inefficacy, comprise psychological dimensions of alienation.
As with the sociological dimension, measures of these subjective

---

89. See Appendix A.

aspects should be of importance (as Thompson and Horton show) in predicting <u>direction</u> of the vote as well as in assessing predispositions toward other types of political activity. Thus alienation is also related to the personality model employed in this book. The relationship, however, is complex, for both self-actualizing and deprived personalities may be social isolates and political deviants—the former as a reaction to unhealthy objective conditions, the latter reacting to psychic deprivation as well.

Political Efficacy, Socialization
and Participation

In the sections above, an attempt has been made to show a theoretical connection between Maslow's need hierarchy and a wide spectrum of sociopsychological research variables. In this final section, we are concerned with more directly political measurements, in order to make our discussion more relevant to the system of human relationships we call political.

In the various voting studies done under the direction of the Survey Research Center, a constant concern has been the measurement of political efficacy—"a feeling of potency about affecting political affairs" (Berelson, Lazarsfeld and McPhee, 1954, p. 25). Specifically, a sense of political efficacy is defined as

> The feeling that individual political action does have, or can have, an impact upon the political process, i.e., that it is worth while to perform one's civic duties. It is the feeling that political and social change is possible, and that the individual citizen can play a part in bringing about this change. (Campbell, Gurin and Miller, 1954, p. 187)

The sense of political efficacy, as measured by this scale, has been repeatedly shown to be significantly related to political participation.[90] In the 1952 election study, for example, the relationship held with eight demographic variables controlled.[91] Almond and Verba (1963) have also shown political efficacy to be related to culture, with citizens of Great Britain and America expressing more competence than citizens of Germany, Mexico or Italy.

In the study of political activity, apathy—and its correlate, a lack of efficacy—have been a constant theme of importance. In chap-

---

90. Easton and Dennis (1967) have discussed three uses of "political efficacy": "as a norm, as a psychological disposition or feeling, and as a form of behavior." This article includes a discussion of the relationships of this variable in a study of 12,052 children between grades 3 and 8.

91. Also see Eulau and Schneider (1956), Janowitz and Marvick (1953), who studied its relationship to authoritarianism, Milbrath (1965, pp. 58-70); also Agger, Goldstein and Pearl (1961).

ter 2, evidence was presented which indicates that such a lack of efficacy is part of the "philosophy of deprivation" adhered to by persons with unfulfilled basic needs. It appears that there is a psychically meaningful connection between a sense of personal competence and both the belief that one lives in a manageable, manipulable world (a world with which one has a positive, meaningful relationship) and behavior congruent to this belief.

Thus political efficacy is an important dimension to include in considering personality and political activity. It should provide an index of a person's ability and desire to take part in political and social activity. Its specific relationship to alienation has been previously discussed and the suggestion was offered that lack of political efficacy may result in "diffuse displeasure at being powerless and mistrust of those who do wield power" (Thompson and Horton, 1960, p. 190). Lack of political efficacy should therefore be related to both lack of faith in people and anomia, and hence point to the direction which the behavior that those low in efficacy is likely to take, should they be aroused to political action.

It has earlier been hypothesized that Maslow's need hierarchy corresponds to a continuum whose end points could be indicated by "concern with self" and "concern with environment (and self in relation to it)." In a society that values democratic theory—that is, whose members are socialized to believe in the possibility and necessity of political action by all—political efficacy should offer a measure of the political dimension of the existence of such a continuum. In the research discussed in chapter 4, therefore, the political efficacy scale developed by SRC is employed,[92] with the hypothesis that it will bear an inverse relationship to Maslow's need hierarchy.

In addition to political efficacy, SRC has developed a second, commonly-used measure of political involvement which is labeled a "sense of citizen duty." It is defined as "the feeling that oneself and others ought to participate in the political process, regardless of whether such political activity is seen as worth while or efficacious" (Campbell, Gurin and Miller, 1954, p. 194). Although the scale is always reported to be highly skewed in an agree direction, a direct relationship has been found to hold between a sense of citizen duty and political participation, variously measured. Again, in the original SRC study for example, the relationship held up well when demographic factors were controlled.

The Citizen Duty Scale[93] has a particular interest here because it is the only scale included in the research below which is not <u>directly</u> relevant to intrapsychic dynamics. It is probably a rather clear measure of the degree of an individual's manifest po-

---

92. See Appendix A.

93. See Appendix A.

litical socialization[94]—the extent to which a person has learned
the lesson of American democracy. Therefore it offers several
useful aspects. It should correlate with political participation and
social activity in general, <u>insofar as these types of behavior are</u>
learned through the socialization <u>process and encouraged by vari-</u>
<u>ous types of social control</u>. When analyzed in terms of politically
relevant attitudes and behavior which engage a psychic dimension,
however, the relationship should be weak or nonexistent.

It has earlier been suggested that it is self-actualizing persons who are likely to learn most (and longest) from the educational process. For this reason, one might hypothesize that self-actualizers should also be most socialized to American political beliefs regarding the value of participation per se. On the other hand,
the drop-out process in education does not begin to be noticeable
until the seventh grade—after a great deal of classroom instruc-
tion has occurred. In these early years, we know that much politically important learning has already taken place. Is it then likely
that psychic factors will be unimportant in predicting degree of political learning? Greenstein (in a study of 659 New Haven children
between 4th and 8th grade) found two interesting relationships
(1965). First "wherever consistent class differences appeared
they showed that upper-status children exceed lower-status children in capacity and motivation for political participation" (p. 94).
Similar politically relevant differences appear in the Hess and
Torney data (1968). These findings would suggest that, even among
young children, selective life experiences are observable and measurable.

Second, however, in the Greenstein study (as generally in the
literature) both upper and lower status groups are similar in "explicit statements about personal willingness to participate in politics and the 'importance' of politics. Both groups are quite likely
to say that they will vote when they are of age (almost no children
deny that they will vote; the remaining responses are largely 'don't
knows') and to say that elections are important" (Greenstein, 1965,
p. 99). Hence, it is also likely that—in spite of personality differences—children and adults will offer near unanimous agreement
with modal American values, <u>regardless of whether their person-</u>
<u>ality health allows them to act out those values</u>.

The Citizen Duty scale was included in the research below in
an attempt to clarify the relationships between political learning
and personality type. Because of the strong agree tendency, it is
assumed that there will be, at best, a weak relationship between
personality needs and expressions of citizen duty.

Finally, because the concern of this book is with the relationship between personality motivation and political <u>behavior</u>, it is

---

94. For the distinction between "latent" and "manifest" political socialization, see Almond's (1960) discussion.

necessary to include a measure of actual political participation. In another attempt to tie the original research reported in chapter 4 to other work in the field, the frequently used Woodward and Roper (1950) "Political Participation Index" has been included as the major measure of behavior (as opposed to attitude). The index includes five dimensions: (1) voting, (2) supporting pressure groups by membership, (3) personally communicating with legislators, (4) party activity and (5) "engaging in habitual dissemination of political opinions through word-of-mouth communications to other citizens."

The Index was used originally in a pretest with a national sample of 500 and then in a nationwide study (n = 8,000). On a 12-point scoring system, only 10 percent had a score of 6 or better and 73 percent were below 4.[95] While college people were found to be much more likely to be active (the top 27 percent of the scorers were defined as "active"), less than half of Woodward and Roper's activists had a college education.

It is always possible that distortion may take place in reporting one's activities.[96] However, because this index has been shown to be discriminating and because it does not tap personally sensitive areas, it is assumed that this measure of reported behavior is a close approximation of scores that would be gained should the individuals be observed directly. The expected relationship between political participation and the fulfillment of basic needs has been spelled out in chapter 2, under the separate need levels. It has been hypothesized that there is a direct relationship between psychic competence and general social and political participation. It should also be again remarked, however, that participation in broadly popular political activities is likely to be a function of one's place in the social structure and of one's socialization, as well as of personality factors.

In the literature of political behavior, mention has increasingly been made of the usefulness of personality. Occasionally, as has been discussed here, these comments have been expanded to express, in detail, a particular perspective from which politics and personality may be assessed (anomia, dogmatism, et cetera). In addition to covering the various perspectives in current use, an

---

95. The scoring system used in this book is reported in Appendix B. Scoring changes were made because of the paucity of high scores reported originally. Generally, the scoring system here is both less discriminating (giving, for example, one point for voting at all in the past four years as opposed to additional points for more frequent voting) and deflates the level of activity (giving one point, for example, for ever working for the election of a candidate, instead of limiting this to the last four years).

96. This was another reason for giving no additional points for degrees of exceptional activity.

attempt has been made here to integrate our particular viewpoint — Maslow's need hierarchy—with major dimensions now employed in the study of behavior and attitude. The theoretical bases of the scales that were used have been presented in considerable detail so that the reader is aware of the rationale for their inclusion in the research design discussed in the next chapter—as well as of the fact that their similarity of concern is often greater than their scale items alone would imply and exists on a theoretical level as well.

The applicability of Maslow's ideas to a wide range of political concerns has been illustrated in this chapter and an attempt has been made to show that Maslow offers not a separate approach, but a theory which synthesizes previous behavioral work in political science, sociology and psychology. As a good theory should, it shows us how far we have come. Through its framework, bits and pieces of knowledge can be meaningfully related. In addition (and equally important) Maslow's motivation theory shows us the directions in which to make future research efforts. It gives us knowledge with which to phrase the questions we must answer as well as a foundation for understanding what those answers might be.

4

Mental Health and
the Democratic Participant Procedures

An examination of behavioral studies shows that there are
many underlying similarities in the empirical findings and theoretical approaches of various popular research perspectives.
Further, the personality theory of Abraham Maslow is a useful
means of bringing these disparate studies into a consistent focus.

But a reasoned theoretical discussion is one thing—and an
empirical demonstration of these possibilities is quite definitely
something else. Before this, various political scientists have con-
ceded that personality study would offer valuable insights for those
concerned with political behavior, and have illustrated this point
by in-depth studies of selected individuals. The question, rather,
has centered around the feasibility of employing an inclusive personality model in field studies. Of particular concern has been
the problem of working with an impossibly complicated research
model. Sidney Verba (1961) discusses this problem of "the economics of research design" in an essay on decision-making models in the international system. Specifically, he questions whether
the increased explanatory power of a model which includes "non-
rational" (that is, personality) variables justifies its increased
complexity.

The force of the preceding argument has been that Maslow's
personality theory, based as it is on five distinct personality need
areas, allows the inclusion of personality in behavioral models in
a manner that is both sophisticated and rich (that is, based on a
complex theory of psychic need groups) and also simple in relation to the number of variables which must be considered. Thus it
does initially appear feasible to utilize Maslow's theory in the
study of political behavior. This chapter reports a field study
which is an original attempt to do so, in order to test the hypotheses outlined in previous chapters.

Procedures

Pecuniary concerns, as always, were a major limitation in
setting up a research project which would allow the empirical use
of Maslow's personality theory and its relation to other currently
employed research interests. In the best of all possible research
worlds, a carefully selected and individually studied nationwide
probability sample would have been employed. In addition to ob-
taining scores on the various scales discussed in the first half of

this book, measures of actual political behavior would have also
been taken. As with almost all of the research reported previously, however, the research design is considerably more modest.
Its results, therefore, must be regarded as tentative and their
value as primarily heuristic. The preceding theoretical discussion
—based as it is on a great variety of studies over a period of many
years—is more likely to be an accurate portrayal of the relationship of Maslow's personality theory to politically relevant behavior than are the results of this one unrepresentative field study.
However, the similarities and differences between the results presented here and the hypothesized relationships discussed earlier
in this book give a clear understanding of fruitful areas for further
research work, as well as underlining the accuracy of predictions
which have been made. In addition, this field study involves a direct test of Maslow's ideas, a clear requirement in view of the in-
ferential nature of the preceding chapters.

Thus, the absolute distribution of personality types in terms
of degrees of psychic competence remains an intriguing but unknown area in psychology—an area of great political relevance. Indeed, the significance of much of the following can only be finally
understood in terms of the percentage of psychically deprived individuals in any given population, as well as their positions within
the social structure. On the positive side, however, it is now possible to more accurately assess the relationships between predisposing psychic factors and precipitating conditions and to achieve
a clearer understanding of the supportive function which personality may or may not play in any given social system.

Two concerns were uppermost in selecting the subjects for
this study. One was to use persons who were not students—to
avoid the obvious bias of measuring politically relevant attitudes
of individuals from whom little (or no) political behavior is possible. Too often, reviews have been written which, ignoring the value of the relationships uncovered, could be summarized under the
heading of "But are students people?" It was also felt desirable
to avoid studying members of organized groups—that other easily
available research commodity. As Hyman and Sheatsley have
pointed out, sampling of organized group members can inflate relationships between attitude and personality.

It is only to be expected that individuals selected from the
ranks of organized groups would be more likely to show both
some patterning of their sentiments and some greater relationship between sentiments and personality factors. The patterning would be a function of the influence of the group; the relationship to personality factors would reflect the individual's
initiative in joining the group. A person who shows sufficient
motivation to participate in a group is more likely to regard
political and social questions as central concerns, and thus
to imbue these aspects of life with energies derived from

more central factors of personality. On the other hand, a person who is so politically inert as to avoid or refrain from group membership is likely to be an individual to whom social and political questions are peripheral and thus not penetrated by more fundamental values and energies. (Hyman and Sheatsley in Christie and Jahoda, 1954, p. 63)

For these reasons, the method of selection was narrowed to a consideration of residence or place of work. Finally, because the problem of lack of staff was second only to that of lack of funds, it was decided to contact subjects through their place of work.

The second concern was to make the sample as large and varied as possible—in order to enhance the reliability of the results obtained. The goal set was a sample size with a minimum of 500, to include both men and women of diversified socioeconomic status. Such a sample would also hopefully include a diversity of personality needs. (However, as the sample was to be based on individual cooperation, it was recognized at the outset that it would likely include an unrepresentatively large number of self-actualizing individuals.)

An additional problem concerned the method of employing the research design. As one of the basic aims here is to show that personality can be made a useful dimension in survey research, our choice was already limited. But what of the method of administration? Should the subjects be asked the various questions in a personal interview situation, or should they be given questionnaires to fill out individually? What about the factor of anonymity? (If respondents' names were obtained, additional information could be secured from personnel files and voter registration information.)

The bulk of the evidence is in favor of using anonymous, written questionnaires in this type of personality-sensitive research work. Pearlin (1961) attempted to assess this problem directly, using as a sample the nursing force (below the level of supervisor) of a large federal mental hospital. The self-administered questionnaire (which had an 86 percent return) gave each subject the option of anonymity and was unsigned by 38 percent of the subjects. In conformity to the results of other studies which he reviewed, Pearlin found that anonymity made no apparent difference in response to questions regarding judgments about an objective situation. For.example, in answering questions concerning sensitive areas of hospital administration, whether the respondents were critical or positive in attitude was no indicator of whether they opted for signing. Thus fear of the threatening quality of the questions didn't enter into the subjects' considerations.

Nonsigning, however, did appear to be a personality characteristic. In an analysis of the response differences between signers and nonsigners, Pearlin notes three trends:

1.   The nonsigners scored lower in competence (as measured

by their lower scores on self-regard, their reported reluctance to state their opinions at work to their superiors and their reported difficulty in answering the questionnaire).

2. The nonsigners were more negative in their views toward other people. (Nonsigning was positively correlated with low scores on the previously discussed "Faith-in-People" scale devised by Morris Rosenberg.)

3. The nonsigners expressed less interest and involvement in issues covered by the questionnaires and less enthusiasm for their work.

Thus individuals who are low in such qualities as self-esteem and faith-in-people (that is, who are likely to be motivated by unfulfilled basic needs) were more likely to leave their questionnaire unsigned—suggesting that an anonymous questionnaire would be more apt to elicit the cooperation of this personality type.

Eysenck also discusses this problem. He notes that employing half interview and half secret ballot, the American Institute of Public Opinion has found that by using the secret ballot "there was a marked decrease in the number of undecided votes. . . . (1954, p. 65). He also mentions a study by Turnbull,[1] in which some questionnaires were marked privately and placed in a box marked "Secret Ballot" and others followed standard interview form. On the basis of this experiment, Turnbull concluded that

the methods of the interview and the secret ballot do produce marked differences in answers under certain conditions. These differences cast some doubt on the validity of the results obtained by the interview method when the subject feels that his answer, if known, would affect his prestige. The discrepancy is probably great enough to warrant the use of the secret ballot whenever questions which have acquired high social prestige are involved, particularly when the questions are of a highly controversial nature, and of deep personal or social significance. (Turnbull in Eysenck, 1954, pp. 65-66)

In their massive study of Soviet refugees, Inkeles and Bauer (1961) employed both oral and written questionnaires for a subgroup of forty-six subjects now residing in the United States. They concluded that "the printed questionnaire minimizes the tendency of respondents to slant answers on which their own prestige or that of the interviewer may be involved. That is to say, the face-to-face situation is an invitation for the respondent to manipulate the interviewer" (pp. 53-54). However, they also found that more confiden-

---

1. Reference is to W. Turnbull. 1944. "Secret Versus Non-Secret Ballots," in H. Cantril (ed.), Gauging Public Opinion. Princeton: Princeton University Press.

tial information (in this case, membership in a Communist Party affiliate) was obtained from the oral interview. While in neither of these situations was anonymity a factor, it again appears that in the individualized, written questionnaire situation, respondents are more likely to be free from concern with giving the socially desirable answer. Further, in the study presented here, no confidential information was being solicited which might be more likely to be derived from an interview situation.

Finally, in this connection, we should note the defense of McClosky and Schaar (1965b) to criticism of their use of an anonymous mailed-back questionnaire. The authors state:

> There is powerful evidence that the self-administering procedure works and that for some types of attitude and personality assessment it is superior to the standard oral interview. Although the procedure is unorthodox by conventional standards, its unorthodoxy can be regarded not as a shortcoming, but as a potentially valuable advance in research design. It combines survey and clinical testing procedures in a way that can enhance both. While some potential respondents may be lost because the task is a demanding one, the large gain in depth and breadth of information collected on each respondent more than compensates for the loss in sampling representativeness. With sufficient responses, of course, even this loss can be minimized.

For these reasons, it was decided to employ an individually filled-out, anonymous questionnaire. In order to increase the sample size as much as possible, it was also decided to utilize a questionnaire which was completed and mailed back at the respondent's leisure.[2] It was immediately realized that this method would allow some important fish to get away. Especially because of our concern with psychological variables, it is likely (as mentioned above) that such a procedure inflated the number of self-actualizing persons in our sample. This is a limitation which can only be openly acknowledged.

The three places of work which were used were: (1) a large wood and paper processing plant in Eugene, Oregon (n = 2674), (2) the teachers of the Junction City School District in Oregon (n = 156) and (3) the lay personnel of Sacred Heart Hospital—the major hospital in Eugene (n = 248). In the case of the teachers, the questionnaires were placed in their boxes. To each questionnaire a page of explanation was affixed. Included in this explanation was mention that the study had been explained to and cleared with the school and district administration. It was also mentioned that the pretest the previous year had involved the entire high school se-

---

2. All questionnaires that were returned came back within five weeks. The data were gathered in the Spring of 1967.

nior class of that city and that the results would soon appear in a professional publication (Knutson, 1967).

In the case of the hospital staff, the situation was somewhat different. With the assistance of the Director of the Nursing Service, I was able to accompany the payroll clerk on her rounds for each shift, handing out the questionnaires, and offering a word of explanation at each floor station. (Additional explanation was printed on the first page of the questionnaire itself.) The returns from these two groups (38 percent for the teachers [n = 60] and 35 percent for the hospital staff [n = 87] indicate perhaps an average amount of acceptance and interest on the part of busy individuals of whom one to two hours of time was being asked.

For the lumber plant, however, the situation was somewhat complicated by uneasy labor relations.[3] Both the plant management and the leaders of both union locals involved received detailed explanations in which all questions were freely answered. Both groups offered their cooperation and were most helpful in facilitating this research project. The open letter which appeared on the front page of the questionnaire stated this approval. Yet, it was apparent in many ways that the extremely low cooperation here was in part due to the men's concern that this study was a technique of management to investigate them and that, somehow, they would be identified. (The questionnaires were stapled to each payroll envelope and then distributed to two plants, all sections, all shifts.) It is now felt that the response would have been much greater if (1) a personalized, dittoed letter from the union leaders had been affixed to the front of the questionnaire and (2) the distribution of the questionnaire had not involved using the company payroll and company employees. The return from the lumber company was 13 percent (n = 348).

Because of this situation, the overall percentage of response was quite small and undoubtedly additionally reduced by the noncooperation of people who feel anxious and threatened. (The generally low SES of lumber company employees—although the respondents included administrators as well as workers—was undoubtedly also a factor.) After all of the returned questionnaires from all three sample groups (n = 507, 495 useable) were coded and read through, however, it was apparent that each personality type was represented and the questionnaire results would allow a suggestive analysis of the relationships outlined in the first part of this book. Thus in concluding the remarks about the sample, it must once more be stated that neither is the original sample representative of any parent group of workers, employees, Oregonians, et cetera, nor are the respondents representative of the sample selected. The value of the results herein reported lies,

3. Having also talked to the management of several other nearby plants, I concluded that this situation was typical of such plants generally.

rather, in the relationships which were found which relate to the theoretical discussion previously presented. How reliable the conclusions are will have to await future replication. (However, because so many frequently used research instruments have been employed, it is possible for the careful reader to note similarities here to many other studies—some of which have employed more representative samples.)

The questionnaires were returned by mail to the "People and Politics Poll" at the University of Oregon. Of the 495 which were received and useable, all appeared to be most carefully completed. Many of the questions evoked additional comments, which were assessed in the coding.[4]

The questionnaire included the various measures discussed previously as well as several groups of questions written especially for this study. The indices which were used in this study are listed in Appendix B. In addition to the previously discussed Woodward-Roper Political Participation Scale, several others are employed. One is a traditional socioeconomic status index, based equally on measures of income, occupation and education. A second is an Index of Leadership, composed both of questions regarding actual behavior as well as questions asking the respondent for a self-assessment. Finally, an index for each of Maslow's five need levels was constructed. For the four deprived categories, specific questions were used which are theoretically justifiable on the basis of the discussion presented in chapter 2.[5]

The Index of Self-Actualization used is a composite index of mental health. Because, according to Maslow's personality theory, an individual cannot be psychically deprived and mentally healthy, in order to achieve the minimal status of being self-actualizing (that is, growth- rather than deficiency-motivated), a respondent had to show no evidence of any of the four lower needs (based on cut-off points determined by the score distribution for each need). Such individuals were further subdivided on the basis of their total score (from 0 to 6) on the questions which composed the Indices of Psychic Deprivation. Persons who evidence no psychic deprivation and whose total score on these measures fell between 0-3 are hereafter referred to as "high self-actualizers." Persons

---

4. All coding was done twice by two different individuals. All key punching was also verified by a second individual.

5. In a few cases, as noted, these questions are taken from scales which were included in the questionnaire. These questions appeared to be a strong indicator of a particular need, in addition to being theoretically connected to other personality dimensions. In noting the relationships which are reported, therefore, the reader should keep in mind this overlap. Analysis has shown, however, that the results are not affected to any important degree by this overlap.

who had higher overall scores (4-6) and who also showed no evidence of a lower need are categorized as "low self-actualizers."[6]

A word of explanation should be offered at this point concerning the reason why persons motivated by the need for self-actualization were not identified by specific questions designed to elicit the major facets of this need syndrome, as discussed by Maslow. First of all, it was felt that knowledge about the higher reaches of this need is fragmentary and speculative. Indeed, in an "open-ended" personality model, no limits can be set on human growth and development. Similar to the history of long-distance runners, as man learns more about the conditions which stimulate his competent functioning, he will hopefully excel and exceed presently envisioned "limits" of psychic competence.

Second, I see the four deficiency needs as specific, delimitable areas of need which humans require in order to function optimally. Self-actualization, on the other hand, is not definable by a limitable group of human requirements, but is rather a process of growth, the end point of which is individually determined by a person's accumulation of psychic strengths and the sociocultural environment in which he lives.

Last, it was felt that what is important in an exploratory analysis of the relationship between personality and political behavior is to identify those persons who have begun this process—persons whose inner requirements allow behavior that is functional and adaptive in terms of the values and goals of the person himself. Thus, similar to the problems raised in the study of intelligence, the higher reaches of self-actualization are speculative in extent and assumed here to affect a numerically very small group. (As the division of self-actualizers in this study into Low and High indicates, however, it appears that there is considerable value in refining the analysis of self-actualization into those who have just begun the process of personal fulfillment and those who are further down the road.)

Thus a natural continuum of mental health appears, as shown in Table 4.1. It is of interest to note that psychically deprived persons predominantly responded to one need area. (There is no empirical reason why threatened individuals could not answer positively the few questions composing each of the four Indices of Psychic Deprivation, instead of responding predominantly to one dimension of deprivation.) Hence, in the research discussed below, only 17 percent of the subjects are typified by salience of more than one basic need in their psychic economy; based on Maslow's view that people generally move on to a higher need after lower needs cease to be motivating, this figure would appear to be within reason.

---

6. It is assumed that an assessment of such factors as creativity, curiosity and empathic ability would have further differentiated the High Self-Actualizers.

Table 4.1

CONTINUUM OF MENTAL HEALTH

	Percent	N
High self-actualizers	20.4	102
Low self-actualizers	24.3	120
Individuals with any one need	38.3	189
Individuals with any two needs	13.8	68
Individuals with three-four needs	3.2	16
	100%	495

Results

The Need for Physiological Satisfaction

Persons who are primarily motivated by unsatisfied physiological needs have previously been pictured as existing on the extreme lower end of our hypothetical continuum marked by "concern with self" versus "concern with environment (and self in relation to it)." Overwhelmingly preoccupied with physical survival, they do not have enough psychic energy remaining to become mentally or physically concerned with their environment. Thus, in the preceding theoretical discussion, persons motivated by physiological needs were considered to be apathetic and uninvolved. While this inactivity stems from a fixation with survival, it also is caused by a general distrust of human relationships as well as a disbelief in the amenability of one's environment to improvement through human activity.

Their apathy is related then to a basic anxiety and accompanying hostility (to use Horney's terms) which lead to a view of the world as threatening and overpowering. Action is thus seen as an extreme response to threat—in addition to being essentially and profoundly futile. Such heightened anxiety and hostility are symptomatic of psychic deprivation, of neuroticism. Are we accurate in so describing individuals who exist at the base of the need hierarchy? An important factor in answering this question is whether their view of the world as a jungle reflects their life situation accurately—whether, in other words, they are objectively and currently deprived. Also to be considered are their scores on the Manifest Anxiety scale and the Security-Insecurity Inventory—general measures of mental health.

Fifty-two individuals in our field study exhibited unfulfilled physiological needs. Of these fifty-two individuals with unfulfilled physiological needs, twelve (or 23.1 percent, as opposed to 10.2 percent for the rest of the subjects) also displayed a need for safety. Thus physiological and safety needs were correlated (r = +.14), a relationship which would be expected because of an overlap of life experiences causing both types of psychic deprivation. The fact that forty persons in the lowest need group (76.9 percent) did not show a need for safety, however, indicates that the two dimensions are separate and isolable (though weakly related).

There was a lack of relationship (r = .01) between the Needs for Physiological Satisfaction and for Affection. Here, of the fifty-two persons with physiological needs, 16 (or 30.8 percent, as opposed to 25.5 percent in the rest of the group) show a need for affection as well. Because economic deprivation has been associated with authoritarian child-rearing methods, it was expected that some overlap would occur. Because the need for affection can occur as well in homes that are not economically deprived, it would not be expected that a great deal of association between these two needs would be found.

Finally, between the Need for Physiological Satisfaction and an unfulfilled Need for Esteem, a relationship (r = +.16) again exists, with an overlap of twenty-three individuals (44.2 percent, as opposed to 26.4 percent in the rest of the group). Again, the common factor of economic deprivation is assumed to account for a good deal of the overlap that exists here also.[7]

As expected, the physiological need area bears a clear inverse relationship (r = -.32, p = .001) to the index of social economic status. With the categories collapsed for added clarity, the relationship is as follows:

Table 4.2

PHYSIOLOGICAL NEED versus SES[*]

	Low	Middle	High	
All other subjects	18.7%	41.5%	39.8%	100%
Physiological need group	51.9%	38.5%	9.6%	100%

[*] As just stated, there are fifty-two individuals with physiological needs. Thus the N's for the tables in this section (4.1-4.11) are 443 and fifty-two, for the total of 495 subjects.

What is important to note here is not the expected, strong relationship which Physiological Need has to socioeconomic status. In view of the situational factors causing this need, what is important is the fact that half of the group—whatever the status of their econom-

7. Using Spearman correlation coefficients, the significance levels between physiological need are: with safety, .001; with affection, .371; and with esteem, .001.

ic origin—are <u>not</u> found in the lower status group. Their expressed needs, however, would make it appear that they were <u>in actuality</u>—not relatively—still economically deprived. Now, however, the deprivation has become psychic instead of economic.[8] This agrees with Maslow's theory that unfulfilled needs can be life-long motivating factors, in spite of improvements which may have occurred in a person's life situation. Thus by employing both variables that are psychological (that is, Physiological Need) and others that are sociological (that is, status), it is possible to achieve a clearer understanding of the factors motivating the commonly labeled "lower class" attitudes and behavior.

While roughly half of this group of individuals are objectively deprived, then, it is important to note that half are not. Nevertheless, the group as a whole should (theoretically) be typified by insecurity and anxiety. What do the results indicate? First of all, there is a clear relationship ($r = .16$, $p = .001$) between Physiological Needs and insecurity, as measured by Maslow's Security-Insecurity Inventory. (Analysis of the components of this Inventory indicates that it is a good general measure of psychic deprivation, although it appears to bear no direct relationship to physiological needs.) This relationship is greatest at the extreme of the insecurity scores[9] where individuals with physiological needs are more than twice as likely (19.2 percent versus 8.8 percent) to be found, compared with individuals in the rest of the group.

An even closer relationship exists, however, between this most basic need area and high scores on the Taylor Manifest Anxiety Scale ($r = .23$, $p = .001$), pointing to the lack of control which has been hypothesized to typify the low end of the need hierarchy.

Table 4.3

PHYSIOLOGICAL NEED versus MANIFEST ANXIETY

	Low			High			
	1	2	3	4	5	6	
All other subjects	19.6	23.2	26.4	15.8	9.3	5.6	100%
Physiological need group	21.2	9.6	15.4	21.2	19.2	13.5	100%

---

8. One is also reminded here of Bettelheim's (1950) disturbed children who, though from economically secure homes, could never secure enough food.

9. The Inventory scores were collapsed into five groups.

Thus persons exhibiting unfulfilled physiological needs as here defined tend to be both insecure and anxious on measures that have been clinically derived and widely employed in field as well as diagnostic research.

With intolerance of ambiguity, the relationship is also significant ($r = .28$, $p = .001$), suggesting the importance for this need group of structuring the phenomena of a world which is frightening in its unpredictability. Indeed, it was suggested in the theoretical discussion that intolerance of ambiguity could be considered as a coping mechanism—or a means by which deep-seated anxieties are made manageable—used by individuals operating at the base of the need hierarchy.

Because of the theoretical similarity between intolerance of ambiguity and the manifestations of closed-mindedness, one would expect to find—and one does—a similarly clear relationship ($r = .29$, $p = .001$) between unresolved physiological needs and Rokeach's Dogmatism Scale. (Indeed, one of the major hypotheses directing this research is the close relationship between dogmatism, as described by Rokeach, and psychic deprivation, as delimited by Maslow.) With the categories collapsed to add clarity, we see that there is a significant difference between the dogmatism displayed by individuals with unresolved physiological needs and that of the rest of the subjects. Further, this difference is primarily due to their average need to take a definite stand, rather than to a lower percentage of undogmatic answers in relation to the rest of the group.

Table 4.4

PHYSIOLOGICAL NEED versus DOGMATISM

	Undogmatic	Neutral	Dogmatic	
All other subjects	5.8	47.9	46.3	100%
Physiological need group	0.0	34.6	65.4	100%

If further research bears out the strong relationship between this area of psychic deprivation and dogmatism, we will know a great deal more about the factors causing the formation of an individual's central beliefs that the world is hostile and threatening and, concurrently, about the cognitive functioning of persons who operate at the base of Maslow's need hierarchy.

Both Rokeach's Dogmatism Scale and the Intolerance of Ambiguity Scale allow a person to impose rigid categories by his choice of alternative answers. The cause for this rigidity has been hypothesized to be the nature of the individual's central beliefs

about the nature of his environment and others, as well as himself.
A direct measure of the degree to which the world is perceived as
threatening is the Threat Orientation Scale which was devised by
Martin and Westie. If the reason that physiologically deprived individuals are dogmatic and intolerant of ambiguity is because they
view the world as hostile and threatening, we would expect to find
a significant relationship here also, as is the case ($r = .19$, $p =$
.001). With the categories collapsed for clarity, we can see that
individuals expressing this type of deprivation clearly tend to positively state that the world is threatening.

Table 4.5

PHYSIOLOGICAL NEED versus THREAT ORIENTATION

	Unthreatened	Neutral	Threatened	
All other subjects	32.7	27.3	40.0	100%
Physiological need group	11.6	26.9	61.5	100%

While the Threat Orientation Scale deals with the individual's
perception of the world as threatening, the Interpersonal Threat
Scale is specifically concerned with a person's declared sensitivity to socially threatening situations. We have earlier suggested
the existence of a continuum of concern with the world which parallels Maslow's need hierarchy. Persons existing at the base of the
need hierarchy are assumed to operate at the low end of this continuum—that is, to be concerned with self rather than with their environment and to be apathetic rather than socially active. Nevertheless, these physiologically deprived individuals exhibit a heightened sensitivity toward threat in interpersonal relationships ($r =$
.21, $p = .001$) which corresponds to their view of their environment
as being likewise threatening and hostile.

The inward states of anxiety and fear, we are told by psychologists, are intimately connected with outwardly directed hostility
and intolerance. If the physiologically deprived group is so beset
by inner insecurities, it should thus be correspondingly found to be
generally intolerant and authoritarian.

The F-scale, as has been noted previously, is both a measure
of a particular personality type whose major concern is with power and also an indication (because of personality needs) of generalized intolerance. As would be theoretically predicated, unfulfilled
physiological needs and authoritarianism are clearly related ($r =$
.34, $p = .001$), with people in this need group twice as likely to
agree with authoritarian items. Collapsed into three categories
for clarity, the scores are:

Table 4.6

PHYSIOLOGICAL NEED versus F-SCALE

	Nonauthoritarian	Neutral	Authoritarian	
All other subjects	51.9	31.2	16.9	100%
Physiological need group	38.8	40.4	30.7	100%

While these individuals are only 10.5 percent of the total group of subjects, they account for over 17 percent of the persons whose answers on F-scale questions indicate authoritarianism. To anticipate our discussion these most psychically deprived individuals are also the most likely to be authoritarian of all the groups in this study. When the scores are collapsed in three categories (see Appendix C); in mean score (mean = 4.08) this group is second highest in authoritarianism.

The questionnaire of Subject 0458 reflects in many ways the scores of individuals who are physiologically deprived. As a lumber grader and trimmer, this subject is a semiskilled operative whose age group (forty-six to fifty-five) and the number of years at his present job (eleven) suggest the limits of his socioeconomic mobility. In spite of his completion of high school, his total annual family income ($4,000-5,000) combined with his occupation, place him in the low SES group. Not only does he recall a childhood of poverty in Missouri, he states that spiritual and financial problems are of utmost concern to him now. When given a choice, he opts for a simplistic solution to complex problems, agreeing that "if we had enough policemen, there wouldn't be any race riots"; that "we shouldn't waste good tax money educating bearded 'beatniks'"; and that Goldwater's "get tough" line with Communists was the path to take because "power is all they respect."

Anxious and insecure, Subject 0458 is in the top 9.5 percent of all the subjects on dogmatism (with a score of 215), shares with only six other subjects the distinction of receiving the highest possible score on Threat Orientation and—out of 495 subjects—is the only one to agree emphatically with every item of the F-scale. (Indeed, "emphatically" hardly suggests the intolerance of this subject who drew special over-agreement categories and then checked them on two of the items.) Finally, this subject (who is a Republican as were his parents before him) is active in the Pentecostal church (where he attends every Sunday and also belongs to a social club), belongs to a fraternal organization—and, under "offices held" lists "C.I.O. Union President." While such a leadership position (and his high political participation score) are unusual for a

psychically deprived individual, in this case his personal philosophy corresponds in its hostility and suspiciousness with the views
of many of his fellow workers and his activity may be seen as a
natural extension of his threatened and punitive views. Furthermore, his participation is accompanied by a clear belief in the inefficacy of political activity.

 With this thumbnail portrait of a physiologically deprived individual before us, let us turn next to more directly sociopolitical
attitudes expressed by this psychically deprived group. Because
of the clear tendency of this group to be intolerant of others (as
expressed by their F-scale scores), it might be assumed that
their scores on Rosenberg's Faith-in-People Scale would be similarly high. Here, however, the relationship is weaker ($r = .12$,
$p = .005$). Perhaps this weak relationship occurs because a lack of
faith in people may be dependent upon an individual's degree of
concern with others and his need for interpersonal relationships.

 The Political Efficacy Scale, it will be remembered, is a measure of a person's belief that the political world is manipulable and
amenable to his activity. It has been found to be strongly related to
actual political participation. We have hypothesized that Maslow's
need hierarchy also corresponds to a second continuum, one that
can be entitled "Control over Self—Perceived Control over Environment" and going from low to high. Persons who operate at the
base of the need hierarchy were conceptualized not only as being
politically nonparticipant, but as being nonparticipant because of
their view of the world as unmanageable. In support of this hypothesis, we find a significant relationship ($r = .33$, $p = .001$) between
Physiological Needs and lack of political efficacy:

Table 4.7

PHYSIOLOGICAL NEED versus POLITICAL
EFFICACY SCALE

	High			Low		
	1	2	3	4	5	
All other subjects	23.0	35.9	23.9	10.4	6.8	100%
Physiological need group	15.4	17.3	26.9	28.8	11.5	100%

Indeed, this need group—of all five of our need groups—is not only
the most intolerant, it is also most lacking in a sense of competence.

 In the first part of this book, issue was taken with some measures of anomie (the objective social state) on the grounds that
anomic individuals are nevertheless likely to express agreement

with modal values. In connection with this, in spite of a strong
tendency for individuals with unfulfilled physiological needs to
feel that their political action would be ineffective, we find a lack
of relationship between this need and lack of citizen duty (r = -.01,
p = .45), with almost all the scores clustering (as usual) around
the agree end.

Table 4.8

PHYSIOLOGICAL NEED versus CITIZEN DUTY SCALE

	High		Low			
	1	2	3	4	5	
All other subjects	57.6	37.7	3.2	0.7	0.9	100%
Physiological need group	46.2	48.1	1.9	0.0	3.8	100%

As Merton has pointed out, however, it is when agreement on modal values does not harmonize with possibilities for social action
that anomie is encouraged—and here psychological factors (for example, lack of political efficacy) can be seen as limitations (perceived and therefore real) on social action. Thus socialization un-
accompanied by psychic strength is largely meaningless. This is
a telling blow on an educational system that measures its success
in terms of verbal agreement.

　　Another measure of social concern is the Esteem Scale, which
taps a desire to be important and obvious in the eyes of others. It
has been hypothesized that persons operating at the base of
Maslow's need hierarchy are, in a profound sense, antisocial. We
find evidence for this in the significant, inverse relationship between physiological need and concern with esteem of others (r =
-.23, p = .001). This scale, like the Political Efficacy Scale, has
also been found to be an effective measure of an individual's proclivity to participate politically. Hence, thus far the performances
of this group of deprived individuals conforms to theoretical expectations. They tend to be insecure and anxious, dogmatic and intolerant. Not only is their environment perceived as threatening, but
their interpersonal relationships are also grounds for anxiety. Further, on two scales which had been widely related to political participation (Efficacy and Esteem), their performance indicates that
activity will likely be blocked by psychic need.

　　The questions relating to Status Concern also are related to
a social dimension—in this case, to the person's desire for social
mobility and status improvement. Here the relationship is weak
and inverse (r = -.09, p = .027). Not only is it unlikely that social
mobility will be appealing to individuals who lack social security

and are primarily concerned with self-preservation, it is also
probable that status striving (remembering the relationship between this group and low SES) will be more likely to be a middle-
class attitude. However, it is an interesting point to consider
whether in our achievement-oriented, affluent society, status-concern is not an indication that the socialization process has been
successful. In any event, the negative relationships with Esteem
and Status Concern can be considered suggestive of a general
withdrawal (based on anxiety and hostility) from interpersonal relations.

Srole's Anomia Scale has been variously characterized as a
measure of despair over life chances and as an expression of the
meaninglessness of life. Anomia was described in chapter 3, above,
as "a diffuse feeling of separation from formal, institutionalized
society and from the informal society of their social milieu by persons who cannot discern a social interest, apart from their individual interests." As such, it appears to be an accurate expression
of the world view of persons who are primarily concerned with
self-preservation and who, concurrently, perceive themselves as
lacking in ability to control their world. The clear relationship
(r = .24, p = .001) between unfulfilled physiological need and Srole's
Anomia Scale further underlines the psychic constriction and an-
guish of those with unfulfilled physiological needs.

Table 4.9

PHYSIOLOGICAL NEED versus ANOMIA SCALE

	Low			High			
	1	2	3	4	5	6	
All other subjects	37.0	23.5	20.8	10.4	6.3	2.0	100%
Physiological need group	23.1	17.3	19.2	17.3	17.3	5.8	100%

Thus far, we have been concerned with proclivities, with various measures previously shown to be predictive of activity and attitude. If these measures are valid—that is if they measure what
they are supposed to measure—this deprived group concurrently
should tend to be socially isolated and politically nonparticipant on
more directly behavioral measures. The Woodward-Roper Political Participation Scale, as has been discussed, registers a variety
of political activity in addition to voting (such as contributing money, attending meetings, et cetera). As would be expected from the
lack of political efficacy and lack of esteem expressed by individuals with unfulfilled physiological needs—as well as from their

tendency toward low status—we find a significant <u>inverse</u> relationship (r = - .24, p = .001) between this need and political participation scores. Collapsing the Index of Political Participation into
three categories for clarity, we see that while they tend to vote
(though believing in the inefficacy of such activity), they are very
unlikely to join with others in more personally involving types of
political activities.

Table 4.10

PHYSIOLOGICAL NEED versus INDEX OF
POLITICAL PARTICIPATION

	Low	Middle	High	
All other subjects	32.3	35.2	32.5	100%
Physiological need group	40.4	53.8	5.7	100%

Our Index of Leadership is composed both of offices which the
person has held since school, and his assessment of his position
in relation to his associates in general and in informal discussion
groups. Again we find an inverse relationship (r = -.17, p = .001)
between this need at the base of Maslow's hierarchy and social activity. Though individuals in this group may participate in some
political activities, the likelihood exists that they will not assume
positions of even informal leadership among their peers. By their
scores on other measures, such nonparticipation becomes understandable—to be inconspicuous is a necessary concomitant of safety.

Table 4.11

PHYSIOLOGICAL NEED versus INDEX OF LEADERSHIP

	Low		High		
	1	2	3	4	
All other subjects	18.3	47.0	32.3	2.5	100%
Physiological need group	30.8	51.9	13.5	3.8	100%

In summary, although the relationships are not uniformly
strong, the empirical evidence presented here is congruent with
the theoretical discussion of these individuals which has been pre-

sented previously. In various ways, persons motivated by physiological need indicate a clear tendency to hold the belief that their existential state is one of threat and insecurity—a belief which disallows positive social concern. When they do consider their environment, it tends to be with hostility, intolerance and dogmatism—for their world is perceived as threatening and uncertain. Their anxieties lead to mental, as well as behavioral, constriction. Perhaps, if verbalized, their inner state might be described as follows:

> In anxiety we do not fear nothingness. We fear something; we do not know it and feel unable to know what it is. This nothing is still something, though it is deprived of any definite character. It fits no scheme; it is beyond our reach. It deprives us of our trust in any order. It is not absolute nothingness but absolute "otherness." It would not be frightening if it were "nothing." It is frightening because it is still "something"—though not to be known, not to be acted upon. (Reizler, 1964, p. 148)

Although these individuals have been taught to believe in the duty of every citizen to participate in the political system, questions reveal that such activity is likely believed to be futile in a world which is meaningless, and unresponsive to individual activity. In short, persons with unfulfilled physiological needs can be typified as social, political and psychic isolates: undemocratic and nonparticipant, they tend to be persons whose psychic needs have negated the politicization which they have received and the democratic values to which they have been exposed in school.

The Need for Safety and Security

It has been hypothesized that individuals motivated by the need for safety and security are, in many ways, similar to the individuals with unfulfilled physiological needs whom we have just considered. As they operate near the base of the need hierarchy, their concern with self should also outweigh their concern with their environment. Further, their hypothesized lack of control over their own impulses should be concurrent with a perceived lack of control over the world around them. Yet these persons operate one step higher on the hierarchy of basic needs and some differences should also mark their attitudes and behavior. Most important, the "flavor" of this need should emphasize—where our questions allow for such a concern—the need for security in an insecure world.

Because of the similarity of causal conditions between one type of insecurity (as discussed in chapter 2) and physiological need, it is not surprising to find a relationship ($r = .14$, $p = .001$) between the two lowest basic needs. Of the fifty-seven individuals with a need for security, twelve (21.1 percent, as opposed to 9.1 percent in the rest of the group) also exhibit a need for physiological satisfaction. On the other hand, there is a clear inverse relationship ($r = -.33$, $p = .001$) between the Need for Safety and

Security and the Need for Affection, with an overlap of seven individuals (12.3 percent, as opposed to 27.9 percent for the rest of the group). Finally, there is a weak relationship (r = .08, p = .04) between the Need for Safety and the Need for Esteem, with an overlap of twenty-one persons (36.8 percent, as opposed to 27.2 percent for the rest of the group). The relationship between Safety and Physiological Needs, as explained above, is not unexpected—given the overlap of causal life situations. This relationship between causal conditions of physical deprivation and the need for security is probably also responsible for the perceived lack of esteem from others in some of the individuals expressing a need for security. The clear inverse relationship to the Need for Affection is perhaps best explained as a fear of involvement—for affection needs are relational needs—by individuals so lacking in basic security.

There is a much weaker, but again inverse relationship between socioeconomic status, as measured by our index of occupation, income and education, and this area of psychic deprivation (r = -.12, p = .005). However, compared to the figures presented for the first need group, we notice the beginnings of a shift away from the low status group and into the high status group (reflected in a much lower correlation), so that close to a third of this second need group is found in each status category.

Table 4.12

NEED FOR SAFETY versus SES*

	Low	Middle	High	
All other subjects	20.3	42.0	37.7	100%
Safety need group	36.8	35.1	28.1	100%

*Thus the N's for the tables in this section (4.12-4.19) are 438 and fifty-seven, with the total = 495.

Thus, to answer the question as to whether persons with a need for safety can be typified as lower class, we would have to answer, "in general, no more than they can be typified as middle or upper class."

In turning first to a consideration of the psychological measures, a nonsignificant and slightly negative relationship exists between the Need for Safety and Maslow's Security-Insecurity Inventory. Upon reflection, it appears likely that this nonsignificant relationship is due to the lack of questions in our Index of Security which deal with an active sense of threat. (Such questions were excluded because of their content overlap with other measures that were employed.) A nonsignificant relationship, probably due to the same cause, is also found when this safety Index is correlated with the Manifest Anxiety Scale (r = .01, p = .37). However, here a weak trend toward manifest anxiety is present.

Table 4.13

NEED FOR SAFETY versus MANIFEST ANXIETY

	Low			High			
	1	2	3	4	5	6	
All other subjects	20.1	22.1	25.6	16.2	10.0	5.9	100%
Safety need group	17.5	19.3	22.8	17.5	12.3	10.5	100%

That these persons are insecure and anxious, however, frequently can be seen in the statements that they made in response to the question "What are the kinds of things that you worry about most? (What are some of the problems that really concern you now?)"[10] Frequently the concern is personal—dealing with such areas as "Having a good job; providing a good home for my family" (Subject 0167); "Job security—ability to do my job well" (Subject 0301); and "Keeping good health" (Subject 0272—in the fifty-six to sixty-five age group). Often, however, the concern of these subjects turns outward, as in the case of Subject 0199, who listed "(A) Lack of enough money to do what I want, (B) Lack of respect in most young people; (C) Lack of disciplinary action in our court system." Subject 0005 worries about "The aparent disregard for law and order," and Subject 0014 has anxieties in similar dimensions: "Crooked politics   education system   government spending   lack of teeth in our laws   judges to soft." That the world has not provided these subjects with adequate security is clear; that this felt insecurity is a "rational" response to the chaos and disorder in their environment is also apparent.

It was earlier hypothesized that there is a strong relationship between an unfulfilled Need for Security and intolerance of ambiguity, as the need to impose an artificial structure on the world can be a means of coping with the lack of order which such individuals perceive to exist. Although there is an overlap of one question here, there obviously exists a relationship between these two measures (p < .001, X^2 = 27.4552, d.f. = 5), thus providing some support for this contention (r = .20, p = .001).[11] As Subject 0432 states,

---

10. To give the reader a better feeling for the human dimension of our data, subjects' statements are reported in the original —without corrections for grammar or spelling or distracting Latin phrases which indicate our awareness of such matters.

11. A significant relationship was also found to be present be-

in regard to what he worries about, "I wish they would finish the war one way or another. [Also] they keep taking men away from jobs and putting more work on you." Ambiguity on the macro- or micro-level is clearly intolerable.

A relationship between the Need for Safety and dogmatism also exists, although this relationship (r = .07, p = .06) is considerably weaker than that which occurred on need level one. These scores show a strong similarity to those of the physiological need group.

Table 4.14

NEED FOR SAFETY versus DOGMATISM

	Undogmatic	Neutral	Dogmatic	
All other subjects	5.0	48.6	46.4	100%
Safety need group	7.0	29.8	63.2	100%

Persons expressing physiological or safety needs thus exhibit similar needs to view the world dogmatically and to be intolerant of ambiguity. Do they likewise (as the subjects' worries would suggest) share a view of the world as hostile and threatening?

In turning to the Threat Orientation scores, it should be kept in mind that the reason for dogmatism and intolerance of ambiguity is hypothesized to be anxieties stemming from existence in a world which is perceived as hostile and threatening. It is most interesting, in view of the lack of relationship between the Need for Safety and Maslow's Security-Insecurity Inventory, to note the relationship (r = .13, p = .002)[12] between the Need for Safety and the Threat Orientation Scale.

Table 4.15

NEED FOR SAFETY versus THREAT ORIENTATION

	Unthreatened	Neutral	Threatened	
All other subjects	32.0	29.2	38.9	100%
Safety need group	19.3	12.3	68.5	100%

---

tween physiological need and intolerance of ambiguity, although there was no overlap in that case.

12. p < .001, X^2 = 29.4260, d.f. = 6.

However, while persons motivated by a need for safety feel that the world is threatening and hostile, they do not express the same fear of interpersonal (that is, social) relationships. Here, in contrast to the scores of persons with unresolved physiological needs, there is a nonsignificant relationship (with a weak trend) between the Need for Safety and the Interpersonal Threat Scale. Perhaps the lack of a clear positive or negative trend represents an ambivalence about social relationships by individuals who are beginning to show some concern for their environment.

Another indication that, in spite of the lack of significant relationship with Maslow's Inventory and the Manifest Anxiety Scale, this group is psychically deprived is the relationship between the Need for Safety and scores on the F-scale ($r = .19$, $p = .001$).[13] Authoritarian in outlook, these individuals show a marked concern with the power dimension as they try to establish meaning in a world which is basically insecure and hostile. Illustrative of the authoritarianism of these subjects is the concern of Subject 0434 with "secrecy of our government toward the people of the U.S."— a personal statement of the well-known F-scale item "Most people don't realize how much our lives are controlled by plots planned in secret places."

To turn to the more directly sociopolitical attitudes, we find that—as would be expected from their F-scale scores—individuals with an unresolved need for safety likewise have a tendency to express a lack of faith-in-people ($r = .12$, $p = .004$). Indeed, there is a logical as well as a psychological connection between a view of the world as threatening and a lack of faith in the people who compose this world.

Theoretically, one would expect to find in persons whose view of the world and of others is fearful and distrusting a concurrent belief that their actions would be ineffective in attempting to control or direct their political system. Empirically, we find a weak relationship ($r = .08$, $p = .04$) between this level of psychic deprivation and lack of political efficacy—although not as many individuals express the extreme lack of efficacy which we found in the first need group. (As this group includes many more individuals whose work—for example, nursing supervisor, foreman, school counselor—would lead them to a belief in their competence, the somewhat reduced inefficacy scores are a likely result of personal experience reducing inner anxiety and heightening an individual's sense of competence.) (See Table 4.16.)

While these psychically deprived individuals tend to express the belief that political activity is futile, however, they tend to agree with the participatory norms which they have doubtless been taught in school, for among the persons who most strongly believe that a citizen has a duty to participate "whether such political activity is seen as worth while or efficacious," one is more likely to

---

13. $p < .001$, $X^2 = 47,2415$, d.f. = 6.

Table 4.16

NEED FOR SAFETY versus POLITICAL
EFFICACY SCALE

	High			Low		
	1	2	3	4	5	
All other subjects	22.8	36.1	23.3	10.7	7.1	100%
Safety need group	17.5	17.5	31.6	24.6	8.8	100%

find individuals with a need for security than those without this
need (r = .11, p = .009), in spite of their avowed belief in the futility of such activity.

Table 4.17

NEED FOR SAFETY versus CITIZEN DUTY SCALE

	High			Low		
	1	2	3	4	5	
All other subjects	55.5	39.3	3.4	0.5	1.4	100%
Safety need group	63.2	35.1	0.0	1.8	0.0	100%

However, given the lack of political efficacy of this group, as well
as their tendency to be politically nonparticipant, figures such as
these again impress the lesson that <u>for democratic values to be
actualized in an individual's life, it is necessary to have a combination of both socialization into these values and psychic strength
in order to exercise them as democratic norms require.</u>
        The Esteem Scale is another indirect measure of a person's
ability to participate politically, though its questions are specifically concerned with an individual's willingness to be obvious in
social situations. The Need for Safety shows an <u>inverse</u> relationship (r = -.07, p = .07) to the Esteem Scale, but the relationship
to this scale is considerably weaker than it was with the first
group. This relationship between the Need for Safety and the Esteem Scale is perhaps a reflection of basic insecurity which would
cause persons so motivated to shun situations in which their personal worth would be measurable (as well as a somewhat greater
concern for interpersonal relationships than the physiological need
group has). The weak <u>inverse</u> relationship (r = -.09, p = .03) be-

tween individuals with a need for safety and the questions tapping
a concern with status mobility is perhaps also a reflection of a
constriction of social concern as a posture of defense.

Table 4.18

NEED FOR SAFETY versus STATUS CONCERN

	Low			High			
	1	2	3	4	5	6	
All other subjects	0.9	5.9	24.4	47.3	20.3	1.1	100%
Safety need group	5.3	14.0	36.8	29.8	12.3	1.8	100%

Although subjects with a need for safety have, on the average, higher social-economic status than do the individuals who are found in
the physiological need group (and thus might be expected to show a
greater interest in status mobility), these figures in Table 4.18 indicate that they tend to have—for understandable psychological reasons—a desire to turn down advancement and remain in the social
position which has already been achieved. This emphasis on job security is epitomized by Subject 0456, a teacher who has been so
employed for thirty-seven years, who lists first (under what three
things he would most like to have or to change in his life "To have
a steady job"!

Finally, although these persons have moved further up the hierarchy to self-actualization, they still share many of the same
anxieties and fears of the individuals with unfulfilled physiological
needs, although these anxieties are muted (we may hypothesize by
increased need satisfaction). Thus the scores of these individuals
on Srole's Anomia Scale (which has a distribution very similar to
those of the first need group) show a positive, but weak relationship ($r = .06$, $p = .11$).

One of the best pieces of evidence which can be offered here
of the existence of a continuum of growing social concern which
parallels Maslow's need hierarchy is the changing relationship to
the Index of Political Participation as we move up the need hierarchy to psychic fulfillment and self-actualization. In the case of
first need, there was a strong inverse relationship. With the second need, this inverse relationship grows much weaker ($r = -.06$,
$p = .08$). We can hypothesize here that as psychic factors tend
to depress participation grow weaker, other factors (particularly socioeconomic status) grow more important in determining
who will participate in political activity. (See Table 4.19.)

Simple participation, however—particularly the anonymity of
voting—is of a different quality from the assumption of positions

Table 4.19

NEED FOR SAFETY versus INDEX OF
POLITICAL PARTICIPATION

	Low	Middle	High	
All other subjects	31.3	37.9	30.8	100%
Safety need group	47.4	31.6	21.1	100%

of leadership, even among one's closest associates. Thus it is not surprising that there continues to exist an <u>inverse</u> relationship between psychic deprivation (in this case, the Need for Safety) and scores on our Index of Leadership (r = -.09, p = .02). As hypothesized earlier, it appears that persons who operate near the base of the need hierarchy are likely to be followers, rather than leaders, both socially and politically.

While this Need for Safety group may participate somewhat more in political life than the lowest need group, their insecurities keep them from desiring the social prominence which is a feature of public office and of leadership roles generally. Tending to view the world as threatening and the phenomena which surround them as unmanageable, persons who operate on this need level are likely to react with dogmatism and intolerance of ambiguity—to be inflexible and fearful in situations of crisis. Lacking faith-in-people and expressing the intolerance that is found to be associated with authoritarian personalities, such individuals, like the first group, are also likely to be numbered among our society's "undemocrats."

The Need for Affection and Belongingness

As a person moves up the need hierarchy toward self-actualization, a measurable, qualitative change takes place in his perspective of the world. This change is dictated by his own psychic needs. It has been conceptualized in chapter 2 that individuals who operate at the need for affection and belongingness level have arrived at an important psychological plateau. For at this point, their psychic needs dictate a desire for satisfaction which can only come from interpersonal activity. Therefore, while they still perceive the world as basically hostile and ungratifying, persons operating on this level are beginning a reaching out in interpersonal relationships. However, it is an anxious and uncertain reaching out motivated by psychic deprivation.

We have previously noted that of the 129 individuals who have been classified as expressing a need for affection, only sixteen (12.4 percent as opposed to 9.8 percent for the rest of the group)

concurrently exhibited a need for physiological satisfaction. Thus
there is little overlap and a nonsignificant relationship between
these two need groups. Between the Need for Safety and this third
need, it has been noted that there is a strong inverse relationship
(r = -.33, p = .001) with an overlap of seven (5.4 percent, as opposed to 13.7 percent for the rest of the group). Finally, there is
again a nonsignificant relationship between the Need for Affection
and the Need for Esteem, although there is an overlap of forty individuals (31.0 percent, as opposed to 27.3 percent for the rest of
the group). Thus the affection dimension, as it operates here, appears discrete from that of the other need areas.

As with the Need for Safety, we also find an inverse relationship (r = -.12, p = .005) between this psychic need and socioeconomic status—a relationship that is considerably weaker than that
to Physiological Need. Again, however, we must also note that it
is almost as likely that a subject motivated by this need is found
in any of the three socioeconomic groups (almost, because there
is an increased tendency here toward the middle status group).

Table 4.20

NEED FOR AFFECTION versus SES*

	Low	Middle	High	
All other subjects	18.6	40.2	41.3	100%
Affection need group	32.6	44.2	23.3	100%

*Thus the N's for tables in this section (4.20-4.28) are 366
and 129, with a total of 495.

Thus, although a clear tendency exists for increasing status to be
associated with lack of psychic deprivation, this is far from a one-
to-one relationship. As one ascends the status ladder in our society, it appears that one also ascends the ladder of psychic fulfillment. (Causality, however, cannot be imputed without further study.
While it is likely that social deprivation causes psychic deprivation, it is also possible that lack of mental strength adversely affects an individual's life chances.)

Turning now to the psychological dimensions of this field
study, we find a significant relationship (r = .21, p = .001) between
this group and scores on Maslow's Security-Insecurity Inventory.
Indeed, the relationship between the need for affection and Maslow's measure of general psychic deprivation is stronger than it
was in the case of the group exhibiting unfulfilled physiological
needs. (It will be remembered that the Need for Affection and Belongingness was clearly stated by Maslow as a dimension which
the Inventory was designed to tap.)

Table 4.21

NEED FOR AFFECTION versus SECURITY-
INSECURITY INVENTORY

	Security		Insecurity			
	1	2	3	4	5	
All other subjects	29.8	28.4	18.0	16.7	7.1	100%
Affection need group	17.8	19.4	20.2	24.8	17.8	100%

Paralleling this indication of psychic deprivation, there is a similarly significant relationship between the Need for Affection and scores on the Taylor Manifest Anxiety scale ($r = .17$, $p = .001$). The scores on insecurity and anxiety indicate that these subjects have psychic weaknesses similar to those of individuals who were motivated by a Need for Physiological Satisfaction. But if Maslow's need hierarchy is to be of value in understanding human behavior, the scale performance of persons motivated by an unfulfilled Need for Affection should differ in important ways from that of the lowest need groups. As we will see, this is indeed the case.

While the first two need groups exhibited a clear tendency to be intolerant of ambiguity, no relationship occurs between the Need for Affection and this scale ($r = .01$, $p = .42$). In other words, it appears that with increased mental health these individuals (although scoring high on two well-known tests of psychic ill-health) are nevertheless much more able to tolerate ambiguity. This finding suggests an increased ability to be flexible, adaptable and politically useful in situations marked by changing conditions and uncertainty in decision-making.

These persons who are motivated by a need for affection still, however, show a tendency to be closed-minded in their cognitive functioning ($r = .13$, $p = .002$), although the collapsed scores below show that this tendency is not as extreme as occurred in the two lower need groups. (See Table 4.22.) Thus individuals expressing a need for affection, while lacking optimal mental health in terms of their general insecurity and anxiety, are nevertheless somewhat more cognitively flexible than (at least) the lowest need group, as the reduced relationship to intolerance of ambiguity and dogmatism indicates.

In examining the scores of this group on the Threat Orientation Scale, one can see an explanation for the noticeable reduction of intolerance of ambiguity and smaller reduction of dogmatism on the part of this group: it appears that their central beliefs about the world differ considerably from those of subjects operating on lower levels of the need hierarchy. For the first time, there is a

Table 4.22

NEW FOR AFFECTION versus DOGMATISM[*]

	Undogmatic	Neutral	Dogmatic	
All other subjects	5.2	50.0	44.8	100%
Affection need group	5.4	36.4	58.2	100%

[*]The reader should keep in mind the one question overlap here, although analysis indicates that it did not prejudice the results in any important degree.

nonsignificant relationship between an area of psychic deprivation and scores on the Threat Orientation Scale. This reduction is in line with our theoretical expectations which led us to assume that it is a particular set of central beliefs about the nature of the world, of other humans and of oneself which is responsible for constriction in cognitive functioning (that is, dogmatism), in positive affect and empathy (that is, intolerance and misanthropy) and in sociopolitical participation. As one's central beliefs (and basic anxieties) become less threatening, therefore, it is likely that one's functioning in several other dimensions will be markedly different.

Again, as in the case of the Need for Safety, there is also a nonsignificant relationship, with a weak positive trend ($r = .05$, $p = .12$), to the Interpersonal Threat Scale. This weak relationship is somewhat surprising in view of the assumed sensitivity of this group to hostility in interpersonal relationships. It is possible that the Need for Affection—a need which can only be reduced by interpersonal relations—requires a reduced sense of interpersonal threat so that activity can be initiated to help satiate this need. (Indeed, their lack of neutral scores gives a slight inverse correlation.)

The increased psychic fulfillment of this group is also seen in the lack of a significant relationship to authoritarianism—in spite of the hypothesized similarity between the primary home life of this group and that of persons who were the focus of the Berkeley study.[14] Again it is assumed that the type of psychic deprivation "flavors" attitudes. Thus, while it has been hypothesized that these individuals are intolerant of others, it is possible that it is difficult to express such punitive attitudes toward others who must be relied upon to assuage one's needs for affection and belonging-

14. Regarding the significant drop in F-scale scores on the part of this group, it is again of value to note Lane's (1962) comments regarding the dimension of homelessness. See chap. 2 above.

ness. This lack of a significant relationship between the need for affection and authoritarianism is congruent with the consistent finding, noted by Lane, that people who score high on McClelland's need for affiliation measure do not score high on the F-scale. Lane (1969) reasons, as I have done here, that persons so motivated "would be likely to hedge on extreme statements of any kind."[15]

Table 4.23

NEED FOR AFFECTION versus F-SCALE

	Nonauthoritarian	Neutral	Authoritarian	
All other subjects	49.0	34.2	18.0	100%
Affection need group	51.2	26.4	22.5	100%

Symptomatic of the psychic requirements of individuals who are motivated by needs for affection and belongingness are the concerns which they expressed in answer to the question about what worries them most. In reading through the responses to this question, it is apparent that several themes occur again and again. One theme is religious; its specific emphasis is brotherhood. To Subject 0073, her worry is "The unsaved souls around me." Subject 0251 says, in a similar vein, "I have no worries, for God has filled my heart with perfect peace. I am burdened, however, for lost souls." With thinly masked hostility toward others and a simultaneous need for belongingness, Subject 0006 lists his major concern as "People having a personal relation with Jesus Christ; the ones that don't will spend eternity in hell and burn for ever and ever." Tied to this theme of brotherhood through religion is a secular theme of the desire for peace and the cessation of all wars.

In addition to a search for belongingness through religion and a desire for the end of all hostilities, a third theme expressed by the Affection Need Group is concern with money. That this theme should be such a common concern of this particular need group appeared puzzling at first; on reflection, it is likely that the desire to be born rich or to have a great deal of money is indicative of a popularly conceived avenue to belongingness in this affluent society.

Another common theme is the concern with the impersonality and automation of the modern world. Subject 0076 puts it this way: "Big business and big government both state and federal Taking our freedom from us and taxing us without any say as to how our

---

15. However, it should be noted that 22.5 percent of this group do fall in the authoritarian column.

taxes will be spent—to many laws—to many tax breaks for big
money and to few for the worker." Subject 0256 (a Senior in college who works at the hospital) states his concern as "Government and society are getting far too complex. Man is only human;
he's not a computer. [He adds] I want to be rich. I want to work
out my personal problems by myself." To Subject 0351, the difficult state of his world centers around "Our Theving Government
and the whites loss of rights."

Finally, the questionnaires of persons expressing a need for
mutuality and interpersonal warmth are marked by the theme of
concern for better communication and more positive relationships
with others, especially one's immediate family. Subject 0194 expresses this concern as "The lack of understanding between the
peoples and honist communication," while Subject 0139 worries
about "companionship with my children" and Subject 0085 states
his major concern as simply "making friends." Similarly, Subject
0425 would most like in life to "cause people to be Loyal and Hon-
est." Thus, in a variety of seemingly unrelated concerns, persons
expressing a need for affection and belongingness indicate through
their worries the core need which flavors (we are hypothesizing)
their attitudes and behavior, a need which keeps them attuned to a
lack of warmth unfilled by government, by religion, by incomes
large or small, by significant others.

Turning now to more directly sociopolitical attitudes, we find
that the significant drop in this group's generalized intolerance,
as measured by the F-scale, has been accompanied by a drop in
lack of faith in people, as measured by Rosenberg's Scale. Although the relationship is still noticeable—as it should be for people whose unfulfilled psychic needs force a primary dependence
on successful interpersonal relationships which never adequately
supply this need—the strength of the relationship has greatly decreased and become nonsignificant ($r = .03$, $p = .24$).

Table 4.24

NEED FOR AFFECTION versus FAITH IN PEOPLE

	High			Low			
	1	2	3	4	5	6	
All other subjects	21.6	23.8	17.8	21.9	9.6	5.5	100%
Affection need group	17.8	18.6	23.3	15.5	14.0	10.9	100%

Individuals with a need for affection are unusual in a number
of respects. While their scores on the Maslow Security-Insecurity
Inventory and the Manifest Anxiety Scale indicate that they are psy-

chically deprived and their tendency toward dogmatism indicates constriction in cognitive functioning, the motivation of a Need for Affection is no predictor of several other measures which would appear to be associated with psychic deprivation (as we have seen with authoritarianism and misanthropy). Still, however, persons who have not reached the level of self-actualization simply do not have the psychic energy, optimism and positive affect that individuals possess who are more psychically competent. Thus with the Need for Affection there is again a relation to lack of political efficacy ($r = .07$, $p = .05$). Like the Need for Safety group, however, the Need for Affection group tends to be more efficacious than those subjects who operate at the bottom of the need hierarchy.

Table 4.25

NEED FOR AFFECTION versus POLITICAL EFFICACY

	High		Low			
	1	2	3	4	5	
All other subjects	23.5	35.2	22.1	12.0	7.1	100%
Affection need group	18.6	30.2	30.2	13.2	7.8	100%

In relation to the scores on the Citizen Duty Scale, there is again a nonsignificant relationship. As in the case of the Need for Security group, we also find that the expression of a citizen's duty more likely to be made by individuals with this psychic need than those in the rest of the group!

Table 4.26

NEED FOR AFFECTION versus CITIZEN DUTY SCALE

	High		Low			
	1	2	3	4	5	
All other subjects	54.9	41.0	2.5	0.5	1.1	100%
Affection need group	60.5	32.6	4.7	0.8	1.6	100%

With an increase in mental health, it might seem likely that subjects in this group would express a desire to be visible in the eyes of significant others so that their scores would show a positive relationship to the Esteem Scale. However, there is still a definite _inverse_ relationship between psychic deprivation, in this case the Need for Affection, and scores on the Esteem Scale (r = -.10, p = .01). While their rejection of others (as expressed through their misanthropy and authoritarianism scores), has grown much weaker, this group nevertheless lacks the psychic strength to desire prominence in the eyes of those others.

In our Status Concern scores, it is now possible to see a trend developing as we ascend the need hierarchy. In the Physiological and Safety Need Areas, there was a significant, _inverse_ relationship between an unfulfilled need and the desire for social mobility. In the case of the Need for Affection, we find that while the trend is still weakly negative, no statistical relationship exists (r = -.01, p = .41). It appears that insecurity in interpersonal relationships and the need primarily for warmth and affection (rather than status) in one's associations with others breed a negative attitude toward advancement per se—particularly advancement that would require giving up old friendships and forming new ones.[16] On the scale of values of this need group, such a choice would be most unsatisfactory.

In spite of the generally improved psychic competence of this group, there are numerous clues to the fact that persons with a need for affection still suffer from a constricted and anxious view of the world. Perhaps the most obvious example of this is the remaining, though weak, relationship (r = .08, p = .05) between this need and scores on Srole's Anomia Scale. It appears that persons in any group which can be termed psychically deprived (with the possible exception of the Need for Safety Group) can be typified by despair over the meaninglessness of their life situation—though these people certainly _cannot_ be considered as uniformly objectively deprived.

One of the clearest indications of the value of Maslow's personality theory to the concerns of political scientists is the relationship between each of the need groups and the Index of Political Participation. As was mentioned in connection with the Need for Safety, a definite trend also appears here in the changing scores as we move up the need hierarchy. With the Need for Affection, there is no relationship (however, the trend, for the first time, is positive [r = .0039, p = .47]). (See Table 4.27.) Most interestingly, another shift can also be seen—one which is in line with the theoretical discussion presented previously. For subjects in this group cannot be classified as inactive; rather their needs appear to force them into activity beyond what their psychic capabilities would allow; it is only in the high range that they are somewhat less participant than the rest of the subjects. Considering their scores in both the middle and high ranges, therefore, it is appar-

---

16. See Appendix A for a review of the type of choices confronting respondents to these questions.

Table 4.27

NEED FOR AFFECTION versus INDEX OF
POLITICAL PARTICIPATION

	Low	Middle	High	
All other subjects	33.9	34.9	31.4	100%
Affection need group	31.0	44.2	24.8	100%

ent that persons with a need for affection are more participant
than any of the deprived groups which have been considered thus
far.

Thus the Need for Affection, while psychically debilitating in
a number of important ways, is not predictive of an individual's
political participation. This corresponds to our theoretical discussion, in which it was hypothesized that persons exhibiting unfulfilled belongingness and affection needs would—in comparison with
other deprived individuals—tend to be "joiners." While it was also
hypothesized that such persons might be found relatively more frequently in leadership roles than members of lower need groups, it
is assumed that their psychic needs will prevent long-term success in these roles. In keeping with this line of reasoning, from
their Index of Leadership Scores, it can be seen that while persons
exhibiting a need for affection tend to be more participant than the
two lower need groups, they still tend to be followers rather than
leaders. Statistically the relationship has become non-significant
(r = -.03, p = .29).

Table 4.28

NEED FOR AFFECTION versus INDEX OF LEADERSHIP

	Low		High		
	1	2	3	4	
All other subjects	17.2	49.2	30.6	3.0	100%
Affection need group	26.4	42.6	29.5	1.6	100%

As hypothesized in chapter 2, therefore, it is likely that individuals with a Need for Affection, compared with members of other psychically deprived groups, will be prominent in sociopolitical
activities as their psychic needs both push them to seek satisfaction in interpersonal relationships and, further, as their greater

mental health (seen in relation to intolerance of ambiguity, faith in people, authoritarianism and threat orientation, for example) allows them to function more adequately in the world of politics. From the scores on the Index of Leadership, however, it appears likely that these persons will seek social satisfaction through group membership rather than through group leadership. Finally, in various ways—such as their scores on Maslow's Inventory, Manifest Anxiety and Anomia—it is apparent that these individuals also tend to deserve the label of "psychically deprived."

The Need for Esteem

Individuals who are motivated by a Need for Esteem occupy a halfway house: the most healthy of the psychically deprived group, they are hypothesized to be best able to manage their anxieties and needs and to engage in participatory roles in the world around them. Yet, motivated as they are by unfulfilled personality needs, these individuals, like those we have just examined, also partici-pate with an unhealthy purpose: they are driven by the need to compensate for an unfulfilled need for esteem. Further, like the proverbial miser with his unsatiable desire for gold, no amount of such values as respect, power or admiration will bring to the person with a need for esteem the life satisfaction possessed by a person who is growth-motivated.

As with the other psychically deprived groups, here too there is a clear inverse relationship ($r = -.18$, $p = .001$) between the Need for Esteem and SES. It can be seen that the distribution is very similar to that of the group characterized by the Need for Affection.

Table 4.29

NEED FOR ESTEEM versus SES[*]

	Low	Middle	High	
All other subjects	19.2	40.0	40.8	100%
Esteem need group	30.0	44.3	25.7	100%

[*] In the tables in this section (4.29-4.39), the N's are 140 (for the Esteem Group), and 355 (All Other Subjects), with the total = 495.

Again, while psychic deprivation is related to low SES, it is note-worthy that this group (at least in this field study) is predominant-ly middle and upper status.

Although this need is found at the top of the deprived category, there is nevertheless a significant relationship ($r = .22$, $p = .001$)

between this need and insecurity, as measured by Maslow's Inventory.[17]

Table 4.30

NEED FOR ESTEEM versus SECURITY-
INSECURITY INVENTORY

	Security		Insecurity			
	1	2	3	4	5	
All other subjects	30.1	28.5	17.7	15.8	7.9	100%
Esteem need group	17.9	20.0	20.7	26.4	15.0	100%

Insecure—but insecure in a different way than the groups which we
have previously considered—their psychic needs can also be expected to "flavor" their behavior and attitudes.

As has been true in the other groups, the direction of the relationships of a group's scores on Maslow's Inventory and their
scores on Taylor's Manifest Anxiety Scale are similar here also.
The Need For Esteem Group's scores show a clear tendency (r =
.24, p value = .001) to express manifest anxiety, as well as to be
insecure as defined by Maslow's inventory. Thus, although these
individuals are hypothesized to be—because of their increased
psychic health—much better able to manage both their own anxieties and their environment, according to their manifest anxiety
scores, they are as psychically crippled in these respects as are
persons who operate on the lowest need levels.

Table 4.31

NEED FOR ESTEEM versus MANIFEST ANXIETY

	Low			High			
	1	2	3	4	5	6	
All other subjects	23.1	22.3	27.6	15.2	7.6	4.2	100%
Esteem need group	11.4	20.7	19.3	19.3	17.1	12.1	100%

---

17. The reader should note the one question overlap here,
though the relationship would stand otherwise.

Thus, at this point in our analysis, we can see that—with the possible exception of the group characterized here as motivated by a Need for Safety (which may be an artifact of the Index construction)—each of the deprived groups can be typified by insecurity and manifest anxiety, two standard measures of neuroticism and unfulfilled needs.

In assessing cognitive functioning, we have two scores to consider: intolerance of ambiguity and dogmatism, both of which can be considered symptomatic of a compulsive need to structure the world. While persons expressing a Need for Affection appear to be relatively tolerant of ambiguity, we find that here there is a weak relationship between esteem needs and intolerance of ambiguity ($r = .12$, $p = .005$).

In view of the increased psychic competence of this group, and the somewhat lower scores by the affection and esteem groups in intolerance of ambiguity, it might be assumed that the group motivated by a Need for Esteem would be similarly low in dogmatism. Instead, we find that individuals motivated by a Need for Esteem are by far the most dogmatic of all our groups, in a relationship that is well beyond the .001 level ($X^2 = 51.3378$, d.f. = 5). (The Spearman correlation coefficient is .35.) This tendency can be clearly seen.

Table 4.32

NEED FOR ESTEEM versus DOGMATISM

	Undogmatic	Neutral	Dogmatic	
All other subjects	6.5	54.4	39.2	100%
Esteem need group	2.1	26.4	71.4	100%

As previously discussed, Rokeach has hypothesized that such persons may tend to be highly dogmatic as a psychic mechanism of gaining power and security. The relationship here gives support for this hypothesis.

Accompanying this relationship both psychologically and logically is an equally significant relationship, again well beyond the .001 level ($X^2 = 42.4083$, d.f. = 6)[18] between the Need for Esteem and the Threat Orientation Scale. Thus there appear to be empirical grounds to support the hypothesis that increased dogmatism is associated (causally we assume but cannot illustrate from these figures) with increased belief in hostility and threat pervading one's environment.

---

18. The Spearman correlation coefficient is .28.

Table 4.33

NEED FOR ESTEEM versus THREAT ORIENTATION

	Unthreatened	Neutral	Threatened	
All other subjects	36.9	27.3	35.8	100%
Esteem need group	14.2	27.1	58.6	100%

In terms of Maslow's personality model, individuals with a Need
for Esteem have come a long way on the road to self-actualization.
And yet their scores on this scale indicate that to this group also,
the world is as threatening and hostile a place in which to exist as
it is for the persons who are motivated by physiological and safety
needs. Such a central belief about the world helps to explain the
extreme closed-mindedness which typifies the cognitive functioning of this group.

Persons who seek the means of compensating for unsatisfied
esteem needs must seek such compensation from others. The
scores of individuals needing affection were unrelated to the Interpersonal Threat Scale. Will those who seek approval, recognition,
deference and power from others likewise see no threat in interpersonal relations? Here a weak but positive trend (r = .06, p =
.08) suggests that individuals lacking esteem may tend to fear anger and ridicule of others.

As we have ascended the need hierarchy, we have seen a corresponding decrease in the F-scale scores of deprived individuals,
with the correlation dropping from .34 (Need for Physiological Satisfaction), to .19 (Need for Safety) to a negative .07 (Need for Affection). It is of interest, therefore, to ascertain whether persons
needing esteem will evidence an even weaker tendency to be authoritarian. Given their high dogmatism scores, as well as the authoritarian tendencies of political leaders with unsatisfied esteem
needs, authoritarian tendencies seem likely.

Hence, it is not surprising to find that there appears a significant relationship beyond the .001 level (X^2 = 46.1458, d.f. = 6) between the Need for Esteem group and F-scale scores (r = .28, p =
.001). Collapsed into three categories for clarity, this trend is
seen in the differences between the averages in authoritarian and
nonauthoritarian responses. (See Table 4.34.) Thus, except for the
Need for Affection Group (whose low scores could be either an
artifact of the Index construction or due to personality needs which
depress intolerance because of desire for acceptance, there is a
positive relationship between authoritarian personality and psychic
deprivation, as employed in this study.

Theoretically, it can be expected that individuals who are intolerant of others (as shown by F-scale scores) will likewise tend

Table 4.34

NEED FOR ESTEEM versus F-SCALE

	Nonauthoritarian	Neutral	Authoritarian	
All other subjects	55.2	33.0	11.8	100%
Esteem need group	35.0	30.0	35.0	100%

to be misanthropic. Hence it is not surprising that we have seen in this study that scores on these two scales vary in similar ways. Thus the Physiological and Safety Groups were high in both authoritarianism and misanthropy, while the Need for Affection Group's scores were nonsignificantly related to faith-in-people and weakly inversely related to authoritarianism. Based on these results, one could expect covariance in these scores by the Esteem Group, which is indeed the case.

Congruent with high F-scale scores by the Esteem Group, we find a significant tendency for these same subjects to likewise lack faith-in-people ($r = .17$, $p = .001$). Thus, while the relationship is not consistently clear, there is a tendency for each psychically deprived group to express a lack of faith in people. Existing in a world which appears forever unable to offer the gratification which their personalities need, it is understandable that the deprived groups should express such generalized misanthropy. It is also likely to follow, of course, that these same persons are antihumanitarian and undemocratic.

At this point, it is useful to pause again in the discussion of scale scores and sample various subjects' own statements, in an effort to bring the reported data alive. In spite of the idiosyncratic way in which individual worries and concerns are phrased, there is a surprising underlying homogeneity in the statements of these respondents, when taken by need group. Here again, several dominant themes are apparent.

The two themes that appear with almost monotonous regularity in the statements of persons expressing a Need for Esteem are a desire for money in order to buy status items and a desire for enhanced education and/or improved occupational status. Subject 0158, for example, lists under the things in life he would like to have or change "Sell present home and obtain larger one" and under his worries "1. Saving for future—children's education, etc. 2. Doing well in job—getting ahead." Subject 0198, in words used by several respondents, simply longs for "better education, better job." Subject 0225 worries about "getting my bills paid so I can buy some of the things we want most," possessions which he lists as "new home, pickup camper." To Subject 0261, occupational concern is pressing. He is worried about "getting another job—I was fired as a supervisor for [company] for reasons unknown to me ([company's] theory is to tell someone when they aren't efficiently carrying out their duties—theory must not apply at [company].)" While Subject 0063 longs for "a better paying job; a new home," Subject 0090 is more specific: "I always wanted to be a civil engineer" (he is a logger with two years of college). Subject 0066 worries about "getting ahead; the government" and his desires are "education; social standing."

Not only through the themes of the desire for increased income and enhanced occupational status, but also in their more general concerns, a feeling of resentment is often apparent. In addition, the Need for Esteem can also be seen to flavor their responses in ways expressive of this motivational syndrome. Subject 0204 is openly hostile, centering his negativism around undeserved recognition and attention granted to others. He states that he is concerned about "(1) The majority of Negroes that want something for nothing. (2) People that yell police brutality bug me. It bugs me to see people demonstrate against Viet Nam. I don't like the creeps at Berkeley college." The theme of the capriciousness of the awards of power, dominance, prestige, status, et cetera, flows through the statements of other subjects as well, as the following comments illustrate (in answer to what worries them most):

Subject 0209 (Supervisor of forestry department)

> How to solve the problems which lead to war and other conflicts in the world. How to cope with the rapidly increasing tendency for large corporation employers to treat their employees like disposable cogs in a machine rather than as people.

Subject 0239 (a female computer operator)

> The very poor education my son is getting in public school. The constant "Give away" policy (Give away and war drain our prosperity—everything going out, "nothing" coming in); the strong influence of the common market—and (Germany)!!

Subject 0345 (a conservation officer)

> Feel that if we are to be blamed for the world's troubles, We should use our power to stop others from getting strong enough to some day be our victors, stop acting the American Father.

Finally, as in the case of concerned individuals expressing a Need for Affection, subjects in the Need for Esteem Group likewise express anxiety over the impersonality and incomprehensibility of the complex modern world—a world in which one feels like a "disposable cog" rather than as esteemed individual. To Subject 0382 (a semiskilled lumber worker), complexity is seen as personally threatening and he worries about "Too many regulations preventing the police from doing a good job protecting us such as the recent supreme court rulings on the rights of the accused. Inflation—Racial problems—Too strong unions." Subject 0093 (also a semiskilled operative) expresses anxiety over

> The passing of laws and ordinances by city, county and state which are taking away our individual freedom as guaranteed by the U. S. Constitution; The increasing Tax load heaped on lower income groups by city, county and state; The increasing influence of big business and lobbiest groups on all phases of government.

Finally, Subject 0414 (a teacher for fifteen years), worries about

> The direction this country is taking in reference to its money spending. Disregard for the individual—too much Big government, federal control—too much power in a few people in Washington—Let the other person (do it) idea.

In the analysis of individualized expressions of worry and concern, the value of employing personality theory in understanding politically relevant attitudes is again illustrated. For personality acts like a magnet suspended over a variety of items in a penny arcade machine—it selectively attracts only those which are composed of a sympathetic material; it remains disengaged from the rest. In a like manner, each individual lives in a world that is complex and fluid, where goods are in limited supply and desires are unlimited, where educational attainment greatly determines socioeconomic mobility and one's occupation shapes one's life style, where he joins with others in a variety of social groups to support and extend a variety of unsatiated needs. Yet, among this diversity of choices, each personality type "selects out" certain themes which are relevant and ignores all the rest.

Attitudes are clues—clues to the direction which activity must take. Equally important is the likelihood that an individual will be moved to act. It has long been assumed, in the literature of political science, that persons with a Need for Esteem will be particularly likely to be propelled to seek psychic compensation through political activity. Thus it is with special interest that we examine such clues as are offered by this field study in this regard. First, in their scores on the Political Efficacy Scale, there is a relationship significant beyond the .001 level (X^2 = 30.8108, d.f. = 4) between the Need for Esteem and lack of efficacy (r = .25). (See Table 4.35.) If indeed these individuals are propelled into political activities, it does not tend to be with the belief that their actions will be efficacious.[19] These scores on the Political Efficacy Scale

---

19. Of course it is recognized that this is not the only reason such individuals would become active social and political participants.

Table 4.35

NEED FOR ESTEEM versus POLITICAL EFFICACY SCALE

	High			Low		
	1	2	3	4	5	
All other subjects	25.9	37.2	22.5	9.3	5.1	100%
Esteem need group	12.9	25.7	28.6	20.0	12.9	100%

are of particular interest as performance on this scale has been widely shown to relate to political participation—and we have hypothesized that, compared to the other deprived groups—the Need for Esteem Group will be most likely to seek compensation through activity. It is possible that persons lacking esteem were particularly responsive to questions relating to whether their voices would be heard or respected by public officials and that they nevertheless seek to participate in an effort to gain esteem.

While there is again a nonsignificant relationship between these individuals and the Citizen Duty Scale, these individuals—like persons motivated by a need for physiological satisfaction—are slightly less likely than the rest of the group to express belief in a citizen's duty.

Table 4.36

NEED FOR ESTEEM versus CITIZEN DUTY SCALE

	High			Low		
	1	2	3	4	5	
All other subjects	57.5	38.0	3.1	0.6	0.8	100%
Esteem need group	53.6	40.7	2.9	0.7	2.1	100%

The Political Efficacy Scale and the Citizen Duty Scale are two measures that have, in other studies, been correlated with actual degree of political participation. From Tables 4.35 and 4.36, we can see that this group—using these two measures—cannot be predicted to be highly participant in relation to all the other subjects. The Milbrath-Klein Esteem Scale is another measure which has been found to be related to participation, particularly to the desire to run for elective office. In the three lower deprived groups, there was an inverse relationship between the deprived group and this Esteem Scale. Now, however, for the first time, there is a weak positive trend (r = .13, p = .003).

Table 4.37

NEED FOR ESTEEM versus MILBRATH-KLEIN
ESTEEM SCALE

	Low			High			
	1	2	3	4	5	6	
All other subjects	9.9	22.8	30.1	22.8	10.7	3.7	100%
Esteem need group	9.3	17.9	20.7	23.6	20.7	7.9	100%

Thus, in spite of various indications of their psychic debilities and their lack of political efficacy, the particular psychological need which Maslow has delimited as motivating this group does appear to dispose them to seek the spotlight in interpersonal relationships, as expressed in their positive responses to the Milbrath-Klein Esteem Scale (Table 4.37).

Another indication that the psychic deprivation of this group has a different "flavor" than that of the other deprived groups is the scores of this group on the status concern scale. While individuals in the Physiological, Safety and Affection Groups showed a clear tendency not to desire status mobility (though this tendency is nonsignificant in the Need for Affection Group), the trend here, though nonsignificant, for the first time, is in a positive direction. It is likely that the insecurities of each of the deprived groups make social mobility a frightening prospect. Yet as the Esteem Group is motivated, at least in part, with a need for status, the impact of their insecurities is apparently depressed when confronted with opportunities which would provide increased social esteem.

Finally, we consider the attitudes of this group as they appear on the Srole Anomia Scale. Although each of the deprived groups has a tendency to give anomic responses, this group—motivated by the Need for Esteem—is as likely to do so as the lowest group (r = .21, p = .001). Increased psychic competence in terms of movement up the need hierarchy has not lessened the despairing view which these deprived persons hold of the world. There is apparently a strong link between anomia and psychic deprivation, considered as a whole.

The scores of the Esteem Group thus far are unclear as to the proclivity of these persons to participate in political activity. While political participation is indicated by their scores on the Milbrath-Klein Esteem Scale, their efficacy and citizen duty scores do not suggest above-average activity. This same lack of clarity is

apparent in the weakly significant negative relationship to the Index of Political Participation (r = -.08, p = .04). Yet this negative
relationship (and the score distributions) mark an important
change—a change which is most noticeable in the group of extreme
activists. Furthermore, this weak relationship is the logical outgrowth of a trend in all of the deprived groups' scores on this Index.

For the two lowest need groups, participation (we can assume)
tends to be abhorrent. Then a switch in score distribution begins
to occur as was predicted, at the level of the Need for Affection.
For in this third group we saw that these deprived individuals tend
to be more active middle-range participants (44.2 percent versus
34.9 percent) than all the other subjects, taken together. Now, for
the first time, a deprived group (Need for Esteem) tends to be as
likely to be highly participant as all the other subjects.

Table 4.38

NEED FOR ESTEEM versus INDEX OF
POLITICAL PARTICIPATION

	Low	Middle	High	
All other subjects	32.7	37.7	29.6	100%
Esteem need group	34.3	35.7	30.0	100%

Thus, in considering the group with a Need for Esteem, this
need appears to be of little predictive ability in assessing political
participation. In view of the voluminous literature describing political activity as primarily stemming from a desire to compensate
for unsatisfied esteem, this inconclusive finding is itself important.
Undoubtedly, the Need for Esteem is a spur to activity, for these
subjects are the most active of the deprived groups. Yet their psychic debilities disallow the activity which is a correlate of self-
actualization—they act in spite of weakness, not on the basis of
strength.

Essentially the same phenomenon can be seen in regard to
this group's scores on the Index of Leadership. If the two high categories are combined, again the Need for Esteem has no predictive ability in determining leadership activity. Yet it is of considerable import to notice that roughly one-third of subjects motivated by a Need for Esteem seek leadership roles—as opposed to only
17.3 percent at the bottom of the need hierarchy. (The clear and
consistent relationship between leadership and increasing psychic
competence can be seen best in Appendix C.) (See Table 4.39.)

As the least psychically deprived of the four groups that are
deficiency-motivated, persons motivated by the Need for Esteem

Table 4.39

NEED FOR ESTEEM versus INDEX OF LEADERSHIP

	Low		High		
	1	2	3	4	
All other subjects	19.2	47.9	31.5	1.4	100%
Esteem need group	20.7	46.4	27.1	5.7	100%

are as likely to participate in sociopolitical activities as they are
to be apathetic (while the lowest two groups are likely to be nonparticipants). Intolerant and dogmatic, tending to feel threatened
by their environment and to hold the belief that life is meaningless
and they are impotent to control the world around them, nevertheless the quality or type of their deprivation demands alleviation
through and only through interpersonal relationships. For esteem,
like affection, is a relational (not an individual) quality and it can
only be acquired in a social situation.[20] Thus though inflexible, undemocratic and nonadaptive, a sizeable group of these individuals
will likely be found among the ranks of political activists—in leadership as well as follower positions.[21]

Generalized Psychic Deprivation

Before turning to the group of self-actualizers, let us briefly
summarize the findings thus far. (Appendix C summarizes these
findings numerically, so that each deprived group's scores can be
assessed relative to those of the other four groups.)

Each of the deprived groups, except the Need for Safety Group,
shows a clear, significant tendency to be insecure, as measured
by Maslow's Security-Insecurity Inventory. Likewise, the Taylor
Manifest Anxiety Scale, again with the exception of the Need for
Safety Group, appears to be a good indicator of psychic deprivation. This finding is congruent with the lack of control hypothesized to be characteristic of psychically deprived individuals.

---

20. This is probably true for self-esteem, as well as social-
esteem. (See the theoretical discussion in chap. 2, section on esteem.)

21. This, of course, is not the same as saying that individuals in this need group are most likely of all individuals to be political activists. (For relative figures, see Appendix C.) Also, as
in the case of the Need for Affection Group, these individuals are
more likely to be followers than leaders.

It is likely that the questions composing the Safety Index (the item content is low in threat and probably peripheral to the anxiety which they experience) failed to enlist the agreement of those deprived persons who are deeply anxious about the insecurity which is an inescapable part of their existence. The performance of this group on several measures indicates a variety of psychic weaknesses. But the lack of relationship to the Security-Insecurity Inventory and the Manifest Anxiety Scale suggests that a number of insecure persons did not feel that the security questions asked in this field study were expressive of their basic insecurity.

Intolerance of ambiguity does not appear to be a phenomenon that is generally associated with psychic deprivation. Instead it appears to be a coping mechanism that is particular to persons who operate at the base of the need hierarchy (need groups one and two), as well as (more weakly related) to the dogmatic Esteem Group. Individuals expressing a Need for Affection, on the other hand, appear to be relatively (that is, in comparison to the other deprived groups) better able to tolerate ambiguity. It is possible that the increased tolerance of ambiguity by the Esteem and Affection Groups is causally related to their increased political participation as ambiguity, in a profound sense, is the essence of politics.

Dogmatism is a characteristic which is general among the psychically deprived groups and in this field study it was most strongly related to the Needs for Physiological Satisfaction and for Esteem. In general, however, all the deprived groups in this study tend to be dogmatic. It was hypothesized earlier in this book that dogmatism would be a symptom of psychic deprivation. It was also suggested that theoretically one could argue either that as people grow toward self-actualization, there will be a weakening of the tendency toward dogmatism, or that each psychically deprived group will be equally defensive and dogmatic. From the results of this field study, it appears that the latter view is correct. As this sample is nonrandom, however, additional research is needed to establish whether the needs of each psychically deprived group necessitate an equally strong closed-minded view of the world or whether, as individuals move up the hierarchy to psychic fulfillment, they do indeed become more open in their cognitive processes even before they reach the level of self-actualization. Certainly the size of the correlation between the Need for Esteem and dogmatism supports Rokeach's contention that individuals so deprived are especially likely to have a closed view of the world.

Another phenomenon which is related to all the groups except for the Need for Affection Group is the view of the world as threatening and hostile. Such an orientation was hypothesized to be an integral part of the philosophy of deprived individuals. While it is indeed significantly related to psychic deprivation taken as a whole (r = .26, p = .001), the lack of correlation here with the Need for Affection bears further investigation.

On the other hand, the Interpersonal Threat Scale does not appear to be generally related to psychic deprivation. There is a clear relationship to Physiological Need and a weak relationship to the Affection and Esteem Need Groups. Further study is needed to determine whether the Interpersonal Threat Scale reliably discriminates personality needs.

However, the F-scale appears, as the results of other studies would indicate likely, to be clearly related to psychic deprivation, again with the exception of the Need for Affection Group. Theoretically, it seems likely that authoritarianism would typify all four deprived groups. It is possible, however, that the desire for affection negates intolerant attitudes on the part of individuals whose prime desire is to belong and to be loved. Again, this is an area deserving of further study.

A similarly intolerant view of people—as expressed in the Faith-in-People Scale—is, like the F-scale scores, related to each psychically deprived group, except for the Affection Group. While it appears psychologically correct that a generalized misanthropy would typify people for whom the world lacks gratification, it is perhaps necessary to maintain a belief that people are likeable if one highly values and neurotically seeks the affection of others. Thus—like the dogmatism and intolerance of ambiguity scores which both tap the dimensions of cognitive rigidity—the similarly oriented measures of misanthropy and authoritarianism covary also. Groups that are high on F-scale scores (Physiological, Safety and Esteem) are likewise high in misanthropy; the Need for Affection Group's scores are unrelated to misanthropy and inversely related to authoritarianism.

Political efficacy also seems to be an important dimension which is related to psychic deprivation. Lack of a sense of political competence is a consistent and strong tendency for people who are psychically deprived, most of all for those whose needs are for physiological or esteem satisfaction. Thus the study of psychic deprivation—a phenomenon found in each SES group—is of particular political relevance. It is likely to be of considerable explanatory value in analyzing the apathetic as well as in predicting what conditions might arouse them to activity and the direction which their activities are likely to take.

Given the lack of political efficacy of deprived individuals, activity becomes futile and rote—or nonexistent. It is against this background that we must assess the general agreement of deprived persons with the duty of a citizen to be participant. Given evidence that deprived persons in fact tend not to be participant, there is an air of unreality surrounding the teaching of democracy when it is divorced from concurrently stimulating psychic growth. (This air of unreality extends to attempts to measure the stability and cohesion of the society or the polity by assessing verbal agreement with modal values.) While the Physiological and Esteem Groups are slightly (and insignificantly) inclined to disagree with democratic participatory norms and the Safety and Affection Groups tend to agree, the outstanding fact is that deprived individuals are not outstanding in differentially accepting norms which they are unable to put into practice.

One of the clearest trends to emerge as we move up the need hierarchy relates to the Esteem Scale of Milbrath and Klein, which measures an individual's desire and ability to be in a position of social prominence. For the first three groups, the relationship is inverse. While it is stronger for the Group with Physiological Needs, it grows somewhat weaker for the Safety and Affection Groups. In a dramatic switch at the highest deprived group (Need for Esteem), the relationship then becomes clearly positive (r = .13, p = .003). As this scale is related to the seeking of elective office, it offers interesting confirmation of the trend of scores of our Index of Political Participation. It also gives strength to the traditional picture of the person seeking compensation for damaged self-esteem as one kind of political activist who particularly seeks one type of activity (positions of prominence).

Another trend which clearly emerges is the relationship between mental health and the lack of rejection of an acquisitive, achievement-oriented status concern. From a weak but significant, inverse relationship between this scale and Physiological Need, the trend grows weaker until, again at the Esteem level, it turns direction and becomes weakly positive. Apparently the psychically deprived lack the security with which social mobility must be positively sought; only esteem needs give weak approval to opportunistic movement toward increased prestige and status. Given the basically competitive nature of American society, one must certainly suspect that a positive relationship between psychic fulfillment and status concern is not a universal phenomenon.

Finally, in reviewing the attitude scales, there is a consistent, positive relationship to Srole's Anomia Scale on the part of each psychically deprived group (nonsignificant only in the case of the esteem group). Apparently this scale is a good measure of lack of psychic health. It is an indication of the generalized, crippling effect of any unsatisfied need that, in spite of increased psychic competence and social-economic status, each psychically deprived group tends to be anomic. (Also, as can be seen by the table in Appendix C, this is the only scale on which the scores consistently fall as one ascends the need hierarchy groups toward self-actualization.)

Directed as this study is to a focus on political behavior, particular attention must be paid here to the Index of Political Participation scores. There is a general trend toward nonparticipation by individuals in these four deprived groups, but this inverse relationship is strongest at the base of the need hierarchy. Further, while there is a clear, inverse relationship between the safety and esteem need areas and political participation, there is no relationship between the Affection Need Area and this form of activity. More important for our interests here, however, are the score distributions.

While a good number of Americans in all categories of mental health are likely to be politically nonparticipant,[22] a tentative description of the psychic factors related to participation would suggest the following: those individuals operating near the base of the need hierarchy (physiological or safety needs) are most likely to be nonparticipant while persons motivated by unfulfilled relational needs are likely to be as participant as self-actualizing individuals (because of the compensation to be won through interpersonal relationships). In other words, as hypothesized earlier, there does appear to be a noticeable increase in political participation when a person reaches the level of the Need for Affection, which is in line with our theoretical discussion of a psychic "reaching-out" which begins to occur at this stage.

A most interesting confirmation of these results is found in a study of participation in voluntary associations reported by Goldhamer (1942). His sample was based on the answers of 5,500 individuals to one-page questionnaires largely distributed through place of employment, plus an additional sample of 1,000 engaged couples. First, he found that frequency of membership and that of leadership were directly related, so that leadership is seen as part of the general phenomenon of participation. Second, Goldhamer notes that education, apart from economic status, was directly related to various forms of participation.

Thus education is likely to stimulate both the interest and the competence necessary for participation. Particularly relevant to our concerns here are the scores on the Thurstone Neurotic Inventory, which Goldhamer administered to his sample of engaged couples. He found that there was an inverse relationship between total neurotic score and membership frequency which held generally with all subgroups—as we have found in the case of different measures of psychic deprivation and a special (political) form of participation. Further, and most vital to our interests, Goldhamer found that there was a U-shaped curve between total neurotic score and "pure" leadership (that is, the number of officerships per organization to which a person belonged): "The data show a declining rate of officerships as total neurotic score increases, but among those with the highest total neurotic scores the rate rises almost to the high point achieved by the persons with the lowest total neurotic scores." (This relationship held among men and women, divided into high school, college and postgraduate groups.) Thus, as hypothesized in our earlier discussion, neuroticism can be either a barrier or a stimulant to participation. However, to achieve such a "U-shaped" score distribution in our study, it would be necessary for those with physiological and safety needs (our most deprived segment) to approximate the activity of the self-actualizers. Instead, we find an increase in participation and

---

22. See Appendix C.

leadership at the <u>affection</u> need level. Could this disparity stem largely from <u>semantic</u> differences?

Fortunately, Goldhamer's analysis did not stop at this point. In line with our theoretical anticipations and empirical evidence, he found that

> the higher total neurotic scores of the High Officership Group are not accounted for indifferently by approximately equal increments of neurotic responses in all the factors; on the contrary there is a very considerable variation in the degree to which the eight factors [on the Thurstone Neurotic Inventory] contribute to the increased neuroticism of the High Group. (p. 84)

For men with High Officership Scores, the only two factors in excess are the inferiority and cycloid components. The inferiority component is described in terms of "feelings of inferiority and lack of self-confidence in general," while the cycloid component which reflects "variability of mood" is especially indicative of "depressive rather than euphoric states." For the women:

> It is the depressive component that ranks first in the case of the women. This is, as compared with the cycloid component, a purer indicator of depression, as it is not mixed with manic or euphoric items. The two items with the highest loadings on the factor are "lonesomeness" items. The Inferiority component ranks second. (pp. 84-86)

In other words, as we have found, Goldhamer's study of the relationship between personality factors and participation in voluntary organizations suggests that (1) there is an inverse relationship between sociopolitical participation and mental health; (2) highly neurotic individuals are almost as likely to assume leadership roles as are mentally healthy individuals, and that (3) it is not all highly neurotic individuals who seem likely to be found in leadership positions, but rather those with types of psychic weakness which could also be described in terms of the Need for Affection and the Need for Esteem.

Further underscoring the similarity between our results and those of the Goldhamer study are the scores on the Index of Leadership employed in this field study. As leadership roles can be assumed to be more psychically requiring than followership roles, it is perhaps to be expected that the relationship between psychic competence and this form of participation is even clearer. Thus there is a negative relationship between leadership and psychic deprivation which grows steadily weaker as one ascends the need hierarchy, with the correlations dropping from -.17, to -.09, to -.03, to -.02.[23] But equally important, there is a sharp increase

---

23. It is realized that the last two differences are not statistically significant.

in the proportion of individuals most active in leadership positions when the level of relational needs is reached (that is, at the Need for Affection), as can be seen from the table in Appendix C. Finally, the most healthy, self-actualizing individuals in our study are only slightly more likely to be found in leadership positions than are persons who express needs for affection and esteem.

Thus, whether or not there are more deprived than self-actualizing persons in our population (which is not a concern of this study) would appear to determine whether individuals in social and political leadership roles will be predominantly self-actualized individuals or largely those motivated by unfulfilled needs for affection and esteem. But while persons in the Affection, Esteem and High Self-Actualization Groups are equally likely to be found in leadership positions, the differing quality of their motivations assures far different philosophies by which to assess their environment. A differential degree of psychic strength with which to meet leadership roles is also assured when one can be characterized as growth-, rather than deficiency-motivated.

Maslow's need hierarchy has thus far been seen to be a useful analytic tool in the study of politically relevant behavior and attitudes, particularly in relation to participation and leadership scores. Not all of the scores on the personality and attitude dimensions show a consistent trend as one ascends the need hierarchy, though two pairs (dogmatism and intolerance of ambiguity; authoritarianism and misanthropy) covary in ways that are psychologically consistent. An attempt has been made to indicate, however, that psychologically there is no reason for all of these scales to either be consistently related to each deprived need group or for the scores to show consistently more psychic strength as the individuals move toward self-actualization. (For example, while a person who has reached the level of esteem needs belongs to the most healthy of our deprived groups, the quality of his psychic needs can also be argued to require a far greater degree of dogmatism and status concern than are expressed by individuals lower on the need hierarchy.) Hence, whether the idea of hierarchy is a valid statement of the relation between deficiency needs cannot be determined on the basis of this study.

Further, it must be frankly admitted that while most of the relationships are statistically significant, many of the correlations are low. Hopefully, more rigorously defined and statistically significant links between personality type and politically relevant attitudes and behavior can be identified by considerably expanding and then factor-analyzing these indices of psychic deprivation, as well as testing them on a variety of subject groups. As such work is indeed on-going,[24] the results reported in this chapter should be con-

24. A recent paper (Knutson, 1971) reports some results of this psychometric process through a study of political leaders in which the data offers considerably stronger statistical relation-

sidered a first step in exploring the research possibilities of employing Maslow's personality model.

As a model of personality, Maslow's need hierarchy does appear to be potentially a valuable tool for the study of the relationships between psychic weaknesses and politically relevant behavior. It not only has considerable explanatory power which is needed to interpret data with which students of behavior must deal; it also is suggestive of the kinds of questions which must be asked in future research, as well as being predictive of many predisposing factors which are relevant to political activity. Finally, as has been shown at various points in the data analysis thus far, it is only by using an inclusive personality theory—rather than traditional single trait or type analysis, that the results can be related in a meaningful way. Thus, in terms of their position on the need hierarchy, a group's performance can be considered in terms of those exhibiting more and less psychic strengths and a nonsignificant relationship (for example, between the Need for Esteem and political participation) becomes a necessary link in a growing trend toward the creative manipulation of one's social and political environment.

The Need for Self-Actualization

By definition, no person can achieve self-actualization who has an unfulfilled basic need. Thus our group of self-actualizers is composed of those persons who fell below the cutoff points[25] on each of the first four Indices (who could not have agreed to more than a total of six of the questions comprising the four indices of psychic deprivation). Skeptics might insist that there are many personality theories and that the answers to a minimum of eleven or a maximum of seventeen questions is not likely to give us results that are psychologically or behaviorally meaningful. If these Indices of Psychic Deprivation did not tap actual psychic dimensions, it is empirically possible that persons here identified as self-actualizing (that is, the balance of our subjects) may also be intolerant, insecure and politically apathetic—unless, that is, Maslow's need hierarchy as utilized here is an accurate assessment of psychological reality.

In analyzing the responses in this category, the subjects were divided into three groups:

1. Psychically deprived (subjects who evidenced at least one of the first four basic needs).

---

ships supporting the hypotheses discussed in this book. Also see Simpson (1971).

25. Determined, in the case of each Index, so as to statistically isolate a small group of subjects to whom such questions were most meaningful.

2. Low self-actualizers (subjects who are not motivated by the Need for Physiological Satisfaction, Safety, Affection or Esteem and whose total score on these four Indices was between four and six).

3. High self-actualizers (subjects who are not motivated by the Need for Physiological Satisfaction, Safety, Affection or Esteem and whose total score on these four Indices was between zero and three).

First of all, a clear relationship (r = .32, p = .001) appears between this "Continuum of Mental Health" and the Index of SES. What is of particular interest throughout this section is the frequent appearance of a continuous trend with <u>increasing</u> self-actualization. Not only are the Psychically Deprived most likely to be found in the low status group, rather than the high status group, but the Low Self-Actualizers fall between the other two groups (although they are usually more similar to the High Self-Actualizers than to the Psychically Deprived, as they theoretically should be). However, it should be noted here that <u>the difference in SES between the Low and High Self-Actualizers is too small to account for the large differences in scales scores of these two groups reported subsequently</u>. Presumably if our research instruments could be further refined for the measurement of self-actualization, an even clearer trend between psychic fulfillment and democratic participatory personality would emerge.

Table 4.40

CONTINUUM OF MENTAL HEALTH versus SES[*]

	Low	Middle	High	
Psychically deprived	28.9	45.8	25.3	100%
Low self-actualizers	15.0	36.7	48.3	100%
High self-actualizers	12.7	34.3	52.9	100%

[*]The N's for the tables in this section (4.40-4.50) are Psychically Deprived = 273, Low Self-Actualizers = 120, High Self-Actualizers = 102, with a total of 495.

This same type of very clear trend can be seen in the <u>inverse</u> relationship (r = -.21, p = .001) to Maslow's Security-Insecurity Inventory. (See Table 4.41.) If it can be assumed that Maslow's S-I Inventory is a good general measure of psychic deprivation versus psychic growth orientation, it is clear from these figures that his personality theory has been utilized in this field study so that it taps dimensions envisioned in his various works.

Table 4.41

CONTINUUM OF MENTAL HEALTH versus S-I INVENTORY

	Security			Insecurity		
	1	2	3	4	5	
Psychically deprived	22.7	20.9	20.1	22.3	13.9	100%
Low self-actualizers	27.5	30.8	17.5	18.3	5.8	100%
High self-actualizers	36.3	34.3	15.7	9.8	3.9	100%

A similarly significant inverse relationship ($r = -.23$, $p = .001$) can be seen to Taylor's Manifest Anxiety Scale, with the figures showing a consistent trend as one moves toward mental health.

Table 4.42

CONTINUUM OF MENTAL HEALTH versus
MANIFEST ANXIETY

	Low			High			
	1	2	3	4	5	6	
Psychically deprived	16.8	17.9	22.7	17.9	15.8	8.8	100%
Low self-actualizers	20.0	24.2	30.0	15.8	5.0	5.0	100%
High self-actualizers	27.5	29.4	26.5	12.7	2.0	2.0	100%

Manifest Anxiety is a type of anxiety which—as its name indicates —is associated with somatic symptoms. It has been hypothesized earlier that individuals who are psychically deprived will not only have more anxieties but they will also have less control over their anxieties, a lack of control which can be seen in somatic symptoms as well as in behavior and attitudes. The scores on the Manifest Anxiety Scale appear as a partial confirmation of this lack of control.

In spite of the lack of relationship which occurred between the Intolerance of Ambiguity Scale and the Need for Affection Group, there is nevertheless here an inverse relationship ($r = -.21$, $p = .001$) between the Continuum of Mental Health and this Scale—a relationship which is clearest at the two end points of the continuum. Again it is important to notice the great and significant difference in performance between the Low and High Self-Actualizers, in spite of their striking similarity in socioeconomic status.

Table 4.43

CONTINUUM OF MENTAL HEALTH versus
INTOLERANCE OF AMBIGUITY

	Low			High			
	2	3	4	5	6	7	
Psychically deprived	0.4	9.9	41.0	42.5	5.9	0.4	100%
Low self-actualizers	0.0	6.7	55.0	36.7	1.7	0.0	100%
High self-actualizers	2.0	25.5	47.1	23.5	2.0	0.0	100%

From these figures, it appears that the High Self-Actualizers, our
most mentally healthy group, are remarkably more able to tolerate ambiguity than are the other two groups. As ambiguity has earlier been hypothesized to be the essence of politics, this trend is a
most important explanation for both the high participation and the
tolerance of our self-actualizers.

One of the major interests of this book has been a hypothesized correlation between Rokeach's concept of dogmatism and
Maslow's concept of psychic deprivation. It will be remembered
that while dogmatism was related to each of our four deprived
groups, this relationship was not equally strong—nor was there a
trend for dogmatism to decrease as one ascended the need hierarchy. Therefore the significant inverse relationship, well beyond
the .001 level (X^2 = 49.2817, d.f. = 10),[26] between our Continuum
of Mental Health and Rokeach's Dogmatism Scale is of particular
interest and the figures are presented here in full.

Table 4.44

CONTINUUM OF MENTAL HEALTH versus DOGMATISM

	Low			High			
	2	3	4	5	6	7	
Psychically deprived	0.0	4.0	36.3	45.8	12.8	1.1	100%
Low self-actualizers	0.8	2.5	55.8	35.0	5.8	0.0	100%
High self-actualizers	0.0	10.8	62.7	24.5	2.0	0.0	100%

---

26. The Spearman correlation coefficient is -.28.

While the specific relationship of dogmatism to each of the deprived groups will have to be subject to further analysis, it appears here that <u>as a person becomes, in Maslow's model, increasingly mentally healthy, he simultaneously becomes, in Rokeach's
conceptualization, increasingly less closed-minded.</u>

A similarly clear inverse relationship, well beyond the .001
level (r = -.21) exists between the Continuum of Mental Health and
the Threat Orientation Scale.

Table 4.45

CONTINUUM OF MENTAL HEALTH versus
THREAT ORIENTATION

	Unthreatened	Neutral	Threatened	
Psychically deprived	24.2	23.8	52.1	100%
Low self-actualizers	39.1	26.7	34.1	100%
High self-actualizers	37.2	37.3	25.5	100%

We have seen that as one becomes more self-actualizing, he becomes more secure, less anxious, and more tolerant of ambiguity.
We have also seen that the type of cognitive functioning changes.
One of the reasons behind these differences now becomes clear:
as individuals move toward self-actualization, their central beliefs about the world change. The adjectives "hostile" and "threatening" have been used so frequently in this book that they have perhaps lost some of their suggestive powers. At this point, therefore,
it is useful for the reader to turn to Appendix A and to reread the
questions in the Threat Orientation Scale. The tenor of the questions to which the Psychically Deprived are assenting make it
forcefully apparent what an unpleasant, Darwinian world this is
for people who lack basic need gratification and how uncomfortable their existence in it must be.

It will be remembered that the relationship between the Interpersonal Threat Scale and the four deprived groups was not uniformly significant. It does show a significant inverse relationship
(r = -.11, p = .008) to the Continuum of Mental Health, however, a
relationship which is most noticeable in the drop of a sense of interpersonal threat by the high self-actualizers. It appears here, in
other words, that there are very few people—even those who are
self-actualizing—who would not be disturbed in socially embarrass-
ing situations, and perhaps this is "normal" for our culture. Whether or not it is "normal" psychologically is another matter—one
which will not be taken up here!

In the theoretical section of this book, a hypothesis was offered concerning authoritarianism. The hypothesis was that if it

was possible to discount the effects of culturally conditioned prejudice (for example, the American South), the authoritarian personality, as measured by the F-scale, would be isomorphic with
Maslow's psychically deprived groups. It is therefore with considerable interest that we note the clear inverse relationship, well beyond the .001 level[27] (X^2 = 57.0320, d.f. = 12) between the Continuum of Mental Health and the F-scale. The self-actualizers, and
most particularly the High Self-Actualizers, have so few "agree"
average scores (four individuals out of an n of 102) that Table 4.44
offers good support for our hypothesis.

Table 4.46

CONTINUUM OF MENTAL HEALTH versus F-SCALE

	Disagree	Neutral	Agree	
Psychically deprived	42.9	29.3	27.9	100%
Low self-actualizers	48.3	42.5	9.1	100%
High self-actualizers	68.7	27.5	3.9	100%

From the various clues to be derived from this field study,
the basis for the frequently found relationship between tolerance
and leadership becomes apparent. It is not that the leadership role
enforces tolerance (although this may be true also)[28] but rather
that the anxieties and hostilities of intolerant, psychically deprived
individuals greatly constrict their ability (1) to be participant socially and politically and, more especially (2) to be active in the
stress and crisis of a leadership role. As would be expected from
the tolerance of self-actualizers expressed in their F-scale scores,
a clear relationship (r = -.19, p = .001) is also found between the
Continuum of Mental Health and the Faith-in-People Scale—a corollary attitude to lack of authoritarianism.

Having reviewed some of the data provided by the more psychically competent respondents, it is of interest to determine
whether their answers to the open ended questions likewise express
greater psychic strength. In an attempt to suggest here the "flavor"
of growth-orientation and increased competence, all of the High
Self-Actualizers' questionnaires were studied for illustrative and
representative comments which typify the concern of individuals
at this level of mental health. This group, interpreting the open-

27. The Spearman correlation coefficient is -.26.

28. Some types of organizations whose leaders were studied
by Stouffer, for instance, are definitely not known for their tolerance of civil liberties. (See Stouffer, 1955).

ended questions at times in terms of immediate problems, frequently said that they had no worries. Almost inevitably, however,
the self-actualizers were likely to add concerns which give evidence of introspection and a recognition of the value of interpersonal relationships—dimensions which were generally lacking in
the comments of the Psychically Deprived. Subject 0214 states,
for example: "I haven't any real worries," but under the three
things in life he would like, adds "I would like to be free of my
physical handicap; be free of arthritis; appreciate people more."
Thus an unskilled logger (Subject 0097) desires "more education,
better job," but also adds "more patience," while an atypical labor-
er with four years of college (Subject 0017) lists under his concerns

> The war in S. E. Asia & worsening U. S. Relations with
> Europe; the alienation of citizens from their governments;
> the unwarranted confidence of political men in the rightness
> of present U. S. political institutions; the lack of humanistic
> goals in American education;

and under the three things in life that he would like to have or to
change:

> More time to read and write; a big crude room where I could
> paint, listen to music, tinker, etc. and where my family could
> do what they wanted to; more social contacts or something
> akin to what Robt. Hutchins is talking about when he refers to
> a "sense of community."

Also of considerable political relevance is the fact that these same
self-actualizing persons—tolerant, open-minded, expressing positive affect toward others—nevertheless frequently also express ardent approval of conservative values which are widely held in rural
Oregon where many of these respondents live and work. (Thus here
again we have evidence that mental health is not an exclusive property of the political left.) Illustrative of the conservative values
with which some of the self-actualizers are concerned are the comments of Subject 0135 (a project engineer), who worries about

> The apparent lack of respect and patriotism of the American
> public toward the Flag of our U.S.A., The great concern of
> some people toward complete separation of church and state;
> racial unrest (ACLU, NAACP & CORE), the health and wel-
> fare of my family

but adds, under the three things that he would like in life

> to have more patience and understanding with people; to have
> more time to play with the children and the patience to do it;
> to be able to instill in people a love of God and our country.

In a similar vein, Subject 0232 is concerned with "The lack of
Christ in people of the World and U.S. Then unrest and war would

be secondary to all people." Under the things that he desires, however, he lists (in contrast to the psychically deprived who emphasize an antihumanistic and punitive view of religion), "I would be a
stronger example for Christ; have enough love to share with some
homeless child." Similarly, Subject 0250 is concerned about the
"Population explosion [number] 1 prob in World; federal control
increasing in all areas; bungling, inept, poorly administrated federal programs," but lists, under her three desires "Compatability
for two people I love, health for my husband, improved communication within our school staff to give us understanding of each other."

Also to be noted is the frequency with which these more psychically competent persons felt called upon to discourse at length
on various dogmatically worded questionnaire items, thus enrich-
ing an understanding of their values and beliefs.[29] (Indeed, one
male respondent added a several thousand word commentary which
easily makes him a candidate for the Northwest's version of Eric
Hoffer.) Thus not only do these self-actualizing persons tend to
deal creatively with the materials with which they work; equally
important, they find it difficult and at times impossible to be simplistic and dogmatic where complex issues are involved.

Finally, the self-actualizing quality of the comments of these
more psychically competent people should be emphasized. Although
these individuals—many low in SES—are also concerned about money and bills and larger homes, they usually include a self-fulfilling
desire, as in the case of Subject 0132 (a wood products supervisor),
who longs for a larger home and a home workshop, and Subject
0181, whose three wishes are "I wish I wasn't diabetic; I would
like to own and be able to operate a real steam locomotive; I wish
they would abolish the Federal Income Tax."

Most noticeable in the comments of the self-actualizers, however, are interpersonal and introspective concerns which are not
in the realm of the material. Subject 0216, for example, wishes
"that my father had lived to train and discipline me; that I had had
a period between high school and college to gain a sense of direc-

---

29. For example, Subject 0395 (a registered nurse) commented on many of the questions, as exemplified by the following:

People who insist upon a yes or no answer just don't know
how complicated things really are. "Like you people for instance."

There are a number of people I have come to hate because of
the things they stand for. "A little bit of 'hate' can be very in-
vigorating."

There is hardly anything lower than a person who does not
feel a great love, gratitude, and respect for his parents. "Depends on the parents."

tion." The sole concern of Subject 0259 (a teacher) is "How to
break through the walls of fear my students have built up"; while
an unmarried librarian in the forty-six to fifty-five age group
(Subject 0287) expresses her worries in this manner: "Am I a success or a failure in my present job and location? Do I measure up
to the average librarian? Will I always live alone or have to live
alone? Who will love me when I get older?" Superficially in contrast, but likewise expressing a lack of materialism, Subject 0322
(an under twenty-one worker in the hospital's central supply room
who has never been married) is concerned about "taking care of
my son; getting to work with my car broke down," but adds, "I
don't wish for thing althought I'm not saying I wouldn't like to have
them—I wouldn't change my life, I love it now. In the future 3 yrs
MAYBE."

In various ways, the comments of the persons typified as self-
actualizers exemplify qualities which theory places in the syndrome
of mental health. Thus they tend to be cognitively flexible, humanistic in value orientation, introspective and concerned with self-
fulfillment and improvement. Equally noteworthy are two relationships that do not appear: first, these self-actualizers are concerned
with self-fulfillment whatever their position in the social structure,
their education, their occupation, their income, their personal interests. Thus individual fulfillment is the goal, but the means are
personally and socially determined. (While the son of a librarian
longs for a room in which to paint and listen to music, an unskilled
stationary boiler fireman whose father was a professional soldier
wants to own and operate a steam locomotive.) Second, while their
value orientation is humanistic, the social means by which to im-
plement these values are shaped by a variety of political orientations—right, left and center. But while the political views of self-
actualizers represent contrasting ideologies, one may hypothesize
that it is their open-mindedness and basic tolerance for others
which makes political consensus possible.

Further evidence of the political relevance of self-actualization can be seen in various other scale scores of these individuals.
In the earlier chapters of this book, it was hypothesized that a continuum of control over self—perceived control over the world parallels the need hierarchy. We have received some confirmation
(for example, the clear relationship to Taylor's Manifest Anxiety
Scale) that psychic deprivation is related to lack of control over
self. When the Political Efficacy Scale is analyzed in relation to
the Continuum of Mental Health, we have additional evidence of
how the view of the world as manageable and amenable to one's individual efforts increases with greater mental health. The relationship here is well beyond the .001 level[30] (x^2 = 40.2682, f.d. = 8).

---

30. The Spearman correlation coefficient is -.25.

Table 4.47

CONTINUUM OF MENTAL HEALTH versus POLITICAL EFFICACY SCALE

	High		Low			
	1	2	3	4	5	
Psychically deprived	17.2	27.8	29.7	16.8	8.4	100%
Low self-actualizers	21.7	43.3	18.3	10.0	6.7	100%
High self-actualizers	36.3	39.2	16.7	2.9	4.9	100%

While causal relationships can only be discussed here in relation to what has been previously established in the field of clinical psychology, it appears that such a dramatic increase in one's belief that the political world is amenable to one's control is causally related to the desire to exercise one's right to participate. This is caused by a reduction in basic anxiety through the increased fulfillment of one's basic needs.

Interestingly, the Citizen Duty Scale continues to show a non-significant relationship to mental health. In fact, the most healthy individuals are no more likely to express the belief in such a duty than the least healthy individuals. Perhaps, in the case of our most healthy individuals, participation per se is not met with increased approval because of their (hypothesized) greater freedom from specific cultural norms.[31]

Table 4.48

CONTINUUM OF MENTAL HEALTH versus CITIZEN DUTY SCALE

	High		Low			
	1	2	3	4	5	
Psychically deprived	54.9	39.2	3.7	0.7	1.5	100%
Low self-actualizers	62.5	35.8	0.8	0.0	0.8	100%
High self-actualizers	52.9	41.2	3.9	1.0	1.0	100%

---

31. In the data taken as a whole it is of interest to note that (at significance levels beyond .001) the Citizen Duty Scale is positively related (r = .16) to political participation but negatively re-

In the preceding sections of this chapter, we noted that the Esteem Scale showed an inverse relationship to the first three need areas and then, with the Need for Esteem, suddenly was significantly positive. When analyzed in terms of the Continuum of Mental Health, the relationship remains weakly positive and significant (r = .08, p = .03). It appears that no group on our continuum has a strong desire <u>for</u> esteem, as measured by this scale. Rather, as one becomes more psychically competent, <u>the aversion to social prominence grows weaker.</u>

The same analysis could be offered concerning the near non-relationship between the Continuum of Mental Health and the questions on status concern (r = .07, p = .07). No group indicates a strong positive desire for status mobility.[32] Rather, it is assumed here, the increase in security that comes with increasing mental health requires less negative response to these questions— questions which are reflective of pervasive American values.

Finally, in this review of the attitude measures, there is a clear, inverse relationship, beyond the .001 level (X^2 = 43.7524, d.f. = 10), between the Continuum of Mental Health and Srole's Anomia Scale (r = -.26). Although the most noticeable drop occurs between the Psychically Deprived and the Low Self-Actualizers, the drop continues as one moves up to the High Self-Actualizers. (Further, in the lowest column, the least anomic are the <u>Low</u> Self-Actualizers, the drop for the High Self-Actualizers perhaps again suggesting the cultural separation which Maslow has found to occur among the menally healthy.) (See Figure 4.49.)

If anomia is a psychological measure (and it appears to be so here), it is apparent that self-actualizing individuals are not despairing of their life situation—nor should they be. Competent people are not likely to be anomic—and in this study, the anomia scores are closely related to those on the Political Efficacy Scale.[33] But it is also apparent that whether or not individuals feel competent or full of despair has a much lower relationship to the degree of their political socialization—if the Citizen Duty Scale can be considered

_____

lated (r = -.14) to political efficacy. This suggests that teaching democratic values does increase political participation (whether or not participation is accompanied by a sense of competence), but that the competent—perhaps more realistic, perhaps husbanding their energies—do not feel that one should be active when activity is futile or inconsequential.

32. It will be remembered that Melvin Seeman has found individuals expressing a strong concern for status highly likely to be prejudiced.

33. In this field study, the Anomia Scale is related to the Political Efficacy Scale far beyond the .001 level of significance (X^2 = 200.7353, d.f. = 20) with a correlation of -.56.

Table 4.49

CONTINUUM OF MENTAL HEALTH versus ANOMIA SCALE*

	Low			High			
	1	2	3	4	5	6	
Psychically deprived	25.6	22.3	23.4	15.8	9.9	2.9	100%
Low self-actualizers	50.8	16.7	18.3	5.8	5.8	2.5	100%
High self-actualizers	44.1	31.4	15.7	4.9	2.9	1.0	100%

*The totals for columns 1 and 2, summed, are: Psychically Deprived = 47.9 percent, Low Self-actualizers = 67.5 percent, High Self-Actualizers = 75.5 percent.

an adequate measure of this dimension.[34] In other words, it is likely that individuals can be psychically anomic—that is, alienated from the sociopolitical world and from its inhabitants in Srole's terminology, but not be social anomic—that is, personally contributing to "a disintegration of political belief systems" or disagreeing over what social values are and should be. Admittedly, the Citizen Duty Scale is an incomplete measure of modal values for which agreement may be assessed. However, this is a testable hypothesis which could help to clarify the present discussion regarding anomia versus anomie.

Is anomia then an indicator of the existence of anomie in our society? It is suggested here that this depends on the opportunities which such psychically deprived persons have to act out their anxieties and insecurities (that is, on the strength of the social structure and their position in it) rather than to register agreement with the values into which they have been socialized. (In other societies, for example, Nazi Germany, cultural values may, of course, correspond to individual anomia.) Anomia, in other words, is lack of competence, lack of faith in people, threat orientation, concern with self—that is, psychic deprivation: in short, anomia is alienation from others. Whether or not a society is anomic, however, depends upon more than the psychic state of its citizenry. It depends upon what social values typify that society and what opportunities there are to express one's concern with self (over one's concern with environment and self in relation to it). It is also of interest to note, as the psychic dimension of alienation was earlier hypothe-

---

34. There is a correlation of -.20 (p = .001) between the Anomia and Citizen Duty Scales.

sized to be measurable by tapping anomia, efficacy and misanthropy, the strong correlations between these variables (See Appendix D).

Finally, let us turn to the relationship between the Continuum of Mental Health and our measures of participation. First, there is a positive relationship (r = .14, p = .001) to the Index of Political Participation. When the scores are collapsed, it is of interest to note that the difference related to mental health is not apparent until the High Self-Actualizers, who are both less nonparticipant and much more highly active.

Table 4.50

CONTINUUM OF MENTAL HEALTH versus
POLITICAL PARTICIPATION

	Low	Middle	High	
Psychically deprived	36.6	37.4	26.1	100%
Low self-actualizers	33.3	40.8	25.8	100%
High self-actualizers	23.5	32.3	44.1	100%

In regard to the Index of Leadership, there is a similarly weak relationship (r = .09, p = .02). While the High Self-Actualizers are most likely not to lack leadership roles, in the combined high leadership categories (3 and 4), it is noticeable (in a trend similar to Anomia and Citizen Duty Scores) that there tends to be a drop-off on the part of the most self-actualizing subjects—who possibly, at this point of mental health, become more concerned in personally creative work than with group activity.

What, then, is the political relevance of self-actualization? In their tendencies toward tolerance, open-mindedness, faith-in-people and lack of authoritarianism, self-actualizers do appear to possess psychic strengths which allow them to work well in situations marked by a diversity of viewpoints, complex and multidimensional problems, and with persons whom they do not choose but with whom they are required to associate. Because of their reduced anxieties and insecurities, as well as a greatly reduced view of the world as hostile and threatening, these more psychically competent individuals have the psychic energy to be participant in their environment, to lead as well as to follow. In short, the results of this study give evidence that the self-actualizer is synonymous (as has been hypothesized) with the democratic personality.

The Effect of SES

The above relationships suggest the value of employing Maslow's personality model in analyzing politically relevant behavior and attitudes. Although the need hierarchy is clearly inversely related to socioeconomic status, the psychically deprived group are certainly not isomorphic with the low status group. Further, the similarity of the Low and High Self-Actualizer Groups in SES and the disparity between these groups in psychic competence also emphasizes the distinction between one's position in society and the degree of one's mental strengths or weaknesses. Further, because high status may encourage political participation by individuals who are psychically deprived, personality theory offers a clarification of relationships which socioeconomic status also suggests.

However, the serious student is undoubtedly interested, at this point, in the specific effect of SES as opposed to the effect of the state of psychic health on the relationships which have been uncovered. While the total sample was too small to run the five need groups with these controls, it was possible to correlate the previously discussed Continuum of Mental Health with each of our variables with SES controlled and then to correlate our Index of SES with our variables with the Continuum of Mental Health controlled. These results, now to be discussed, are also found in graphic form in Appendix D.

Maslow's Security-Insecurity Inventory (to no one's surprise!) appears as a pure personality measure. Even when SES is controlled, the strength of its relationships remain significant and relatively unchanged. With mental health controlled, however, the strength of the relationships is halved and only in the case of the Psychically Deprived does the relationship reach statistical significance. Manifest Anxiety is likewise—as expected—a personality measure, with the strength of its relationships largely unchanged when SES is controlled. When mental health is controlled, however, it is likewise only significantly related to the psychically deprived.

Similarly, with SES controlled, intolerance of ambiguity is clearly related to each status group, giving evidence of a clear psychic dimension. With mental health controlled, however, the size of the relationship becomes considerably reduced, except in the case of the Low Self-actualizers where the relationship remains significant. (The differential in performance between the two groups of self-actualizers, which there will again be occasion to note, should be emphasized.) Dogmatism, on the other hand, appears to be composed rather equally of social and psychic factors, as it is significantly related to each subgroup when controls are applied, although the variation in the high status group should be noted.

Threat Orientation, when analyzed with controls, appears more closely tied to social than psychic factors. With SES controlled, it is significantly related only to the middle status group. With mental health controlled, it remains clearly related to the Psychically Deprived and the Low Self-Actualizer groups. (Again,

the differential performance of the two self-actualizer groups
when mental health is controlled should be noted.) While the relationship between Threat Orientation and SES remains significant
(increasing from -.24 to -.27) in the case of the Low Self-Actualizers, it disappears entirely (r = .01) in the case of the High Self-
Actualizers. This difference gives additional evidence that membership in the High Self-Actualizer group (as opposed to the Low
Self-Actualizer group) is almost purely determined by psychic
considerations. Turning to the Interpersonal Threat Scale, it is
not surprising in view of its low discriminating ability in this
study, that the relationships here are generally nonsignificant for
both sets of controlled figures. (The extremely strong, increased
relationship to low status when SES is controlled, however, suggests that this dimension of psychic threat is particularly meaningful to low status individuals.)

While the F-scale was developed as a measure of a particular personality type, it has—as others have demonstrated previously—a very clear connection with the social press connected
with low status. Thus, with mental health controlled, it nevertheless remains strongly related to each subgroup. With SES controlled, the relationships also remain significant, except in the
case of the low status group—thus giving further evidence that
while a personality dimension is clearly being tapped, for persons
who live at the lower social levels, authoritarian responses are
most likely to be based upon objective considerations and cultural
values. This finding suggests that education toward democratic
values, when combined with more positive life experiences, is
likely to reduce intolerance among lower SES groups, but to be
largely ineffective when directed toward their social superiors.

A somewhat similar pattern can be seen in the lack of faith-
in-people dimension. Again, however, when mental health is controlled, the relationship is reduced to insignificance for the High
Self-Actualizer group (from -.23 to -.08) while remaining clearly
related to SES (r = -.28) in the case of Low Self-Actualizers, suggesting again the social dimension of this group's responses.

To consider the more directly political measures, if upper
status people lack feelings of political efficacy, this lack is likely
to be related to personality factors. However, for all three personality groups, political efficacy is also negatively related to SES.
This suggests that with objective opportunities to control one's environment (that is, as income, occupational level and education
rise) comes a subjective feeling of competence. On the other hand,
the Citizen Duty Scale is a measure which elicits high agreement
from all groups and does not appear to have a personality dimension, when analyzed using the total group or subgroups with SES
controlled. It is, however, related to SES, a relationship which remains only in the case of the psychically deprived group when mental health is controlled, suggesting that some personality factors
are involved in the responses of the self-actualizers to this scale.

The Esteem Scale, in contrast to the Citizen Duty Scale, is significantly related to personality when correlated with total group scores. The relationship is small, however (r = .08) and becomes nonsignificant when SES is controlled. Esteem is, however, significantly and positively related to SES (r = .20), a relationship which remains when mental health is controlled—again with the noteworthy exception of the High Self-Actualizers. These relationships are similar to those which occur when Status Concern is analyzed with controls. (It should be noted that only in the cases of these measures and the Citizen Duty Scale is there a positive relationship to SES.)

Anomia appears to be composed of both psychic and social factors. With SES controlled, the relationship remains significant, though reduced, particularly in the middle status group. With mental health controlled, the scale is significantly related to the psychically deprived and most strongly to the Low Self-Actualizers. The difference between the Low and High Self-Actualizers in this regard is of special interest in view of their close similarity in SES. While the relationship between Anomia and the High Self-Actualizers drops from -.29 to -.10 with mental health controlled, the relationship to the Low Self-Actualizers (r = -.30) remains unchanged.

In the previous pages it has variously been suggested that the addition of personality factors to a model of political behavior will likely tell us little about participation in broadly popular political activities that could not be foretold by employing sociological variables, but will be of great value in predicting the intensity, direction and meaning of such participation. Thus it is of interest that while the Political Participation Index is significantly related (r = .14, p = .001) to the Continuum of Mental Health, this relationship does not hold when SES is controlled. Further, Political Participation is much more strongly related to SES (r = .31, p = .001), a relationship which with controls becomes nonsignificant only in the case (again) of the High Self-Actualizers. What, then, determines political participation? It is, as predicted, a combination of social and psychic factors, with the social factors predominating except in the case of the High Self-Actualizers. In general, the Index of Leadership performs like the Political Participation Index—likely for the same reasons. (It should be noted that while fourteen of these fifteen relationships were significant when correlated with the total sample data, only three remain significant for the High Self-Actualizer group when mental health is controlled, as opposed to ten for the Low Self-Actualizers and twelve for the Psychically Deprived.)

In a recent secondary analysis of the five nation data originally collected for the Almond and Verba (1963) study, plus additional data from India, it was found that two factors largely accounted for political participation (Nie, Powell and Prewitt, 1969a, 1969b). The variable with the greatest predictive strength was organizational involvement; hence here, as in studies discussed previously, political participation is seen as an extension of general social participation.[35] Most interestingly, about 60 percent of this relationship was <u>not</u> accounted for by either social class or attitudinal variables. Thus "many citizens whose organizational involvement propels them into political life are <u>not</u> more politically informed, politically efficacious, or politically attentive than the nonparticipants."[36] In terms of our model and their explanation, it thus appears that involvement in such organizations as trade unions stimulates political activity of many persons who lack necessary psychic strength and would otherwise be generally nonparticipant. Second, Nie, Powell and Prewitt found social status to be of high value in predicting political participation; this relationship, however, was virtually all explainable in terms of intervening attitudinal variables which we have hypothesized to be part of the syndrome of self-actualization. Thus it appears here also that social factors and psychic factors jointly account for political participation—again with social factors predominating.

While these intricacies of the effects of socioeconomic status versus mental health are of considerable significance for the research-oriented reader, they should not cause us to lose sight of the import of the previous section which dealt with the clear relationship between growing psychic competence and a variety of factors which are necessary for tolerant and creative participation in one's environment. For to say, for example, that a man's increasing participation in the world around him is most likely accounted for by <u>socially</u> related factors (that is, income, occupation and education) does not obviate a <u>psychic</u> explanation. As Glad points out:

> psychoanalytic explanation is in no way competitive with economic, sociological, or political explanation. All human behavior is the result of multiple causation; and explanations can be sought at several levels of analysis. The psychic makeup of any individual is the result of his own nature and his earliest encounters with the culture which helped make him what he is. His behavior at any one moment is the result of his psyche as well as those factors in the environment with which his psyche interacts. This is where psychology connects with sociology and political science. (1968, p. 10)

Not only is it possible that increased education and social opportunities may stimulate psychic growth, it is also likely that growth-motivation may be a precondition to the ability to complete an edu-

---

35. For a study which elaborates this point, see McConaughy and Gauntlett (1967).

36. Also surprising was the lack of relationship between urban residence and political participation.

cation and assume more responsible, psychically demanding (and economically rewarding) socioeconomic roles.

What is of concern are various politically relevant syndromes of behavior, attitudes and personality predispositions. The focus in this section has been the best indicators of where persons may be found who display these syndromes. As has been previously advanced, it has hopefully been illustrated here that it is only by simultaneously considering social and psychic factors that a clear picture of political man can be derived. These factors are complex and not likely to be determined in one research project. The above relationships indicate, however, that the employment of personality theory in political research will enrich the scope and meaning of the research concern without unmanageably complicating the research design.

An Overview

This field study appears to be of use to students of political behavior for several reasons. First, it helps to clarify the relationships between various measures frequently used in behavioral research, by analyzing them in terms of a common framework. Past behavioral research has often given the impression that the world's population can be dichotomized into the "haves" and the "have nots," depending upon the research subjects' scores along a particular dimension. Thus subjects are categorized as misanthropic or not, authoritarian or not, anomic or not, lower status or not. Not only are such simplistic assumptions generally meaningless beyond controlled research situations, they also tend to confuse the already unclear picture of political man. Is the authoritarian also the dogmatist? Is he the isolate or the avid participant? Is he lower status—or is this a factor of personality? Once a special research dimension has been isolated, continual employment of single-interest research is highly unsatisfactory. Only by considering subjects simultaneously from a variety of perspectives is one likely to understand the importance of any one factor in the real world.[37] Further, in a democracy, where all votes are of equal weight, there is no justification for avoiding consideration of any group because their scores do not register on a single dimension. Through an integrated analysis of a variety of personality types we are more adequately considering the universe of wants and needs that shape politically relevant behavior.

In addition, such a multivariate analysis helps to provide a clearer understanding of the relationships between and discriminatory value of sociological versus psychological variables. For example, through confirmation in a variety of studies, it has almost become a political law that political activity is directly re-

---

37. For the inter-correlations of the major variables employed in this study (exclusive of need levels), see Appendix E.

lated to such factors as education, upper status, a primary family
with political interest, and a particular occupation (such as law).
Now it is time to ask, in addition, such questions as why some individuals with all of these traits do not engage in political activity
(or perhaps even more significant, why some individuals with none
of these traits are political activists), and why some activists respond in an anxious, inflexible and personally threatened manner
to every political crisis, while other persons (with or without the
same demographic traits) and open-minded, flexible, tolerant, and
objective.

   This research study is also suggestive of the value which
Maslow's need hierarchy holds for the field of political psychology.
It is freely acknowledged that Maslow's personality theory is but
one of a variety of psychological models by which one can differentiate research subjects.[38] The problems of identity, of marginality,
of inner versus other directedness, of oral versus anal character,
of various types of neuroticism, of mass man versus "spontaneous"
individualism—all of these problems have received considerable
attention in recent years. Like the employment of such variables
as authoritarianism and dogmatism, however, these approaches
also tend to degenerate too often into the "have"-"have not," "either-or" type of proposition.

   Maslow's personality model, on the other hand, offers a rich-
er typology, composed as it is of five basic need groups, yet not
encompassing an unwieldy number of personality types. Perhaps
equally important, it bears a certain inherent theoretical similarity to a variety of concerns long employed in behavioral research.
Thus instead of providing a new research dimension, an attempt
has been made here to show that it simplifies the present research
picture. For example, an examination of the results has disclosed
several striking parallels which are deserving of further study.
Of great interest here is the close relationship between mental
health as delimited by Abraham Maslow and cognitive functioning,
as analyzed by Milton Rokeach. While the specific relationship of
dogmatism to each level of psychic deprivation will require more
discriminating analysis, it seems clear that increasing psychic
health (in Maslow's terms) is strongly related to increasing open-
mindedness (in Rokeach's terms).

   Another constant research concern which parallels Maslow's
need hierarchy is authoritarianism, as defined by F-scale scores.
Again there is a strong and inverse relationship between increasing self-actualization and the generalized intolerance commonly
called authoritarianism. It is indeed likely that, if cultural factors
could be isolated, the intolerant would be isomorphic with the psychically deprived. (The most interesting nonsignificant relationship between the Need for Affection—in view of this group's lack

---

   38. For a good general discussion of other major approaches,
see Hall and Lindzey (1957).

of psychic fulfillment—and F-scale scores is, again, a matter for further study.)

An examination of our group F-scale means is illustrative of the value of considering personality types who have authoritarian tendencies. That the total sample mean (3.49) is somewhat lower than the combined student mean of the Berkeley study (3.56) suggests—as was hypothesized at the beginning of this chapter—that the sample is overly-representative of individuals who are low in anxiety. But while other studies have reported higher means in authoritarian cultures than our deprived groups achieved here,[39] the mean of the Low Self-Actualizers has rarely been equalled and —to our knowledge—that of the High Self-Actualizers is unique in the literature.

Table 4.51

F-SCALE MEANS BY PSYCHIC NEED GROUP[*]

Physiological need	4.08
Safety need	4.21
Affection need	3.47
Esteem need	3.97
Psychically deprived	3.73
Low self-actualizers	3.33
High self-actualizers	2.91
Sample Total	3.49

[*]The dogmatism means, which have a somewhat smaller range and somewhat higher averages, are: Physiological Needs = 4.90; Safety Needs = 4.74; Affection Needs = 4.68; Esteem Needs = 4.91; Psychically Deprived = 4.71; Low Self-Actualizers = 4.43; High Self-Actualizers = 4.18; Total sample mean = 4.53.

Anomia is another research perspective which parallels our concern here with increasing mental health (as well as being related to socioeconomic status). It appears, for example, that at all points on the status ladder, anomia is related to psychic as well as social factors. Further, this feeling of despair and of the meaninglessness of life is closely related to a feeling of lack of competence—of the lack of control over one's hostile environment, as well as to a lack of faith in the people who inhabit it. Thus the isolation of anomic individuals helps to uncover the political apathetic—and the alienated—as well as the psychically deprived.

The importance of anomia, both theoretically and as a predic-

39. See, for example, Prothro and Melikian (1953).

tor of behavior, has been clouded by the lack of concurrence among scholars concerning its conceptualization and the methods by which it can be made operational. The viewpoint held here is that anomia is personal (and hence social) alienation—that is, because the anomic individual lacks faith in other men to satisfy his unfulfilled psychic needs, he lacks faith that the social structure (composed of other men) will be responsive to his needs. Anomia, in other words, is psychic distress writ large. It indeed measures, as Srole intended it to, "self-to-others alienation." Anomia in this field study was found to be directly related to each psychically deprived group (that is, if an individual can be typified as physiologically, safety, affection or esteem deprived, he is much more likely to be anomic than if he does not express any of these needs.) It is not until one reaches the level of self-actualization that the relationship becomes significantly negative. It further appears that as a person grows in self-actualization, his anomic feelings continue to decrease.

Finally, as anomia and misanthropy (with inefficacy) were hypothesized earlier to comprise the psychological dimension of alienation, it is important to note their clear relationship to each other (r = .54) which suggests that they are separate but strongly related factors. It is also of interest to note that both factors are negatively related to political participation (anomia = -.28, lack of faith in people = -.19) as well as to agreement with the Citizen Duty Scale (anomia = -.20, lack of faith in people = -.19). Thus misanthropy and despair over one's existential state are relevant to the dimension of political alienation, although one can admittedly be psychically alienated but socially supportive as well as politically alienated and self-actualizing.

Yet, in spite of the fact that there is a strong relationship between anomia and unfulfilled basic needs, there is here a very weak and generally nonsignificant relationship between mental health and belief in one's duty as a citizen—this being taken as an indicator (though incomplete and hence, unsatisfactory) of degree of politicization. If this tenuous connection can be upheld, it could be of considerable importance for social scientists (as well as educators). First, it suggests in regard to the problem of anomia, that psychological measures rather than value conflict are likely to be indicative of the degree to which the community bonds are inherently weak in our society. (Indeed, other studies have often suggested that it is the superpatriot, who jingoistically defends all of his country's values, who is most likely to be psychically deprived and a danger to a democratic social system.)

This finding also suggests that psychic deprivation is likely to determine one's attitudes toward others, no matter how democratic are the values which one has been socialized to accept. Not only is it likely that growth-motivated persons (for both social and psychological reasons) will stay in school longest and actualize to the greatest degree their education in democratic values, it is also probable that they are the group most likely to use the democratic ideals that they have learned. They will use them not just because they have been taught democratic values are right, but because democratic values correspond to their inner reality (a dimension which education may not affect at all).

Most likely, these self-actualizers will behaviorally and cognitively conform to the participant values they have learned because they feel psychically powerful or competent in relation to an unthreatening, manipulable environment. From this field study data at least, it appears that there is a clear relationship between mental health and political efficacy. Man will rarely devote his time to exercises in futility: lacking a sense of efficacy, the person who is psychically deprived is likely to be an apathetic citizen, no matter what he has learned to be his right and duty as a member of a democratic polity. Yet, political scientists have learned that political participation is also likely to be determined in part by one's place in the social structure. Low status individuals (who often lack a knowledge of the issues as well as the mechanics involved), as well as high status individuals (whose politicized families often give them a special entree into the world of power), will likely have the amount of their political activity—in normal times—partially predetermined by the accident of their births. Thus political participation is a complex phenomenon in which psychological and sociological factors both play a part.

It has been a constant theme here, however, that as important as it is for the political scientist to know who will be active in politics, it is equally important to understand what direction his activities will take—a dimension which is as yet little explored. It is here that personality theory is envisioned to be of the greatest value. Threat Orientation scores, for example, are significantly related to psychic deprivation, to anomia, lack of faith-in-people, dogmatism, authoritarianism, lack of political efficacy and (somewhat more weakly) lack of political participation (See Appendix E). The person who feels that he operates in a secure and manageable environment will respond differently to political events than he "who lives his life out as if he were a spy in enemy territory" (Maslow, 1954, p. 114). A knowledge of personality type is thus an important indicator of both direction and intensity of political activity. Further, it becomes particularly valuable in relation to the problem of assessing the latent possibilities for political activity by the traditionally apathetic.[40]

---

40. McClosky and Schaar (1965), for example, found a high correlation between their Anomy scale and extremist political views. They comment: "Not only does the anomic feel confused and normless, but he also leans toward values and opinions that are rejected in his society." For a useful discussion of the political forms which psychic alienation and resentment may take, see Horton (1960).

One of the major values of using Maslow's need hierarchy in field research can be seen in the basis which it provides for making such causal and relational statements. In so doing, it clarifies the direction which research must take. To mention but one problem, it has long been noted that the political activists on which the strength of our political system rests can be differentiated in many demographic dimensions from the rest of the citizenry. It appears that these individuals can also be differentiated on the more basic level of personality and degree of psychic growth. In turn, a consideration of personality predispositions leads to a deemphasis of the means of "molding" public opinion and values (including formal socialization) and to a focus, instead, on the problem of psychic receptivity—of encouraging the growth of mental health and the reduction of psychic frustration. In a democratic society, Maslow's basic needs are indeed "basic" politically as well as psychologically because their frustration produces a variety of undemocratic attitudes and behavior, while their fulfillment provides the minimal condition for contributory citizenship. It is in tracing out these consequences in political life that we, as students of political behavior, must now be concerned.

5

The Nature of Man Reexamined

[T]he political nature of a man is indistinguishable from
his personality as a whole, and . . . his personality as a
whole is not the sum total of his specific reactions, but
rather a congruent system of attitudes, each element of
which is intelligible only in the light of the total pattern.
A man's political opinions reflect the characteristic
modes of his adjustment to life. (Allport, 1930, p. 238)

In the beginning of this book, it was stated that each political
philosophy which is advanced is inextricably linked with the author's view of the nature of man. As the thesis of this book has
been unfolded, various attempts have been made to show that some
long-held assumptions concerning politics and human nature simply do not relate in a meaningful way to the data that has been
gathered from a variety of behavioral research perspectives employed over a long period of years.

Least supportable is the view that man's nature is all of a
piece—the view that a political system can be designed to meet
the needs of man because his nature is seen as cooperative, or
basically antagonistic, concerned with liberty and freedom of expression, or primarily concerned with equality and freedom from
a variety of physical and social ills. Considering the full range of
human behavior, man is all these things—and more. Taken individually, however, it is apparent that some men are cooperative
and tolerant, while others are antagonistic and hostile to those
around them; some men are primarily concerned with freedom of
expression because their self-actualizing natures allow their major concern to be individual creativity—while other men, mentally
on the run, emphasize security and freedom from such ills as
want and fear. Thus the focus necessarily changes from a discussion of the human nature to a concern with the proportion of personality types and their distribution within the social structure
(particularly with their access to the loci of power and authority).
For it is likely that in specific societies the proportion of individuals of one personality type may be significantly different from
that found elsewhere. Thus the persons of which a polity is composed must be considered in assessing the type of political system
which is both desirable and feasible. In short, it becomes impossible to consider a political theory without first delimiting the human material that it is to order.

Not only is the simplistic view of man's nature as a homoge-
nous entity untenable; the argument concerning the rationality ver-

sus the irrationality of man has also muddied the waters of political discussion (Cook, 1949). If by "rationality" as a basis for political philosophy one means the view that the universe is knowable, orderly and amenable to man's efforts of control[1] and that further, man's acts are determined by "means-ends" calculations, in which he tries to "maximize his utilities" on the basis of a standardized set of values,[2] one immediately runs into several basic difficulties. In the first place, from the preceding chapters it can be seen that one's cosmic view—one's Weltanschauung—is individualistic, and inextricably bound with one's psychic needs. Thus "every person—even a 1 year old child—has his own conception of human nature." Equally important,

> every adjustment, whether bad or good, is already a general solution to the person's problems. Even the most extremely neurotic outlook in the world is functional and purposeful, and orders the individual, his problems, and his world into a coherent, logical structure. (Maslow, 1941-1942, p. 343)

In every society, there have undoubtedly been men to whom the universe was knowable and orderly and others who have perceived their existential state to be hedged by chaos and uncertainty, a state in which each man must build as best he can a fortress behind which to huddle—knowing full well the tenuous and uncertain foundation on which any human edifice rests. With man's increased knowledge and satisfaction of bodily needs, it is probable that the former view has become relatively more important. But nevertheless, in any society there are doubtless a sizeable number of individuals whose personal philosophy is diametrically opposed to the philosophical assumptions underlying their political system—whichever view it is built upon.

Thus, a discussion of the rationality of political man has generally become a meaningless exercise in semantics. Either all men, in the light of their own needs, act rationally or only men whose acts conform to the writer's personal value system are rational. Either way, the theorist is placed in an indefensible position.

M. Brewster Smith (1969a) offers an analysis of the concept of rationality more useful than such simplistic, judgmental notions

---

1. Erikson offers a useful distinction which refines the argument here: "Reality, . . . is the world of phenomenal experience, perceived with a minimum of distortion and with a maximum of customary validation agreed upon in a given state of technology and culture; while actuality is the world of participation, shared with other participants—with a minimum of defensive maneuvering and a maximum of mutual activation" (1964, pp. 164-65).

2. For a thorough-going application of this argument, see Downs (1957).

about human behavior. Smith divides a consideration of rationality into "the <u>products</u> of individual and social decision processes" and "the decision <u>processes</u> themselves." Rationality seen in terms of <u>products</u> of decision-making is inescapably tied to a view from outside the person—that is, it involves the imposition of a set of values by which to measure the costs and utilities of the specific decision. Rationality seen as a process, however, is based on a sociopsychological approach congenial to the focus of this book. Based on his division of the functional bases of attitudes into object appraisal, mediation of self-other relationships and externalization and ego defense, Smith discusses that, in these terms:

> the crux of a processual conception of individual political rationality . . . lies in the relative preponderance of object appraisal in the person's attitudes that enter into his political decisions and actions. As products, his decisions may be defective and irrational if they are based on the appraisal of erroneous or deficient information. But to the extent that they are grounded in processes of object appraisal, they are rational in the sense that they represent a weighing of means-end relationships that is corrigible in principle given the availability of better information.

In these terms, Smith comes to essentially the point which we have been stressing. Instead of categorizing persons as "rational" or not, I am opting for the view that it is more useful to think of them in terms of the degree to which their cognitive, perceptual and conative systems are open-ended (that is, assimilating and creatively using what is available and relevant). As the term "rationality" appears too limiting, I would suggest it more useful to think of this process in terms of an individual's ability to function, of his degree of competence in integrating inner requirements and outer necessities.

As the above quotation suggests, Smith (1969b) ties his analysis of rationality to the milieu in which the person must make his decisions, in his discussion of whether process rationality leads to product rationality. The answer to the measure of decision rationality lies, he points out, in such features of the situation as

> Does the situation pose a meaningful and intelligible political choice? Is information relevant to the choice readily available? How is the citizen to distinguish information from misinformation? . . . And does the situation present the issue in a context of threat and stress, or in a way more conducive to thoughtful deliberation? (p. 29)

Hence the political system, in the mode and degree of its information presentation (as well as the penalties which it attaches to some conclusions rather than others) directly affects individual rationality in addition to having the power to stimulate the psychic growth through which process rationality becomes possible.

Therefore, it appears far better to examine political philosophy in relation to the assumptions which it makes of the mental health of the members of the political system and then to appraise a specific polity in the light of the justifiability of those assumptions. (It is thus possible additionally to gain some fascinating insights into the psychic needs of the originators of certain popular philosophies.) Specifically advanced here is the view that the ideal polity—open, participant, democratic in the widest sense—assumes a personal philosophy of the citizenry which is the essence of self-actualization.

In regard to research problems, the discussion in the preceding chapters is equally relevant. Throughout the earlier discussion, various suggestions were offered as to the practical usefulness of Maslow's personality theory. In the section below, a general analysis is attempted. This overview is by no means exhaustive of the possibilities for the application of personality to the study of politically relevant behavior. Rather it is intended to offer a perspective from which one may proceed.

Clarifying Our Research Designs

It is strange for me, whose habitat is mathematics, to say this, but I think that depth psychology, particularly the contribution of Freud, is the richest area of behavioral science. I only regret that the disparity between the soft-heads and the hard-heads is so great that it is difficult for them to lay out a common program in which intuitive insights can be translated into strict deductions and verifiable generalizations. (Rapoport, 1961, p. 50)

Throughout this book, it has been advanced that the political scientist must consider both the personal and the social aspects of politically relevant behavior, although our interest here has been primarily personality variables and neither aspect—in the deepest sense—denies the validity of the other. Sometimes one group of factors will be of principal importance in the final outcome and sometimes the other group will be the major determinants of action; almost inevitably, however, the results in observable behavior and measurable attitudes will reflect a combination of the two sets of factors interacting in a knowable pattern. Thus it is a model based on such a combination that is advanced here.

The most succinct and incisive statement of our position is found in a thoughtful article by J. Milton Yinger (1963), entitled "Research Implications of a Field View of Personality" (1963).[3] As Yinger points out, neither psychological nor sociological theories are by themselves chiefly focused on behavior. The primary

---

3. Yinger's argument is more richly developed in his Toward a Field Theory of Behavior (1965).

concern of personality theorists is "the inner tendency system of the individual and how it is produced" while sociologists place major emphasis on "sociocultural systems and how they are produced." The variables isolated by either group are alone of predictive and heuristic value in the study of behavior <u>only in stable situations</u>.[4] Thus Yinger points to the need "to incorporate personality variables and environmental variables into the very unit of analysis, with full attention to the fact that neither by itself has 'direct effects upon behavior'—that is, has effects that are not mediated through the other system of influences."

In advancing the view that a social-psychological construct is "a more powerful analytic tool" than either perspective taken alone, Yinger goes on to state:

> The social-psychological point of view can be described in simple mathematical terms by putting the familiar concepts of "predisposing" factors (located in the individual) and "precipitating" factors (located in the situation) into scales. Assume that values can range from zero to ten, which would represent the theoretically limiting cases. The likelihood of suicide (or of any other act being interpreted by the use of this scheme) is measured by the product of the values on these two presumed scales; if either is zero, the act will not occur no matter how high the score on the other measure. Thus a person caught in a thoroughly anomic situation and surrounded by other social forces strongly precipitating him toward suicide will have no likelihood of performing the act if his "predisposal" score is zero. Similarly, if he is as thoroughly predisposed as is theoretically imaginable but is surrounded by a situation that contains no precipitating influences whatever, suicide will not occur.
>
> To think in terms of empirically more likely cases, we can hypothesize a "score" of 50 as the point at which suicide is likely to occur. A person with a "predisposal" score of 1 to 4 will be immune even in the most powerfully precipitating context, as anomic and stressful as one can imagine. If his score rises to 5, however, he becomes vulnerable in situations with the highest possible score. One can successfully predict a high rate (that is, a group measure) when such precipitating influences as anomie are strong (let us say, arbitrarily, about 7), because the product scores of a large number are brought

---

4. As Yinger states, ". . . if one lives in an environment that never falls below $0°$ C. or goes above $100°$ C. he can afford to predict solely on the basis of the 'traits' of H_2O that it is a liquid. This is an adequate way of saying that H_2O, a compound with certain potentialities, is liquid under certain conditions which, being constant, can be disregarded. That does not mean, however, that the conditions are not always involved in producing the results."

above the assumed critical point of 5. A precipitating score
of 5 will affect only these with a predisposal score of 10; but
if the former score rises to 7, all those above 7 in the latter
measure are affected. Knowledge of anomie, therefore, may
allow us better to predict rates but is of no value in the social-psychological task of understanding how particular individuals will behave in the social context. This statement can
be reversed, of course: knowledge of individual tendencies
tells us who is vulnerable but does not indicate the likelihood
of a given act, which is always situationally influenced. (pp.
585-86)

The Yinger article has been quoted at length because it states,
in a very specific and forceful way, the research thesis advanced
here. Such precise quantification is necessarily neither demon-
strably feasible (at this point in our knowledge) nor even, in many
cases, essential (many necessary and valuable subjects of study
are not precisely quantifiable). The value of Yinger's (1965) statement is seen rather in its clear analysis of the interaction between
psychic and social variables. In short, what we must adhere to is
"the principle of multiple possibilities." The causality of personality is modified and determined by the causality of the social, the
cultural and the specific field situation in which an individual operates—as well as simultaneously influencing and structuring this
field. Thus "we have a problem of solving two simultaneous equa-
tions. Both the situation and the individual are 'unknowns' that can
be defined only when the other is also defined."

The use of such a sociopsychological approach will encourage
the refining of both theoretical assumptions and working models,
so that political science can move toward the type of precise understanding so suggestively presented by Yinger. (For example,
external factors are likely to be of primary importance in determining who will take part in political activities in general. Yet it
has also been noted that as individuals move toward psychic fulfillment, they become much more likely to participate in the world
around them. It is certainly within the realm of feasibility to assign weights to these two factors in a field study in order to arrive
at an accurate index of political participation.)

Our concern here has been with one part of Yinger's equation
—the "predisposing" factors. Paralleling Maslow's need hierarchy,
it has been suggested that the following continua also exist. If further research indicates that these continua indeed correspond both
to reality and to each other, the separation of one's subjects into
Maslow's five need categories will indicate (1) their degree of psychic competence in relation to the ideal and to other subjects as
well as (2) their functioning along other relevant dimensions. (See
p. 253.)

In considering the situationally induced "precipitating" factors,
an additional matter must be noted which is relevant to field re-

Maslow's Need Hierarchy:

PSYCHICALLY DEPRIVED — MENTALLY HEALTHY

Physiological   Safety   Affection   Esteem   Self-Actualization

Related Continua:

Concern with self   ——   Concern with environment
                                              (and self in relation to it)

    Low   —   (Control over self, perceived   —   High
                 control over environment)

Acceptance of culture   ——   Detachment from culture[5]

Closed-mindedness   ——   Open-mindedness[6]

Self-to-others alienation   ——   Self-to-others belongingness[7]

Passive   —   (in Cognitive functioning and   —   Active[8]
                 Sociopolitical behavior)

search. The preceding chapters have stressed the connection between such characteristics as intolerance of ambiguity and of others and psychic deprivation. Only tangentially has the point been
made that in anxiety-producing situations, such unhealthy, neurotic
characteristics are more prevalent in all character types. Yet this
is a necessary basis for understanding the rise of such demagogues
as Hitler and Joseph McCarthy, the "white backlash" reaction to
ghetto violence, as well as many types of mob action.[9] As Else
Frenkel-Brunswik Notes:

_____

    5. Derived from Maslow's writings.

    6. Derived from Rokeach's writings.

    7. Derived from Srole's writings.

    8. Derived from the writings of Rokeach, Mussen and Wys-
zinski, and Witkin.

    9. As Pye comments in his work on Burma: "Unfortunately,
in most transitional societies which have been dislocated by the
impact of the world culture, when people begin to put themselves
mentally into the roles of others, they seem to 'learn' that others
have hidden hostile feelings toward them. Suddenly feelings of aggression which were once channeled and controlled by traditional
patterns tend to be released in diffuse and unpredictable directions. We can hypothesize that with the increase in insecurity
which change produces in most transitional societies, there must

external pressures of a traumatic character, be they past or be they presently imposed, are likely not only to bring authoritarian personalities to the fore but to reinforce authoritarian trends in individuals who otherwise would remain democratic-minded. . . . Anxiety-inducing social and political situations such as economic depression or war can bring to the fore irrational elements and feelings of helplessness, and thus create susceptibility to totalitarianism regardless of how democratic the family situation might have been. (1954, p. 177)

Thus behavioral research should benefit additionally from the isolation and comparative measurement of differing amounts of social stress and the effect of this variable on each personality type. (As noted above, it is in this regard that the political system exercises a direct, crucial power over the possibilities for individual rationality.)

In regard to specific research interests, our previous discussion suggests that Maslow's personality theory will be of use in the study of the following behavioral areas:

1. Leadership: Although it is understood that leadership is shaped by situational factors, individuals who seek leadership positions are likely (a) to be higher on the need hierarchy, rather than lower, and (b) to bring their particular psychic "flavor" to the leadership role. It is empirically possible to assess, in specific situations (for example, legislatures, unions, precinct work, central committees, et cetera) the relationship between degree of health and the assumption of and performance in leadership roles. It is also feasible to examine the proposition that—in every type of leadership role—the more open-minded (undogmatic) and self-actualizing the individual, the more successful he will be, in terms of the goals which are personal to him and to his particular group. In relating personality factors to leadership roles, Edinger concurs with the view expressed here, stating (concerning leadership research) that

a holistic approach to the dynamics of personality development and expression which gives consideration to antecedent as well as contemporaneous events, to psychic as well as somatic factors, to the "inner man" as well as the impact of sociopolitical "outside" variables in the patterning of behavioral characteristics seems most appropriate. (1964, p. 675)

Within the decision-making process, the influence of any individual leader's personality will depend on the presence of factors that engage his psychic needs and give him an opportunity to act them out. Greenstein (1967), for example, suggests that psychic needs are more likely to be determining factors in ambiguous situations ("new, complex, contradictory") as well as in "the degree

be a quantitative increase in the degree of aggression and hostility within the society" (1962, p. 54).

that an act is <u>demanding</u> and not just a conventionally expected performance. . . ." It is particularly within the realm of <u>political</u> decision-making that such conditions are likely to be present.

2. <u>Extremism</u>: Various studies have suggested that similar
personality types tend to compose the membership of extremist
(for example, conspiratorial or demagogic and mob-oriented)
groups of both the left and the right and that, further, this phenomenon can be seen in a variety of cultures. As Inkeles states, "In
many different institutional settings and in many parts of the
world, those who adhere to the more extreme political positions
have distinctive personality traits separating them from those taking more moderate positions in the same setting" (1961, p. 193).

In each political system, opinion could logically be arrayed in
terms of "Left," "Right" and "Center." Further, in all political
systems, those at the polar ends advocate change variously ranging from procedural matters to revolutionary upheaval. Certainly,
much of this politically deviant behavior, because it does not rest
principally on simplistic solutions stemming from <u>personality</u> deviance, cannot—in our terms—be labeled "extremist." A study of
the phenomenon of extremism as a unitary dimension would rather
be concerned with certain characteristic modes of response to authority which are unhealthy <u>politically and psychologically</u> because
they are total, dogmatic, self-serving, simplistic and, usually dysfunctional to the political goals of their adherents.[10] Seen in these
terms, for example, the battle cry of "America—love it or leave
it" is <u>not</u> a great psychic distance from "Down with all things Establishment."

Further, it appears that a weakening of the social structure
allows simultaneous and politically disparate expressions of negativism to occur, once hostilities are able to be enacted. William
Kornhauser states, for example:

> We have been able to identify eight European countries . . .
> in which the anti-democratic extremes (communism and fas-
> cism) ran candidates in at least two consecutive national elec-
> tions since 1920. Comparing changes from one election to the
> next for each country, we find that the Communist and Fascist
> vote increased or decreased together 16 times out of a total
> of 24 pairs of elections. In other words, the two anti-demo-
> cratic extremes changed in the same directions twice as often
> as they changed in opposite directions. . . . We may infer that
> changes in conditions that favor one anti-democratic extreme
> also favor the other, that changes that weaken one extreme
> also weaken the other, and that changes in conditions affect

10. It is likely, for example, that extremists could be fruitfully studied in terms of "over-controllers" and "under-controllers" with the former typifying the conservative response and the
latter, the radical. For an exposition of these personality types,
see the works of Jack Block and Jeanne Block cited previously.

the democratic parties in the opposite direction from their effect on the political extremes. This suggests that, in spite of important differences between them, anti-democratic mass movements spring from similar social [and psychic] conditions. (1959, p. 124)

Thus it appears possible to study directly the thesis previously advanced that for anomia and alienation to affect the social and political structures, psychic deprivation requires an opportunity (such as a weakened social structure, or a crisis in politics) through which hostilities may be expressed. Further, it is likely that the particular negativism (for example, left or right extremism) through which rejection of the status quo is expressed by the psychically deprived will be due to an individual's situational and psychic receptivity, rather than to the movement itself.[11] For example, the many organizational similarities among such ideologically disparate extremist groups in our society as the Black Muslims, the Ku Klux Klan, the John Birch Society, the Weathermen and the Communist Party suggest that they serve similar personality types.[12] (In addition, they operate where the social structure is weak.)

That neurotic proclivities exist universally and that, further, they may be channeled into politically significant behavior, has long been regarded as established (in large measure due to the work of Harold Lasswell). What has not as frequently been likewise acknowledged is the interplay of field and personality which produces extremist movements. In his historical analysis of the development of anti-Semitism, Cohn wisely notes that

it is a great mistake to suppose that the only writers who matter are those whom the educated in their saner moments can take seriously. There exists a subterranean world where pathological fantasies disguised as ideas are churned out by crooks and half-educated fanatics for the benefit of the ignorant and superstitious. There are times when this underworld emerges from the depths and suddenly fascinates, captures,

---

11. Conversely, of course, it has previously been noted that it is possible for healthy people to rebel against a sick society.

12. Professor John Howard, in a lecture at the University of Oregon, suggested these similarities: (1) apocalyptic ideology, (2) charismatic leadership, (3) appointment rather than election of local leaders, (4) no accounting for funds given and secretive about membership, (5) progressive isolation of members from non-members, (6) defining membership in terms of a good deal of personal involvement, and (7) a severe condemnation of defectors. Dr. Howard further suggests that these groups do not rely on conversion for new members, but rather that deviant personality types are drawn to a group which meets their particular needs.

and dominates multitudes of usually sane and responsible people, who thereupon take leave of sanity and responsibility. And it occasionally happens that this underworld becomes a political power and changes the course of history.

Not, of course, that myths operate in a vacuum. The myth of the Jewish world-conspiracy would have remained the monopoly of right-wing Russians and a few cranks in western Europe, and the Protocols would never have emerged from obscurity at all, if it had not been for the First World War and the Russian Revolution and their aftermath. And they would never have become the creed of a powerful government and an international movement if it had not been for the great slump and the utter disorientation it produced. On the other hand all these disasters together could never have produced an Auschwitz without the help of a myth which was designed to appeal to all the paranoid and destructive potentialities in human beings. (1966, p. 18)

Thus here again it is an analysis which incorporates both social and psychic factors which orders data in a meaningful way.

3. Cross-cultural research: If, as has been suggested here, mental health is a universal standard similar to physical health, it is then possible to work toward the development of some universally applicable rules of political behavior (in addition to the proclivity to extremist behavior by psychically deprived individuals). By validating the relationship between personality type and specific behavior pattern, such questions as the readiness of a particular country to become a participant, open society can be more accurately assessed.

For example, it is hard to imagine (in the realm of science fiction) a more carefully planned experiment to reduce an entire people for generations to come to the level of physiological and safety needs (with the accompanying primary concern for self, hostility and intolerance toward the outside world and disinterest in political and social activity) than the murderous cross-fire in which the people of northern and southern Vietnam have been forced to live since 1944. According to the thesis advanced here, it is extremely unlikely that—should the hostilities cease—there will be left creative, tolerant individuals who opt for an open political system grounded in humanistic values. Indeed, it is likely that if such a political order were presented to the Vietnamese people, it would be firmly rejected—for sound psychological reasons.[13] If cultural forms are indeed shaped by psychic needs, the

---

13. Such "psycho" logic appears dynamically related to the original acceptance and maintenance of democratic forms of government in Germany and Japan after World War II and periodically in France in these post-war years. This acceptance took place in spite of the insecurities and anxieties which are war's residual

chances of establishing an open society in Vietnam have been lost
for years to come.[14]

In his review of the work to date on personality in various cultures, Alex Inkeles (1961) offers the conclusion that there is substantial and rather compelling evidence of a regular and intimate
connection between personality and the mode of political participation by individuals and groups within any one political system.
Through providing a universally applicable basis of analysis, Maslow's personality theory can offer a more adequate means of cross-
cultural comparison. Indeed, the growing concern with the simplistic analysis and circular reasoning on which much national character research has been based stems in part from an increasing
awareness of the need for a more inclusive model of personality
than has heretofore been employed. As Inkeles and Levinson note,
here—as in the field of political behavior—

> One of the major problems in the empirical study of national
> character . . . is the lack of an explicit, standardized analytic
> scheme, that is, a universally applicable system of concepts
> and descriptive variables in terms of which modal adult per-
> sonality structures can be described and compared. Even the
> more relatively systematic approaches, which have achieved
> a broad conceptual framework, are relatively limited at the
> level of descriptive variables or categories. This is particu-
> larly true of the psychoanalytic viewpoint. (1969, p. 442)

Further,

> it is evident that the choice of personality variables for inclu-
> sion in these recent studies is ordinarily not made on the ba-
> sis of a systematic framework of personality theory. Each in-
> vestigator selects a few variables in which he is particularly
> interested, or for which quantitative measures are available.
> The need remains for a more inclusive, standardized, and the-
> oretically comprehensive analytic scheme in terms of which
> modal personalities can be described and compared cross-
> nationally. (p. 447)

---

because (and only because) the democratic systems in these countries were initially surrounded and substantively subverted by authoritarian leadership at the apex of the power system.

14. Gilbert, in speaking of the frequent historical occurrence
of a reversion to authoritarian rule "after a too drastic attempt to
impose democracy on an authoritarian culture" states: "Since social upheaval invariably accentuates psychological and socioeconomic insecurity, and the acculturation process in personality development is not readily reversed, there is apt to be a persistence
of the older patterns of behavior for at least a generation or two
after the revolution" (1955, pp. 5-6).

Not only does Maslow's personality model offer an undoubted advance over the fragmented approach of much past research in this field of behavior, it has an equally important advantage in overcoming the logical (and psychological) difficulties of the current concept of "modal" personality. Bendix (1952), for example, notes that all western cultures "have the same range of personality types." But if personality predispositions are universal, how then can one account for intra- and inter-nation differences? Bendix suggests that inter-nation differences develop because of differential social expectations which "make demands upon the emotions of the individual." Intra-nation differences, however, are based on differential tolerance for the "psychological tensions of everyday living" that is in turn dependent upon "their character structure as this is related to childhood experience." While personality as behavior is more than character predispositions, the predispositions alone (as we have seen) account for important intra- and inter-nation differences in behavior. Maslow's personality model makes possible intra- and inter-nation analysis on the basis of behavior stemming from different motivational syndromes, as well as suggesting the differential effects that the proportion and distribution of these syndromes in a given population make likely.

In addition, Maslow's personality types can be divorced from the specific political associations connected with some terms now in current use. For example, Inkeles (1961) defines a citizen of a democracy as ideally "accepting of others," "open to new experiences," "tolerant of differences and of ambiguity," et cetera—in short, "at the opposite pole from the authoritarian personality syndrome." The difficulty in using the term "democrat" for such traits of self-actualization can be seen in the confusion which would result in listing such Soviet citizens as Yevtushenko or Pasternak as "democratic" when their political (as divorced from human) values separate them from the Western conception of "democrat." The difficulty is overcome by isolating self-actualizers and relating this personality type to predispositions toward a specific type of social and political behavior. Thus the behavioral differences in various societies can again be discussed in terms of Yinger's model—that is, the predisposing factors (the relative size and distribution of each need group in the population) and the precipitating factors (the specific cultural values and objective situation).

4. The politically apathetic: Many students of political behavior have noted the stability in American politics of the group of traditional nonvoters. In spite of additional leisure, education, mass media influence and the lessening of restrictions, a considerable number of qualified voters refuse to take an active part in political affairs.[15] In view of the pattern of voting that brought

15. In this connection, Berelson et al. (1954, p. 241) in the

Hitler into office as well as the suggestive research in our country, however, it is not possible to equate apathy with contentment for the status quo or lack of political relevance. It appears that political apathy is generally part of a larger phenomenon of personality passivity[16] and further, that apathetics are likely to have a highly undemocratic view of the world. While the following comments are addressed to individuals with severe neuroses, they are descriptive in many ways of the psychically deprived on which so much of our previous discussion has focused:

> I do not believe that one can understand any severe neurosis without recognizing the paralyzing hopelessness which it contains. Some neurotic persons express their exasperation in no uncertain terms, but in others it is deeply covered by resignation or by a show of optimism. It may be difficult then to see that behind all the odd vanities, demands, hostilities, there is a human being who suffers, who feels forever excluded from all that makes life desirable, who cannot enjoy it. When one recognizes the existence of all this hopelessness it should not be difficult to understand what appears to be an excessive aggressiveness or even meanness, unexplainable by the particular situation. A person so shut out from every possibility of happiness would have to be a veritable angel if he did not feel hatred toward a world he cannot belong to. (Horney, 1937, pp. 227-28)

Because the apathetic (the anomic, the threatened, the misanthropic, the nonparticipant) are granted full participatory rights of citizenship in our society, it is crucial to closely examine this prominent phenomenon in our political life. In the sections on psychic deprivation, it was suggested that Maslow's personality theory has much to offer here too. It can provide an understanding of the personality types that are likely to be apathetic, of the events that are likely to arouse these types to political behavior, and what the subsequent political activities of these types are likely to be (such as their proclivities toward extremism).

5. Specific political issues: As stated previously, affiliation with broadly popular political parties is not likely to be related to personality factors. As Glazer and Lipset remark, ". . . political

---

classic Voting study discuss the correlation which was found between media exposure and freedom from personal disorders (as checked by the respondent). It appears from their results, that a major determinant of media exposure to political materials is "freedom from personal maladjustment that allows the individuals to focus on public affairs in addition to private concerns, as represented by a (primitive) index of certain kinds of neuroticism."

16. See the comments regarding "Motivations Obstructing Political Involvement" in Rosenberg (1951).

events, in the large, are the results mainly of what organized
groups do, and this may have little relevance to the sentiments of
their members or supporters considered in the mass" (1955, p.
161). However, in a particular election—especially on the state
and local level—there are certain ideological issues which serve
to engage personality and, in these instances, personality variables will be useful in research work.[17] Issues do arise, in other
words, which clearly mark a mentally unhealthy versus a healthy
world view.

For example, the 1968 California Senatorial primary race
presented such an ideological issue in the Republican primary con-
test between the incumbent, Thomas Kuchel, and the challenger,
Superintendent of Schools Max Rafferty. Dr. Rafferty's speeches
presented a clear appeal to the need for security in a hostile, chaotic and threatening world. Rafferty urged unquestioning defense
of order in America because "if America goes, everything you
know and have goes" and offered himself as a candidate willing
and anxious to defend the "American" values he iterated. Senator
Kuchel, on the other hand, made a reasoned appeal for commitment and responsibility in a challenging world. Both a content
analysis of the contestants' speeches and a voting analysis of this
election's results should be quite illuminating in terms of the role
of personality in deciding elections. It is likely that the skillful manipulation of voters' unfulfilled basic needs was the factor responsible for Dr. Rafferty's initial success.

V. O. Key, Jr. once asked "What, if any, bearing does early
family influence have on the view of a person fifty years of age on
a question that may have been unheard of when he was a boy?"
(1964, p. 35). The answer which is advanced here is: a great deal
—if the issue appeals to the individual's personality needs in a
meaningful way. As Maslow emphasizes, there is an autonomous
quality to developed personality so that, in spite of changing circumstances, a consistent viewpoint tends to adhere to a person's
politically relevant behavior. In concurrence with this, a recent
careful analysis of longitudinal studies has shown that "basic values are likely to remain stable" though "their representation in
particular attitudes, views, and opinions may shift considerably
over time" (Bloom, 1964, p. 173).

6. Political socialization: In an analysis of some research
data, Lester Milbrath (1962) raises and attempts to answer a most
interesting question: "How do children growing up in homes where
they do not get consistent socialization toward one party develop a
party identification?" Although many other factors are involved,
Milbrath suggests a connection between the individual's personality needs and a basic liberal-conservative view of the world which

17. See, for example, the study of two local bond elections in
Horton (1960).

<u>also</u> bears a causal relationship to party affiliation.[18]

Somewhat similarly, Gabriel Almond (1960) has discussed the difference between what he calls "manifest" and "latent" socialization. Manifest socialization "takes the form of an explicit transmission of information, values, or feelings vis-à-vis the roles, inputs, and outputs of the political system." It is the most obvious and frequently studied means of transmitting cultural values and approved norms of behavior. Yet, much earlier, the child has also begun a process of "latent" socialization which "takes the form of a transmission of information, values, or feelings vis-à-vis the roles, inputs, and outputs of other social systems such as the family which affect attitudes toward analogous roles, inputs, and outputs of the political system."

Much of our discussion of the value of Maslow's personality theory is related to such latent inculcation of values.[19] For by the time a child begins his formal education, he has developed personality needs which, in turn, have shaped a definite world view and value hierarchy. Such "tacit systems of presuppositions" (to use Bernard Williams' phrase)[20] are politically relevant and likely to remain present in all the individual's subsequent behavior and attitudes. They are relevant because personality needs shape the way in which an individual perceives the world. As W. I. Thomas has succinctly stated: "if men define situations as real, they are real in their consequences."[21] M. Brewster Smith, in the same vein, has stated:

> A person will tend to perceive and judge the focus of an attitude in terms of one of his personal values to the extent that (a) the value is important to him, occupying a central position in his value hierarchy; (b) the information available to him about the focus contains a basis for engaging the value; and (c) the scope of the value and of the person's interests is

---

18. In this connection, one should note the most interesting essay by Phillips (1956), which outlines similarities in viewpoint between skepticism and conservatism, such as the beliefs that human nature is irrational and that social perfection is unattainable.

19. However, as pointed out in relation to McClosky and Schaar's (1965) work on anomie, "socialization" is a generally inadvisable term to use because it suggests learning—which in turn suggests the possibility of changed beliefs—while one's world view (primary or central beliefs) and cognitive functioning are likely to be an inalienable part of one's self.

20. Williams, in Rejai (1967, p. 164).

21. W. I. Thomas, quoted in Holsti and Fagen (1967). Also see Levinson (1958) for a useful discussion of the relation between politics and personality.

broad enough to extend to the focus of the attitude. (1949, p. 486)

In short, the personality of the individual, as it is shaped in the first few years of his life, will be a more important though less obvious source of his "information, values, or feelings vis-à-vis" the basic ground rules by which all human systems—social, political and economic—work and relate to him than will the concurrent and later manifest socialization to which he is subjected. This "latent philosophy" is a self-consistent body of beliefs that, in turn, shapes the meaning which yet distant events of major concern to him will have. Indeed, I believe it is of greater import for the political researcher to learn how a person views the nature of the world than to assess the person along any more obvious political dimension.

Thus in various basic fields of political research, Maslow's personality theory offers an economic research model which can clarify and enhance the work presently being done. Further, considering the interaction between individual and social forces, political scientists should be better able to both understand and to predict the actions and attitudes of political men.

Refining Our Theoretical Assumptions

The intellectual abstractions of pure reason may be adequate for the highly educated few, though even this is open to question. They are not adequate for the overwhelming majority who for a greater or less portion of their lives are moved by passion. Basically, the problem of a democracy is one of the acceptance of attitudes and customs which will channel passion into constructive lines. (Griffith, in Rejai, 1967, p. 231)

As has been pointed out at the beginning of this chapter, there are several basic difficulties involved in the reconciliation of political philosophy with what is today known of the nature of man. Such reconciliation does not focus on the obvious differences between the earlier rationalistic assumptions and the more recent "irrational" models (Cook, 1949; Verba, 1961). The basic issue rather centers on the recognition that any unitary view of man is too simplistic to be usefully employed. Human nature can indeed be spoken of as a whole—theoretically and originally. Through individually patterned development, however, the results (adult political men) are disparate types which must be considered separately. Furthermore, the predominant type of personality will vary by society and over time.

Perhaps even more vital is the recognition that the assumptions of classic democratic theory are the assumptions of mental health or psychic competence.[22] While only a brief sketch can be

---

22. The view presented here is in contrast to that of Frenkel-

offered here, this point is so important that it deserves further analysis in the light of what is considered to be the body of "political theory." In brief, there are at least two viable "operational codes" in use which are politically relevant. The code of the self-actualizer is the code of classical democratic theory.[23] (There is a very good reason for this similarity. It is likely that it is primarily creative, self-actualized, mentally healthy individuals who will have the psychic interest or energy to reflect upon the nature and purposes of political organization.)[24] Other political theories—such as the Stalinist version of communism and the nationalist ideologies of the underdeveloped countries—reflect the point of view of the psychically deprived.

In a modern discussion of classic theoretical interest, Bennis and Slater speak of democracy as "The Temporary Society" that "becomes a functional necessity whenever a social system is competing for survival under conditions of chronic change" (1968, p. 4). What is the nature of this form of ordering human relationships? Bennis and Slater see democracy as seeking "no new stability, no end point; it is purposeless, save that it purports to ensure perpetual transition, constant alternation, ceaseless instability." Further,

> Democracy is a superior technique for making the uncommitted more available. The price it exacts is the pain of uninvolvement, alienation, and skepticism. The benefits it gives are flexibility and the joy of confronting new dilemmas. (pp. 12-14)

And it is because they see the American experience today as composed of "temporary systems, nonpermanent relationships, turbulence, uprootedness, unconnectedness, mobility, and above all, un-

---

Brunswik, who stated: "It is conceivable that in the study of certain social and political movements, especially the more matter-of-fact or rational ones, psychology will have little to say. Thus psychology may not play an obvious or prominent role in the explanation of the formation and structure of the American Constitution" (1954).

23. Throughout, the term "democracy" is used to include more than a system in which the majority rules. Rather, the term refers to a participant, open society, similar to the "polity" described by Aristotle—a polity, in other words, grounded in humanistic values. Thus our concern is with substantive rather than procedural democracy.

24. Yet even at our Constitutional Convention and among the literature of political philosophy, there are interesting evidences of fear of human nature and of chaos which is but loosely controlled.

exampled social change . . ." that they suggest education for self-
fulfillment within such an existential state (pp. 124, 127-28).

To sample but one additional modern writer whose focus is
democratic politics, Bunzel suggests that

> Political action is always based on imprecise knowledge, nev-
> er able to take account of all the factors entering into any sit-
> uation. . . . Politics in a democracy deals with the contingent
> and the unknown. . . . The spontaneity, variety, and continu-
> ous unrest of democratic politics is a contradition of every
> canon of order. . . . The conception of politics as a continuing
> flow of compromises between groups, with the accent on inno-
> vation, clashes sharply with the static and disciplined world
> of the closed society, where the accent is on stability. (1967,
> pp. 9-12)

In short, democratic politics operates "in a context of conflict, ambiguity, and change. . . ." (p. 291). Indeed, "The commitment to
democratic politics implies the acceptance of the conflict between
loyalty to society and loyalty to one's inner necessity as a free and
human being" (p. 243).

The purpose of selecting various statements from the work of
three recent authors is to suggest, as clearly as possible, how impossible it is to request or expect the support of the anxious and
the insecure for a political system based on an ordering principle
that there be no firm order. Further, as Daniel Bell (1947-48) has
noted, democracy implies much more than participation and a
sense of affiliation—the cornerstones of totalitarian systems—for
". . . a democratic leader seeks to instill understanding rather
than obedience. . . ." But here again an author is making psychologically relevant statements which are not universally applicable,
for understanding in a democracy is rooted in appreciation of difference and tolerance of divergence. In short, the essence of democracy is the essence of the philosophy of self-actualization, as
delimited in the preceding chapters.

The literature of democratic theory can be considered from
a variety of perspectives. Perhaps the most obvious perspective
is the seemingly eternal discussion over the necessary and essential procedural requirements of a democratic system. Under this
heading would be included such things as division of power, rule
of law, majority rule, choice of alternatives, popular sovereignty
and guarantee of individual rights. But even more vital to the existence of democracy is the spirit behind the procedures—the
view of man and of his existential state. In reading the literature
of democratic theory, one is struck with the consistency of assumptions which the authors make about the nature of man and,
equally important, with the consistency of the writers' views of
what is both desirable and feasible in the ordering of human relationships for the resolution of political conflict.

A recent compilation of writings on democratic theory (Rejai,

1967) offers a variety of examples of the assumptions upon which
the theory of democracy rests. The clearest illustration of just
how much democratic philosophy rests upon the need for and belief in the self-actualization of the individuals who will operate
such a system can be seen in the discussion by Zevedei Barbu.[25]
Barbu thoughtfully notes that the foundation of democracy is not a
group of procedures, but rather "a specific frame of mind" which
he sees as being composed of four elements. The first element is
"the feeling of change" shared by members of a democratic community, the belief that "their personal and their communal life as
well are in a state of permanent transformation and readjustment."
Concurrent with this is a shared "habit of mind" by the members
"to adjust themselves and to adjust the structure of their society,
to the ever-changing conditions of life." The welcomed acceptance
of change as a necessary and useful element of personal and social life is, however, not possible for all personality types. It requires a mental security and—as Barbu notes—a willingness and
ability to adjust to change. Psychically deprived individuals will
not feel comfortable in such a system; rather, they will opt for a
society which emphasizes the security of order, predictability
and regularity.

Barbu gives the second element in a democratic frame of
mind as the belief that "this change is the direct result of their
own activities" or the "conviction that each individual is a maker
of his own society." Such a conviction is based on a concurrent belief in social cooperation: it makes possible the doctrines of equality and of freedom. Here too, we see that Barbu is making certain
psychological assumptions that are not universally applicable. For
a feeling of political efficacy, a belief in the cooperativeness of
human nature—in short, the belief that acting together, men are
the active agents of their own destiny, again is an inherent part of
self-actualization.

Third, Barbu lists "a feeling of the instability and relativity
of power and authority." He notes that authority based on absolute
power has been, with the rise of democracy, replaced by "the internal authority of reason and conscience"—that is, by "confidence
in and reliance on the powers of human reason and conscience."
Yet, as has been discussed in previous chapters, persons who are
psychically deprived have a strong emotional and cognitive need
for stable and absolute external authority. Further, they lack a belief in and confidence of their own powers of reason. To live in a

---

25. Zevedei Barbu, "Democracy as a Frame of Mind," from
Democracy and Dictatorship, New York, Grove Press, Inc., 1956,
in Rejai (1967, pp. 173-79); also see Karl Mannheim, "Integrative
Behavior and Democratic Personality," from Freedom, Power,
and Democratic Planning, New York, Oxford University Press, in
Rejai (1967, pp. 282-87).

world where one must totally rely on human efforts is a frightening prospect for such individuals.

Finally, Barbu lists the "last category of the democratic
frame of mind" as "an attitude of confidence in reason." He rightly notes that

> the feeling of confidence in reason is necessary as a balanc-
> ing factor in the mind of the individual who has to adjust him-
> self to a world of change and novelty; it is necessary for this
> individual to develop the belief that there is an order and sta-
> bility behind the change, and that there are certain regulative
> principles which put a check upon change.

Again we return to the necessity for the existence of the belief that
man operates in a rational, manageable and orderly world: only
thus is it possible for man to psychically manage constant personal and social change. Barbu also correctly notes that the belief in
the rationality of the universe is intimately connected with open-
mindedness in cognitive functioning:

> Reason presupposes a high degree of mental flexibility which
> enables the individual to compare things, to establish differ-
> ences and identities, and finally to compromise. . . . [Indeed]
> this type of adjustment would hardly have been possible with-
> out the feeling of confidence in the ability of humankind, and
> without a strong feeling of security, both individual and col-
> lective.

Thus, in a kind of philosophical Darwinism, democracy becomes a method of organizing political relationships which is only
desirable or even tolerable for the self-actualizing—for those who
can face (and perhaps enjoy) the prospect of life in a world marked
by flux and relativity, where total reliance must be placed on the
efforts of individual man, working cooperatively. Moreover, to
survive in such a system demands cognitive flexibility for "New
events demand new relations, and consequently readjustment."[26]
Our thesis is that such a political system (and the assumptions on
which it is based) are anathema to persons whose basic needs are
unsatisfied and unsatisfiable. To these individuals, such a system
is not challenging, optimal or even possible: it is a deeply frightening spectre. (In this context, Erik Erikson offers a particularly
insightful statement that ". . . in creative adult men lack of political passion turns out to be antipolitical action" [1942, p. 486].)

Let us carry this analysis a bit further. In the volume collected by Rejai, several other threads run through the discussion of
classical democratic theory. One of these threads could be sub-

---

26. Concurrently, a theme of the present book has been that
when psychically deprived individuals become politically active,
it is often with the aim of forcing social-political change in an effort to create greater stability and security.

sumed under the heading of "toleration"—a concept which is of
particular importance in our pluralist society. As Yinger points
out:

> A heterogeneous society . . . requires tolerance as part of its
> minimum cultural unity, which in turn probably depends upon
> the sharing of several broad goals or core values; for it is
> doubtless true that we are never tolerant of values that seem
> to us to be fundamentally in error. (1964, p. 168)

R. F. M. Durbin, for example, states flatly that "Democracy may
be defined by the toleration of opposition" (Durbin in Rejai, 1967,
pp. 88-94). Durbin goes on to say that "the ultimate cause of stable democratic habits" is the predominance of a certain personality type that "alone makes democracy possible." It is a personality type which operates on the basis of mutual toleration.

Bernard Williams (in Rejai, 1967, pp. 162-70) also is concerned with the relationship between tolerance and democracy. He
first tortuously divides tolerance into "essential" (for the functioning of the democratic system) and "nonessential" (or broadly humanitarian). After discussing that they do not necessarily have to
go together, however, Williams finally is forced to conclude that
"the grounds of belief in liberal democracy are closely bound up
with the grounds of belief in toleration in general."

Thus the belief that tolerance is essential for democracy is
tied into the second thread which runs through democratic theory:
that of the intrinsic value of each human being. A. D. Lindsay
states (in Rejai, 1967, pp. 124-30) that "democracy is based on
the assumption that men can agree on common action which yet
leaves each to live his own life—that if we really respect one another's personality we can find a common framework or system
of rights within which the free moral life of the individual is possible." Thus tolerance and mutual respect are also tied into another great pillar of democracy: natural, inalienable, individual
rights. Ernest Barker concurs in the emphasis placed by Lindsay.
He states:

> The assumption is that in our human world, and under God,
> the individual personality of man alone has intrinsic and ulti-
> mate worth, and having also the capacity of development has
> also an intrinsic and ultimate claim to the essential condi-
> tion of its development. Liberty will then be that essential
> condition; and the essence of liberty will be that it is a con-
> dition, or status, or quality, which individual personality
> must possess in order that it may translate itself from what
> it is to what it has the capacity of becoming. (in Rejai, 1967,
> pp. 131-35)

Barker also emphasizes fraternity or community: "the general
sense of cooperation in a national society which impels its members to create, in the spirit of a family, the common framework

or equipment, both material and mental, which is the necessary condition of the good life of the society and of each and all of its members."

Thus we have gone the full round and returned, in examining the assumptions of classical democracy, to Plato and Aristotle's view of the polity as the place where man is able to develop to his fullest potentialities. Yet, the emphasis here is not on the formal role of the polity in man's development (for example, education), but rather in providing the necessary conditions—the nurture, if you will—so that man can individually become all that he is able to be.

The foregoing assumptions of democratic theory are summarized by John H. Hallowell, who declares:

> The principles of classical realism might be summarized in this way. There exists a meaningful reality whose existence does not depend upon our knowledge of it. . . . The world in which we live is an orderly universe—a cosmos, not a chaos.
>
> A second principle of classical realism is that man is endowed with a faculty which enables him, at least dimly, to grasp the meaning of this reality. . . . Knowledge does not involve the making or constructing of anything, but rather the discovery of what already exists. . . .
>
> A third principle is that being and goodness belong together. Through knowledge of what we are, we obtain knowledge of what we ought to do. To know what man is, is to know what he should be and do. The knowledge of what man should do in order to fulfill his human nature is embodied in what has traditionally been called the "law of nature" or the "moral law." This law . . . provides universally applicable principles in terms of which we can guide our individual and social life toward the perfection of that which is distinctively human. This principle denies that there is any natural opposition between individual good and the common good; the restraints that are necessary for the development of a good man are identical with the restraints that make life in society possible. (in Rejai, 1967, pp. 79-81)

Throughout this section, the discussion has centered on the philosophical assumptions which, implicitly or explicitly, underlie the theory of democracy (using "democracy" in its broadest sense). It is apparent that these assumptions coincide with the world and human nature as seen by the self-actualizer and that they are diametrically opposed to the views held by the psychically deprived. As Lipset has noted, "Acceptance of the norms of democracy requires a high level of sophistication and ego security" (1954, p. 108).

Maslow has discussed at length the fact that for the creative, growth-motivated person, the world is knowable, manageable, "not overwhelmingly dangerous and powerful." Further, to self-

actualizers, human beings in their own right are worthy of toleration and respect. Thus self-actualizers, I am suggesting, will
feel comfortable in and supportive of an open political system
based on the principles discussed above, because such principles
coincide with their personal world view.[27] To individuals who are
psychically deprived, however, life in such a system will heighten
their insecurities.[28] David Riesman, for example, speaks of the
powerless, marginal man as "seldom able to rise above animal
cunning" (1953, p. 245). And such cunning cannot cope with wholly
novel, unanticipated situations. It is again an undifferentiated map,
not individualized, and hence no matter how rebellious the individual may feel himself to be, he is incapable of fruitful nonconform-
ity."[29]

To such individuals, an open political system will be a frightening prospect; to them such a social order will be unstable and
susceptible to dangers of all kinds. For to these individuals, the

27. Throughout this book, I have spoken of personal philosophies (or "operational codes") which form part of need level syndromes in the manner in which Clyde Kluckhohn uses "value orientation"—that is, "a generalized and organized conception, influencing behavior, of nature, of man's place in it, of man's relation
to man, and of the desirable and non-desirable as they relate to
man-environment and interhuman relations." Clyde Kluckhohn,
"Values and Value-Orientations in the Theory of Action," in Tal-
cott Parsons and Edward Shils, eds., Toward a General Theory of
Action (New York: Harper Torchbooks, 1951, p. 395), quoted in
Lane, Political Thinking and Consciousness, p. 20.

28. Symptomatic of this is the political behavior of Goldwater
and his associates. As Hofstadter (1965, p. 101) rightly notes (referring to Goldwater's political bad manners upon losing), "By
complying with the code, but grudgingly and tardily, he expressed
his suspicion that the whole American political system, with its
baffling ambiguities and compromises, is too soft and too equivo-
cal for this carnivorous world" (1965, p. 101). In a similar (paranoid) vein can be seen Richard Nixon's famous tantrum at the "conspiracy" of the press upon his loss of the California gubernatorial
race.

29. Block (1965) discusses this point in terms of "resilien-
cy": "An individual who is unresilient will not be in a state of anxiety if the circumstances in which he functions are for him safe
and predictable. Yet, it may be expected that, inevitably, an adap-
tively inelastic individual will find a wider range of environmental
happenings to be disruptive of his personal economy, and distress-
ing. Accordingly, he will present himself as more anxious, more
maladjusted, less appropriate, less attuned to his world and, not
least, as possessing personal attributes which society agrees are
undesirable."

world is _not_ amenable to individual effort, nor is it predictable, orderly, rational. People are _not_ trustworthy: this is a jungle world in which—at every turning of the path—you may be seriously hurt, or even devoured. Thus tolerance is dangerous because it is not based on realistic assumptions.

Both psychically fulfilled and psychically deprived individuals may be outwardly loyal to their democratic system (be, for example, equally aware of a citizen's duty). (That self-actualizers will tend to be loyal to democracy does _not_ imply an inability to distinguish between the value of the system and the value of a particular government or of particular governmental decisions. Further, unquestioning acceptance is a trait which _certainly_ does not fall within the syndrome of self-actualization.) Yet while both growth- and deficiency-motivated persons may be loyal to democracy, the psychically deprived person is loyal with reservations. He is loyal because his citizenship came with his birth or his immigration in search of bettering the conditions of his life space; to date, he has not suffered under the system. On the other hand, the urban violence, the Communist menace, the indecision in high places, the political assassinations—indeed the whole process of democratic debate—all these things are deeply frightening.

The self-actualizer, however, is loyal to a democratically organized polity because the assumptions upon which it is based coincide with his own personal philosophy. Thus he is able to tolerate freedom of speech because he does not exist in a Manichean world. He is willing to trust his future to majority decisions because of his view of the trustworthy nature of the majority of his fellow humans. He is also, however, capable of seeking change in the manner in which his system operates and the direction in which it is going because he is creative, undogmatic and nonauthoritarian and thus realizes that what is given is not immutable, or always necessary or even right. Finally, his humanistic values are the cause of his loyalty to his government (whereas for the psychically deprived, causality is reversed); thus his political system—as Thomas Jefferson declared to the world—must ever earn its right to exist through its employment of those humanistic values.[30]

In a different connection, Erich Fromm has stated:

---

30. This most _definitely_ does not imply that self-actualizers are—_regardless_ of the social, cultural or political situation—system conforming or socially "adjusted." As Maslow bluntly puts it: "We have learned to ask whether we are going to advocate adjusting to the dope addicts down the block, the Nazis around the corner, or the Negro haters in the next city. To be adjusted to stinkers is to be a stinker yourself. A requisite of Eupsychia [a mentally healthy society] is that adjustment is a neutral concept. To adjust to good would be good; to adjust to bad would be bad." Maslow, "Eupsychia—The Good Society" (unpublished manuscript).

> Psychologically, faith has two entirely different meanings. It can be the expression of an inner relatedness to mankind and affirmation of life; or it can be a reaction formation against a fundamental feeling of doubt, rooted in the isolation of the individual and his negative attitude toward life. (1941, p. 97)

The loyalty and faith of the psychically deprived to an open democratic society are of a different quality and staying power than is the faith of the self-actualizing citizen. The faith of the psychically deprived is tentative because the democratic way of life does not coincide with his personal hierarchy of values and "the angle of vision" through which he sees the world. As George Homans has pointed out: "One is not loyal to a society in which one has been lonely and anxious" (1950, pp. 458-59). Thus the person whose basic psychic requirements have been unmet is, at best, a passive or reserved proponent of democratic beliefs (no matter how he may cling blindly to "the American way of life").

Democratic theory has in mind a particular population—a utopia in which tolerant, secure citizens are active participants in the world around them while, at the same time, manifesting the mutual respect which allows each to make his idiosyncratic contribution. Such a philosophy will provide a workable system of government to the extent to which the citizens of a country are self-actualizing. In the real world, the longevity of a system based on such assumptions will also be dependent upon the procedural restraints which limit the opportunities for persons lacking psychic fulfillment to act out their anxieties and hostilities, as well as the limitation of those forces which create and maintain anxiety.[31]

A Call for Commitment

> In the personal system centering on the self . . . attitudes of hope and of self-respect are at the crux of competence. Are

31. Merelman (1969) comes to similar conclusions in his assessment of democracy: "Democracy demands much with its emphasis on openness, flexibility, gradual reform, progress through secular endeavor, and tolerance for those on the margins of society. Most people do not reach a high-enough level of moral or cognitive development to maintain a long-run commitment to such a system. Either democracy must support itself by assuring material well-being for most of its citizens or it must extract commitment at the cost of developing in its people a sense of nationalism. Both forms of support may eventually come into conflict with the norms of the system itself. We are led to the conclusion that diverse kinds of democratic commitment, resting as they do on different modes of perception and evaluation, provide considerable potential for fission and fragmentation. As Lasswell argued long ago, insufficient cognitive and moral development constitute continuing threats to democracy."

there corresponding features of a person's location in the social system that play an equally strategic role? I think there
are such strategic aspects of location in the social structure:
opportunity, respect, and power. Opportunity corresponds to
hope and provides its warrant. Respect by others—more important in this regard than love or approval—provides the social ground for respect of self. And Power is the kingpin of
the system. Power receives respect and guarantees access
to opportunity. (Smith, 1968, p. 313)

In a timely and useful statement, Christian Bay (1965) has
called for a recognition of the distinction between two types of political activities: one type, which is truly "political," is aimed at
providing the good life according to "some universalistic scheme
of priorities" regarding human needs. The other, much more frequently emphasized type of "pseudopolitical" activity is concerned
solely with private wants within a situation of interest conflict
where the political system acts as a broker. "Yet," Bay states,
"only analysis of data on wants in terms of a theory of needs will
permit us to evaluate wants and aspects of wants with a view to
longer-term consequences of their relative satisfaction or frustration." Bay is also concerned, in this essay, with the lack of
"political responsibility of political scientists."[32] He argues that
the disinterested reporting of the status quo in behavioralist research is based on the "antipolitical" assumption "that politics,
or at any rate American politics, is and must always remain primarily a system of rules for peaceful battles between competing
private interests, and not an arena for the struggle toward a more
humane and more rationally organized society."

In the last section, an attempt was made to indicate the similarity between the democratic theorists' portrayal of the "good
society" (along Aristotelian lines) and assumptions of mental
health. On another level, it has been indicated in chapters 2 and 3
that the behavioralists' concern with the concomitants of a participant pluralistic society is also based upon the dimension of mental health: by dividing individuals into participant versus apathetic,
tolerant versus intolerant, anomic versus socially integrated, researchers are again making psychologically relevant distinctions.

Although there may be some argument over the specific definitions of these phenomena, there is general agreement among the
scientific community that both physical and mental health are universally desirable objectives, the obverse of which can be empirically shown to result in human misery. In this book, mental health
is viewed as the fulfillment of need areas defined as physiological,
safety, affection and esteem. Maslow (1959) has summarized the

---

32. That this concern is becoming widespread is discussed
by Easton (1969).

reasons why these need areas can be regarded as "basic" and their lack of fulfillment can be equated with psychic deprivation:

1. The person yearns for their gratification persistently.
2. Their deprivation makes the person sicken and wither, or stunts his growth.
3. Gratifying them is therapeutic, curing the deficiency-illness.
4. Steady supplies forestall these illnesses.
5. Healthy people do not demonstrate these deficiencies.

Indeed, the personal philosophy of the psychically deprived group can be characterized in the terms used by Maslow to describe the subjects which various studies have found to be high in authoritarianism:

> Their sickness is a character sickness; they have a sick philosophy of life, which is to say a false, incorrect one. It is understandable that they should have formed such a philosophy when we understand their jungle childhood. But their jungle philosophy doesn't change even when they grow up and come out of the jungle. It resists new facts. It is sick because it reacts to an outgrown past, rather than to the real present. (Of course, for those who actually live in a jungle-like world— and there are plenty who do today—a jungle philosophy is realistic and reasonable.) (1957b, p. 130)

The underlying theme of this book has been the necessity of recognizing the importance of psychic competence, not just on the individual level where its value has been proven, but on the political level, where the necessity for its presence has only been implicitly recognized. Eckstein, in his essay entitled A Theory of Stable Democracy (1961), equates systemic stability (and longevity in most cases) with the congruence of the authority pattern of the government to the authority patterns prevalent in the society. It appears here, however, that congruence of authority patterns is only a manifestation (a "presenting symptom," if you will) of a more elemental congruence of values, philosophy and need requirements as the basis of political stability.[33]

---

33. Eckstein also advances that a democratic system will only be stable if its governmental authority pattern "is to a significant extent impure" (that is, contains authoritarian elements as well) and intermediate associations exist as means of lessening the tensions between governmental democracy and the "social relations in which most individuals are engaged most of the time —family life, schools, and jobs"—relations which are necessarily authoritarian. It is certainly unwise to so limit one's definition of an authority pattern that the existence of a central authority figure makes it necessary to characterize families, schools and most economic activities as "authoritarian."

An attempt has been made in this book to indicate that the self-actualizing citizen makes a positive contribution to the social order and harmony of a democratically organized society (that is, to its stability) by his dedication to humanitarian values, his tolerance of viewpoints other than his own and his ability to participate in the educational process as well as his social and political world. On the other hand, the psychically deprived are likely to feel supportive of an authoritarian system which provides the illusion—if not the reality—of stability, order and predictability which more open systems obviate. To be specific: a governmental system is likely to be stable to the extent to which the philosophy upon which it is founded and its activities and decisions (systemic output) are congruent with the personality needs of its citizens.

Thus while the means by which the individual citizen's full psychic growth can be maximized are doubtless debatable[34] (for example, benevolent government aid versus the increased recognition of the responsibility of citizens for their fellow man), the end, however, has long been an implicit value of political science. It is essential now for the implications of the relationship between a democratic polity and personality to be made clear. For example, it has been repeatedly shown that education and democratic values are strongly related. As Lipset (1959) notes, in a variety of studies, conducted in disparate cultures, "the most important single factor differentiating those giving democratic responses from others has been education." It has been suggested in the preceding sections, however, that continuing education and the corresponding training in democratic beliefs are likely to be largely available to those individuals whose basic psychic needs have been fulfilled to a point where they are able to become ego-involved by the educational process. Thus education does not become simply a matter of providing a learning experience; the mental receptivity of the individual to this educational process must be also considered. It is questionable whether greater "endorsement of democratic principles" is due to a "greater acquaintance with the logical implications of the broad democratic principles" (Prothro and Grigg, 1960). It is more plausible that espousal of democratic values is concomitant with the view of reality of such educated individuals.[35]

---

34. Kariel (1967), for example, discusses how employment of a personality theory the end-point of which is self-actualization defined in idiosyncratic, personal terms frustrates attempts to offer political "solutions" to human needs. But one cannot agree with Kariel that "growth-oriented" psychology "provides no theory for discriminating between competing forms of restraint, no scale for weighing the consequences of alternative [political] decisions," for numerous conditions which help satisfy basic needs and thus stimulate human growth are known today.

35. For an excellent analysis of other reasons for the slip-

Lipset (1959) also notes that "men who belong to associations are more likely to hold democratic opinions on questions concerning tolerance and party systems, and are more likely to participate in the political process—to be active or to vote." McClosky sees the significantly different increased support for democratic values which is a characteristic of activists as having "to do with the differences in the political activity, involvement and articulateness. . . ." (in Rejai, 1967, p. 276). These differences, however, are likely to be symptomatic of the psychic fulfillment of these individuals which is the <u>precondition</u> of their participation.

In the literature on democracy, a great deal of emphasis has also recently been placed on the close correlation between the emergence and stability of democratic systems of government and the economic development of a country. In an oft-quoted essay, Lipset has spelled out this relationship in considerable detail. Is it not possible that it is not economic development per se that is responsible for the emergence of participant democracy, but rather the fulfillment of man's most basic needs which is the result of economic development? Industrialization has at least one primary advantage over an agrarian economy: greatly increased regularity of payment to the worker and the release from complete dependence on the physical environment. It is likely that industrialization thus provides the basis for the satisfaction of more and more people's needs for physiological satisfaction and for safety and security; that it, in other words, provides a psychic basis of security through which they may begin an active reaching out for further satisfaction in the world around them. And this basic psychic satisfaction may well be the sine qua non of participant society.

For example, Joel Aronoff has found (in a recent follow-up analysis of the sociocultural institutions in a West Indian community[36] that there was a dramatic inter-generational difference in psychic need satisfaction. This was due to increased health standards, a declining death rate, reduced emigration and more stable primary families. The new, younger workers operated on a higher level of need motivation (in Maslow's hierarchy) than did the previous generation. Concurrently, Aronoff found that the pattern of the work group had changed from that of an authoritarian relationship between the head cane cutter and each man, to that of a participant group in which the incentive, initiative and desires of each

---

page between the explicit function of the schools in this regard and the resultant output in citizen behavior, see Hess (1968). Along these lines, Stinchcombe (1968) reports some very interesting data bearing on the relationship between education and competence —the general thesis of which, however, suffers from a lack of consideration of the relevance of personality development.

36. Aronoff, "Psychological Needs as a Determinant in the Formation of Social Structure," unpublished manuscript.

worker were obviously important factors.

Aronoff thus supports the view that a change in man's motivational level may be at the root of a variety of cultural and political differences. Robert Dahl (in Rejai, 1967, pp. 267-68) for example, points out that the "peaceful opposition among organized, permanent political parties" is an "exotic historical phenomenon" which has only been possible within most recent human history. Could it be that the conditions fostering widespread humanization (that is, psychic fulfillment) and a participant, mutually tolerant society have but recently appeared and that they bear a mutually dependent relationship?

A similar process may underlie the growth of participant society as discussed by Daniel Lerner. Through empirical historical analysis, Lerner (1958) shows that participant society evolves through a regular sequence involving three phases: first urbanization, then literacy and media growth. He illustrates that it is the individual possessing empathy and opinions (and, I suggest, psychic security) who responds to the siren call of participant society. He also shows that as urbanization spreads, additional empathic individuals emerge to take part in the growing participant society. Again it is possible that urbanization and industrialization, by bringing psychic satisfaction and greater security, thus release growing numbers of men from these basic concerns and provide the opportunity for men to seek different and higher psychic satisfactions through social intercourse. Certainly the picture which Lerner presents of the typical traditional figuratively pulling his forelock with shock over the interviewer's assumption that he has opinions—so psychically ingrown is he—has a personality that is of a different quality from the opinionated, alert and outgoing individual who participates with interest in his changing culture.

But fulfillment of basic needs is not only necessary for a person's active membership in a participant society, such fulfillment is particularly necessary for him to feel a positive attachment to a democratic political order, because of the uncertainties that are inherent in a pluralistic democracy. (Indeed, it has previously been advanced that crisis and uncertainty are the essence of politics.) It is in this vein that George Kennan (1954) points to the particular danger which is present in our country because extremist groups have held that our government's role is not to be a moderator of change, but rather that it should provide the security of permanence. The desire for "total security," according to Kennan, holds "particular danger for a democracy, because it creates a curious area between what is held to be possible and what is really possible—an area within which government can always be plausibly shown to have been most dangerously delinquent in the performance of its tasks."

This danger will not be averted, Kennan goes on to state, "until many of our people can be brought to understand that what we have to do is not to secure a total absence of danger but to balance

peril against peril and to find the tolerance degree of each. . . ."
This danger to the stability of our political system, however, is
not primarily a matter of understanding and learning, but rather
of the cognitive and emotional capacity to tolerate insecurity.
This issue indicates in a very clear way that the assumptions of
mental health made by democratic theorists have a great practical relevance. Kennan implicitly realizes this personality dimension in his thoughtful concluding remarks concerning the personal relevance of security:

> The first criterion of a healthy spirit is the ability to walk
> cheerfully and sensibly amid the congenital uncertainties of
> existence, to recognize as natural the inevitable precarious-
> ness of the human condition, to accept this without being dis-
> oriented by it, and to live effectively and usefully in its shad-
> ow. [37]

Given the necessity of a self-actualizing citizenry for the stability of an open society, our concern as political scientists should
be—as Christian Bay has indicated—with the social and political
conditions which encourage and nurture the growth of healthy personalities. Here the emphasis must rest on the vital (but not exclusive) significance of the early years. [38] As Erik Erikson notes

> if we want to make the world safe for democracy, we must
> first make democracy safe for the healthy child. . . . We have
> learned not to stunt a child's growing body with child labor;
> we must now learn not to break his growing spirit by making
> him the victim of our anxieties.

> If we will only learn to let live, the plan for growth is all
> there. (1959, p. 100)

Bloom, in his examination of the stable characteristics of personality, gives three reasons for the "crucial importance" of the
early environment. The first reason has to do with the "very rapid
growth of selected characteristics during these years." The second "has to do with the sequential nature of much of human development. Each characteristic is built on a base of that same characteristic at an earlier time or on the base of each characteristics which precede it in development." In other words, unfulfilled

---

37. The effect of this concern for security by extremist
groups on the functioning of our government is a specific example
of Aronoff's hypothesis that "the deprivation of a basic need will
cause the individual to organize or utilize an institution in such a
way as to achieve some measure of gratification for that deprived
need" (1967).

38. One need only to read such a book as Bettelheim's Love
Is Not Enough (1950) to realize how very difficult it is to change
character once its development has been severely thwarted.

needs tend to be cumulative in effect, and life experiences are selectively perceived so that their effect is reinforcing to the personal philosophy formed earlier. Third, Bloom relates the importance of the early years to learning theory: it is much easier to
learn something new than it is to stamp out one set of learned behaviors and replace them by a new set" (1964, pp. 215-16).

To this, Maslow adds an additional reason for social concern
with the provision of a positive environment in which the development of mental health is a concomitant:

> These impulses and directional tendencies toward self-fulfill-
> ment, though instinctive, are very weak, so that, in contrast
> with all other animals who have strong instincts, these im-
> pulses are very easily drowned out by habit, by wrong cultural
> attitudes toward them, by traumatic episodes, by erroneous
> education. Therefore, the problem of choice and of responsi-
> bility is far, far more acute in humans than in any other spe-
> cies. (1962b, pp. 154-55)

(None of this, however, is meant to deny the efficacy of competent
social and psychiatric intervention in human lives.)

In addition to a healthy milieu, however, it is also necessary
(as noted previously) to inculcate democratic values and here
again, our political system has a positive role to play. Yet of the
two factors—the encouragement of a humanizing environment and
the inculcation of democratic values—the former is undoubtedly of
primary importance. Throughout human lives, growth-stimulating
values need to be present in order to assure political health in an
open society as well as health on a personal, psychic level. This is
a political truth which Harold Lasswell, more than anyone else, has
worked to establish (and is thus rightly called by Arnold Rogow a
"radical social thinker"). As Lasswell has emphasized in his writings, shared power and wealth are not alone a sufficient egalitarian
base for the maintenance of an open society. Other major values
must be likewise shared; there must be a "democratization" of such
values as insight and respect.[39]

For it otherwise appears that deprived individuals become psychically isolated in an open society and are largely unable to participate in its dominant values and activities once they have passed
the formative years. Indeed, it is likely that life in our open society
adds to their anxieties and to their desire for insulation, if not to
their social and political alienation. Thus the role which our polity
must play, in the interests of its self-preservation, is to discour-

---

39. See the summary of this line of Lasswell's writing in
Rogow (1969). As Kelman (1970) notes: ". . . democratic communal decision-making and participation are not merely a means to
the end of a good society but also a part of the good society itself.
Men feel better and fuller as human beings through participating
with their fellows in deciding things for the group."

age the process by which individuals <u>become</u> and tend to <u>remain</u> inhabitants of this debilitating psychic ghetto. Here again Maslow has clearly stated the alternatives:

> Whether character education can take place in the classroom, whether books, lectures, catechisms, and exhortations are the best tools to use, whether sermons and Sunday schools can produce good human beings, or rather whether the good life produces the good man, whether love, warmth, friendship, respect, and good treatment of the child are more consequential for his later character structure—these are the alternatives presented by adherence to one or the other theory of character formation. (1954, pp. 114-15)

There has been a growing awareness that various sectors in our society breed psychic deprivation and that remedial measures must be adopted which will help to create a more healthy social foundation for psychic growth. Undoubtedly, fundamental social and economic measures can effect a general increase in the potentialities for psychic fulfillment, and should be directed to this end. As in every society, however, psychically deprived persons will still remain of potential or actual political importance, because the quality of child care and emotional security in the primary family varies greatly and has numerous idiosyncratic determinants. Democratic society will thus always have to operate with potential extremists, assassins and bigots in its midst. Hence, while personality theory suggests the means by which a more stable foundation for our polity may be encouraged, it also suggests the concurrent necessity for two types of preventive measures.

In the first place, it is apparent that the tolerance of anxiety is directly and strongly related to mental health and will vary greatly within any given population. Today, as never before, the ambiguities and uncertainties of politics become personally obvious to every person who is a member of a participant society. With terrifying immediacy, television particularly makes otherwise distant events of urgent personal concern. Reporting of current events will always necessitate the discussion of ambiguities which must be tolerated, hostilities that cannot be averted and crises which are not settled. Voices of concern have been raised from various directions about the lack of self-constraint on the part of the mass media. In this area an open society should insist, in the interest of its own stability, on a measure of restraint and responsibility not in evidence today.[40] A corollary of this is the manner in which the political system makes use of information

---

40. The concern for media responsibility is a problem of long-standing. After Theodore Roosevelt had been superficially shot in the chest (during the Bull Moose campaign of 1912), he commented: "It is a very natural thing that weak and vicious minds should be inflamed to acts of violence by the kind of foul mendacity

and dispenses it. At a basic level, the only control for the ever-
present strain of irrationality in any given population "is, in fact,
a leadership which is competent in the use of political communication and yet also enlightened enough to avoid—for its own good—
the glib exploitation of non-rational thinking" (Erikson, 1964, p.
214).

A second area for application of preventive measures lies in
the opportunities provided by a weakened social and political structure for psychically deprived individuals to act out their hostilities
and authoritarian predispositions, and to encourage undemocratic
tendencies in self-actualizing persons. One of the prime functions
of a political system is the provision of order and today—as never
before—it is sadly apparent how the lack of order in our society
provides the opportunity for the activation of undemocratic predispositions and political polarization (which disallow the discussion
of opposing ideas to be carried out in any meaningful way). Lack
of order and stability foster behavior and attitudes which are the
antithesis of democracy. The contribution of the political system
to the climate of violence today is indeed worthy of thoughtful study.
A variety of politically sponsored and regulated relationships (in
addition to that of media regulation) need reassessing: the relationship of the policeman to his community, of the educational system
both to students and to the basic goals of the society it serves, of
political parties as means for the distillation and implementation
of sentiment, of the individual and the sociopolitical order of which
he is a part—but from which he must remain forever separate and
distinct.

At many sensitive points within our political system, the impact of personality predispositions can be seen to operate in measurable ways. Through studies which have been done in the field of
psychology, we should become more cognizant of the vital difference which different personality types can make, located at different places within the social structure and political system and operating under different conditions. Most important, our goal should
be not only to understand political behavior as it is, but what—under more favorable psychic conditions—it might become. Our concern should be the encouragement of the preconditions for psychic
growth as the basis for a more stable and creative open society.

---

and abuse that have been heaped upon me in the last three months
in the interest not only of Mr. Debs, but of Mr. Wilson and Mr.
Taft. . . . I wish to say seriously to the speakers and the newspapers representing both the Republican and Democratic and Socialist parties that they cannot, month in and month out, make the kind
of slanderous, bitter and malevolent assaults that they have made
and not expect that brutal and violent characters, especially when
the brutality is accompanied by a not-too-strong mind—they cannot expect that such natures will be unaffected by it."

Bibliography

Abcarian, G. and S. M. Stanage. 1965. "Alienation and the Radical Right," The Journal of Politics, 27 (November), 776-96.

Aberbach, J. D. 1969. "Alienation and Political Behavior," The American Political Science Review, LXIII, 1 (March), 86-99.

Adelson, J. 1953. "A Study of Minority Group Authoritarianism," The Journal of Abnormal and Social Psychology, 48, 4, 477-85.

Adelson, J. and R. P. O'Neil. 1966. "Growth of Political Ideas in Adolescence: The Sense of Community," Journal of Personality and Social Psychology, 4, 3, 295-306.

Adorno, T. W., E. Frenkel-Brunswik, D. J. Levinson and R. N. Sanford. 1950. The Authoritarian Personality. New York: John Wiley & Sons.

Agger, R. E., M. N. Goldstein and S. A. Pearl. 1961. "Political Cynicism: Measurement and Meaning," The Journal of Politics, 23, 3 (August), 477-506.

Alexander, F. 1959. "Emotional Factors in Voting Behavior," in Eugene Burdick and Arthur J. Brodbeck (eds.), American Voting Behavior. Glencoe: The Free Press.

Alker, H. A. 1969. "A Quasi-paranoid Feature of Extreme Attitudes Against Colonialism," paper presented to the 19th International Congress of Psychology.

Allport, G. W. 1929-1930. "The Composition of Political Attitudes," The American Journal of Sociology, XXXV, 220-38.

_____. 1954. The Nature of Prejudice. Garden City: Doubleday & Company.

Allport, G. W., J. S. Bruner and E. M. Jandorf. 1941-1942. "Personality Under Social Catastrophe: Ninety Life Histories of the Nazi Revolution," Character and Personality, X, 1-27.

Almond, G. A. and J. S. Coleman (eds.). 1960. The Politics of the Developing Areas. Princeton: Princeton University Press.

Almond, G. A. and S. Verba. 1965. The Civic Culture. Boston: Little, Brown and Company.

Anderson, B., M. Zelditch, Jr., P. Takagi and D. Whiteside. 1965. "On Conservative Attitudes," Acta Sociologica, 8, 189-204.

Anderson, J. and R. W. May. 1952. McCarthy, The Man, the Senator, the "Ism." Boston: The Beacon Press.

Anonymous. 1964. A Dictionary of the Social Sciences. Ed. by J. Gould and W. L. Kolb. Glencoe, Ill.: The Free Press.

Arendt, H. 1951. The Origins of Totalitarianism. New York: Harcourt, Brace and Company.

Aronoff, J. 1967. Psychological Needs and Cultural Systems. Princeton: D. Van Nostrand Company.

____. Psychological Needs as a Determinant in the Formation of Social Structure. Unpublished manuscript.

The Autobiography of Malcolm X. 1964. New York: Grove Press.

Barber, J. D. 1965. The Lawmakers. New Haven: Yale University Press.

____. 1968a. "Adult Identity and Presidential Style: The Rhetorical Emphasis," Daedalus, 97, 3 (Summer), 938-68.

____. 1968b. "Classifying and Predicting Presidential Styles: Two 'Weak' Presidents," Journal of Social Issues, XXIV, 3 (July), 51-80.

Barker, E. N. 1963. "Authoritarianism of the Political Right, Center, and Left," The Journal of Social Issues, XIX, 2 (April), 63-74.

Bass, B. M. 1955. "Authoritarianism or Acquiescence?" The Journal of Abnormal and Social Psychology, 51, 3 (November), 616-23.

____. 1956. "Development and Evaluation of a Scale for Measuring Social Acquiescence," The Journal of Abnormal and Social Psychology, 53, 3 (November), 296-99.

Bay, C. 1965a. "Politics and Pseudopolitics: A Critical Evaluation of Some Behavioral Literature," The American Political Science Review, LIX, 1 (March), 39-51.

___. 1965b. The Structure of Freedom. New York: Atheneum.

___. 1968. "Needs, Wants, and Political Legitimacy," Canadian Journal of Political Science, I, 3 (September), 241-60.

Beiser, M. 1965. "Poverty, Social Disintegration and Personality," Journal of Social Issues, 2, 56-78.

Bell, D. 1947-1948. "The Study of Man," Commentary, V, 368-75.

Bell, W. 1957. "Anomie, Social Isolation and the Class Structure, Sociometry, 20, 2 (June), 105-16.

Bender, G. J. 1967. "Political Socialization and Political Change," The Western Political Quarterly, XX, 2, Part I (June), 390-407.

Bender, I. E. 1953. "The Development of a Scale for Attitudinal Motives," The Journal of Abnormal and Social Psychology, 48, 4 (October), 486-94.

Bendig, A. W. 1958. "Identification of Item Factor Patterns Within the Manifest Anxiety Scale," Journal of Consulting Psychology, 22, 2 (April), 158.

Bendix, R. 1952. "Compliant Behavior and Individual Personality," The American Journal of Sociology, LVIII, 3 (November), 292-303.

Bennis, W. G. and P. E. Slater. 1968. The Temporary Society. New York: Harper & Row.

Bensman, J. and B. Rosenberg. 1960. "The Meaning of Work in Bureaucratic Society," in M. R. Stein, A. J. Vidich and D. M. White (eds.), Identity and Anxiety, pp. 181-97. New York: The Free Press.

Bentler, P. M., D. N. Jackson and S. Messick. 1965. "The Identification of Content and Style: A Multidimensional Interpretation of Acquiescence," unpublished paper, Educational Testing Service.

Berelson, B. R., P. F. Lazarsfeld and W. N. McPhee. 1954. Voting. Chicago: The University of Chicago Press.

Berelson, B. R. and G. A. Steiner. 1964. Human Behavior: An Inventory of Scientific Findings. New York: Harcourt, Brace & World.

286   Bibliography

Berg, I. A. 1955. "Response Bias and Personality: The Deviation
    Hypothesis," The Journal of Psychology, 40 (July), 61-72.

Berger, E. M. 1952. "The Relation between Expressed Accep-
    tance of Self and Expressed Acceptance of Others," The Jour-
    nal of Abnormal and Social Psychology, 47, 4 (October), 778-82.

Berkowitz, N. H. and G. H. Wolkon. 1964. "A Forced Choice
    Form of the F Scale—Free of Acquiescent Response Set,"
    Sociometry, 27, 54-65.

Bettelheim, B. 1943. "Individual and Mass Behavior in Extreme
    Situations," The Journal of Abnormal and Social Psychology,
    38, 4 (October), 417-52.

____. 1947. "The Dynamism of Anti-Semitism in Gentile and Jew,"
    The Journal of Abnormal and Social Psychology, 42, 2 (April),
    153-68.

____. 1950. Love Is Not Enough. New York: Collier Books.

____. 1952. "Remarks on the Psychological Appeal of Totalitarian-
    ism," The American Journal of Economics and Sociology, 12,
    1 (October), 89-96.

____. 1955. Truants from Life. New York: The Free Press.

____. 1960. The Informed Heart. Glencoe, Ill.: The Free Press.

____. 1962. Dialogues with Mothers. New York: The Free Press.

Bettelheim, B. and M. Janowitz. 1964. Social Change and Preju-
    dice [including Dynamics of Prejudice]. New York: The Free
    Press.

Block, J. 1950. "An Experimental Investigation of the Construct
    of Ego-Control." Unpublished Ph.D. dissertation, Stanford
    University.

____. 1965. The Challenge of Response Sets. New York: Appleton-
    Century-Crofts.

Block, J. and J. Block. 1951. "An Investigation of the Relation-
    ship between Intolerance of Ambiguity and Ethnocentrism,"
    Journal of Personality, 19, 3 (March), 303-11.

Block, J. H. 1951. "An Experimental Study of a Topological Rep-
    resentation of Ego-Structure." Unpublished Ph.D. dissertation,
    Stanford University.

Bloom, B. S. 1964. Stability and Change in Human Characteristics. New York: John Wiley & Sons.

Boehner, S. 1965. "Defining Intolerance of Ambiguity," The Psychological Record, 15, 393-400.

Bordue, D. J. 1961. "Authoritarianism and Intolerance of Nonconformists," Sociometry, 24, 198-216.

Borel, J. C. 1964. "Security as a Motivation of Human Behavior," Archives of General Psychiatry, 10, 2 (February), 105-8.

Boulding, K. 1967. "The Learning and Reality-Testing Process in the International System," Journal of International Affairs, XXI, 1-15.

Breland, K. and M. Breland. 1961. "The Misbehavior of Organisms," The American Psychologist, 16, 681-84.

Brim, O. G. and D. B. Hoff. 1957. "Individual and Situational Differences in Desire for Certainty," The Journal of Abnormal and Social Psychology, 54, 2 (March), 225-29.

Brodie, B. 1957. "A Psychoanalytic Interpretation of Woodrow Wilson," World Politics, IX, 3 (April), 413-22.

Brodie, F. M. 1966. Thaddeus Stevens. New York: W. W. Norton & Company.

Browning, R. P. 1968. "The Interaction of Personality and Political System in Decisions to Run for Office: Some Data and a Simulation Technique," Journal of Social Issues, XXIV, 3 (July), 93-109.

Browning, R. and H. Jacob. 1964. "Power Motivation and the Political Personality," The Public Opinion Quarterly, XXVIII, 1 (Spring), 75-90.

Budner, S. 1962. "Intolerance of Ambiguity as a Personality Variable," Journal of Personality, XXX, 1 (March), 29-50.

Bunzel, J. H. 1967. Anti-Politics in America. New York: Alfred A. Knopf.

Burns, J. M. 1956. Roosevelt: The Lion and The Fox. New York: Harcourt, Brace & World.

Butler, D. 1958. The Study of Political Behavior. London: Hutchinson University Library.

Campbell, A. 1962. "The Passive Citizen," Acta Sociologica, 6, 9-21.

___. 1964. "Who are the non-Voters?" New Society, 68 (January 16), 11-12.

Campbell, A., P. E. Converse, W. E. Miller and D. E. Stokes. 1960. The American Voter. New York: John Wiley & Sons.

Campbell, A., G. Gurin and W. E. Miller. 1954. The Voter Decides. Evanston, Ill.: Row, Peterson and Company.

Campbell, D. T. and B. R. McCandless. 1951. "Ethnocentrism, Xenophobia and Personality," Human Relations, IV, 185-92.

Canning, R. R. and J. M. Baker. 1959. "Effect of the Group on Authoritarian and non-Authoritarian Persons," The American Journal of Sociology, LXIV, 6 (May), 579-81.

Cantril, H. 1940. The Invasion from Mars. New York: Harper & Row.

___. 1961. Human Nature and Political Systems. New Brunswick: Rutgers University Press.

___. 1963. The Psychology of Social Movements. New York: John Wiley & Sons.

Carlson, H. B. and W. Harrell, 1942. "An Analysis of Life's 'Ablest Congressmen' Poll," The Journal of Social Psychology, 15, 153-58.

Carstensen, R. N. 1963. Job: Defense of Honor. New York: Abingdon Press.

Cervantes, L. F. 1965. The Dropout, Causes and Cures. Ann Arbor: The University of Michigan Press.

Chapman, L. J. and D. T. Campbell. 1957. "Response Set in the F Scale," The Journal of Abnormal and Social Psychology, 54, 1 (January), 129-32.

Christie, R. 1955. "A Book Review: The Psychology of Politics," The American Journal of Psychology, LXVIII, 4 (December), 702-4.

___. 1956a. "Eysenck's Treatment of the Personality of Communists," Psychological Bulletin, 53, 6 (November), 411-30.

____. 1956b. "Some Abuses of Psychology," Psychological Bulletin, 53, 6 (November), 439-51.

Christie, R. and J. Garcia. 1951. "Subcultural Variation in Authoritarian Personality," The Journal of Abnormal and Social Psychology, 46, 4 (October), 457-69.

Christie, R., J. Havel and B. Seidenberg. 1958. "Is the F Scale Irreversible?" The Journal of Abnormal and Social Psychology, 56, 2 (March), 143-59.

Christie, R. and M. Jahoda (eds.). 1954. Studies in the Scope and Method of "The Authoritarian Personality." Glencoe, Ill.: The Free Press.

Christie, R. and R. K. Merton. 1958. "Procedures for the Sociological Study of the Values Climate of Medical Schools," The Journal of Medical Education, 33, 10, Part 2 (October), 125-53.

Clark, J. P. 1959. "Measuring Alienation within a Social System," American Sociological Review, 24, 6 (December), 849-52.

Clark, J. V. 1961. "Motivation in Work Groups: A Tentative View," in Paul Lawrence et al. (eds.), Organizational Behavior and Administration, pp. 229-46. Homewood: The Dorsey Press.

Clark, L. P. 1933. Lincoln, A Psycho-Biography. New York: Charles Scribner's Sons.

Clinard, M. B. (ed.) 1964. Anomie and Deviant Behavior. New York: The Free Press.

Coffman, T. L. 1967. "Personality Structure, Involvement, and the Consequences of Taking a Stand." Unpublished Ph.D. dissertation, Princeton University.

Cohen, J. 1960. "Individuality of Thought," in M. R. Stein, A. J. Vidich and D. M. White (eds.), Identity and Anxiety, pp. 540-51. New York: The Free Press.

Cohn, N. 1966. Warrant for Genocide. New York: Harper & Row.

Coles, R. 1970. Erik H. Erikson: The Growth of His Work. Boston: Little, Brown and Company.

Connelly, G. M. and H. H. Field. 1944. "The Non-Voter—Who He Is, What He Thinks," The Public Opinion Quarterly, 8, 2 (Summer), 175-87.

Cook, T. I. 1949. "Democratic Psychology and a Democratic World Order," World Politics, I, 4 (July), 553-64.

Coopersmith, S. 1967. The Antecedents of Self-Esteem. San Francisco: W. H. Freeman and Company.

Couch, A. and K. Keniston. 1960. "Yeasayers and Naysayers Agreeing Response Set as a Personality Variable," Journal of Abnormal and Social Psychology, 60, 2, 151-74.

Cronbach, L. J. 1946. "Response Sets and Test Validity," Educational and Psychological Measurement, 6, 4 (Winter), 475-94.

Crutchfield, R. S. 1955. "Conformity and Character," The American Psychologist, 10, 191-98.

Dahl, R. A. 1969. "The Behavioral Approach in Political Science: Epitaph for a Monument to a Successful Protest," in H. Eulau (ed.), Behavioralism in Political Science, 68-92. New York: Atherton Press.

Dallmayr, F. R. 1968. "Empirical Political Theory and Personal Identity," paper delivered to the 1968 American Political Science Association Convention.

Davids, A. 1955a. "Alienation, Social Apperception, and Ego Structure," The Journal of Consulting Psychology, 19, 1 (February), 21-27.

____. 1955b. "Generality and Consistency of Relations between the Alienation Syndrome and Cognitive Processes," The Journal of Abnormal and Social Psychology, 51, 1 (July), 61-67.

____. 1955c. "Some Personality and Intellectual Correlates of Intolerance of Ambiguity," The Journal of Abnormal and Social Psychology, 51, 3 (November), 415-20.

____. 1963. "Psychodynamic and Sociocultural Factors Related to Intolerance of Ambiguity," in Robert W. White (ed.), The Study of Lives, 160-77. New York: Atherton Press.

Davids, A. and C. W. Eriksen. 1957. "Some Social and Cultural Factors Determining Relations between Authoritarianism and Measures of Neuroticism," Journal of Consulting Psychology, 21, 2 (April), 155-59.

Davies, A. F. 1966. Private Politics. London: Melbourne University Press.

Davies, J. C. 1954. "Charisma in the 1952 Campaign," The American Political Science Review, XLVIII, 4 (December), 1083-1102.

___. 1959. "A Note on Political Motivation," The Western Political Quarterly, XII, 2 (June), 410-16.

___. 1963. Human Nature in Politics. New York: John Wiley and Sons.

___. 1965. "The Family's Role in Political Socialization," The Annals of The American Academy of Political and Social Science, 361 (September), 10-19.

Davis, A. 1948. Social-Class Influences upon Learning. Cambridge: Harvard University Press.

Davis, K. 1940. "Extreme Social Isolation of a Child," The American Journal of Sociology, XLV, 4 (January), 554-65.

Dawson, R. E. and K. Prewitt. 1969. Political Socialization. Boston: Little, Brown and Company.

Dean, D. G. 1960. "Alienation and Political Apathy," Social Forces, 38, 3 (March), 185-89.

___. 1961. "Alienation: Its Meaning and Measurement," American Sociological Review, 26, 5 (October), 753-58.

___. 1965. "Powerlessness and Political Apathy," Social Science, 40, 1 (January), 208-13.

De Charms, R. 1968. Personal Causation. New York: Academic Press.

De Grazia, S. 1948. The Political Community, A Study of Anomie. Chicago: The University of Chicago Press.

Diab, L. N. 1965. "Some Limitations of Existing Scales in the Measurement of Social Attitudes," Psychological Reports, 17, 2 (October), 427-30.

Dicks, H. V. 1950. "Personality Traits and National Socialist Ideology," Human Relations, III, 2, 111-54.

___. 1952. "Observations on Contemporary Russian Behavior," Human Relations, V, 2, 111-75.

Dickson, W. J. and F. J. Roethlisberger. 1966. Counseling in an Organization: A Sequel to the Hawthorne Researches. Boston: Harvard University.

Di Palma, G. and H. McClosky. 1970. "Personality and Conformity: The Learning of Political Attitudes," The American Political Science Review, LXIV, 4 (December), 1054-73.

Dixon, J. J., C. De Monchaux and J. Sandler. 1957. "Patterns of Anxiety: An Analysis of Social Anxieties," The British Journal of Medical Psychology, XXX, Part 2, 107-12.

Dobzhansky, T. 1959. "Human Nature as a Product of Evolution," in Abraham H. Maslow (ed.), New Knowledge in Human Values, 75-85. New York: Harper & Row.

Dohrenwend, B. P. 1966. "Social Status and Psychological Disorder: An Issue of Substance and an Issue of Method," American Sociological Review, 31, 1 (February), 14-34.

Douvan, E. and A. M. Walker. 1956. "The Sense of Effectiveness in Public Affairs," Psychological Monographs, v. 70, no. 22, 1-19.

Downs, A. 1957. An Economic Theory of Democracy. New York: Harper & Row.

Dulles, A. W. 1966. "A Foreign-Affairs Scholar Views the Real Woodrow Wilson," Look Magazine, 30, 25 (December 13), 50.

Dyson, J. W. and D. St. Angelo. 1968. "Personality, Perception, and Ideology: Leaders and Citizens," unpublished paper delivered to the 1968 APSA Convention.

Easton, D. 1964. The Political System. New York: Alfred A. Knopf.

___. 1969. "The New Revolution in Political Science," The American Political Science Review, LXIII, 4 (December), 1051-61.

Easton, D. and J. Dennis. 1967. "The Child's Acquisition of Regime Norms: Political Efficacy," American Political Science Review, LXI, 1 (March), 25-38.

Easton, D. and R. D. Hess. 1962. "The Child's Political World," Midwest Journal of Political Science, VI, 3 (August), 229-46.

Eckstein, H. 1961. A Theory of Stable Democracy. Princeton
University: Center of International Studies.

___. 1963. "A Perspective on Comparative Politics, Past and
Present," in H. Eckstein and D. E. Apter (eds), Comparative
Politics, A Reader, 3-32. New York: The Free Press.

Edinger, L. J. 1964a. "Political Science and Political Biography:
Reflections on the Study of Leadership (I)," The Journal of
Politics, 26, 2 (May), 423-39.

___. 1964b. "Political Science and Political Biography (II)," The
Journal of Politics, 26, 3 (August), 648-76.

___. 1965. Kurt Schumacher. Stanford: Stanford University
Press.

Erbe. W. 1964. "Social Involvement and Political Activity: A Replication and Elaboration," American Sociological Review, 29,
2 (April), 198-215.

Eriksen, C. W. 1951. "Perceptual Defense as a Function of Unacceptable Needs," The Journal of Abnormal and Social Psychology, 46, 4 (October), 557-64.

Erikson, E. H. 1942. "Hitler's Imagery and German Youth," Psychiatry, I, 475-93.

___. 1954. "Wholeness and Totality—A Psychiatric Contribution,"
in C. J. Friedrich (ed.), Totalitarianism, 156-71. Cambridge:
Harvard University Press.

___. 1956. "The Problem of Ego Identity," Journal of the Ameri-
can Psychoanalytic Association, IV, 1 (January), 56-121.

___. 1958. Young Man Luther. New York: W. W. Norton & Com-
pany.

___. 1959. "Identity and the Life Cycle," Psychological Issues, I,
1, Monograph 1.

___. 1963. Childhood and Society (rev. ed.) New York: W. W.
Norton & Company.

___. 1964. Insight and Responsibility. New York: W. W. Norton
& Company.

___. 1968a. Identity: Youth and Crisis. New York: W. W. Norton
& Company.

___. 1968b. "On the Nature of Psycho-Historical Evidence: In Search of Gandhi," Daedalus, 97, 3 (Summer), 695-730.

___. 1969. Gandhi's Truth. New York: W. W. Norton & Company.

Eulau, H. 1956. "The Politics of Happiness: A Prefatory Note to 'Political Perspectives—1956,'" The Antioch Review, XVI, 3 (September), 259-64.

___. 1963. The Behavioral Persuasion in Politics. New York, Random House.

Eulau, H. and P. Schneider. 1956. "Dimensions of Political Involvement," The Public Opinion Quarterly, XX, 1 (Spring), 128-42.

Eysenck, H. J. 1954. The Psychology of Politics. London: Routledge & Kegan Paul, Ltd.

___. 1956a. "The Psychology of Politics: A Reply," Psychological Bulletin, 53, 2 (March), 177-82.

___. 1956b. "The Psychology of Politics and the Personality Similarities between Fascists and Communists," Psychological Bulletin, 53, 6 (November), 431-38.

Farber, M. L. 1955. "The Anal Character and Political Aggression," The Journal of Abnormal and Social Psychology, 51, 3 (November), 486-89.

___. 1960. "Toward a Psychology of Political Behavior," The Public Opinion Quarterly, XXIV, 458-64.

Farris, C. D. 1956. "'Authoritarianism' as a Political Behavior Variable," The Journal of Politics, 18, 1 (February), 61-82.

Feldman, M. J. and S. M. Siegel. 1958. "The Effect on Self Description of Combining Anxiety and Hostility Items on a Single Scale," Journal of Clinical Psychology, XIV, 1 (January), 74-77.

Feuer, L. 1962. "What Is Alienation?; The Career of a Concept," New Politics, 1, 3 (Spring), 116-34.

Fey, W. F. 1955. "Acceptance by Others and Its Relation to Acceptance of Self and Others: A Revaluation," The Journal of Abnormal and Social Psychology, 50, 2 (March), 274-76.

Fillenbaum, S. and A. Jackman. 1961. "Dogmatism and Anxiety in Relation to Problem Solving: An Extension of Rokeach's Results," The Journal of Abnormal and Social Psychology, 63, 1, 212-14.

Finifter, A. W. 1970. "Dimensions of Political Alienation," The American Political Science Review, LXIV, 2 (June), 389-410.

Finlay, D. J., O. R. Holsti and R. R. Fagen. 1967. Enemies in Politics. Chicago: Rand McNally & Company.

Flavell, J. H. 1963. The Developmental Psychology of Jean Piaget. Princeton: D. Van Nostrand.

Foote, N. N. 1951. "Identification as the Basis for a Theory of Motivation," American Sociological Review, 16, 1 (February), 14-22.

Foulkes, D. and S. H. Foulkes. 1965. "Self-Concept, Dogmatism, and Tolerance of Trait Inconsistency," Journal of Personality and Social Psychology, 2, 1, 104-10.

Frady, M. 1968. Wallace. New York: The World Publishing Company.

Frenkel-Brunswik, E. 1942. "Motivation and Behavior," Genetic Psychology Monographs, 26, 121-65.

____. 1948. "A Study of Prejudice in Children," Human Relations, I, 3, 295-306.

____. 1949-1950. "Intolerance of Ambiguity as an Emotional and Perceptual Personality Variable," Journal of Personality, XVIII, 108-43.

____. 1952. "Interaction of Psychological and Sociological Factors in Political Behavior," The American Political Science Review, XLVI, 44-65.

____. 1954a. "Environmental Controls and the Impoverishment of Thought," in Carl J. Friedrich (ed.), Totalitarianism, 171-202. Cambridge: Harvard University Press.

____. 1954b. "Social Tensions and the Inhibition of Thought," Social Problems, 2, 2 (October), 75-81.

Freud, S. and W. C. Bullitt. 1967. Thomas Woodrow Wilson: A Psychological Study. Boston: Houghton Mifflin Company.

296   Bibliography

Froman, L. A., Jr. 1961. "Personality and Political Socializa-
    tion," The Journal of Politics, 23, 2 (May), 341-52.

Fromm, E. 1941. Escape from Freedom. New York: Avon Books.

___. 1947. Man for Himself. Greenwich: Fawcett Publications.

___. 1955. The Sane Society. Greenwich: Fawcett Publications.

Fromm-Reichmann, F. 1960. "Psychiatric Aspects of Anxiety,"
    in M. R. Stein, A. J. Vidich and D. M. White (eds.), Identity
    and Anxiety, 129-44. New York: The Free Press.

George, A. L. 1967. The "Operational Code," a Neglected Ap-
    proach to the Study of Political Leaders and Decision Making.
    The Rand Corporation, Memorandum RM-5427-PR (Septem-
    ber).

___. 1968a. "Political Leadership and Social Change in Ameri-
    can Cities," Daedalus, 97, 4 (Fall), 1194-1217.

___. 1968b. "Power As a Compensatory Value for Political Lead-
    ers," Journal of Social Issues, XXIV, 3, 29-49.

George, A. L. and J. L. George. 1956. Woodrow Wilson and Col-
    onel House: A. Personality Study. New York: Dover Publica-
    tions, Inc.

Gerth, H. 1940. "The Nazi Party: Its Leadership and Composi-
    tion," The American Journal of Sociology, XLV, 4 (January),
    517-41.

Gibb, C. A. 1955. "The Principles and Traits of Leadership;" in
    A. P. Hare, E. F. Borgatta and R. F. Bales (eds.), Small
    Groups, 87-95. New York: Alfred A. Knopf.

Gilbert, G. M. 1950. The Psychology of Dictatorship. New York:
    Ronald Press Company.

___. 1955. "Dictators and Demogogues," The Journal of Social
    Issues, XI, 3, 51-53.

Glad, Betty. 1966. Charles Evans Hughes and the Illusions of In-
    nocence. Urbana: University of Illinois Press.

___. 1968. "The Role of Psychoanalytic Biography in Political
    Science," paper delivered to the 1968 meeting of the Ameri-
    can Political Science Association.

Gladstone, A. I. 1955. "The Possibility of Predicting Reactions to International Events," The Journal of Social Issues, XI, 1, 21-28.

Gladstone, A. I. and M. A. Taylor. 1958. "Threat-related Attitudes and Reactions to Communications about International Events," The Journal of Conflict Resolution, II, 1 (March), 17-28.

Glazer, N. and S. M. Lipset. 1955. "The Polls on Communism and Conformity," in Daniel Bell (ed.), The New American Right, 141-65. New York: Criterion Books.

Goldfried, M. R. 1963. "Feelings of Inferiority and the Depreciation of Others: a Research Review and Theoretical Reformulation," Journal of Individual Psychology, 19, 1 (May), 27-48.

Goldhamer, H. 1942. "Some Factors Affecting Participation in Voluntary Associations." Unpublished Ph.D. dissertation, University of Chicago.

____. 1950. "Public Opinion and Personality," The American Journal of Sociology, LV, 4 (January), 346-54.

Goodstein, L. D. 1953. "Intellectual Rigidity and Social Attitudes, The Journal of Abnormal and Social Psychology, 48, 3 (July), 345-53.

Gottfried, A. 1955. "The Use of Psychosomatic Categories in a Study of Political Personality," The Western Political Quarterly, VIII, 2 (June), 234-47.

____. 1962. Boss Cermak of Chicago. Seattle: University of Washington Press.

Gough, H. G. 1948. "A Note on the Security-Insecurity Test," The Journal of Social Psychology, 28, 257-61.

____. 1951a. "Studies of Social Intolerance: I. Some Psychological and Sociological Correlates of Anti-Semitism," The Journal of Social Psychology, 33 (May), 237-46.

____. 1951b. "Studies of Social Intolerance: II. A Personality Scale for Anti-Semitism," The Journal of Social Psychology, 33 (May), 247-55.

____. 1951c. "Studies of Social Intolerance: III. Relationship of the Pr Scale to Other Variables," The Journal of Social Psychology, 33 (May), 257-62.

____. 1951d. "Studies of Social Intolerance: IV. Related Social Attitudes," The Journal of Social Psychology, 33 (May), 263-69.

Gough, H. G., H. McClosky and P. E. Meehl. 1951. "A Personality Scale for Dominance," The Journal of Abnormal and Social Psychology, 46, 3 (July), 360-66.

Greenstein, F. I. 1965a. Children and Politics. New Haven: Yale University Press.

____. 1965b. "Personality and Political Socialization: The Theories of Authoritarian and Democratic Character," The Annals of The American Academy of Political and Social Science, 361 (September), 81-95.

____. 1967a. "The Impact of Personality on Politics: An Attempt to Clear Away Underbrush," The American Political Science Review, LXI, 3 (September), 629-41.

____. 1967b. "Personality and Politics: Problems of Evidence, Inference, and Conceptualization," American Behavioral Scientist, XI, 2 (November-December), 38-53.

____. 1968. "The Need for Systematic Inquiry into Personality and Politics: Introduction and Overview," Journal of Social Issues, XXIV, 3 (July), 1-14.

____. 1969. Personality and Politics. Chicago: Markham Publishing Company.

Grusky, O. 1962. "Authoritarianism and Effective Indoctrination: A Case Study," Administrative Science Quarterly, 7, 1 (June), 79-95.

Hall, C. S. and G. Lindzey. 1957. Theories of Personality. New York: John Wiley & Sons.

Hanely, C. and M. Rokeach. 1956. "Care and Carelessness in Psychology," Psychological Bulletin, 53, 2 (March), 183-86.

Hargrove, E. C. 1966. Presidential Leadership: Personality and Political Style. New York: The Macmillan Company.

Harlow, H. F. 1958. "The Nature of Love," The American Psychologist, 13, 12 (December), 673-85.

____. 1959. "Love in Infant Monkeys," Scientific American, 200, 6 (June), 68-74.

Harlow, H. F. and M. K. Harlow. 1962. "Social Deprivation in Monkeys," Scientific American, 207 (November), 136-46.

Harned, L. 1961. "Authoritarian Attitudes and Party Activity," The Public Opinion Quarterly, XXV, 3 (Fall), 393-99.

Harris, I. D. 1961. Emotional Blocks to Learning. New York: The Free Press.

Hartmann, H. 1947. "On Rational and Irrational Action," Psychoanalysis and the Social Sciences, I, 359-92.

___. 1964. "The Application of Psychoanalytic Concepts to Social Science," in Essays on Ego Psychology, 90-98. New York: International Universities Press.

Hastings, P. K. 1954. "The Non-Voter in 1952: A Study of Pittsfield, Massachusetts," The Journal of Psychology, 38, 301-12.

___. 1956. "The Voter and the Non-Voter," American Journal of Sociology, LXII, 3 (November), 302-7.

Haythorn, W., A. Couch, D. Haefner, P. Langham and L. F. Carter. 1956. "The Behavior of Authoritarian and Equalitarian Personalities in Groups," Human Relations, IX, 1 (February), 57-74.

Hennessy, B. 1959. "Politicals and Apoliticals: Some Measurements of Personality Traits," Midwest Journal of Political Science, III, 4 (November), 336-55.

Henry, W. E. 1949. "The Business Executive: The Psycho-Dynamics of a Social Role," The American Journal of Sociology, LIV, 4 (January), 286-91.

Hess, R. D. 1968. "Discussion: Political Socialization in the Schools," Harvard Educational Review, 38, 3 (Summer), 528-36.

Hess, R. D. and J. V. Torney. 1967. The Development of Political Attitudes in Children. Chicago: Aldine Publishing Company.

Himelhoch, J. 1950. "Tolerance and Personality Needs: A Study of the Liberalization of Ethnic Attitudes among Minority Group College Students," American Sociological Review, 15, 1 (February), 79-88.

Hodge, R. W. and D. J. Treiman. 1966. "Occupational Mobility and Attitudes toward Negroes," American Sociological Review, 31, 1 (February), 93-102.

Hoffer, E. 1951. The True Believer. New York: Harper & Brothers.

Hoffman, M. L. 1953. "Some Psychodynamic Factors in Compulsive Conformity," The Journal of Abnormal and Social Psychology, 48, 3 (July), 383-93.

Hofstadter, R. 1965. The Paranoid Style in American Politics. New York: Alfred A. Knopf.

Holsti, O. R. 1962. "The Belief System and National Images: A Case Study," The Journal of Conflict Resolution, VI, 244-52.

Homans, G. C. 1950. The Human Group. New York: Harcourt, Brace & World.

Honigmann, J. J. and R. J. Preston. 1964. "Recent Developments in Culture and Personality," The Annals of the American Academy of Political and Social Science, 354 (July), 153-62.

Horney, K. 1937. The Neurotic Personality of Our Time. New York: W. W. Norton & Company.

Horton, J. E. 1960. "The Angry Voter, A Study in Political Alienation." Unpublished Ph.D. dissertation, Cornell University.

____. 1964. "The Dehumanization of Anomie and Alienation: A Problem in the Ideology of Sociology," The British Journal of Sociology, XV, 283-300.

Horton, J. W. and W. E. Thompson. 1962. "Powerlessness and Political Negativism: A Study of Defeated Local Referendums," The American Journal of Sociology, LXVI, 5 (March), 485-93.

Hyman, H. 1942. "The Psychology of Status," Archives of Psychology, 38, 269 (June), 1-94.

____. 1959. Political Socialization. Glencoe: The Free Press.

____. 1960. "Reflections on Reference Groups," The Public Opinion Quarterly, XXIV, 3 (Fall), 383-96.

Inkeles, A. 1961. "National Character and Modern Political Systems," in F. Hsu (ed.), Psychological Anthropology: Approaches to Culture and Personality. Homewood: The Dorsey Press.

Inkeles, A. and R. A. Bauer. 1961. The Soviet Citizen. Cambridge: Harvard University Press.

Inkeles, A. and D. J. Levinson. 1969. "National Character: The Study of Modal Personality and Sociocultural Systems," in Gardner Lindzey and Elliott Aronson (eds.), The Handbook of Social Psychology, IV, 2nd ed. Reading, Mass.: Addison-Wesley Publishing Co.

Jacob, H. 1962. "Initial Recruitment of Elected Officials in the U.S.—A Model," The Journal of Politics, 24, 4 (November), 703-16.

Jackson, D. N. and S. J. Messick. 1957. "A Note on 'Ethnocentrism' and Acquiescent Response Sets," The Journal of Abnormal and Social Psychology, 54, 1 (January), 132-34.

Jahoda, M. 1959. "Conformity and Independence," Human Relations, XII, 2, 99-120.

Jahoda, M. and S. W. Cook. 1954. "Ideological Compliance as a Social-Psychological Process," in C. J. Friedrich (ed.), Totalitarianism, 203-22. Cambridge: Harvard University Press.

Janowitz, M. 1954. "The Systematic Analysis of Political Biography," World Politics, VI, 3 (April), 405-12.

Janowitz, M. and D. Marvick. 1953. "Authoritarianism and Political Behavior," Public Opinion Quarterly, XVII (Summer), 185-201.

Janowitz, M. and D. Wright. 1956. "The Prestige of Public Employment: 1929 and 1954," Public Administration Review, XVI, 1 (Winter), 15-21.

Jennings, M. and R. G. Niemi. 1968. "Patterns of Political Learning," Harvard Educational Review, 38, 3 (Summer), 443-67.

Jones, R. M. 1960. An Application of Psychoanalysis to Education. Springfield: Charles C. Thomas.

Kanwar, U. 1958. "Social Perception in Authoritarian and Non-Authoritarian Personality," Education & Psychology, V, 1, 15-23.

Kardiner, A. 1945. "The Concept of Basic Personality Structure as an Operational Tool in the Social Sciences," in Ralph Linton (ed), The Science of Man in the World Crisis. New York: Columbia University Press.

Kariel, H. A. 1967. "The Political Relevance of Behavioral and Existential Psychology," The American Political Science Review, LXI, 2 (June), 334-42.

___. 1968. "The Pluralistic Personality as Political Goal," paper presented to the APSA Convention.

Katz, D. 1960. "The Functional Approach to the Study of Attitudes," The Public Opinion Quarterly, XXIV, 2 (Summer), 163-204.

Katz. E. and P. F. Lazarsfeld. 1955. Personal Influence. New York: The Free Press.

Kaufman, W. C. 1957. "Status, Authoritarianism, and Anti-Semitism," The American Journal of Sociology, LXII, 4 (January), 379-82.

Kecskemeti, P. 1951. "The Study of Man: Prejudice in the Catastrophic Perspective," Commentary, II, 3 (March), 286-92.

Kelly, E. L. 1955. "Consistency of the Adult Personality," The American Psychologist, 10, 659-81.

Kelman, S. 1970. Push Comes to Shove: The Escalation of Student Protest. Boston: Houghton Mifflin Company.

Kemp, C. G. 1961. "Changes in Patterns of Personal Values," Religious Education, LVI, 1 (January-February), 63-69.

Kendall, P. L. and K. M. Wolf. 1949. "The Analysis of Deviant Cases in Communications Research," in Communications Research, 1948-1949, 152-79. New York: Harper & Brothers.

Kendall, W. 1958. "Comment on McClosky's Conservatism and Personality," American Political Science Review, LII, 2 (June), 506-10.

Kennan, G. F. 1954. "The Illusion of Security," The Atlantic Monthly, 194, 2 (August), 31-34.

Key, V. O., Jr. 1964. Public Opinion and American Democracy. New York: Alfred A. Knopf.

___. 1966. The Responsible Electorate. New York: Random House.

Kirscht, J. P. and R. C. Dillehay. 1967. Dimensions of Authoritarianism. Lexington: University of Kentucky Press.

Knapp, R. H. 1963. "The Psychology of Personality," in Bernard Berelson (ed.), Behavioral Sciences Today. New York: Basic Books.

Knupfer, G. 1947. "Portrait of the Underdog," The Public Opinion Quarterly, 11, 1 (Spring), 103-14.

Knutson, J. N. 1967. "Psychological Deprivation and Its Effect on School Behavior," Bulletin of the Oregon School Study Council, 11, 4 (October).

Knutson, J. N., ed. The Handbook of Political Psychology. San Francisco: Jossey-Bass, Inc., forthcoming.

___. 1971. "Personality Correlates of Political Beliefs: Left, Right and Center," unpublished paper presented to the Annual Convention of the American Political Science Association, Chicago.

___. 1972. "The Political Relevance of Self-Actualization," in Allen R. Wilcox (ed.), Public Opinion and Political Attitudes: A Reader. New York: John Wiley & Sons.

Kohlberg, L. 1966. "Moral Education in the Schools: A Developmental View," The School Review, 74, 1 (Spring), 1-30.

___. 1968. "The Child as a Moral Philosopher," Psychology Today (September), 25-30.

Korchin, S. J. 1946. "Psychological Variables in the Behavior of Voters," unpublished Ph.D. dissertation, Harvard University.

Kornhauser, W. 1959. The Politics of Mass Society. New York: The Free Press.

Kroeber, T. C. 1963. "The Coping Functions of the Ego Mechanisms," in Robert S. White (ed.), The Study of Lives, 178-99. New York: Atherton Press.

Kroll, A. and J. W. Dunlap. 1937. "The Arrangement of Statements in an Attitude Scale," The Psychological Bulletin, XXXIV, 544-45.

304   Bibliography

Lane, R. E. 1953. "Political Character and Political Analysis,"
    Psychiatry, 16, 387-98.

___. 1955. "Political Personality and Electoral Choice," The
    American Political Science Review, XLIX, 1 (March), 173-90.

___. 1957. "Depth Interviews on the Personal Meanings of Poli-
    tics," PROD, I, 1, 10-13.

___. 1959. Political Life. New York: The Free Press.

___. 1962. Political Ideology. New York: The Free Press of
    Glencoe.

___. 1965. "The Need to be Liked and the Anxious College Liber-
    al," The Annals of The American Academy of Political and
    Social Science, 361 (September), 71-80.

___. 1968. "Political Education in the Midst of Life's Struggles,"
    Harvard Educational Review, 38, 3 (Summer), 468-94.

___. 1969. Political Thinking and Consciousness. Chicago:
    Markham Publishing Company.

Langton, K. P. 1967. "Peer Group and School and the Political
    Socialization Process," The American Political Science Re-
    view, LXI, 3 (September), 751-58.

___. 1969. Political Socialization. New York: Oxford University
    Press.

Langton, D. B. and M. K. Jennings. 1968. "Political Socializa-
    tion and the High School Civics Curriculum in the United
    States," The American Political Science Review, LXII, 3
    (September), 825-67.

Lasswell, H. D. 1939. "Person, Personality, Group, Culture,"
    Psychiatry, 2 (November), 533-61.

___. 1948. Power and Personality. New York: The Viking Press.

___. 1951a. "Democratic Character," in The Political Writings
    of Harold D. Lasswell. Glencoe, Ill.: The Free Press.

___. 1951b. "Personality, Prejudice, and Politics," World Poli-
    tics, III, 3 (April), 399-407.

___. 1959. "Political Constitution and Character," Psychoanaly-
    sis and the Psychoanalytic Review, 46, 4 (Winter), 3-18.

___. 1960. Psychopathology and Politics. New York: The Viking
Press.

___. 1968. "A Note on 'Types' of Political Personality: Nuclear,
Co-Relational, Developmental," Journal of Social Issues,
XXIV, 3 (July), 81-91.

Lazarsfeld, P., B. Berelson and H. Gaudet. 1944. The People's
Choice. New York: Duell, Sloan and Pearce.

Lazarus, R. S. 1963. Personality and Adjustment. Englewood
Cliffs: Prentice-Hall.

Lefcourt, H. M. 1966. "Internal versus External Control of Reinforcement," Psychological Bulletin, 65, 4, 206-20.

Leites, N. 1948. "Psycho-Cultural Hypotheses About Political
Acts," World Politics, I, 1 (October), 102-19.

Lerner, D. 1958. The Passing of Traditional Society. New York:
The Free Press of Glencoe.

Leventhal, H., R. L. Jacobs and N. Z. Kudirka. 1964. "Authoritarianism, Ideology, and Political Candidate Choice," The
Journal of Abnormal and Social Psychology, 69, 5, 539-49.

Levin, M. B. 1966. The Alienated Voter: Politics in Boston. New
York: Holt, Rinehart and Winston.

Levin, M. B. and M. Eden. 1962. "Political Strategy for the
Alienated Voter," Public Opinion Quarterly, XXVI, 1 (Spring),
47-63.

Levinson, D. J. 1957. "Authoritarian Personality and Foreign
Policy," The Journal of Conflict Resolution, I, 1 (March),
37-47.

___. 1958. "The Relevance of Personality for Political Partici-
pation," The Public Opinion Quarterly, XXII, 1 (Spring),
3-10.

Lichtenstein, E., R. P. Quinn and G. L. Hover. 1961. "Dogmatism and Acquiescent Response Set," The Journal of Abnormal and Social Psychology, 63, 3, 636-38.

Lifton, R. J. 1967. Death in Life: Survivors of Hiroshima. New
York: Random House.

Lindesmith, A. L. and A. L. Strauss. 1950. "A Critique of Culture—Personality Writings," American Sociological Review, 15, 5 (October), 587-600.

Lippitt, G. L. and D. A. Sprecher. 1960. "Factors Motivating Citizens to Become Active in Politics as Seen by Practical Politicians," The Journal of Social Issues, XVI, 1, 11-17.

Lipset, Seymour Martin. 1959a. "Democracy and Working-Class Authoritarianism," American Sociological Review, 24, 4 (August), 482-501.

___. 1959b. "Social Stratification and 'Right-Wing Extremism,'" The British Journal of Sociology, X, 4 (December), 346-82.

___. 1959c. "Some Social Requisites of Democracy: Economic Development and Political Legitimacy," American Political Science Review, LIII (March, 1959) in Institute of Industrial Relations, Reprint No. 126.

___. 1959-1960. "The Political Animal: Genus Americana," Public Opinion Quarterly, XXIII, 4 (Winter), 554-62.

___. 1960. Political Man, The Social Bases of Politics. New York: Doubleday & Company.

Lipset, S. M., P. F. Lazarsfeld, A. H. Barton and Juan Linz. 1954. "The Psychology of Voting: An Analysis of Political Behavior," in Gardner Lindzey (ed.), Handbook of Social Psychology, II. Reading: Addison-Wesley Publishing Company.

Lipsitz, L. 1965. "Working-Class Authoritarianism: A Reevaluation," American Sociological Review, 30, 1 (February), 103-9.

Litt, E. 1963. "Political Cynicism and Political Futility," The Journal of Politics, 2, 25 (May), 312-23.

Loevinger, J. 1966. "The Meaning and Measurement of Ego Development," American Psychologist, 21, 195-206.

Lopreato, J. 1967. "Upward Social Mobility and Political Orientation," American Sociological Review, 32, 4 (August), 586-92.

Luchins, A. S. 1950. "Personality and Prejudice: A Critique," The Journal of Social Psychology, 32, 79-94.

Lynd, H. M. 1958. On Shame and the Search for Identity. New York: Harcourt, Brace and Company.

Maccoby, E. E., J. P. Johnson and R. M. Church. 1965. "Community Integration and the Social Control of Juvenile Delinquency," Journal of Social Issues, XIV (1958), 38-51, reprinted in
J. David Singer (ed.), Human Behavior and International Politics. Chicago: Rand McNally.

MacKenzie, N. 1964. "Alienation," New Society, 74 (February 27),
27-29.

MacKinnon, W. J. and R. Centers. 1956-1957. "Authoritarianism
and Internationalism," The Public Opinion Quarterly, XX, 4
(Winter), 621-30.

___. 1956. "Authoritarianism and Urban Stratification," Ameri-
can Journal of Sociology, LXI, 610-20.

Manheim, E. 1965. "Reaction to Alienation," The Kansas Journal
of Sociology, 1, 3 (Summer), 108-11.

Manheim, H. L. 1959. "Personality Differences of Members of
Two Political Parties," The Journal of Social Psychology, 50,
261-68.

Martin, J. G. 1961. "Tolerant and Prejudiced Personality Syndromes," Journal of Intergroup Relations, 2, 171-76.

Martin, J. G. and F. R. Westie. 1959. "The Tolerant Personality,"
American Sociological Review, 24, 4 (August), 521-28.

Masling, J. M. 1954. "How Neurotic is the Authoritarian?" The
Journal of Abnormal and Social Psychology, 49, 2 (April),
316-18.

Maslow, A. H. 1937. "Personality and Patterns of Culture," in
R. Stagner (ed.), Psychology of Personality, 408-28. New
York: McGraw-Hill Book Company.

___. 1941-1942. "The Dynamics of Psychological Security-Inse-
curity," Character and Personality, X (September-June),
331-44.

___. 1942a. "Liberal Leadership and Personality," Freedom, 2,
27-30.

___. 1942b. Social Personality Inventory for College Women.
Stanford: Stanford University Press.

___. 1943a. "A Theory of Human Motivation," Psychological Re-
view, 50, 370-96.

____. 1943b. "The Authoritarian Character-Structure," The Jour-
nal of Social Psychology, 18, 401-11.

____. 1943c. "Dynamics of Personality Organization: I," Psycho-
logical Review, 50, 5 (September), 514-39.

____. 1943d. "Dynamics of Personality Organization: II," Psycho-
logical Review, 50, 6 (November), 541-58.

____. 1951. "Resistance to Acculturation," Journal of Social Is-
sues, I, 26-29.

____. 1952. The Security-Insecurity Inventory. Stanford: Stanford
University Press.

____. 1954. Motivation and Personality. New York: Harper & Row.

____. 1957a. "A Philosophy of Psychology," in J. E. Fairchild (ed.),
Personal Problems & Psychological Frontiers. New York:
Sheridan House.

____. 1957b. "Power Relationships and Patterns of Personal De-
velopment," in A. Kornhauser (ed.), Problems of Power in
American Democracy, 92-144. Detroit: Wayne State University Press.

____. 1959. "Psychological Data and Value Theory," in A. H. Mas-
low (ed.), New Knowledge in Human Values, 119-36. New York:
Harper & Row.

____. 1962a. "Critique of Erich Fromm" (Review of J. H. Schaar's
Escape from Authority), Humanist, 22, 1 (January-February),
34-35.

____. 1962b. Toward a Psychology of Being. Princeton: D. Van
Nostrand Company.

____. 1963. "The Need to Know and the Fear of Knowing," The
Journal of General Psychology, 68, 111-25.

____. 1964a. "Criteria for Judging Needs to be Instinctoid," in A.
M. Jones (ed.), International Motivation Symposium. Lincoln:
University of Nebraska Press.

____. 1964b. "Synergy in the Society and in the Individual," Jour-
nal of Individual Psychology, 20, 153-64.

____. 1965. Eupsychian Management. Homewood, Ill.: Richard D.
Irwin.

___. 1967. "A Theory of Metamotivation: The Biological Rooting of the Value-Life," Journal of Humanistic Psychology, 7, 2 (Fall).

___. 1969a. "The Farther Reaches of Human Nature," The Journal of Transpersonal Psychology, 1, 1 (Spring).

___. 1969b. "Theory Z," in W. G. Bennis and E. H. Schein (eds.), New Developments Within the Human Side of Enterprise. New York: McGraw-Hill.

___. "Eupsychia—The Good Society." Unpublished manuscript.

Maslow, A. H. and R. Diaz-Guerrero. 1960. "Adolescence and Juvenile Delinquency in Two Different Cultures" (reprinted from Festschrift for Gardner Murphy). Ed. by J. Peatman and E. Hartley. New York: Harper.

Maslow, A. H., E. Hirsh, M. Stein and I. Honigmann. 1945. "A Clinically Derived Test for Measuring Psychological Security-Insecurity," The Journal of General Psychology, 33 (July), 21-41.

Matthews, D. R. 1960. U. S. Senators & Their World. New York: Vintage Books (Random House).

Matthews, D. R. and J. W. Prothro. 1967. "Social and Economic Factors and Negro Voter Registration in the South," in Harry A. Bailey, Jr. (ed.), Negro Politics in America, 178-210. Columbus: Charles E. Merrill.

May, R. 1950. The Meaning of Anxiety. New York: The Ronald Press Company.

Mayzner, M. S., Jr., E. Sersen and M. E. Tresselt. 1955. "The Taylor Manifest Anxiety Scale and Intelligence," Journal of Consulting Psychology, 19, 5, 401-3.

Mead, G. H. 1934. Mind, Self, and Society. Chicago: University of Chicago Press.

Meier, D. L. and W. Bell. 1959. "Anomia and Differential Access to the Achievement of Life Goals," American Sociological Review, 24, 2 (April), 189-202.

Merelman, R. M. 1969. "The Development of Political Ideology: A Framework for the Analysis of Political Socialization," The American Political Science Review, LXIII, 3 (September), 750-67.

Meresko, R., M. Rubin and F. C. Shontz. 1954. "Rigidity of Attitudes Regarding Personal Habits and its Ideological Correlates," The Journal of Abnormal and Social Psychology, 49, 1 (January), 89-93.

Merton, R. K. 1949. "Social Structure and Anomie," in Social Theory and Social Structure, 125-49. Glencoe, Ill.: The Free Press.

____. 1964. "Anomie, Anomia, and Social Internation: Contexts of Deviant Behavior," in M. B. Clinard (ed.), Anomie and Deviant Behavior, 213-42. New York: The Free Press.

Merton, R. K. and A. S. Kitt. 1957. "Reference Groups," in L. A. Coser and B. Rosenberg (eds.), Sociological Theory, 264-72. New York: The MacMillan Company.

Middleton, R. 1960. "Ethnic Prejudice and Susceptibility to Persuasion," American Sociological Review, 25, 5 (October), 679-86.

Milbrath, L. W. 1960. "Predispositions Toward Political Contention," The Western Political Quarterly, XIII, 1 (March), 5-18.

____. 1962. "Latent Origins of Liberalism-Conservatism and Party Identification: A Research Note," The Journal of Politics, 24, 4 (November), 679-88.

____. 1965. Political Participation. Chicago: Rand McNally & Company.

Milbrath, L. W. and W. W. Klein. 1962. "Personality Correlates of Political Participation," Acta Sociologica, 6, 1-2, 53-66.

Mills, C. W. 1960. "On Reason and Freedom," in M. R. Stein, A. J. Vidich and D. M. White (eds.), Identity and Anxiety, 110-19. New York: The Free Press.

Mizruchi, E. H. 1960. "Social Structure and Anomia in a Small City," American Sociological Review, 25, 5 (October), 645-54.

Money-Kyrle, R. E. 1951. Psychoanalysis and Politics: A Contribution to the Psychology of Politics and Morals. London: Gerald Duckworth & Co., Ltd.

Moos, M. and B. Koslin. 1952. "Prestige Suggestion and Political Leadership," The Public Opinion Quarterly, 16, 1 (Spring), 77-93.

Murray, E. 1968. "The Teacher as a Person," Journal of Home Economics, 60, 8 (October), 645-47.

Mussen, P. H. and A. B. Wyszynski. 1952. "Personality and Political Participation," Human Relations, V, 1, 65-82.

McClelland, C. A. 1960. "The Function of Theory in International Relations," The Journal of Conflict Resolution, IV, 3, 303-37.

McClelland, D. C. 1961. The Achieving Society. Princeton: D. Van Nostrand Company.

McClosky, H. 1958. "Conservatism and Personality," The American Political Science Review, LII, 1 (March), 27-45.

___. 1960. "Perspectives on Personality and Foreign Policy," World Politics, XIII, 1 (October), 129-39.

McClosky, H. and H. E. Dahlgren. 1959. "Primary Group Influence on Party Loyalty," The American Political Science Review, LIII, 3 (September), 757-76.

McClosky, H. and J. H. Schaar. 1965a. "Psychological Dimensions of Anomy," American Sociological Review, 30, 1 (February), 14-40.

___. 1965b. "Reply to Srole and Nettler," American Sociological Review, 30, 5 (October), 763-67.

McConaughy, J. B. 1950. "Certain Personality Factors of State Legislators in South Carolina," The American Political Science Review, XLIV, 4 (December), 897-903.

McConaughy, J. B. and J. H. Gauntlett. 1967. "The Influence of the S Factor upon the Voting Behavior of South Carolina Urban Negroes," in H. A. Bailey, Jr. (ed.), Negro Politics in America, 296-309. Columbus: Charles E. Merrill Publishing Co.

McDill, E. L. 1960. "Anomie, Authoritarianism, Prejudice, and Socio-Economic Status: An Attempt at Clarification," Social Forces, 7, 3 (September), 239-45.

McDill, E. L. and J. C. Ridley. 1962. "Status, Anomia, Political Alienation, and Political Participation," The American Journal of Sociology, LXVIII, 2 (September), 205-13.

McEvoy, J., M. Chester and R. Schmuck. 1967. "Content Analysis of a Super Patriot Protest," Social Problems, 14, 4 (Spring), 455-63.

McGregor, D. 1961. "The Need Hierarchy: A Theory of Motivation," in P. Lawrence, J. C. Bailey, R. L. Katz, J. A. Seiler, C. Orth, J. V. Clark, L. B. Barnes and A. N. Turner (eds.), Organizational Behavior and Administration, 224-28. Homewood: The Dorsey Press.

McLeod, J., S. Ward and K. Tancill. 1965-1966. "Alienation and Uses of the Mass Media," The Public Opinion Quarterly, XXIX, 4 (Winter), 583-94.

Nardini, J. E. 1952. "Survival Factors in American Prisoners of War of the Japanese," The American Journal of Psychiatry, 109, 4 (October), 241-48.

Neal, A. G. and S. Rettig. 1963. "Dimensions of Alienation Among Manual and Non-Manual Workers," American Sociological Review, 28, 4 (August), 599-608.

Neal, A. G. and M. Seeman. 1964. "Organizations and Powerlessness: A Test of the Mediation Hypothesis," American Sociological Review, 29, 2 (April), 216-26.

Nett, E. M. 1965. "An Evaluation of the National Character Concept in Sociological Theory," Social Forces, XXXVI (1958), 297-303, in J. D. Singer (ed.), Human Behavior and International Politics. Chicago: Rand McNally.

Nettler, G. 1957. "A Measure of Alienation," American Sociological Review, 22, 6 (December), 670-77.

____. 1965. "A Further Comment on 'Anomy,'" American Sociological Review, 30, 5 (October), 762-63.

Nettler, G. and J. R. Huffman. 1957. "Political Opinion and Personal Security," Sociometry, 20, 1 (March), 51-66.

Neumann, F. 1960. "Anxiety and Politics," in M. R. Stein, A. J. Vidich and D. M. White (eds.), Identity and Anxiety, 269-90. New York: The Free Press.

Neuringer, C. 1964. "The Relationship Between Authoritarianism, Rigidity, and Anxiety," The Journal of General Psychology, 71, 169-75.

Newcomb, T. M. 1943. Personality & Social Change. New York: Holt, Rinehart and Winston.

___. 1953. "Motivation in Social Behavior," in Current Theory and Research in Motivation, 139-61. Lincoln: University of Nebraska Press.

Newmann, F. M. 1968. "Discussion: Political Socialization in the Schools," Harvard Educational Review, 38, 3 (Summer), 536-45.

Nie, N. H., G. Powell, Jr. and K. Prewitt. 1969a. "Social Structure and Political Participation: Developmental Relationships, Part I," The American Political Science Review, LXIII, 2 (June), 361-78.

___. 1969b. "Social Structure and Political Participation: Developmental Relationships, II," The American Political Science Review, LXIII, 3 (September), 808-32.

Nisbet, R. A. 1965. Emile Durkheim. Englewood Cliffs: Prentice-Hall.

Olsen, M. E. 1965. "Alienation and Political Opinions," The Public Opinion Quarterly, XXIX, 2 (Summer), 200-212.

___. 1962. "Liberal-Conservative Attitude Crystallization," Sociological Quarterly, 3, 17-26.

O'Neil, W. M. and D. J. Levinson. 1953. "A Factorial Exploration of Authoritarianism and Some of Its Ideological Concomitants," Journal of Personality, 22, 449-63.

Pannes, E. D. 1963. "The Relationship Between Self-Acceptance and Dogmatism in Junior-Senior High School Students," The Journal of Educational Sociology, 36, 9 (May), 419-26.

Paul, I. H. 1956. "Impressions of Personality, Authoritarianism, and the Fait-Accompli Effect," The Journal of Abnormal and Social Psychology, 53, 3 (November), 338-44.

Peak, H. 1953. "Problems of Objective Observation," in L. Festinger and D. Katz (eds.), Research Methods in the Behavioral Sciences. New York: The Dryden Press.

Pearlin, L. I. 1961. "The Appeals of Anonymity in Questionnaire Response," Public Opinion Quarterly, 25, 4 (Winter), 640-47.

Perkins, J. E. and L. R. Goldberg. 1963. "Contextual Effects on the MMPI," ORI Research Bulletin, 3, 2 (May), Oregon Research Institute.

Perlmutter, H. V. 1954. "Relations between the Self-Image, the Image of the Foreigner, and the Desire to Live Abroad," The Journal of Psychology, 38, 131-37.

Pettigrew, T. F. 1965. "Personality and Sociocultural Factors in Intergroup Attitudes: A Cross-National Comparison," The Journal of Conflict Resolution, II (1958), 29-42, in J. D. Singer (ed.), Human Behavior and International Politics. Chicago: Rand McNally.

Phillips, N. R. 1956. "The Conservative Implications of Skepticism," The Journal of Politics, 18, 1 (February), 28-38.

Pinner, F. A. 1965. "Parental Overprotection and Political Distrust," The Annals of the American Academy of Political and Social Science, 361 (September), 58-70.

Plant, W. T., C. W. Telford and J. A. Thomas. 1965. "Some Personality Differences Between Dogmatic and Nondogmatic Groups," The Journal of Social Psychology, 67, 67-75.

Polsby, N. W. 1960. "Towards an Explanation of McCarthyism," Political Studies, VIII, 250-71.

Postman, L., J. S. Bruner and E. McGinnies. 1948. "Personal Values as Selective Factors in Perception," The Journal of Abnormal and Social Psychology, 43, 142-54.

Powell, F. A. 1962. "Open- and Closed-Mindedness and the Ability to Differentiate Source and Message," The Journal of Abnormal and Social Psychology, 65, 1 (January), 61-64.

Prewitt, K. 1965. "Political Socialization and Leadership Selection," The Annals of The American Academy of Political and Social Science, 361 (September), 96-111.

Prewitt, K., H. Eulau and B. H. Zisk. 1966. "Political Socialization and Political Roles," Public Opinion Quarterly, XXX, 4 (Winter), 569-82.

Prothro, E. T. 1952. "Ethnocentrism and Anti-Negro Attitudes in the Deep South," The Journal of Abnormal and Social Psychology, 47, 105-8.

Prothro, E. T. and L. Melikian. 1953. "The California Public
    Opinion Scale in an Authoritarian Culture," The Public Opin-
    ion Quarterly, 17, 3, 353-62.

Prothro, J. W. and C. M. Grigg. 1960. "Fundamental Principles
    of Democracy: Bases of Agreement and Disagreement," The
    Journal of Politics, 22, 2 (May), 276-94.

Putney, S. and R. Middleton. 1962. "Ethical Relativism and Ano-
    mia," American Journal of Sociology, LXVII, 4 (January), 430-
    38.

Pye, L. W. 1961. "Personal Identity and Political Ideology," in
    D. Marvick (ed.), Political Decision-makers, 290-313. Glen-
    coe, Ill.: The Free Press.

___. 1962. Politics, Personality, and Nation Building. New
    Haven: Yale University Press.

Quinney, R. 1964. "Political Conservatism, Alienation, and Fa-
    talism: Contingencies of Social Status and Religious Funda-
    mentalism," Sociometry, 27, 3 (September), 372-81.

Rankin, R. E. and E. A. Quarrick. 1964. "Personality and Atti-
    tude Toward a Political Event," Journal of Individual Psychol-
    ogy, 20, 2 (November), 189-93.

Rapoport, A. 1961. "Various Meanings of 'Theory,'" in J. N.
    Rosenau (ed.), International Politics and Foreign Policy.
    New York: The Free Press.

Rejai, M. 1967. Democracy, The Contemporary Theories. New
    York: Atherton Press.

Restle, F., M. Andrews and M. Rokeach. 1964. "Differences Be-
    tween Open- and Closed-Minded Subjects on Learning-Set and
    Oddity Problems," Journal of Abnormal and Social Psychol-
    ogy, 68, 6, 648-54.

Rhodes, A. L. 1961. "Authoritarianism and Alienation: The F-
    Scale and the Srole Scale as Predictors of Prejudice," The
    Sociological Quarterly, 2, 3 (July), 193-202.

Riesman, D. 1953. "Marginality, Conformity, and Insight," Phy-
    lon, XIV, 3, 241-57.

Riezler, K. 1960. "The Social Psychology of Fear," in M. R.
    Stein, A. J. Vidich and D. M. White (eds.), Identity and Anx-
    iety, 144-57. New York: The Free Press.

Riker, W. 1965. "Theory and Science in the Study of Politics: A Review," The Journal of Conflict Resolution, IX, 3, 375-79.

Roberts, A. H. and M. Rokeach. 1956. "Anomie, Authoritarianism, and Prejudice: A Replication," The American Journal of Sociology, LXI, 4 (January), 355-58.

Robin, S. S. 1957. "Executive Performance and Attitudes Toward Mobility." Unpublished M.A. Thesis, The Ohio State University.

Robinson, W. S. 1952. "The Motivational Structure of Political Participation," American Sociological Review, 17, 1 (February), 151-56.

Rodgers, T. C. 1960. "The Evolution of an Active Anti-Negro Racist," The Psychoanalytic Study of Society, I, 237-47.

Rogers, C. R. 1961. On Becoming A Person. Boston: Houghton, Mifflin Company.

Rogow, A. A. 1963. James Forrestal: A Study of Personality, Politics and Policy. New York: The Macmillan Company.

___. 1968. "Review of 'The Revolutionary Personality: Lenin, Trotsky, Gandhi,'" The American Political Science Review, LXII, 2 (June), 604-6.

___. 1969b. "Toward a Psychiatry of Politics," in Politics, Personality, and Social Science in the Twentieth Century, 123-46. Chicago: The University of Chicago Press.

___ (ed.). 1969b. Politics, Personality, and Social Science in The Twentieth Century. Chicago: The University of Chicago Press.

Rokeach, M. 1951a. "Prejudice, Concreteness of Thinking, and Reification of Thinking," The Journal of Abnormal and Social Psychology, 46, 1 (January), 83-91.

___. 1951b. "Toward the Scientific Evaluation of Social Attitudes and Ideologies," The Journal of Psychology, 31, 97-104.

___. 1954. "The Nature and Meaning of Dogmatism," Psychological Review, 61, 3 (May), 194-204.

___. 1956. "Political and Religious Dogmatism: An Alternative to the Authoritarian Personality," Psychological Monographs: General and Applied, 70, 18, whole no. 425, 1-43.

___. 1960. The Open and Closed Mind. New York: Basic Books.

___. 1961. "Belief Versus Race as Determinants of Social Distance: Comment on Triandis' Paper," The Journal of Abnormal and Social Psychology, 62, 1, 187-88.

___. 1964. The Three Christs of Ypsilanti. New York: Alfred A. Knopf.

___. 1968. Beliefs, Attitudes and Values. San Francisco: Jossey-Bass, Inc.

Rokeach, M. and C. Hanley. 1956. "Eysenck's Tender-Mindedness Dimension: A Critique," Psychological Bulletin, 53, 2 (March), 169-76.

Rorer, L. C. 1965. "The Great Response-Style Myth," Psychological Bulletin, 63, 3 (March), 129-56.

Rose, A. M. 1959. "Attitudinal Correlates of Social Participation," Social Forces, 37, 3 (March), 202-6.

___. 1962. "Alienation and Participation: A Comparison of Group Leaders and the 'Mass,'" American Sociological Review, 27, 6 (December), 834-38.

___. 1966. "Prejudice, Anomie, and the Authoritarian Personality," Sociology and Social Research, 50, 2 (January), 141-47.

Rose, G. 1966. "Anomie and Deviation—a Conceptual Framework for Empirical Studies," The British Journal of Sociology, XVII, 1 (March), 29-45.

Rosenberg, H. 1960. "The Orgamerican Fantasy," in M. R. Stein, A. J. Vidich and D. M. White (eds.), Identity and Anxiety, 319-28. New York: The Free Press.

Rosenberg, M. 1951. "The Meaning of Politics in Mass Society," The Public Opinion Quarterly, 15, 1 (Spring), 5-15.

___. 1954-1955. "Some Determinants of Political Apathy," The Public Opinion Quarterly, 18, 4 (Winter), 349-66.

___. 1956. "Misanthropy and Political Ideology," American Sociological Review, 21, 6 (December), 690-95.

___. 1962. "Self-Esteem and Concern with Public Affairs," The Public Opinion Quarterly, XXVI, 2 (Summer), 201-11.

Rosenzweig, R. M. 1957. "The Politician and the Career in Politics," Midwest Journal of Political Science, I, 2 (August), 163-72.

Rotter, J. B. 1966. "Generalized Expectancies for Internal versus External Control of Reinforcement," Psychological Monographs, 80, 1, No. 609.

Rovere, R. H. 1959. Senator Joe McCarthy. New York: Harcourt, Brace and Company.

Saenger, G. H. 1945-1946. "Social Status and Political Behavior," The American Journal of Sociology, LI, 103-13.

Saenger, G. H. and S. Flowerman. 1954. "Stereotypes and Prejudicial Attitudes," Human Relations, VII, 2, 217-38.

Salisbury, H. E. 1969. The 900 Days. New York: Harper & Row.

Sampson, R. V. 1966. The Psychology of Power. New York: Random House.

Sanai, M. 1952. "The Relation Between Social Attitudes and Characteristics of Personality," The Journal of Social Psychology, 36 (August), 3-13.

Sanford, F. 1950. Authoritarianism and Leadership. Philadelphia: Stephenson Brothers.

Sanford, F. H. 1951-1952. "The Use of a Projective Device in Attitude Surveying," The Public Opinion Quarterly, 14, 4 (Winter), 697-709.

Sarason, I. G. 1960. "Empirical Findings and Theoretical Problems in the Use of Anxiety Scales," Psychological Bulletin, 57, 5 (September), 403-15.

Sarbin, T. 1964. "Anxiety: Reification of a Metaphor," Archives of General Psychiatry, 10, 6 (June), 630-38.

Sarnoff, I. 1960. "Psychoanalytic Theory and Social Attitudes," The Public Opinion Quarterly, XXIV, 2 (Summer), 251-79.

Sarnoff, I. and D. Katz. 1954. "The Motivational Bases of Attitude Change," The Journal of Abnormal and Social Psychology, 49, 1 (January), 115-24.

Schaar, J. H. 1961. Escape from Authority. New York: Basic Books.

Schaff, A. 1967. "Alienation and Social Action," Diogenes, 57 (Spring), 64-82.

Schoenberger, R. A. 1968. "Conservatism, Personality and Political Extremism," The American Political Science Review, LXII, 3 (September), 868-77.

Scodel, A. and P. Mussen. 1953. "Social Perceptions of Authoritarians and Nonauthoritarians," The Journal of Abnormal and Social Psychology, 48, 2 (April), 181-84.

Scott, M. B. 1963. "The Social Sources of Alienation," Inquiry, 6, 1 (Spring), 57-69.

Scott, W. A. 1965. "Empirical Assessment of Values and Ideologies," American Sociological Review, XXIV (1959), 299-310, in J. D. Singer (ed.), Human Behavior and International Politics. Chicago: Rand McNally & Company.

Sears, D. O. and J. L. Freedman. 1967. "Selective Exposure to Information: A Critical Review," Public Opinion Quarterly, XXXI, 2, 194-213.

Sears, R. R. 1951a. "Social Behavior and Personality Development," in Toward a General Theory of Action, 465-78. Cambridge: Harvard University Press.

____. 1951b. "A Theoretical Framework for Personality and Social Behavior," The American Psychologist, 6, 9 (September), 476-83.

Seeman, M. 1958. "Social Mobility and Administrative Behavior," American Sociological Review, 23, 6 (December), 633-42.

____. 1959. "On the Meaning of Alienation," American Sociological Review, 24, 6 (December), 783-91.

____. 1963. "Alienation and Social Learning in a Reformatory," The American Journal of Sociology, 69 (November), 270-84.

____. 1966. "Alienation, Membership, and Political Knowledge: A Comparative Study," Public Opinion Quarterly, XXX, 3 (Fall), 353-67.

____. 1967a. "On the Personal Consequences of Alienation in Work," American Sociological Review, 32, 2 (April), 273-85.

____. 1967b. "Powerlessness and Knowledge: A Comparative Study of Alienation and Learning," Sociometry, 30, 2 (June), 105-23.

Seeman, M., D. Rohan and M. Argeriou. 1966. "Social Mobility and Prejudice: A Swedish Replication," Social Problems, 14, 2 (Fall), 188-97.

Seligman, L. G. 1950. "The Study of Political Leadership," The American Political Science Review, XLIV, 4 (December), 904-15.

Seligman, M. E. 1970. "On the Generality of the Laws of Learning," Psychological Review, 77, 5 (September), 406-18.

Sewell, W. H. and A. O. Haller. 1959. "Factors in the Relationship between Social Status and the Personality Adjustment of the Child," American Sociological Review, 24, 4 (August), 511-20.

Sheerer, E. T. 1949. "An Analysis of the Relationship between Acceptance of and Respect for Self and Acceptance of and Respect for Others in Ten Counseling Cases," Journal of Consulting Psychology, 13, 169-75.

Sherif, M. and C. W. Sherif. 1964. Reference Groups. New York: Harper and Row.

Shibutani, T. 1955. "Reference Groups as Perspectives," The American Journal of Sociology, LX, 6 (May), 562-69.

Shils, E. 1969. "Reflections on Deference," in A. A. Rogow (ed.), Politics, Personality, and Social Science in the Twentieth Century, 297-346. Chicago: The University of Chicago Press.

Shostrom, E. L. 1964. "An Inventory for the Measurement of Self-Actualization," Educational and Psychological Measurement, XXIV, 2, 207-18.

Siegel, S. M. 1956. "The Relationship of Hostility to Authoritarianism," The Journal of Abnormal and Social Psychology, 52, 3 (May), 368-72.

Siegel, S. 1954. "Certain Determinants and Correlates of Authoritarianism," Genetic Psychology Monographs, 49 (May), 187-29.

Silberman, C. E. 1964. Crisis in Black and White. New York: Random House.

Silberstein, F. B. and M. Seeman. 1959. "Social Mobility and Prejudice," The American Journal of Sociology, LXV, 3 (November), 258-64.

Simmons, J. L. 1965. "Liberalism, Alienation, and Personal Disturbance," Sociology and Social Research, 49, 4 (July), 456-64.

Simon, W. B. 1959. "Motivation of a Totalitarian Mass Vote," The British Journal of Sociology, X, 4 (December), 338-45.

Simpson, E. L. 1971. Democracy's Stepchildren: A Study of Need and Belief. San Francisco: Jossey-Bass, Inc.

Singer, J. D. 1968. "Man and World Politics: The Psycho-Cultural Interface," Journal of Social Issues, XXIV, 3 (July), 127-56.

Smelser, N. J. 1968. "Personality and the Explanation of Political Phenomena at the Social System Level: A Methodological Statement," Journal of Social Issues, XXIV, 3 (July), 111-25.

Smith, B. F. 1967. Adolf Hitler. Stanford: The Hoover Institution on War, Revolution and Peace.

Smith, B. L. 1969. "The Mystifying Intellectual History of Harold D. Lasswell," in A. A. Rogow (ed.), Politics, Personality, and Social Science In the Twentieth Century, 41-106. Chicago: The University of Chicago Press.

Smith, C. U. and J. W. Prothro. 1957. "Ethnic Differences in Authoritarian Personality," Social Forces, 35, 4 (May), 334-38.

V Smith, M. B. 1949. "Personal Values as Determinants of a Political Attitude," The Journal of Psychology, 28, 477-86.

____. 1958. "Opinions, Personality, and Political Behavior," The American Political Science Review, LII, 1 (March), 1-17.

____. 1968a. "Competence and Socialization," in J. A. Clausen (ed.), Socialization and Society, 270-320. Boston: Little, Brown and Company.

____. 1968b. "A Map for the Analysis of Personality and Politics," Journal of Social Issues, XXIV, 3 (July), 15-28.

____. 1969a. "Personality in Politics: A Conceptual Map, with Application to the Problem of Political Rationality," in Social Psychology and Human Values, 14-32. Chicago: Aldine Publishing Company.

___. 1969b. "Rationality and Social Process," in Social Psychology and Human Values, 370-79. Chicago: Aldine Publishing Company.

___. 1971. "A Psychologist's Perspective on Public Opinion Theory," The Public Opinion Quarterly, 35 (Spring), 36-43.

Smith, M. B., J. S. Bruner and R. W. White. 1956. Opinions & Personality. New York: John Wiley & Sons.

Spitz, D. 1958. "Power and Personality: The Appeal to the 'Right Man' in Democratic States," The American Political Science Review, LII, 1 (March), 84-97.

Spitz, R. A. 1945. "Hospitalism," The Psychoanalytic Study of the Child, I, 53-74.

___. 1946. "Anaclitic Depression," The Psychoanalytic Study of the Child, II, 313-42.

Srole, L. 1956. "Social Integration and Certain Corollaries: An Exploratory Study," American Sociological Review, 21, 6 (December), 709-16.

___. 1965. "A Comment on 'Anomy,'" American Sociological Review, 30, 5 (October), 757-62.

St. Angelo, D. and J. W. Dyson. 1968. "Personality and Political Orientation," Midwest Journal of Political Science, XII, 2 (May), 202-23.

Stagner, R. 1954. "Attitude Toward Authority: An Exploratory Study," The Journal of Social Psychology, 40, 2 (November), 197-210.

Stein, D. D. 1966. "The Influence of Belief Systems on Interpersonal Preference: A Validation Study of Rokeach's Theory of Prejudice," Psychological Monographs: General and Applied, 80, 8, 1-29.

Stewart, D. and T. Hoult. 1959. "A Social-Psychological Theory of The Authoritarian Personality," The American Journal of Sociology, LXV, 3 (November), 274-79.

Sticht, T. C. and W. Fox. 1966. "Geographical Mobility and Dogmatism, Anxiety, and Age," The Journal of Social Psychology, 68 (February), 171-74.

Stinchcombe, A. L. 1968. "Political Socialization in the South American Middle Class," Harvard Educational Review, 38, 3 (Summer), 506-27.

Stock, D. L. 1949. "An Investigation into the Interrelations between the Self Concept and Feelings directed toward other Persons and Groups," Journal of Consulting Psychology, 13, 176-80.

Stogdill, R. M. 1948. "Personal Factors Associated with Leadership: A Survey of the Literature," The Journal of Psychology, 25, 35-71.

Stogdill, R. M., O. S. Goode and D. R. Day. 1963. "The Leader Behavior of United States Senators," The Journal of Psychology, 56, 3-8.

Stokes, D. E. 1962. "Popular Evaluations of Government: An Empirical Assessment," in H. Cleveland and H. D. Lasswell (eds.), Ethics and Bigness, 61-72. New York: Harper & Brothers.

Stouffer, S. A. 1955. Communism, Conformity, and Civil Liberties. New York: John Wiley & Sons.

Struening, E. L. and A. H. Richardson. 1965. "A Factor Analytic Exploration of the Alienation, Anomia and Authoritarianism Domain," American Sociological Review, 30, 5 (October), 768-76.

Suchman, E. A. and H. Menzel. 1955. "The Interplay of Demographic and Psychological Variables in the Analysis of Voting Surveys," in P. F. Lazarsfeld and M. Rosenberg (eds.), The Language of Social Research, 1948-55. New York: The Free Press.

Sullivan, P. L. and J. Adelson. 1954. "Ethnocentrism and Misanthropy," The Journal of Abnormal and Social Psychology, 49, 2 (April), 246-50.

Tannenbaum, R. and F. Massarik. 1958. "Leadership: A Frame of Reference." Reprint No. 68, Institute of Industrial Relations: University of California at Los Angeles.

Taylor, J. A. 1953. "A Personality Scale of Manifest Anxiety," The Journal of Abnormal and Social Psychology, 48, 2 (January), 285-90.

Templeton, F. 1966. "Alienation and Political Participation: Some Research Findings," Public Opinion Quarterly, XXX, 2 (Summer), 249-61.

Thibaut, J. W. and H. W. Riecken. 1955. "Authoritarianism, Status, and the Communication of Aggression," Human Relations, VIII, 2, 95-120.

Thompson, W. E. and J. E. Horton. 1960. "Political Alienation as a Force in Political Action," Social Forces, 38, 3 (March), 190-95.

Treiman, D. J. 1966. "Status Discrepancy and Prejudice," The American Journal of Sociology, LXXI, 6 (May), 651-64.

Triandis, H. C. 1961. "A Note on Rokeach's Theory of Prejudice," The Journal of Abnormal and Social Psychology, 62, 1, 184-86.

Troldahl, V. C. and F. A. Powell. 1965. "A Short-Form Dogmatism Scale for Use in Field Studies," Social Forces, 44, 2 (December), 211-14.

Tugwell, R. G. 1968. Grover Cleveland. New York: The Macmillan Company.

Tumin, M. M. and R. C. Collins, Jr. 1959. "Status, Mobility and Anomie: A Study in Readiness for Desegregation," The British Journal of Sociology, X, 3 (September), 253-67.

Ulmer, S. S. (ed.). 1961. Introductory Readings in Political Behavior. Chicago: Rand McNally & Company.

Verba, S. 1961a. "Assumptions of Rationality and non-Rationality in Models of the International System," in K. Knorr and S. Verba (eds.), The International System. Princeton: Princeton University Press.

___. 1961b. Small Groups and Political Behavior. Princeton: Princeton University Press.

Vidulich, R. N. and I. P. Kaimon. 1961. "The Effects of Information Source Status and Dogmatism Upon Conformity Behavior," The Journal of Abnormal and Social Psychology, 63, 3, 639-42.

Wada, G. and J. C. Davies. 1957. "Riots and Rioters," Western Political Quarterly, X, 4 (December), 864-74.

Wallas, G. 1962. Human Nature in Politics. Lincoln: University of Nebraska Press.

Weatherly, D. 1964. "Some Personality Correlates of Authoritarianism," The Journal of Social Psychology, 64, 161-67.

Wedge, B. 1964. "Social Psychiatry and Political Behavior," Bulletin of the Menninger Clinic, 28, 2 (March), 53-61.

Weissman, P. 1958. "Why Booth Killed Lincoln: A Psychoanalytic
Study of a Historical Tragedy," Psychoanalysis and the Social
Sciences, V, 99-115.

Weitman, M. 1962. "More Than One Kind of Authoritarian," Journal of Personality, 30, 2 (June), 193-208.

Welsh, G. S. 1952. "An Anxiety Index and an Internalization Ratio
for the MMPI," Journal of Consulting Psychology, 16, 1 (February), 65-72.

White, J., R. D. Alter and M. Rardin. 1965. "Authoritarianism,
Dogmatism, and Usage of Conceptual Categories," Journal of
Personality and Social Psychology, 2, 2, 293-95.

White, R. W. 1959. "Motivation Reconsidered: The Concept of
Competence," Psychological Review, 66, 5, 297-333.

____. 1963. "Sense of Interpersonal Competence: Two Case Stud-
ies and Some Reflections on Origins," in R. W. White (ed.),
The Study of Lives. New York: Atherton Press.

Wiebe, G. D. 1952. "Responses to the Televised Kefauver Hear-
ings: Some Social Psychological Implications," The Public
Opinion Quarterly, 16, 2 (Spring), 177-200.

Wilson, J. Q. 1962. The Amateur Democrat. Chicago: The University of Chicago Press.

Witkin, H. A., R. B. Dyk, H. F. Faterson, D. R. Goodenough and
S. A. Karp. 1962. Psychological Differentiation. New York:
John Wiley & Sons.

Witkin, H. A., H. B. Lewis, M. Hertzman, K. Machover, P. B.
Meissner and W. Wapner. 1954. Personality Through Perception. New York: Harper & Brothers.

Wolfenstein, E. V. 1967. The Revolutionary Personality: Lenin,
Trotsky, Gandhi. Princeton: Princeton University Press.

____. 1969. Personality and Politics. Belmont: Dickenson Pub-
lishing Company.

Wolff, H. G. 1957. "A Scientific Report on What Hope Does For Man," Saturday Review, 40 (January 5), 42-45.

Wolin, S. S. 1960. Politics and Vision. Boston: Little, Brown and Company.

Woodward, J. L. and E. Roper. 1950. "Political Activity of American Citizens," The American Political Science Review, XLIV, 4 (December), 872-85.

Yinger, J. M. 1963. "Research Implications of a Field View of Personality," American Journal of Sociology, LXVIII, 5 (March), 580-92.

____. 1964. "On Anomie," Journal for the Scientific Study of Religion, 3, 158-73.

____. 1965. Toward a Field Theory of Behavior. New York: Mc-Graw-Hill Book Company.

Zink, H. 1938. "A Case Study of a Political Boss," Psychiatry, I, 527-33.

Zinker, J. C. 1966. Rosa Lee, Motivation and the Crisis of Dying. Painesville, Ohio: The Lake Erie College Press.

Scales Used in Field Study

Anomia Scale (Srole)

1. There's little use writing to public officials because often they aren't really interested in the problems of people like me.

2. Nowadays a person has to live pretty much for today and let tomorrow take care of itself.

3. In spite of what some people say, the lot of the average man is getting better all the time.*

4. It's hardly fair to bring children into the world with the way things look for the future.

5. These days a person doesn't really know whom he can count on.

---

*Reversed from original wording, as suggested in Tumin and Collins (1959).

Citizen Duty Scale (SRC)

1. It isn't so important to vote when you know your party doesn't have a chance to win.

2. A good many local elections aren't important enough to bother with.

3. So many other people vote in the national elections that it doesn't matter much to me whether I vote or not.

4. If a person doesn't care how an election comes out, he shouldn't vote in it.

Esteem Scale (Milbrath-Klein)

1. I like to be the center of attention.

2. I tend to act out a story I am telling.

3. It makes me uncomfortable to put on a stunt or play a game at a party, even when others are doing the same sort of thing.

4. It is hard for me to tell anyone about myself.

5. As long as the job gets done, I don't mind if someone else gets the credit.

Faith-In-People Scale (Rosenberg)

1. Some people say that most people can be trusted. Others say you can't be too careful in your dealings with people. How do you feel about it?
2. Would you say that most people are more likely to help others or more likely to look out for themselves?
3. If you don't watch yourself, people will take advantage of you.
4. No one is going to care much what happens to you, when you get right down to it.
5. People are basically good and helpful.

Modified F-Scale (Derived from the Berkeley Study)

1. Most people don't realize how much our lives are controlled by plots planned in secret places.
2. Sex crimes, such as rape and attacks on children, deserve more than just imprisonment—such criminals ought to be publicly whipped.
3. The law is far too easy on draft dodgers, conscientious objectors and draft card burners. If a person won't fight for his country, he deserves a lot worse than just prison or a work camp.
4. There is hardly anything lower than a person who does not feel a great love, gratitude, and respect for his parents.
5. Every person should have complete faith in some type of God or Fate whose decisions he obeys without question.
6. Young people sometimes get rebellious ideas, but as they grow up they ought to get over them and settle down.
7. Homosexuals are hardly better than criminals and ought to be severely punished.
8. It's important to obey and respect authority because people in positions of authority know best.
9. People can be divided into two distinct classes: the weak and the strong.
10. Nowadays when so many different kinds of people move around and mix together so much, a person has to be careful not to catch an infection or disease from them.
11. The trouble with letting everybody have a say is that so many people are just naturally stupid or full of wild ideas.
12. A real insult to your honor should always be punished.
13. A person who has bad manners, habits and breeding can hardly expect to be liked and accepted by decent people.
14. Even if people say they are 100 percent Americans, they shouldn't be allowed to picket and demonstrate against policies our government has already decided on.
15. Certain religious groups who don't salute the flag should be forced to be a part of such a patriotic ceremony.

Interpersonal Threat Scale (Rosenberg)

1. I would be deeply disturbed if someone were to laugh at me for my political opinions.
2. I often prefer to say nothing at all than to say something that will make a bad impression.
3. I try to avoid saying things that will make people angry with me.

Political Efficacy Scale (SRC)

1. I don't think public officials care much what people like me think.
2. Voting is the only way that people like me can have any say about how the government runs things.
3. People like me don't have any say about what the government does.
4. Sometimes politics and government seem so complicated that a person like me can't really understand what's going on.

Status Concern (Adapted from Silberstein-Seeman)

1. I'd turn down a real job advancement, if the people doing the hiring had the reputation of wanting a "yes man" who would go along with their ideas.
2. I wouldn't let my friendships in town stand in the way of moving on to a higher position (a better job).
3. If you've got a good job where you are now, you shouldn't be tempted if a bigger job comes your way.
4. It's often a good idea to move to a new job after a few years in one place, because you tend to come up against more and more problems.
5. One thing that keeps you from wanting to move up in your job is the thought of the increased responsibility breathing down your neck in the top jobs.

Threat Orientation Scale (Martin and Westie)

1. When you come right down to it, it's every man for himself in this world.
2. If a person doesn't look out for himself nobody else will.
3. A person has to be very careful these days to avoid being gypped or cheated by other people.
4. Human nature being what it is, there will always be war and trouble.
5. Most of the people on public relief are just too lazy to work.
6. You can talk about humanity and all that, but in reality,

life is a matter of the survival of the fittest—of the strongest winning.

    7. A little charity is all right, but most people will just ask for more if you give them something.

    8. Life is basically a struggle for survival.

Indices Used in Field Study

Index of Political Participation (Woodward and Roper)

Scoring method used here:

Voting once or more times in the last four years (since 1963)	1 point
Frequently discussing public issues with others and either taking an equal share in the conversation or, usually trying to convince others he is right	1 point
Belonging to any organization that takes a stand on public issues	1 point
Having ever written or talked to an elected official regarding a public issue	1 point
Having ever worked for the election of any candidate	1 point
Having ever contributed money to a political party or candidate	1 point
Having attended any meetings in the last four years at which political speeches were made	1 point
Total Possible Points	7 points

Index of Socioeconomic Status

The following scores were summed and averaged:
1. Score on level of schooling attained
    1 = 7th grade or less
    2 = finished eighth grade
    3 = some high school
    4 = finished high school
    5 = vocational school (such as Beauty or Business School)
    6 = some college (and 3 year R.N. course)
    7 = finished college
    8 = graduate work
2. Score on level of occupation
    (from 1 through 9, coding sheet adapted to specific sample)
3. Income
    (from 1 through 8, in categories checked by respondent from "Less than $3,000" to "$9,000 and over"

Index of Leadership

The following scores were summed and averaged:
1.   One point if any offices held since school
2.   One point if, in relation to friends, respondent checked either "a leader" or "sometimes a leader"
3.   One point if, in discussion with friends, individual checked "I do more than just hold up my end of the conversation; I usually try to make the others see my opinions are right." (Also a part of the Political Participation Scale.)

Index of Physiological Need

1. One point if the respondent agreed or agreed strongly (on a 5-point scale) with "I'd be very happy in life if I always could count on enough money for food, clothes, house payment, et cetera —the basics.

2. One point if the respondent checked "Not as well off as most people" or "Very poor; sometimes didn't have enough to eat" to the question "Which of the following describes your family's financial life when you were a child?"

3. One point if the respondent checked either "Good pay, so I don't have to worry about money" or "A steady job that you can count on keeping" in answer to "What is the most important thing to you about a job? (Check one.)"

Index of Safety, Security Needs

1. One point if the respondent agreed or agreed strongly (on a 5-point scale) to "The biggest cause of happiness is being able to know what you are going to be doing next month, next year and in ten years."

2. One point if the respondent disagreed or disagreed strongly (on a 5-point scale) to "It is better to buy what you can get of the good things in life than to put money in the bank."

3. One point if the respondent disagreed or disagreed strongly (on a 5-point scale) to "It is better to have good friends than money in the bank."

4. One point if the respondent "agreed very much" or "agreed mostly" (on a 7-point scale) with "A person who leads an even, regular life in which few surprises or unexpected happenings arise, really has a lot to be grateful for." (Also in Intolerance of Ambiguity Scale.)

Index of Need for Affection

1. One point if the answer is agree or agree strongly (on a 5-point scale) to the question "It is better to have good friends than money in the bank."

2. One point if the answer is disagree or disagree strongly (on a 5-point scale) to the question: "It is possible to be very happy in love."

3. One point if the answer is agree very much or agree mostly (on a 7-point scale) to the statement "Basically, the world we live in is a pretty lonesome place." (Also in Dogmatism Scale.)

4. One point if the answer checked is "No Close Friends" to the question "Compared to the people that you know, how many friends do you think you have?"

5. One point if the answer checked was "Not as happy as most families" or "Very unhappy" to the question: "Which of the following describes your family life as a child."

6. One point if the answer checked was "A job where you can work with friends that you really like" to the question "What is the most important thing to you about a job?" Check one.

Index of Need for Esteem

1. Give one point if the answer is agree or agree strongly (on a 5-point scale) to the statement "The most important satisfaction in life is being able to do something so well that everyone looks up to you."

2. One point if the answer is agree or agree strongly (on a 5-point scale) to the statement "It really makes you mad how you never get any appreciation for a job well done."

3. One point if the answer is no or undecided to the question "Do you feel that you get enough praise?" (Also in S-I Inventory.)

4. One point if the answer checked is "A job with authority, so the other workers will look up to you" to the question "What is the most important thing to you about a job?" (Check one.)

Index of Need for Self-Actualization

All people who have none of the above needs (as determined by cut-off points) and whose total score on the above indices is 3 or less = high self-actualizers.

All people who have none of the above needs (as determined by cut-off points) and who total score on the above indices is 4 - 6 = low self-actualizers.

Field Study Scores by Need Hierarchy

In this Appendix, the field study scores for the major variables are presented in a different arrangement from what has been discussed in chapter 4. In an attempt to help the reader assess the <u>relative standing</u> of each need group, the scores for each group on the same variable have been combined into one table. (The scores for the Psychically Deprived serve somewhat like an average of the first four groups, the difference being the fact that each individual here is only counted once, while in the first four groups 17 percent of the total subjects appear in more than one need group.) At the bottom of each table some general comments are offered and at the right of the table the high scores are summed, so that the reader can more easily note trends. The N's for Appendix C are, as in chapter 4, Physiological Need = 52, Safety Need = 57, Affection Need = 129, Esteem Need = 140, Psychically Deprived = 273, Low self-actualizers = 120 and High self-actualizers = 102.

SECURITY-INSECURITY INVENTORY

	Security			Insecurity		4-5
	1	2	3	4	5	
Physiological need	28.8	15.4	17.3	19.2	19.2	38.4
Safety need	33.3	19.3	14.0	21.1	12.3	33.4
Affection need	17.8	19.4	20.2	24.8	17.8	42.6
Esteem need	17.9	20.0	20.7	26.4	15.0	41.4
Psychically deprived	22.7	20.9	20.1	22.3	13.9	36.2
Low self-actualizers	27.5	30.8	17.5	18.3	5.8	24.1
High self-actualizers	36.3	34.3	15.7	9.8	3.9	13.7
Totals	26.7	26.1	18.6	18.8	9.9	28.7

1. Steady drop as mental health increases.

2. Drop <u>not</u> even by need groups. Increase in Affection and Esteem groups.

ANOMIA SCALE

	Low			High			4-5-6
	1	2	3	4	5	6	
Physiological need	23.1	17.3	19.2	17.3	17.3	5.8	40.4
Safety need	26.3	12.3	28.1	15.8	15.8	1.8	33.4
Affection need	27.9	22.5	19.4	17.8	8.5	3.9	30.2
Esteem need	19.3	22.1	31.4	14.3	10.7	2.1	27.1
Psychically deprived	25.6	22.3	23.4	15.8	9.9	2.9	28.6
Low self-actualizers	50.8	16.7	18.3	5.8	5.8	2.5	14.1
High self-actualizers	44.1	31.4	15.7	4.9	2.9	1.0	8.8
Totals	35.6	22.8	20.6	11.1	7.5	2.4	21.0

1.   Steady drop by mental health and <u>by each need</u> as mental health increases.

MANIFEST ANXIETY SCALE

	Low			High			4-5-6
	1	2	3	4	5	6	
Physiological need	21.2	9.6	15.4	21.2	19.2	13.5	53.9
Safety need	17.5	19.3	22.8	17.5	12.3	10.5	40.3
Affection need	14.7	16.3	24.0	17.1	20.2	7.8	45.1
Esteem need	11.4	20.7	19.3	19.3	17.1	12.1	48.5
Psychically deprived	16.8	17.9	22.7	17.9	15.8	8.8	42.5
Low self-actualizers	20.0	24.2	30.0	15.8	5.0	5.0	25.8
High self-actualizers	27.5	29.4	26.5	12.7	2.0	2.0	16.7
Totals	19.8	21.8	25.3	16.4	10.3	6.5	33.2

1.   Steady drop as mental health increases.

2.   Drop not even by need groups: increases for affection and esteem groups.

STATUS CONCERN

	Low			High			4- 5- 6
	1	2	3	4	5	6	
Physiological need	1.9	11.5	15.4	50.0	21.2	0.0	71.2
Safety need	5.3	14.0	36.8	29.8	12.3	1.8	43.9
Affection need	2.3	8.5	28.7	38.0	18.6	3.9	60.5
Esteem need	2.1	7.9	22.1	43.6	22.9	1.4	67.9
Psychically deprived	2.2	7.3	28.9	39.9	19.4	2.2	61.5
Low self-actualizers	0.8	10.0	20.0	51.7	17.5	0.0	69.2
High self-actualizers	0.0	2.0	24.5	52.0	21.6	0.0	73.6
Totals	1.4	6.9	25.9	45.3	19.4	1.2	65.9

1. All groups are relatively concerned with status, except Safety.

2. Steady increase as mental health increases, and by needs—except for the very high scores of the physiological need group.

ESTEEM SCALE

	Low			High			4- 5- 6
	1	2	3	4	5	6	
Physiological need	11.5	34.6	28.8	15.4	7.7	1.9	25.0
Safety need	19.3	22.8	28.1	21.1	5.3	3.5	29.9
Affection need	11.6	29.5	25.6	19.4	10.1	3.9	33.4
Esteem need	9.3	17.9	20.7	23.6	20.7	7.9	52.2
Psychically deprived	11.7	24.5	23.8	20.5	14.3	5.1	39.9
Low self-actualizers	7.5	23.3	28.3	25.8	10.8	4.2	40.8
High self-actualizers	6.9	10.8	36.3	26.5	14.7	4.9	46.1
Totals	9.7	21.4	27.5	23.0	13.5	4.8	41.3

1. Steady increase as mental health increases.

2. Increase steady among groups 1-4, then a drop for self-actualizer groups because of high scores for esteem group.

FAITH-IN-PEOPLE SCALE

	High			Low			4-5-6
	1	2	3	4	5	6	
Physiological need	9.6	17.3	30.8	19.2	13.5	9.6	42.3
Safety need	15.8	8.8	19.3	26.3	17.5	12.3	56.1
Affection need	17.8	18.6	23.3	15.5	14.0	10.9	40.4
Esteem need	15.7	14.3	22.9	22.1	15.7	9.3	47.1
Psychically deprived	16.1	17.6	21.2	22.0	13.9	9.2	45.1
Low self-actualizers	30.0	26.7	15.8	15.0	7.5	5.0	27.5
High self-actualizers	21.6	30.4	17.6	21.6	5.9	2.9	30.4
Totals	20.6	22.4	19.2	20.2	10.7	6.9	37.8

1. Self-actualizers have more faith-in-people than psychically de-
    prived, but low self-actualizers have more than high self-actual-
    izers.

2. No pattern by needs: safety group has least faith-in-people.

DOGMATISM SCALE

	Low			High			5-6-7
	2	3	4	5	6	7	
Physiological need	0.0	0.0	34.6	40.4	25.0	0.0	65.4
Safety need	0.0	7.0	29.8	47.4	14.0	1.8	63.2
Affection need	0.0	5.4	36.4	43.4	14.0	0.8	58.2
Esteem need	0.0	2.1	26.4	51.4	18.6	1.4	71.4
Psychically deprived	0.0	4.0	36.3	45.8	12.8	1.1	59.7
Low self-actualizers	0.8	2.5	55.8	35.0	5.8	0.0	40.8
High self-actualizers	0.0	10.8	62.7	24.5	2.0	0.0	26.5
Totals	0.2	5.1	46.5	38.8	8.9	0.6	48.3

1. Steady drop as mental health increases.

2. Steady drop by needs except for esteem group, which is the highest
    of all.

INTOLERANCE OF AMBIGUITY SCALE

	High			Low			5-6-7
	2	3	4	5	6	7	
Physiological need	0.0	5.8	34.6	50.0	7.7	1.9	59.6
Safety need	1.8	1.8	29.8	59.6	5.3	1.8	66.7
Affection need	0.0	11.6	45.0	37.2	6.2	0.0	43.4
Esteem need	0.0	10.7	40.7	42.1	6.4	0.0	48.5
Psychically deprived	0.4	9.9	41.0	42.5	5.9	0.4	48.8
Low self-actualizers	0.0	6.7	55.0	36.7	1.7	0.0	38.4
High self-actualizers	2.0	25.5	47.1	23.5	2.0	0.0	25.5
Totals	0.6	12.3	45.7	37.2	4.0	0.2	41.4

1.   Steady decrease as mental health increases.

2.   Decrease not even by needs: safety is highest, physiological need is second.

THREAT ORIENTATION SCALE

	Low				High			5-6-7
	1	2	3	4	5	6	6	
Physiological need	0.0	3.8	7.7	26.9	42.3	11.5	7.7	61.5
Safety need	0.0	3.5	15.8	12.3	31.6	28.1	8.8	68.5
Affection need	0.8	12.4	20.2	22.5	27.1	10.9	6.2	44.2
Esteem need	0.0	2.1	12.1	27.1	40.7	10.0	7.9	58.6
Psychically deprived	0.4	7.7	16.1	23.8	34.1	12.1	5.9	52.1
Low self-actualizers	0.8	10.8	27.5	26.7	20.0	13.3	0.8	34.1
High self-actualizers	4.9	9.8	22.5	37.3	16.7	7.8	1.0	25.5
Totals	1.4	8.9	20.2	27.3	27.1	11.5	3.6	42.2

1.   Steady drop as mental health increases.

2.   Drop not even by needs: safety is the highest.

F-SCALE

	Low			High			5-6-7
	2	3	4	5	6	7	
Physiological need	0.0	1.9	26.9	40.4	25.0	3.8	69.2
Safety need	0.0	10.5	19.3	29.8	21.1	17.5	68.4
Affection need	3.9	20.2	27.1	26.4	19.4	3.1	48.9
Esteem need	0.7	7.9	26.4	30.0	28.6	5.7	64.3
Psychically deprived	2.2	13.6	27.1	29.3	22.0	5.5	56.8
Low self-actualizers	3.3	12.5	32.5	42.5	5.8	3.3	51.6
High self-actualizers	6.9	30.4	31.4	27.5	3.9	0.0	31.4
Totals	3.4	16.8	29.3	32.1	14.3	3.8	50.2

1.   Steady drop as mental health increases.
2.   Drop not even by needs only because of very low affection score.

POLITICAL EFFICACY SCALE

	High		Low			4-5
	1	2	3	4	5	
Physiological need	15.4	17.3	26.9	28.8	11.5	40.3
Safety need	17.5	17.5	31.6	24.6	8.8	33.4
Affection need	18.6	30.2	30.2	13.2	7.8	21.0
Esteem need	12.9	25.7	28.6	20.0	12.9	32.9
Psychically deprived	17.2	27.8	29.7	16.8	8.4	25.2
Low self-actualizers	21.7	43.3	18.3	10.0	6.7	16.7
High self-actualizers	36.3	39.2	16.7	2.9	4.9	7.8
Totals	22.2	33.9	24.2	12.3	7.3	19.6

1.   Steady decrease with increase in mental health.
2.   Needs drop evenly except for very low affection scores.

CITIZEN DUTY SCALE

	High		Low		
	1	2	3	4	5
Physiological need	46.2	48.1	1.9	0.0	3.8
Safety need	63.2	35.1	0.0	1.8	0.0
Affection need	60.5	32.6	4.7	0.8	1.6
Esteem need	53.6	40.7	2.9	0.7	2.1
Psychically de-prived	54.9	39.2	3.7	0.7	1.5
Low self-actual-izers	62.5	35.8	0.8	0.0	0.8
High self-actual-izers	52.9	41.2	3.9	1.0	1.0
Totals	56.4	38.8	3.0	0.6	1.2

INTERPERSONAL THREAT SCALE

	Low		High		3-4
	1	2	3	4	
Physiological need	15.4	23.1	50.0	11.5	61.5
Safety need	15.8	33.3	40.4	10.5	50.9
Affection need	27.1	24.0	41.1	7.8	48.9
Esteem need	22.1	27.9	37.9	12.1	50.0
Psychically de-prived	23.1	27.1	40.3	9.5	49.8
Low self-actual-izers	23.3	30.0	38.3	8.3	46.6
High self-actual-izers	28.4	41.2	24.5	5.9	30.4
Totals	24.2	30.7	36.6	8.5	45.1

1. Steady decrease as mental health increases.

2. Decrease by needs except for esteem group (increases 1.1 percent).

INDEX OF SOCIOECONOMIC STATUS

	Low	Middle	High
Physiological need	51.9	38.5	9.6
Safety need	36.8	35.1	28.1
Affection need	32.6	44.2	23.3
Esteem need	30.0	44.3	25.7
Psychically deprived	28.9	45.8	25.3
Low self-actualizers	15.0	36.7	48.3
High self-actualizers	12.7	34.3	52.9
Totals	22.2	41.2	36.6

1. Psychically deprived group has one-half as many high status; twice as many low status; 10 percent more middle status.

2. Physiological group is lowest; groups 2-4 are very similar; there is very little difference between the groups of actualizers—thus SES differences do not account for the differences in their performance on most scales.

INDEX OF POLITICAL PARTICIPATION

	Low	Middle	High
Physiological need	40.4	53.8	5.7
Safety need	47.4	31.6	21.1
Affection need	32.0	44.2	24.9
Esteem need	34.3	35.7	29.9
Psychically deprived	36.6	37.4	26.1
Low self-actualizers	33.3	40.8	25.8
High self-actualizers	23.5	32.3	44.1
Totals	33.1	37.1	29.6

1. Steady increase by need groups and by mental health for high activity, except for .3 percent decrease from Psychically Deprived or 4.1 percent decrease from esteem score for low self-actualizers.

2. Groups 1 and 2 are most inactive (safety most of all).

INDEX OF LEADERSHIP

	Low		High		3-4
	1	2	3	4	
Physiological need	30.8	51.9	13.5	3.8	17.3
Safety need	38.6	38.6	21.1	1.8	22.9
Affection need	26.4	42.6	29.5	1.6	31.1
Esteem need	20.7	46.4	27.1	5.7	32.8
Psychically de-prived	23.1	47.3	26.4	3.3	29.7
Low self-actual-izers	16.7	44.2	38.3	0.8	39.1
High self-actual-izers	13.7	52.0	31.4	2.9	34.3
Totals	19.6	47.5	30.3	2.6	32.9

1. Steady decrease in lack of leadership (#1) by need and by mental health, except for increase in safety scores.

2. Steady increase in activity (#3 and 4) by need and by mental health, except for 4.8 percent decrease for high self-actualizers.

APPENDIX D

RELATIONSHIPS AND SIGNIFICANCE LEVELS WITH CONTROLS

Part I: Major Variables Run against Continuum of Mental Health, with SES Controlled

	Low Status (N = 110)	Middle Status (N = 204)	High Status (N = 181)	Total Group, No Controls (N = 495)
Security-Insecurity Inventory	-.16, p = .04	-.20, p = .003	-.19, p = .006	-.21, p = .001
Anomia Scale	-.15, p = .06	-.21, p = .001	-.19, p = .006	-.26, p = .001
Manifest Anxiety Scale	-.22, p = .01	-.21, p = .001	-.16, p = .02	-.23, p = .001
Status Concern	.08, p = .22	.04, p = .27	.06, p = .20	.07, p = .07
Esteem Scale	.08, p = .20	.05, p = .24	.0003, p = .50	.08, p = .03
Faith-in-People Scale	-.06, p = .27	-.18, p = .004	-.13, p = .04	-.19, p = .001
Dogmatism Scale	-.27, p = .002	-.32, p = .001	-.14, p = .03	-.28, p = .001
Intolerance of Ambiguity Scale	-.16, p = .05	-.16, p = .01	-.21, p = .002	-.21, p = .001
Threat Orientation Scale	-.10, p = .16	-.24, p = .001	-.10, p = .10	-.21, p = .001
F-Scale	-.14, p = .08	-.21, p = .001	-.21, p = .003	-.26, p = .001
Political Efficacy Scale	-.11, p = .13	-.11, p = .06	-.30, p = .001	-.25, p = .001
Citizen Duty Scale	.03, p = .38	.004, p = .48	-.04, p = .32	.02, p = .35
Interpersonal Threat Scale	-.21, p = .01	-.06, p = .18	-.08, p = .14	-.11, p = .008
Political Participation Index	.06, p = .26	.08, p = .12	.03, p = .32	.14, p = .001
Index of Leadership	-.05, p = .31	.13, p = .03	-.14, p = .32	.09, p = .021

RELATIONSHIPS AND SIGNIFICANCE LEVELS WITH CONTROLS

Part II: Major Variables Run against Index of Socioeconomic Status, with Mental Health Controlled

	Psychically Deprived (N = 273)	Low Self-Actualizers (N = 120)	High Self-Actualizers (N = 102)	Total Group, No Controls (N = 495)
Security-Insecurity Inventory	-.10, p = .05	-.09, p = .16	-.11, p = .14	-.19, p = .001
Anomia Scale	-.17, p = .003	-.30, p = .001	-.10, p = .17	-.29, p = .001
Manifest Anxiety Scale	-.14, p = .01	-.05, p = .31	-.06, p = .26	-.19, p = .001
Status Concern	.06, p = .16	-.04, p = .32	.14, p = .09	.07, p = .05
Esteem Scale	.19, p = .001	.18, p = .02	.08, p = .21	.20, p = .001
Faith-in-People Scale	-.10, p = .04	-.28, p = .001	-.08, p = .20	-.23, p = .001
Dogmatism Scale	-.20, p = .001	-.19, p = .02	.15, p = .06	-.20, p = .001
Intolerance of Ambiguity Scale	-.09, p = .07	-.16, p = .05	-.06, p = .27	-.17, p = .001
Threat Orientation Scale	-.14, p = .01	-.27, p = .001	.01, p = .47	-.24, p = .001
F-Scale	-.20, p = .001	-.33, p = .001	-.27, p = .003	-.31, p = .001
Political Efficacy Scale	-.17, p = .002	-.31, p = .001	-.26, p = .004	-.30, p = .001
Citizen Duty Scale	.12, p = .02	.05, p = .30	.06, p = .29	.10, p = .02
Interpersonal Threat Scale	-.09, p = .06	-.007, p = .47	.06, p = .26	-.06, p = .09
Political Participation Index	.30, p = .001	.24, p = .004	.13, p = .10	.31, p = .001
Index of Leadership	.21, p = .001	.18, p = .02	.16, p = .05	.24, p = .001

APPENDIX E

INTER-CORRELATIONS BETWEEN MAJOR VARIABLES
(exclusive of need levels)

	1	2	3	4	5	6	7	8	9	10	11	12	13	14	15	16
1. Security-Insecurity Inventory	X	+.32	+.72	-.11	-.15	+.25	+.21	+.06	+.24	+.06	-.27	-.13	+.06	-.18	-.21	-.19
2. Anomia	+.32	X	+.34	-.11	-.13	+.54	+.32	+.20	+.47	+.39	-.56	-.20	+.10	-.29	-.28	-.26
3. Manifest Anxiety	+.72	+.34	X	-.15	-.13	+.25	+.28	+.08	+.24	+.16	-.34	-.08	+.17	-.19	-.23	-.16
4. Status Concern	-.11	-.11	-.15	X	+.11	+.01	-.13	-.12	+.07	-.13	+.09	-.03	-.10	+.07	+.04	+.10
5. Esteem (Milbrath-Klein)	-.15	-.13	-.13	+.11	X	-.02	-.06	-.19	+.01	-.15	+.11	+.05	-.16	+.20	+.21	+.28
6. Faith-in-People	+.25	+.54	+.25	+.01	-.02	X	+.24	+.15	+.52	+.23	-.36	-.19	+.01	-.23	-.19	-.24
7. Dogmatism	+.21	+.32	+.28	-.13	-.06	+.24	X	+.22	+.38	+.49	-.33	-.05	+.20	-.20	-.15	-.02
8. Intolerance of Ambiguity	+.06	+.20	+.08	-.12	-.19	+.15	+.22	X	+.11	+.38	-.18	+.07	+.18	-.17	-.16	-.06
9. Threat Orientation	+.24	+.47	+.24	+.07	+.01	+.52	+.38	+.11	X	+.42	-.42	+.16	+.03	-.24	-.15	-.09
10. F-Scale	+.06	+.39	+.16	-.13	-.15	+.23	+.49	+.38	+.42	X	-.40	-.02	+.20	-.31	-.19	-.06
11. Political Efficacy	-.27	-.56	-.34	+.09	+.11	-.36	-.33	-.18	-.42	-.40	X	-.14	-.17	+.30	+.30	+.24
12. Citizen Duty	-.13	-.20	-.08	-.03	+.05	-.19	-.05	+.07	+.16	-.02	-.14	X	-.07	+.10	+.16	+.08
13. Interpersonal Threat	+.06	+.10	+.17	-.10	-.16	+.01	+.20	+.18	+.03	+.20	-.17	-.07	X	-.06	-.18	-.13
14. SES Index	-.18	-.29	-.19	+.07	+.20	-.23	-.20	-.17	-.24	-.31	+.30	+.10	-.06	X	+.31	+.24
15. Political Participation Index	-.21	-.28	-.23	+.04	+.21	-.19	-.15	-.16	-.15	-.19	+.30	+.16	-.18	+.31	X	+.40
16. Leadership Index	-.19	-.26	-.16	+.10	+.28	-.24	-.02	-.06	-.09	-.06	+.24	+.08	-.13	+.24	+.40	X

Other Applications
of Maslow's Personality Model

The following is offered as an aid to the research oriented reader. It is a brief summary of the value from a political point of view of several studies which have employed Maslow's personality model.

Least useful is the report by Clark (1961) on motivation in a work group. Clark works with the idea that it is the environment which determines need level (so that, for example, the need for safety is the determinant of work behavior in depression with the result that men work hard because security is all-important). The study generates some useful ideas by Clark's consideration of personality needs as group needs. However, if there is any meaning in the study of personality for political scientists, it is the differential effect of a social situation.

In a study with a similar focus, Dickson and Roethlisberger (1966) have adapted and applied Maslow's need hierarchy to another industrial situation. Physical needs are not considered, as their satisfaction is assumed. The hierarchy employed consists (in ascending order) of (1) safety needs, (2) friendship and belonging needs, (3) needs for justice and fair treatment, (4) dependence-independence, and (5) needs for achievement.

In the preceding pages, use has also been made of the lengthy theoretical discussion by Davies (1963) concerning the possible applications of Maslow's ideas to the study of politics. Here, as in his other writings (1965), Davies does not consider the need for safety and security as a separate need, stating that he regards this need "as a need for being secure in the satisfaction of the physical, social, self-esteem, and self-actualization needs." (Lengthy theoretical discussions of the applicability to politics of Maslow's personality model can also be found in works by Bay [1965] and Lane [1969].)

A fourth use of Maslow's ideas is found in Joseph Zinker's (1966) most unusual longitudinal study of a terminal cancer patient. (Therein Zinker offers his own summary of the meaning of Maslow's need hierarchy.) This study lends empirical support to the internal consistency of Maslow's hierarchy. Specifically, Zinker found a significant inverse relationship between the importance of physiological needs and, at different times, both esteem needs and self-actualization.

Fifth, in a field study concerning the relationship between personality and economic culture in a West Indian village, Aronoff (1967) illustrates the relationship between prevailing psychic needs and corresponding cultural forms. Aronoff sees institutions as being determined by three factors: physical environment, historical sociocultural institutions and present mental needs. While Aronoff offers useful material regarding Maslow's need hierarchy as a whole; it is particularly valuable in its description of the effects and causes of the need for safety. In the cane cutters, for example (the economic group in which the need for safety predominated), Aronoff found significant differences in such disparate variables as mating patterns, choice of marriage partner and father's role in the family, physical and social access of their homes to strangers, and behavior patterns. Most interestingly, Aronoff found individuals with a need for safety unable to cooperate or conflict. "Having experienced the dangers of this mode of experience so fully in childhood, he fears forming ties or confronting another directly. Instead, he tends to withdraw from a threatened clash, as he tends to withdraw from all significant human bonds." This concurs with the hypothesis presented in chapter 2 that individuals with a need for safety will tend to be politically inactive except in times of crisis, when they are likely to become followers.

Finally, of special interest to the readers of this book is Simpson's (1971) study analyzing the relationship between Maslow's personality model and the development of democratic social and political values in the high school. The author (using students from three geographically and culturally varied high schools as a sample) measured Maslow's need levels by a considerably expanded and refined version of the Indices of Psychic Deprivation employed in this book. Of particular interest is Simpson's use of separate indices to measure self- and social-esteem, as well as her reports of scores on some dimensions (such as the Dogmatism Scale and Rotter's Internality-Externality Scale) that have been of concern to us. Her findings suggest that institutional democratic socialization will not produce a democratic personality unless preceded or accompanied by an environment which gratifies the basic psychic needs of the child.

Name Index

Subject Index